ANTITRUST POLICY

An Economic and Legal Analysis

This is the seventh and last in a series of studies on competition and monopoly in American industry financed by a grant from the Merrill Foundation for the Advancement of Financial Knowledge. The series was planned to include a number of studies focusing on the effectiveness of competition in particular industrial markets accompanied by certain investigations into the effect on competition of various elements of market structure and business practice common to many industries. Although each volume was an independent study representing only the views of its author, all have contributed to the central objective of the whole project: an evaluation of monopoly policy in the United States.

ANTITRUST POLICY

An Economic and Legal Analysis

Carl Kaysen and Donald F. Turner

Harvard University Press, Cambridge
1 9 5 9

Distributed in Great Britain by
Oxford University Press, London

Library of Congress Catalog Card Number 59–12973

Printed in the United States of America

Foreword

Views on antitrust policy, perhaps even more than views on economic policy in other fields, rest heavily on judgments of value and on disputable conclusions about the way the economic mechanism works. Ideally, proponents of a new policy or critics of an old one should carefully distinguish the elements of evaluation, speculation, supposition, well-established fact, and analytical framework out of which their position is compounded. Actually, these are in practice so intertwined as to make a complete separation impossible. Nonetheless, we have done as much as we can to let our readers see the bases of our criticisms and recommendations, in the hope that our discussion will be useful even to those who do not agree with us.

If what we have done has any special merit in our own eyes, it lies in the fact that we have tried to relate our policy proposals, on the one hand to an economic analysis of markets as they do and might function, and on the other to a legal and administrative analysis of what the presently and potentially available instruments of policy can do. In this way, we have tried to avoid equally merely tinkering with the present operations of antitrust law and merely advancing utopian blueprints of no practical relevance to policy.

One of us is an economist, the other a lawyer; while each bears special responsibility for those parts of the work which rest on his own discipline, the whole is the result of a collaborative effort in which each has freely criticized and revised the other's work. During the long period in which this study has been in various stages of gestation, we have received assistance from many sources. As Dean Mason has indicated in the Preface, the discussion group in which we participated taught us much; and the process of defending our ideas before its members, or abandoning them when we could not, sharpened and clarified our views greatly. We owe a special debt to Edward S. Mason, Kingman Brewster, Jr., and Donald Trautman, with whom we have shared at various times the teaching of a seminar in the economic and legal problems of the antitrust laws, and to the students in law and economics who have participated in it. The brunt of the considerable research that went into Chapter II was borne by Merton J. Peck; he was assisted at various times by Maureen Brunt and William R. Hughes. Robert L. Bishop's notes and unpublished writing on the patent system were particularly useful to us in dealing with this area, and much of what is novel in our proposals is due to him. M. A. Adelman and Hugh Scott were particularly helpful on problems of exemption and regulation. James W. McKie and Stuart Land contributed substantial memoranda on problems of patents, price discrimination, and mergers. We cannot succeed in listing all our debts, and we do not try. Any writer on a subject that has been studied as long as antitrust policy has is inevitably in debt to his colleagues and predecessors. We must leave it to our readers to judge what we have added to that which has already been said. Finally, we wish to record the generous and long-continued support of the Merrill Foundation for the Advancement of Financial Knowledge, which made possible our own work, the previous studies in this series, and the discussion group out of which so many of our ideas were drawn. For what we have made of all this help, we alone are of course responsible; the ultimate conclusions to which we have come are our own and are not necessarily shared by those who have helped us to reach them.

April 1959 C.K.
Cambridge, Massachusetts D.F.T.

CONTENTS

TABLES

Preface by Edward S. Mason

It requires an unusual degree of temerity to present the public with another study of antitrust policy, particularly with a study that proposes substantial legislative amendment. Antitrust is by far our most comprehensive and complex piece of economic policy, and it has by now been subjected to nearly seventy years of interpretation and adjudication. It might therefore be presumed that, in this process, everything worth saying has been said and many times over. Since, moreover, the area in question covers an infinite variety of business situations and practices, any new legislation, like the old, must be general in character and subject to case-by-case interpretation. This means that a long period elapses before the law is "known." The merger statute of 1951 has now been on the books for eight years and as yet no case under the statute has reached the Supreme Court. Despite this, it is my view that the authors have something new to say and, in extenuation of their presumption in proposing legal changes, it may be suggested that these changes are in a direction already indicated by recent judicial decisions. Lawyers, in particular, are allergic to novelties, but it is to be hoped that they will see in the proposals of this study an extension of what is in process of becoming a traditional view of the monopoly problem.

Although antitrust is our most complex and comprehensive bit of public economic policy, it is, in my judgment, rather far from being the most important. In the field of business organization there is a test that can usefully be applied in determining the position and emoluments of a man in the management hierarchy — how much would it cost the firm if the man makes a serious mistake. If we apply this same test in the area of public economic policy and ask the question what difference would stupid policy make to the functioning of the economy, I suspect that both labor-management relations and stabilization policy would rank ahead of antitrust. But to say that antitrust is not as important as certain other fields of economic policy is not to say that it is unimportant.

The structure of American industry and the behavior of firms are markedly different than they would have been if Sherman, Clayton, and Federal Trade were names unknown to the statute books. The proliferation of agreements restraining competition and the prevalence of restrictive practices in other industrial economies give some indication of what we have been spared in the United States. Even with respect to large firms, where the impact of antitrust is supposedly small, some credit is due. The struggle against size was largely lost in the merger movement of 1897–1901; but since the turn of the century there has been little, if any over-all increase in concentration in the American economy. Cases against monopolization, it is true, have been few in number and dissolutions have been even fewer. But countless mergers and amalgamations that might well have taken place in the absence of antitrust have been scotched in the office of corporate counsel. It is, in fact, to the advice that lawyers give their clients that the laws against monopoly must look for their chief impact.

It is of course impossible to produce vigorously competitive behavior by legislation. A search for those "springs of action" of American enterprise that have produced a rapidly expanding volume of output would take us much deeper into American institutions and culture than a study of antitrust policy. But negative restraints can channel activity into productive pursuits and away from mere transfers of income, and this has been the primary function of antitrust.

An evaluation of any branch of economic policy must consider the objectives sought, the means considered to be appropriate, and the state of knowledge concerning relationships among the variables to be manipulated and the ends to be attained.[1] The literature of antitrust and the decisions of the courts exhibit substantial differences of opinion concerning both the ends to be sought and the means considered appropriate, though a fairly clear line of development has become visible within the last twenty years. But it is the third area, involving the state of knowledge of relationships between market structure, business behavior, and the monopolistic and competitive consequences of structure and behavior, that presents the greatest difficulties. One school of thought, representing many antitrust lawyers and a few judges, would like to reject economic analysis and the presentation of economic evidence as mere philosophizing. On the other hand, the dominant view appears to be that the substantive issues in the antitrust field are essentially economic. It

[1] See Erik Lundberg, *Business Cycles and Economic Policy* (Cambridge, Mass. 1957), chapter IV.

follows that if improvement in the choice of means is attainable, it will come about largely through improvements in the techniques of economic analysis and the presentation of economic evidence.

It is unnecessary here to reassess public opinion and Congressional intentions, circa 1890, in order to assert with some confidence that the Sherman law was aimed at two targets: "unreasonable" market power (a situation), and "unfair" — exclusionary, restrictive, oppressive — practices (a type of conduct). Opinions differed then — as they differ now — on which was the main target and on the reciprocal relationship between power and practices. But neither target has, for long, been out of sight. One can, of course, quote Senator Hoar to the effect that oppressive practices was the wrong to be remedied, while monopoly achieved without benefit of such practice was unobjectionable. Equally valid and prestigeful testimony, however, supports the view that the principal evils to be remedied were those huge agglomerations of capital, the trusts.

Justice Holmes, in his much quoted dissent in the *Northern Securities* case, aptly observed that, "The Act says nothing about competition."[2] Neither does it mention monopoly. The operational words are "restraint" and "monopolizing." But it was the emphasis given by the Court in previous cases to another word in the statute, "every," that led eventually to the enunciation of the "rule of reason." To many, the rule of reason represented an abandonment of the attack on monopoly in favor of a much attenuated rule relating to conduct. Good trusts were distinguished from bad trusts. But, of course, the questions of size and market power were always relevant since conduct on the part of a small competitor does not, necessarily, have the same significance as similar conduct by a large one.

The Court, in 1920, somewhat gratuitously, found that "size is no offense." And indeed, during the ensuing twelve years of Republican administration, which embraced our second merger movement, size was not much of an offense. But by 1932 Justice Cardozo was proclaiming that "size carries with it an opportunity for abuse that is not to be ignored when the opportunity is proved to have been utilized in the past."[3] And from then on, a long series of decisions, including *Tobacco, Alcoa,* and *United Shoe,* has laid increasing emphasis on market power. Monopoly (or market power) "without more" is still no offense under the antitrust laws, but the "more" is

[2] Northern Securities Co. v. United States, 193 U.S. 197 (1904).
[3] United States v. Swift and Co., 286 U.S. 106 (1932).

being attenuated into what mathematicians might call the second order of smalls.

There is a school of thought that, while holding the limitation of monopoly to be the chief objective of antitrust policy, believes that all undesirable market situations can, in fact, be reached by a rule on restrictive conduct. The contention is that the history of every large firm will, on examination, reveal practices that can legitimately be made the basis of an antitrust suit. If one is willing to become an antitrust archaeologist, this may well be true. But if the undesirability lies primarily in the situation, i.e., the market power structure, rather than in the conduct, this procedure somewhat resembles an attack on kidnaping by prosecuting kidnapers for income tax violation. And when, as in *United Shoe,* the conduct complained of is that which is not "economically inevitable," extensive reliance on a rule of conduct appears somewhat misplaced. Moreover, while a careful study of the ancient history of existing firms may reveal derelictions on which a charge can be based, this may not hold true in the future.

There is another school of thought that favors subsuming both the market situation of a firm and its conduct under a rule of "intent." [4] According to its leading practitioner, "The distinction between 'market control' and 'restriction of competition' is not only elusive, it is nonexistent." Neither "control" nor "restriction," moreover, provides an adequate test of violation. "It is inadequate because it focuses the issue on the pattern of market structure, the possession of market power, and ignores the animus lying behind the development of that structural pattern. Intent provides an appropriate *primary* criterion of compliance with or violation of the law, because of the nature of the antitrust law itself. The Sherman Act prescribes a rule of conduct. It does not condemn monopoly; it prohibits monopolizing." [5] In further elaboration of the meaning of "intent" it is asserted that "intent, in law, is always an inference drawn from *conduct.* Personal motives are irrelevant. It is the pattern of conduct in a specific set of circumstances that reveals the intent, according to common experience, on which turns the issue of whether an offense has been committed." [6]

[4] See Myron W. Watkins, review of "Economic Concentration and the Monopoly Problem" by Edward S. Mason, *American Economic Review* (September 1957), pp. 747–753; and Alfred E. Kahn, "Standards for Antitrust Policy," *Harvard Law Review* (November 1956), p. 28.

[5] Watkins, p. 749.

[6] Watkins, p. 751.

But, when we turn to the "specific set of circumstances" in which a specified type of conduct may or may not evidence an "intent to monopolize," the market position of the firm inevitably looms large. Unless we are to prohibit these specified types of conduct as illegal per se, they must be judged with reference to some situation. Let us quote from another advocate of the primacy of intent. "A state medical association expels some doctors for 'a breach of medical ethics.' A publishing company which owns a morning and an evening newspaper refuses to accept advertisements in either one separately. A number of cement manufacturers quote identical delivered prices. A chain store reduces its margins in a particular locality at a particular time. A pipe line company owned by an oil refiner establishes minimum tenders. A man standing in front of a bank which is being robbed whistles loudly when a policeman comes into view. How does one decide when to exonerate, when to condemn these courses of action?" [7]

The primary answer to be given to these questions, I submit, is that the conduct is to be condemned when the actor is shown to have the power or the capabilities to make his conduct effective. If the rule of "intent" means merely that the legal significance of action is to be judged largely with reference to the market power of the actor, I have no fault to find with it, though I do not think that subsuming, and confusing, both elements under the term "intent" gets us very far forward.[8] But that "intent to monopolize," inferred exclusively from conduct, either is, or should be, the law I would strongly deny.

After all, is it necessary at this late date to argue that mergers, agreements, and various types of business practices have a significance with respect to the maintenance of competition that de-

[7] Kahn, p. 51.

[8] This discussion reminds me of the differences between the alleged practices of American and British military intelligence officers during World War II. The Americans extolled the merits of their formulation of the central problem, defined as an evaluation of enemy "capabilities," as against an alleged British evaluation of enemy "intentions." According to the American officers, an evaluation of intentions leads toward a subjective assessment of "desires" and away from a hard core and objective assessment of what the enemy can do. I do not know, in fact, whether the choice of "intentions" led the British in this direction, but there is no reason why it should have. A proper assessment of intentions includes both capabilities and interests. A reasonable man does not "intend" what he manifestly cannot do. Nor does he use his capabilities in the pursuit of aims in which he has no interests. Obviously, an evaluation of both capabilities and interests (whether or not exhibited by previous conduct) is necessary to a sensible evaluation of intentions.

pends largely on the market position of the merging, agreeing, or practicing firms? The attention paid in recent cases to defining the relevant market and assessing the position of firms in this market is sufficient indication that the courts, at least, are aware of this dependence.

An evaluation of market power, or control, or monopoly, as an essential element in the assessment of the competitive significance of business conduct, obviously presents economic analysis with a set of problems it is not very well equipped to handle. We shall have more to say on this later. But whatever the difficulty, it is a set of problems that cannot be avoided. It has not, in fact, ever been avoided in cases involving large firms, though the emphasis on conduct was much stronger thirty years ago than it is today. It cannot be avoided in the selection of cases by the Antitrust Division and the Federal Trade Commission unless the Division and the Commission abdicate their positive role in the enforcement of antitrust in favor of a mere follow-up of the complaints that flow in from business quarters. An assessment of the relation between power and practices is unavoidable in remedy proceedings. The choice between an injunction or a "cease and desist" order as against some form of divestiture depends on the anticipated consequences for competition of a prohibition of particular practices. And this, in turn, depends largely on the power of the relevant firms or the structure of the market. If the power is large, injunction may be without effect.

Finally, an assessment of market power is of the essence of merger policy. How else can the line be drawn between permitted and prohibited mergers other than by assessing the probable consequences of a proposed or an accomplished merger on the "level" or "vigor" of competition, i.e., by assessing the change in the distribution of market power?

While the problem of market power cannot be — and has not been — avoided in the administration of the antitrust laws, it would admittedly be a long step to advocate a market power standard "without more" as a test of violation, in addition to the present "market power plus conduct" standard; and indeed, the authors, recognizing certain "justifications" of market power, do not go quite that far. The Sherman Law is a criminal as well as a civil statute, and as Justice Holmes has said, "The words cannot be read one way in a suit which is to end in fine and imprisonment and another way in one which seeks an injunction." [9] In fact, they have been increasingly so read, which is perhaps one of the difficulties with the attenuated "conduct" standard used in recent antitrust cases. In any case, a criminal statute is obviously inappropriate when the wrong to be remedied is a situation rather than a type of conduct. Consequently the authors in their draft of a proposed "market power" statute have eliminated criminal liability.

There remains, however, the large question of whether current tools of analysis are adequate to make an acceptable distinction between permissible and nonpermissible situations of market power. Returning to our earlier discussion of the task of evaluating any branch of economic policy, we are here concerned with the state of knowledge concerning relationships among the variables to be manipulated and the ends to be attained. Without anticipating at this point the lengthy discussion of these matters in the text, it may be useful to attempt to clear away certain obvious misconceptions.

The espousal of a standard aimed at the avoidance of "unreasonable" market power or the preservation of a minimum "level of competition" is most decidedly not an argument for the acceptance of tests of business performance. Business performance, as the term is currently used, is a normative concept; performance is either "good" or "bad." Goodness and badness obviously have to be judged with reference to their approach to — or departure from — some ideal type, and in the search for the ideal, one of two standards or both are customarily brought forward. The first is a performance consistent with the existence of pure competition, or of some variant that may take account of a "real" desire on the part of buyers for some degree of product differentiation. The second is "progressiveness," "dynamism," or some rate of innovation.

The first ideal type of performance has the merit of being more or less clearly defined and is backed by a respectable body of analysis having to do with the behavior of prices and quantities of goods and resources under conditions of static equilibrium. Unfortunately, the situations and types of conduct we have to deal with are not static. But the second ideal type of performance cannot even be defined. There is no known way of ascertaining whether the progressiveness of firms or the rate of innovation in a particular industry constitutes good or bad performance in a given situation. This inability, however, has not prevented many admirers of the "new" or

[9] His dissent in the Northern Securities Case, 193 U.S. 197 (1904).

"dynamic" competition from advocating performance tests of antitrust violation, with heavy weight given to evidences of "progressive" behavior. As I have suggested elsewhere, a proposal to rely on such tests is an invitation to nonenforcement.

The fact that we cannot directly measure the goodness or badness of business performance, however, does not mean that we are uninterested in performance. The ultimate justification of an antimonopoly policy rests heavily on the belief that the maintenance of competition has an important contribution to make to efficiency in resource use and to continuous product and process improvement. Efficiency and progressiveness enforced by the market, rather than dispensed as largess by publicly minded custodians of private power, have been the traditional objectives. Unless it can be assumed that antitrust has some significant effect of this sort on the functioning of the economy, it is little more than a device for policing business morality. But it does not follow that an analysis of these effects can provide us with acceptable tests of antitrust violation.

The other main misconception is that market power or the plane of competition can be inferred directly and exclusively from data relating to the structure of the market. As the phrase is currently used, market structure refers to those permanent, or slowly changing, competitive limitations of which a firm must take account in formulating its own policies. The most important of these limitations are the number and size distribution of buyers and sellers in the market, the conditions of entry of new firms, and the extent of product differentiation, including geographical dispersion.

Despite Stigler's observation that "an industry which does not have a competitive structure will not have competitive behavior," [10] a study of structure is not enough. This is so for two reasons. Many if not most of the markets with which antitrust is concerned do not approach very closely the only two models, pure competition and pure monopoly, that permit us to infer with assurance — at least under equilibrium conditions — behavior from structure. Secondly, if we include, as elements of market structure, data on growth trends and susceptibility to cyclical variations, as we frequently must if we are to explain the behavior of firms, we are fairly far removed from the universe of static market models.

If we reject both performance and structure-without-more as

[10] George J. Stigler, "The Case Against Big Business," *Fortune* (May 1952), p. 167.

inadequate, where are we to find evidence of market power? The answer given by the authors is essentially that it is to be found in the combined study of market structure and business behavior. The critical problem — and the chief difficulty confronting anyone who wishes to reassess antitrust policy — is presented by oligopoly. A large fraction of manufacturing output in the United States is produced in industries in which three or four or five firms account for sixty percent or more of the total. And if the industry data are "adjusted" to take account of market realities, a serious degree of concentration still remains. The exclusive application of structural standards — at least on certain definitions — might condemn all such markets. On the other hand, the application of performance standards might excuse all. To those who believe, as the authors do, that there is a substantial monopoly problem in the oligopolistic structure of American industry, but that not all highly concentrated markets fall under the ban, there is presented the problem of separating the sheep from the goats. How successfully this separation is here accomplished must be judged by the reader.

Although this volume has been written by the two authors whose names are appended, the study is, in an important sense, the product of the discussion of a group of lawyers and economists extending over several years.[11] The authors would be the first to admit that the contribution of the group to the formulation of the ideas here presented has been large. At the same time, the study is, as any study that says something must be, an individual rather than a group product. And it would be unfair to the reader not to indicate that, on the central proposal of a market power standard, there was considerable disagreement in the group. The principal objections had to do with the vagueness of the proposed standard and the possible disincentive effects of a policy laying greater emphasis on size and market power. Some, but not all, of the lawyers found the standard too unclear for effective adjudication. Some, but not all, of the economists feared that the checks to business growth implied in the proposed limitation of market power might seriously impair competitive incentives.

That the antitrust laws are uncertain is a charge of long standing. A greater degree of certainty has been achieved in recent years

[11] The members of the group (not all of whom participated continuously) were Morris Adelman, Joe Bain, Robert Bishop, Robert Bowie, Kingman Brewster, David Cavers, Kermit Gordon, Lincoln Gordon, Carl Kaysen, John Lintner, Edward Mason (chairman), Albert Sacks, Donald Trautman, Donald Turner.

through the specification of various types of conduct that the courts have been willing to find illegal per se. A still greater degree of certainty could be achieved by legislation limiting the absolute size of firms or their market share or prohibiting branch plants. Although a few extremists espouse such "limitist" views,[12] considerations of possible economies of scale and disincentive effects have heavily weighed against their acceptance. Greater certainty could, no doubt, also be achieved by the adoption of "performance" or other standards — that would essentially make the antitrust laws unenforceable. If we reject both these extremes, we are pushed back to some kind of rule of reason. Whether adding "unreasonable market power" to the other unreasonablenesses of the rule of reason would make antitrust law still more uncertain is at least a debatable question. In the first place, it can be pointed out that in all cases under the present law involving monopolizing, parallel action, or merger, and in all remedy proceedings in which dissolution or divestiture are proposed, an assessment of the market power position of the firms in action is inevitable. Secondly, it can be maintained, as the authors do, that the presentation of economic evidence relevant to the market power of firms can be much improved and that the adoption of a market power standard would force improvement in this direction.

Speaking as an economist, I should have to admit that an effective antimonopoly policy is handicapped by our relative ignorance of the relationships between market structure and business behavior; between the structure-behavior complex and the "level" of competition or degree of market power; and between the level of competition and that efficiency of resource use that must be assumed to be the principal ultimate desideratum. However, in this respect we are, I think, not worse off in this area than in other important fields of economic policy. The relationships between changes in interest rates and business behavior or between increases and decreases in taxation and entrepreneurial incentives are not, to say the least, perfectly known. It must be recognized that there is an element of faith in the proposition that maintaining competition substantially improves the efficiency of resource use. And a substantial amount of guesswork is involved in forming a judgment on market power or the plane of competition based as it is on the available evidence of market structure and business practices. Such elements of faith and guesswork, however, are the inevitable concomitants, in the present

[12] See Fred I. Raymond, *The Limitist* (New York, 1947).

state of our knowledge, of any economic policy, the alternative being no policy at all.

All this, of course, has a bearing on the question of how much difference the introduction of a market power standard would make. And this in turn has a bearing on the question of the disincentive effects, if any, involved in such a policy. The authors clearly believe that the proposed change would make a substantial difference; that it represents a considerable tightening of antitrust policy. A number of firms that now escape dissolution would, in their opinion, be broken up. This may well be, but against this view would have to be set not only the difficulties in the presentation of economic evidence but the institutional conservatism of the judicial process. The Courts have hitherto shown themselves to be notably reluctant to break up going concerns, and even such a nudge by Congress, assuming Congress is willing to act, might have a relatively small effect. The authors are, of course, aware of this possibility and suggest the creation of special enforcement machinery, including adjudication by a special court, to carry out a program against unreasonable market power. The pros and cons of this proposal are discussed in Chapter VIII.

If we assume that the impact of a market power standard would be substantial, what disincentives, if any, to competitive vigor would be involved? Although the monopolistic significance of a given share of the market will vary from market to market, depending on other considerations, it may be conjectured that the proposed standard might substantially reduce, in many industrial markets, the share of output that the largest firms could safely acquire without running foul of the law. Would this check to growth in a particular market seriously impair the drive for cost reduction and product and process improvement? The authors propose to minimize disincentives by exempting market power attributable to economies of scale, patents, or innovation.

Furthermore, though it may well be true that the imposition of a limit to the growth of going concerns would adversely affect managerial incentives, this is not proposed. Firms in jeopardy in one market are free to expand in other directions. Nevertheless, when these and other considerations are taken into account, it is possible that in certain markets and for certain firms the proposed standard would adversely affect managerial incentives. No doubt this is also true to some extent of present antitrust policy. The question raised is one not very amenable to rational argument. Is it worth while to accept a slight loss in efficiency in order to limit the growth in the economy of positions of private power? This is a question on which reasonable men may well differ.

This preface has paid particular attention to unreasonable market power as a test of antitrust violation because it is the central and the most controversial of the proposals. The study, however, undertakes a thorough reassessment of antitrust policy, and offers a number of suggestions for improvement, which are summarized in the introduction to Chapter III. The substantive proposals have mainly to do with mergers, price-fixing and price-influencing agreements, patents and patent licensing, and price discrimination. All these proposals relate to conduct, but to conduct contributing to market power. It is the reciprocal relation between market power and business conduct that forms the theme of the study.

Chapter I lays out the assumptions on which the subsequent analysis is based and discusses the ultimate aim of an antimonopoly policy. Chapter II undertake an assessment of market structures in the American economy and attempts an identification of monopoly and oligopoly markets, and of the size and location of the sectors of the economy that are exempt from antitrust policy. Chapter III contains the first statement of the authors' proposed reformulation of antitrust policy. As a first approximation, unreasonable market power is defined as market power greater than justified by economies of scale. The concept of market power is analyzed in terms of market structure, business behavior, and performance. In Chapters IV and V the policy is applied: in Chapter IV to size, integration, and mergers; in Chapter V to per se practices, to patents, and to price discrimination. Chapter VI surveys the principal areas of exemption from antitrust policy. Chapter VII examines the relevance of other public policies to the plane of competition and the existence of market power. Finally, Chapter VIII considers the procedural questions raised by the policy proposals and assesses alternative formulations.

In conclusion, let me express, on behalf of the authors and myself, the deep appreciation we all feel to the members of the group who gave up so many of their evenings to a discussion of the questions here at issue. The authors have not attempted a consensus of the views expressed. To have done so would have produced a series of eminently sound observations of little interest to anyone. They have, however, benefited at every stage from the counsel of their peers. And they have, I believe, produced a provocative and suggestive study of antitrust policy.

Cambridge, Massachusetts EDWARD S. MASON

ANTITRUST POLICY

An Economic and Legal Analysis

I

Introduction

This analysis of United States antitrust policy has two aims: the proposal of a strengthened antitrust policy, worked out in enough detail to indicate the changes in law and administration necessary to apply it; and a statement of the logic of the policy proposal — in terms of the presumptions, factual judgments, and analytical reasoning on which it rests — in such a way that it will be useful even to those who disagree with the value judgment inevitably involved in it. In this chapter we shall examine some general presumptions of antitrust policy, discuss the possible aims of such a policy, and indicate the organization of the whole essay.

SOME UNDERLYING ASSUMPTIONS

Certain broad propositions must be taken as true to warrant any antitrust policy. We make these explicit here, in part to indicate our justification of them, in part to set bounds to the scope of our discussion.

As the context of our discussion we take for granted the present mixed economy, in which the largest part is organized on the decentralized lines of private property and private enterprise. The market is thus the central institution regulating economic activity. The use to a significantly greater extent than at present of other methods of economic organization — including nationalization, direct government control in detail of individual firms, consumer cooperation, or worker-manager guild organization — is ruled out as a real policy alternative. Indeed, only in this context is it worth while to place much emphasis on antitrust policy.

Further, we assume that the sectors of the economy in which government monopoly, or private monopoly controlled in more or less detail by government (to which antitrust policy is not applicable), are limited, and are not growing rapidly relative to the rest of the economy. Thus we posit a market-controlled sector and a distinct and identifiable government-controlled sector,[1] in the first of which antitrust policy is the primary form of extramarket regulation, while in the second various kinds of more specific controls apply.[2] Although the boundaries between the two sectors cannot be easily specified in general terms, we must be able to say of any specific industry or industrial activity that it falls on one or the other side of the boundary.[3] We further assume that the size of the government-controlled sector and its interrelations with the market-controlled one are not, and will not become, such as to make a successful antitrust policy impossible. This is by no means an obvious truth. The government-regulated sector is not so large in a crude sense as to leave no room for market forces; this is clear from what follows in Chapter II. But the problem of interrelations between regulation in the one area and competition in the other is more complex. It will be examined in some detail in Chapter VII. Here we can only point out the difference between the existence of regulated monopoly in an industry like electric power, which does not affect the structure or market operations of power-users, although it does affect their costs; and the kind of regulation involved in crude-oil prorationing, or in collective bargaining as now established, which may have powerful impacts on industrial markets, in the first case in the oil industry, in the second case, generally.

We assume that some kind of antitrust policy is necessary or desirable. Again, though this proposition is often taken as obvious, it is not necessarily so. Other industrial nations, with few exceptions, have not had such policies in the past, although in recent years interest in them has grown. Belief in the need for a procompetitive public policy rests on two propositions. First, there is some minimum level of competition which it is necessary to achieve in the market-controlled sector if that sector is to be allowed to remain a market-regulated rather than a government-controlled one. Second, this level is not self-maintaining: in the absence of antitrust, the level of

1. See Chapter II for a discussion of the size and limits of the two.

2. See Chapter VI for a discussion of regulated industries and exemptions from the antitrust laws.

3. To be sure, an industry may be regulated in part, and still left to market forces in part. Any hard and fast demarcation of the two sectors will thus contain arbitrary elements.

competition will sink below the minimum. While there are substantial economic arguments for the first proposition, it rests basically on a political judgment. In our democratic, egalitarian society, large areas of uncontrolled private power are not tolerated. The continued freedom of most industries from detailed government regulation rests on their subjection to the control of market forces. This means some level of competition, sufficient to prevent at least the accumulation of visable, unchecked private economic power. It is likely that this level of competition — the politicaly tolerable minimum — is less than the level which could be urged as desirable on economic grounds. We explore this point below. For our present purposes it is necessary only to point out that a complete absence of positive public policy would lead to a drastic decline in the competitiveness of business. A much more widespread pattern of growth by merger, an efflorescence of collusive arrangements of all sorts, and the use of various exclusionary and otherwise anticompetitive practices now forbidden would all follow on the abandonment of a procompetitive public policy.[4] In general, these changes in the structure of markets and the conduct of business firms would lead to declining economic efficiency and shifts in income distribution of a sort which are usually viewed as undesirable. Further, at least part of the competitive spirit and the striving to excel now present in the typical large corporation is the result of the past impact of the antitrust laws on standards of business conduct and business goals. How much of this would persist in the absence of continued antitrust enforcement is hard to say, but certainly some decline is to be expected.

Next, we assume that enforcement of some kind of anti-trust policy is worth its cost. This means that the level of competition which would persist in the absence of any policy is far enough away from what could be achieved so that the administrative, political, and economic costs of government intervention involved in a procompetitive policy are worth incurring. Another way of stating this assumption is to say that an effective antitrust policy is possible, as well as necessary — the alternative being reliance on something other than market regulation over most of the economy. One way

4. The prevalence of some of these either on the fringes of or outside the law at present, the experience of the NRA, or of practices in industries exempted from the antitrust laws, the pattern of market conduct in other countries, as well as the logic of profit — and security — maximization can be cited in support of this statement.

of justifying this assumption is to point to the present antitrust policy, and its application — in changing ways — over the past sixty years. It is fairly clear from the cases that the antitrust law sets a standard of business conduct in respect to anticompetitive practices that is more stringent than would exist in its absence. The relative freedom from cartelization of American industry can also be attributed to the present policy. And, as we have suggested above, the goals of business conduct have probably been affected by the law.

At a deeper level, the assumption that an effective antitrust policy is worth while involves several complex judgments of fact. First, economies of scale under present technology do not indicate the desirability of a radically *greater* concentration of output in a small number of large firms, so that antitrust policy is not hopelessly at variance with the underlying cost situation. Several kinds of evidence support this conclusion. First is the importance of mergers in explaining the present relative size distribution of industrial firms. Second is the fact that all of the technical economies of scale are achieved at the level of the plant rather than of the firm, and the greatest part of the size difference between very large and large firms (say $500 million and over assets in the first class, and $50 to $500 million in the second) lies in the number of plants they operate rather than in the size of the plants themselves. Technical economies of scale are not the only kind; economies at the level of the firm in selling, advertising, research, production planning, personnel recruitment, etc., are also possible. But in many industries in the size range here under discussion, the whole overhead margin is not sufficiently great to permit quantitatively large differences in average unit cost arising simply from economies at the firm level. Third is the large variation in size within the group of "large" firms with modern management organizations, highly developed research and marketing activities, multiplant and multimarket activity. Among integrated steel producers the range is ten to one; among "major" oil producers, twenty to one; among chemical manufacturers it is perhaps fifty to one. This variation shows no tendency to diminish over time; giant firms are not generally outcompeting smaller ones, by any tests now available.[5]

5. For detailed discussion of these matters see C. Kaysen, "Looking Around: Books About Competition," *Harvard Business Review* (May-June 1954); J. F. Weston, *The Role of Mergers in the Growth of Large Firms* (1953); G. J. Stigler, "Monopoly and Oligopoly by Merger," *American Economic Review*, Papers and Proceedings (May 1950), *Report of the Federal Trade Commission on the Divergence between*

What is now true must be expected to continue in the future: no sharp change in technology, including the introduction of large-scale rapid computation and automatic control techniques, will in the near future dictate a substantial increase in concentration among market-controlled firms. The truth of this is, of course, a speculative matter; inventions not now foreseen may lead to radical changes in all our ideas. But insofar as we have any basis of speculation, there appears to be no reason to expect any radical change in the character of scale economies. Indeed, to the extent that the chief visible changes are changes in management techniques and tools, there may well be some reduction in the advantages of large-scale firms. Many of the practices of rational and efficient management have been introduced first in large firms, partly because of the greater need for uniform and relatively objective management practices in a large than in a small organization. Even now, they are spreading, and the availability of computing machines and of consulting firms to provide and direct their services is likely to increase the speed with which the managements of other than the largest firms can avail themselves of superior methods and practices.

In singling out the relation between size and efficiency for discussion, we are acknowledging that competition requires the existence of competitors, in the plural. The vexing question, which will run through a major part of all our discussion, is "how many?" We begin exploring this question by observing that the rigorous model of the perfectly competitive market[6] is the appropriate starting point of any definition, but it cannot be the end of any practically useful one. The model provides us with two important notions: first, a market in which each seller acts as if his own decisions had no influence on any significant market variable — price, supply, the number of other sellers and their sales, etc.; second, a definition of economic efficiency in terms of the relations between costs and prices characteristic of the model. The second result, the efficient use of resources in meeting the demands of consumers, depends on the first and on the logic of profit maximization. In the model, the first result comes about because sellers are many in number and individ-

---

Plant and Company Concentration (1947); J. S. Bain, "Economies of Scale, Concentration, and the Condition of Entry in Twenty Manufacturing Industries," *American Economic Review* (March 1954); and *Barriers to New Competition* (1956).

6. See E. H. Chamberlin, *The Theory of Monopolistic Competition*, chapter II; T. Scitovsky, *Welfare and Competition*, chapters II-VIII, for a detailed discussion of the rigorous model.

ually of insignificant size relative to the total market, the product of any seller is a perfect substitute for that of any other, and new sellers enter and old ones leave freely and quickly in response to profits and losses. In real markets — with very few exceptions — these conditions do not hold. The existence of significant economies of scale at both the plant and the firm level over some size range means that firms are not generally insignificant in relation to the market. The geography of production and consumption reinforces this result: for many products there are local or regional markets in which the number of sellers is relatively small, and which are to a substantial extent isolated from other local and regional markets by the barriers of transport cost. The outputs of one seller are usually ony imperfect substitutes for the outputs of another: product differentiation, advertising, and locational differences among sellers which bring about this result must be taken as permanent features of the economy, answering in some measure to real preferences of consumers. Neither entry nor exit is universally free and speedy. All sorts of barriers to entry, from large capital requirements to high advertising costs and closely held patented technology, are widely characteristic of the economy, though in varying measure in different industries. Frictions, and the influence of uncertainty and risk aversion on business decisions, mean that entry and exit often take place with substantial lags after the changes in profitability which occasion them.

Nonetheless, though the model of competitive market structure is not usable as such in our definition of competition, other concepts of the model are. Where firms can persistently behave over substantial periods of time in a manner which differs from the behavior that the competitive market would impose on competitive firms facing similar cost and demand conditions, they can be identified as possessing market power. Conversely, where, on the average and viewed over long periods of time, the relations of prices, costs, outputs, capacities, and investments among a group of rivalrous firms are such as would be expected in a competitive model, then it can be inferred that the market does constrain the scope of the individual firm's decisions sufficiently to be called competitive. The existence of such constraints depends on many features of a market, which we will discuss in more detail in Chapters III and IV. In general, numbers and conditions of entry are the most important of these features. There is a high correlation between concentration of output in the hands of a small number of large producers and the existence of firms with significant degrees of market power. This is the basic reason for singling out the relation between size and efficiency for rather extended discussion at this point. Were they such as to dictate a very small number of sellers — two, three, four — in most markets, antitrust policy would make little sense.

On the same ground, we must be concerned with differences in the levels of cost curves among enterprises. We must assume that it is not the case that a few firms, managed by men of superior gifts, can and will continue to attract the small number of superior managers, and thus will be enabled to outperform all rivals in all fields, were they permitted and motivated to do so. In other words, large permanent differences in economic efficiency among firms, persisting in time over wide ranges of output and wide product lines, are either nonexistent or rare. This proposition implies something about the distribution of business ability in the population at large and the nature of business activity. On the first point it is assumed that first-grade managerial talent exists sufficient to man a few hundred companies such as Du Pont, General Motor, Standard Oil of New Jersey, etc.: there is a chairman of the board's gavel in the attaché case of every division manager. On the second, it is assumed that where a particular firm does have an advantage in men and methods, rivals can and will copy the methods and hire away the men, and that incentives of pay and promotion will suffice to do so, in that employee loyalties to particular firms will not prove so strong as to make this impossible.[7] It is hard to support this proposition with concrete evidence, and, while we believe it accords with experience, others have expressed different views.[8] Perhaps it is best to label this assumption as an article of democratic faith and leave it at that.[9]

7. Organizations of some types might not find it possible to use the mechanisms of imitation and of hiring away talent to catch up with rivals. Nations do not do so in respect to talent because of the strength of nationalist sentiments. Perhaps artistic organizations — ballet companies, theater companies, etc. — provide examples of organizations whose goals constrain them to some extent from imitating more successful competitors. But the very rationality of business, the objectivity of profit and income, and the strength of income as a measure of prestige in our society all suggest that behavior of this sort is unlikely in the business world, despite the growing institutionalization of lifetime careers in some of the larger corporations.

8. Schumpeter frequently expressed the opposite view. Whether he had any more evidence than a tempermental inclination toward aristocracy is not clear.

9. Some light is cast on the general subject by an examination of an American Institute of Management survey of excellently managed firms, entitled "Manual of Excellent Managements." The 1955 edition lists 389 firms, of which 199 are in manufacturing. The size distribution of these was examined by comparison with the FTC list of 1000 largest manufacturing corporations (1948). The results showed that,

Finally, we must assume that the dependence of business initiative and vigor on the degree of *laissez faire* is not so intimate and important that variations in the amount of government intervention and supervision of the kind involved in antitrust policy will significantly effect it. This is not to say that particular antitrust measures will not vary in their effects on business incentives, and that such variation is not relevant to the choice among them. Rather it is an assertion that over-all we need not fear that the possibility of any effective antitrust policy is foreclosed because of unfavorable repercussions on business vigor. This proposition is broadly supported by the history of the last three (or the last seven) decades, which have witnessed a progressive increase in the scope and detail of federal government intervention in business decisions in areas from labor relations to taxation and security issues, with no worthwhile evidence that over-all business effort has been noticeably

---

while there was a significant correlation between size and the proportion of excellently managed firms, the largest firms were not all listed, nor were all those listed giants. The distribution by group of 50 was:

The 1000 largest manufacturing firms, by size	Number of excellently managed firms (AIM)
1st 50	26
2nd	31
3rd	20
4th	26
5th	17
6th	11
7th	15
8th	9
9th	7
10th	5
11th	35
12th	2
13th	4
14th	2
15th	4
16th	11
17th	4
18th	2
19th	1
20th	3

A variance analysis of the distribution by groups of 10 among 250 firms showed no correlation between size and the proportion of excellently managed firms over this part of the size range. The assets of the 10th firm on the list were about $1150 million, of the 50th firm, $288 million; the 100th, $139 million; the 200th, $68 million; the 250th, $54 million; the 500th, $23 million; and the 1000th, $9 million.

These figures are compatible with the hypothesis suggested above that rational management practices historically began in large corporations, but have been spreading to smaller and smaller ones. (We do not think it necessary to examine the content of the AIM definition of "excellent management" for the present purposes.)

diminished. The past history of antitrust points broadly in the same direction.[10]

THE AIMS OF ANTITRUST POLICY

Antitrust policy may serve a variety of ultimate aims. We can divide the aims against which any policy proposal may be tested into four broad classes: the attainment of desirable economic performance by individual firms and ultimately by the economy as a whole; the achievement and maintenance of competitive processes in the market-regulated sector of the economy as an end in itself; the prescription of a standard of business conduct, a code of fair competition; and the prevention of an undue growth of big business, viewed broadly in terms of the distribution of power in the society at large.

(a) *Desirable Economic Results*

The desirable economic results which we seek refer ultimately to the whole economy. At this level we wish to see: (1) efficiency in the use of resources — the achievement of the largest bundle of desired outputs from the available bundle of resources; (2) progress — growth of total output and of output per head and development of new cheaper production methods and new improved products; (3) stability in output and employment — growth at a relatively stable rate, rather than with large fluctuations; and (4) an equitable distribution of income. Not all of this quartet of virtues are connected to the functioning of markets in an equally intimate way. Efficiency is most closely dependent on the operation of markets. While the existence and character of market competition is one of the forces influencing the pace of innovation, it is only one; and others, including the supply and training of technical personnel, the expenditures by government on industrial research, the attitude of consumers toward new products and of managements and workers toward new methods of production, are in the aggregate of greater importance. To the extent that an equitable distribution of income implies the passing along of the fruits of efficiency and progress to consumers, it is related to the functioning of markets. To the important extent that ideas of equity involve judgments that some

10. We shall take up in Chapters III and IV the more difficult problem of whether certain antitrust measures, such as dissolution and divestment, may have disincentive effects which outweigh their contribution to increasing the level of competition.

income receivers should receive more and some less than they could get from the market—no matter how competitive—equity must be sought by policies (such as taxation) other than those which affect the operation of markets. Finally, fluctuations in output and employment are primarily responses to fluctuation in aggregate demand rather than to events in particular markets, and again, policies designed to promote stability find their primary means outside the sphere of market organization. Thus, to the extent that we conceive of antitrust policy as designed to promote certain desirable economic ends, we should measure its impact in the areas of economic efficiency and progress. The particular contribution to equity in income distribution which is made by the promotion of competitive markets is the bringing down of prices to costs. Since this result also appears as an aspect of efficiency, no separate treatment of it is needed. The effects of different kinds of market situations either on equity, broadly conceived, or on stability are uncertain in direction and probably small enough in relation to the effects of taxes, government transfer payments, and fiscal and monetary policies so that they may safely be neglected.

Efficiency is ideally a distributive or relational concept, which embraces the whole economy. Essentially, it is a state in which no rearrangement of outputs among products and no redistribution of inputs among firms could increase consumer satisfaction. We make the usual assumption that even though economy-wide efficiency is impossible to achieve, because of the existence of natural monopolies, government monopolies, and areas exempted from the requirements of competition for other reasons, it is desirable to make as close an approach to the conditions of economic efficiency in as many sectors of economy as possible.[11] On this basis, we can apply the concept of efficiency to individual industries and firms. Its elements are the efficient relations between prices and costs, capacities and outputs, demands and capacities; and production at efficient scale in efficient locations. The characteristic results of the competitive model define efficiency. In technical terms, prices should equal both long-run average costs (including normal profits) and marginal costs for each product as well as for the enterprise as a whole; capacity should be fully utilized in periods of high demand (excluding

11. The assumption might be called the Pigovian assumption, since it is implicit in the approach of Pigou's *Economics of Welfare*.

obsolete stand-by capacity) and, where capacity is not fully utilized, firms should not be earning positive profits; increases or decreases in the level of demand should call forth corresponding changes in capacity (with an allowance for lags due to uncertainty, and for the slowness with which declines in fixed capital take place); output should be produced at minimum costs, in plants of efficient scale; plants should be at efficient locations (again with allowance for the large lags between changes in costs and market situations, and the growth of new producing centers).[12]

In defining progressiveness as an aspect of desirable economic performance which it might be the goal of antitrust policy to promote, we can add little to what we have said. Progress consists in increasing output, in increasing output per unit of input by the development of new techniques, and in producing new and better final products. These results are achievable in part and are observable at the level of the firm and the industry, as well as aggregatively for the economy as a whole. Some ingredients of progress, such as better technical training, may not be achievable at the firm or industry level, but their effects can be observed there.

To sum up, efficiency and progressiveness are the most important economic results whose achievement can be substantially influenced

12. These points are developed in further detail in Chapter III. There are two further aspects of efficiency which may be mentioned, though they are less directly related to market organizations than those we have listed. First is the relation between private and social costs. Economic efficiency requires that every real cost involved in any resource use be reflected in the cost-price system. This is not always the case. Sometimes inappropriate property institutions, such as the rule of capture in oil, lead to large divergences between social and private costs. Sometimes, as in the case of forest resources, capital rationing and ignorance lead to rates of resource consumption which diverge from the optimum, because the time horizon of the private producer is shorter than the appropriate social time horizon, and thus future income is sacrificed for present income (in real terms) at a too high rate. Given inappropriate property laws, or institutional barriers to business units of an appropriate sort, it may be that the degree and nature of competition has an effect on the efficiency of resource use in this respect. Thus, under the rule of capture, a monopolist would be less wasteful of oil than a horde of competing producers in the same field. But the fundamental remedy for these situations typically lies elsewhere than in the promotion or restriction of competition. Second, there may be a problem of product variety. Under competitive conditions, every (known) variety of product for which producers can cover their costs by charging any uniform price will be produced. There may be some products, however, for which costs cannot be covered by any single price, though they could be under discriminatory pricing. The question then arises as to what is the optimum degree of product variety: the lesser one corresponding to uniform pricing, or the greater one corresponding to discriminatory pricing? Persistent successful discrimination implies monopoly or cooperation among sellers; in general this has been permitted only under regulation.

by antitrust policy. Thus they furnish the criteria by which antitrust policy aimed at producing desirable economic results must be judged.

(*b*) *Promoting competitive processes*

The achievement and maintenance of competitive processes in the market-controlled sector of the economy is the second goal that antitrust policy can serve. In this sense, competition is seen as an end in itself rather than as a means to achieve desirable economic results. An effort to extend as far as possible the market-controlled area and to limit sharply the government-controlled one is directly complementary to this goal; its relation to the goal of achieving desirable economic performance is less clear. Competition as an end in itself draws its justification from the desirability of limiting business power. As we have indicated, this can be achieved either by superimposing control by politically responsible authority or by the internal limitation provided by the competitive market; we have assumed the latter is the preferable alternative. Business power can be viewed either narrowly in terms of economic power, or broadly in terms of power in the society at large. The two aspects are, to be sure, interconnected, but for the purposes of the present topic we focus on the economic power and leave the latter aspect to further discussion below. Again, we can view the economic power of business in relation to the community at large, both consumers and suppliers of labor, or more narrowly in relation to the power of some firms vis-à-vis others in interbusiness transactions. The demand for limiting business power springs more often from those who feel themselves at a disadvantage in interbusiness transactions than it does from households either as consumers or as suppliers of labor.[13] Competition in this context is desirable because it substitutes an impersonal market control for the personal control of powerful business executives, or for the personal control of government bureaucrats. The impersonality of market regulation makes it fair in the eyes of those subject to it; the sense of fairness is greater when the same restriction on conduct is imposed by the market than when it is viewed as the result of a personal decision by a powerful individual. This same attribute of the competitive market is seen in another as-

13. Organized labor generally takes an ideological position favoring the limitation of business power, but the actual pattern of collective bargaining suggests that, in practice, large unions prefer to deal with concentrated industries rather than with atomistic ones. See the further discussion in Chapter VI.

pect for all who deal in the market as the existence of effective alternatives; no one source of supply, no one outlet, confronts buyer or seller with terms that must be met because no alternative exists. The buyer who gets no copper because excessive demand has pushed price to an unprofitably high level does not experience the same sense of unfair treatment as he would if the copper were denied him by the allocation decision of a single supplier. In this sense, competition is a code of fair dealing among business firms.

From the broader perspective of the whole society, this same impersonality appears as the compulsion that the competitive market exercises upon the transactors in it. Rather than having scope to choose more or less desirable patterns of conduct, the firms in the competitive market are compelled along the only economically feasible line of conduct by the constraints of the market.

Logically, constraints and impersonality derive from the model of a profit-maximizing enterprise in a perfectly competitive market. The markets of experience deviate in many ways from the competitive model, and the enterprises of experience likewise deviate from rigorous devotion to maximizing the present value of an unambiguously defined flow of profits. Even in the most competitive of real markets, enterprises retain some scope for discretion in behavior: markets are less than perfect and less than purely competitive; firms must be thought of as maximizing some utility index, in which profits have an important weight, but into which desires for security, growth, and avoidance of various kinds of "trouble" also enter.[14] However, the less competitive the market, the wider the scope of this discretion. The firm with a good monopoly position may well have profits which are both high and stable; a firm in a more competitive market will have little room for choosing between smaller and more secure profits and larger though more fluctuating ones, though it will not be entirely without some discretion in this matter. Competition not only constrains business decisions in general; it forces businesses to move closer to a policy of long-run

14. Logically, profit maximization can be defined unambiguously only under conditions of perfect certainty. When the consequences for the stream of future income of present decisions are not known certainly — as is always the case in the real world — then "profit maximization" might mean maximizing the expected value of profits, or maximizing the expected value of profits subject to some constraint on acceptable probability (risk) of losses of specified sizes, or maximizing the expected utility of profits, or any one of a large number of possible policies. Thus the existence of uncertainty about the future, and the interdependence of present decisions and future income streams, provide the firm with some discretion even in a competitive market.

profit maximization than they would necessarily be under other market conditions.

(c) *"Fair conduct"*

Although competitive processes provide one standard by which fair business conduct can be defined, it is not necessarily the only one. One possible goal of antitrust policy is the maintenance of a standard of business conduct which is considered fair. A policy oriented toward this goal would concern itself with judgments on the way business power was used rather than with whether or not such power existed. The content of fairness is vague once its identification with competitive market processes is abandoned. In general, fairness entails some concept of equal treatment of those in similar situations; but this achieves specific content only if the principles of classification, which determine who are in the same situation, can be stated. Unless there is fairly general social agreement on the relevant classificatory variables — as for instance income and family status in deciding on income tax rates — fairness tends to mean equal treatment for everybody. In practice, in the context of a market, this may mean equal treatment for firms now operating in the market, rather than equal treatment for existing firms and potential entrants, since the realities of administering equal treatment, whether by private or public administrators, can be met only by dealing with existing rather than with potential claimants. Fairness also has the content of fair play or sporting behavior, which in the market context may be translated as not using market power where it exists, and in general seeking reasonable rather than maximum returns. Both "equal treatment" and "reasonable returns" may lead to the rule of preventing any changes in a given situation which are disadvantageous to any participants therein; or which are more disadvantageous to some than to others.[15] It is out of this type of fairness that "grandfather rules" arise, whether expressed in legislation or in business practices of serving old customers in times of shortages, and the like.

Forbidding the use of unfair tactics as a means of acquiring monopoly power has of course been an important element in antitrust policy. Nevertheless, this description of the problem is to some

15. Note that this is different from stating that all changes be no more advantageous to some than to others. It is in general easier to agree that an other-than-equal division of a gain among all parties involved is fair than it is to agree on a similar division of a loss.

extent superficial. If a firm can coerce rivals, suppliers, or customers, there must be some reservoir of force on which it draws that accounts for the acquiescence of the coerced party in a situation that, by definition, is not the result of mutually free bargaining. There are three possible kinds of force which a firm can resort to: violence (or the threat of it), deception, or market power. While the first two are not unknown in the records of antitrust cases, they are illegal in themselves and hardly need be considered in defining the goals of antitrust policy. Typically, then, coercion consists in the ability of a firm with market power to impose terms in a bargain which the other party would refuse, were there an alternative transactor with whom he could deal more advantageously. The normal instruments of business bargaining, delays, refusals to deal, representations which fall short of complete candor, and the like, can be turned uniformly to the advantage of the powerful bargainer, because his partner in the transaction would be even worse off if he did not accept the terms imposed. This is not to say that the use of unfair tactics in this sense in order to increase or maintain a position of power is without significance in particular markets. Rather it is to argue that this meaning of unfairness must be viewed as an aspect of market power, and that if the prevention of unfair conduct is a distinct policy aim, it must refer to the kind of characteristics of transactions discussed above in terms of equal treatment of those similarly situated.

(*d*) *Limiting big business*

The last broad class of goals to which antitrust policy can be directed is the creation of a desirable distribution of social power among business units by changing the relative positions of "large" and "small" firms in the economy. This goal is broader than that of limiting the market power of firms, since it aims at what we have called social power broadly defined, rather than economic power in particular markets. Power in this sense has some relation to economic power in particular markets, but it transcends it and includes political power and general social leadership.

The goal of a "proper" distribution of power between large and small business is rationalized in terms of certain Jeffersonian symbols of wide political appeal and great persistence in American life: business units are politically irresponsible, and therefore large powerful business units are dangerous. The political and social power of the independent proprietor is the foundation of democracy; therefore his power as against that of the corporate bureaucrat must be maintained or re-established. The power of absentee ownership and management in relation to the local community and local and state governments must be diminished, lest the failure of state and local control provoke an increase in federal intervention in both business and local community life, and a corresponding increase in federal power. These doctrines, often in inchoate form, undoubtedly provide an important emotional substratum on which political support for antitrust policy of some kind rests.

Public policy directed to reducing big business power can move along three lines. First, it can reduce the size and relative importance of large business firms directly in one way or another. Second, it can place limitations on the conduct of large businesses, especially on conduct viewed as having a competitive impact on small businesses. Third, it can provide direct subsidies to small businesses. The first two of these fall within, the third falls without, the usual scope of antitrust policy.

AIMS OF PAST AND PRESENT ANTITRUST POLICY

The four possible aims of antitrust policy that we have examined — promoting desirable economic performance, limiting market power, enforcing a standard of fair conduct in business, and reducing the social power of large and promoting that of small business — are in part competitive and in part complementary. An assessment of the extent to which the pursuit of each reinforces or interferes with the achievement of the others is prerequisite to any antitrust policy proposal that purports to rest on an articulated statement of aims. This task we leave to Chapter III. At this point, we wish to describe briefly what the approach and purposes of American antitrust policy seem to have been up to now, with an eye toward what the weaknesses and difficulties might be.

Present antitrust policy is the product of a long evolution, influenced by the views of a succession of Assistant Attorneys General and a more slowly moving succession of Supreme Court majorities, and punctuated only twice, in 1914 and 1936, by major legislative pronouncements. If there has been any persistent policy and approach, it has been that of protecting competitive opportunities and competitive processes by preventing unfair, unreasonable, or coercive conduct, but this is a faulty generalization at best.

It is obvious that in passing the Sherman Act, "Congress was dealing with competition, which it sought to protect, and monopoly, which it sought to prevent." [16] The legislators were well aware of the common law on restraints of trade, and of the power of monopolists to hurt the public by raising price, deteriorating product, and restricting production. At the same time, there was at least equal concern with the fate of small producers driven out of business, or deprived of the opportunity to enter it, by "all-powerful aggregations of capital." There was no obvious inconsistency in these two interests. One could readily have identified free access and large numbers of comparatively small producers with competitive processes, and in turn have identified competitive processes derived from such market structures with beneficial economic results for the public at large. Or, to short circuit the proposition, one could have equated beneficial economic results with the protection of large numbers of small independent producers.

We think it reasonable to suppose that those legislators who dwelt on the matter proceeded on such a premise. Nevertheless, it seems probable that they also desired to protect equal opportunity and equal access for small business for noneconomic reasons: concentration of resources in the hands of a few was viewed as a social and political catastrophe as well. Indeed, if Congress had decided to prohibit "monopoly in the concrete," it might have been reasonable to conclude that dispersion of power was the Sherman Act's primary goal. But this was not done, or so the courts have interpreted the act, unless *Alcoa*[17] means otherwise, which we do not think it does. The Act was deemed by its sponsors not to be applicable to one "who merely by superior skill and intelligence . . . got the whole business because nobody could do it as well." [18] Perhaps it was believed or hoped that the exception would never be of any significance, that few if any positions of monopoly power could be gotten and held so long as anticompetitive behavior was proscribed — a belief akin to the suggestion that beneficial economic results may be equated with competitive market structure. But whatever the premise for it, the exception was an indication that power obtained or maintained by the kind of behavior that competition is thought to

16. Standard Oil Co. v. FTC, 340 U.S. 231, 249 (1951).
17. U.S. v. Aluminum Co. of America, 148 F.2d 416 (C.A. 2, 1945).
18. 21 Cong. Rec. 3146–52, cited in U.S. v. United Shoe Machinery Co., 110 F. Supp. 295, 341 (D. Mass. 1953).

foster, if not compel, was immune even though businesses and business opportunities were destroyed in the process. In short, in the event of conflict in goals, protection of incentives to competitive behavior would prevail over dispersion of market power.

Several factors prevented realization of the hope that regulation of conduct would prevent significant growth and persistence of undue market power, and prevent attenuation of opportunities for "small" businesses in many important areas. Economies of size, in the absolute if not in the relative sense, assumed an importance not foreseen when the Sherman Act was passed. Patent monopolies contributed more to the concentration than to the dispersion of economic power, though a priori there might have been reason to suspect that such would not be the case. Moreover, the courts, in enforcing the Sherman Act, did not sweep into the category of illegal conduct all that could or should have been put there. Unreasonable conduct tended to be confined to behavior, such as price-fixing, which had traditionally come to be thought of as illegal restraints, and to behavior of a predatory or abusive nature that had been or could be readily described as unfair. For some periods at least, the courts were unduly lenient with cooperative trade association activities, with restrictive practices by patentees, and perhaps most important with the growth of market power by peaceful combination. Neither the Clayton Act nor the Federal Trade Commission Act, for reasons that need not be repeated here, had an appreciable impact in these respects.

During these periods of what we advisedly call weak enforcement, when fair conduct was apparently the predominent policy goal, it might be said that a concept of desirable economic performance played a part, but that the role of monopoly (or market) power was in practice an extremely attenuated one. The courts appeared to assume, more than the facts would justify, that efficiency and progressiveness went hand in hand with large size. This assumption at least contributed to decisions in cases where large combinations were either absolved of antitrust charges or protected against dissolution. Market power, on the other hand, rarely appeared to have independent significance as a test of illegality; generally speaking, it was found when unfair conduct was found, and found absent in the absence of abuse.

In the past fifteen or twenty years, some notable changes have been made. The law has been tightened on such conduct as tying arrangements, requirements contracts, collective refusals to deal, patent licensing restrictions, and (presumably) on mergers. Moreover, it is clear that in the *New Tobacco, Alcoa, United Shoe,* and *Cellophane* cases, in the remedy in *Paramount,* and in the opinions on remedy in *National Lead* and *Alcoa,* market elements were given new emphasis in antitrust policy.[19] In one way or another, market structure and market behavior either influenced the court's evaluation of conduct not in itself wrongful under old cases, or led the court to propose or reject a remedy for reasons other than deprivation of wrongfully acquired gains. *Tobacco, Aluminum, United Shoe,* and *Cellophane* involved determinations of liability resting to a larger or smaller degree on an evaluation of market structure (and to some extent market behavior) which supported the conclusion that defendant firms possessed or did not possess monopoly power (in the judges' language) or market power (in ours). *Paramount* showed the rejection by the Supreme Court of one proposed remedy (competitive bidding) and the suggestion of another (dissolution) largely on the ground that the former would not change the market structure sufficiently to produce the desired degree of competition. *National Lead* and the *Alcoa* remedy opinions both involved rejection of a request for dissolution in part on performance grounds: the former as promising no improvement in performance; the latter for the reason that defendant's performance had been good and the proposed remedy threatened to make it worse. Nevertheless, whatever advances have been made, we do not believe that the law on monopoly has reached the point of covering, or could be fairly construed to cover, the case where monopoly power is effectively exercised, wholly without agreed-upon courses of action, by a small group of sellers in an oligopoly market.

But this has not meant that market power, even though legitimate in itself, goes untrammeled. This was the key issue in *United Shoe,* and one that is part of a pervasive, yet still unsettled, problem of antitrust policy. In essence, the decision in *United Shoe* was that a monopolist, though his power was legally acquired, could not

19. American Tobacco Co. v. U.S., 328 U.S. 781 (1946); U.S. v. Aluminum Co. of America, 148 F.2d 416 (C.A. 2, 1945); U.S. v. United Shoe Machinery Co., 110 F. Supp. 295 (D. Mass. 1953); U.S. v. E. I. du Pont de Nemours & Co., 351 U.S. 377 (1956), *affirming* 118 F. Supp. 41 (D. Del. 1953); U.S. v. Paramount Pictures, Inc., 334 U.S. 131 (1948); U.S. v. National Lead Co., 332 U.S. 319 (1947).

indulge in practices, though otherwise legal, that unnecessarily raised the barriers to growth or entry of competitors. As we indicated above, the Sherman Act has been interpreted — and properly, we think — to leave room for legal monopolies, that is, for monopolies acquired solely by competitive merit (within which patents should be included). Nevertheless, a decision that monopoly power is legal does not compel the acceptance as legal of everything the monopolist does. It may be desirable to curb the uses to which monopoly power is put, particularly in light of the aim of antitrust policy to protect competition. The reward for successful competitive endeavor should not be destroyed, but it may be lowered by restrictions on the use of power without noticeably diminishing the efforts to achieve power. If so, the clear benefits to be derived from such curbs are a net economic gain; even if there were some losses in incentive, the gains might still outweigh them.

In any event, the courts have proceeded, albeit erratically, on the premise that an accommodation must be made between the economic interests of those possessing legitimately acquired power, and the economic interests of others. The legality of many practices — tying arrangements, lease-only arrangements, requirements contracts, and the like — has at one time or another turned on the existence of monopoly power in the hands of the practitioner.

It is in this connection that the second historic aim of antitrust policy — that of preserving the opportunities of smaller businesses competing with, buying from, or selling to the "monopolist" — has retained continuing vitality, and a vitality that has been renewed from time to time by legislative enactment. The Robinson-Patman Act and the recent automobile dealer franchise act are clearly of this genus. And while resale price maintenance may have other motivations and other effects, invidious or praiseworthy depending on one's point of view, we would be inclined to identify it also as being conceived of in part as another method of curbing the misuse of market power that cannot be directly dealt with by dissolution. Thus, whatever need there may be for statutes of this kind (concerning which we shall say more later), the scope of the need is directly related to the lack of success in coping with undue market power.

We think it fair to say that the antitrust laws have not been notably successful in this respect, and it is on this premise that we proceed to consider how they might be improved.

PLAN OF THE STUDY

Before examining the interrelations among the four possible goals of policy, and selecting some combination of them as our own policy goal in Chapter III, we survey the occurrence in the American economy of market structures of different kinds. This material occupies Chapter II. In Chapters IV and V, we indicate how the policy proposal of Chapter III is applied to the major problem areas of antitrust, and compare it with policy under the present laws. Chapter IV covers size, integration, and mergers; Chapter V, business practices and per se rules, patents, and price discrimination. In Chapter VI the exemptions to antitrust are surveyed. In Chapter VII, we examine the impact of other public policies than antitrust on the functioning of markets, including taxation, government procurement, and international trade policies. Chapter VIII contains a discussion of the administration machinery required to put our policy proposal into practice, and a rough draft of a statute that would put our various recommendations into effect.

II

A Survey of Market Structures in the American Economy

Some knowledge of the size, location, and significance of the monopolistic and competitive sectors in the economy is a prerequisite to discussion of antimonopoly policy. The purpose of this chapter is to furnish such information. In so doing, we have avoided two procedures as inconsistent with the conclusions reached in the following chapter on policy.

First, we do not attempt to produce one single number representing the quantitative division of the economy between monopoly and competition. Such an all-inclusive index has little meaning in the assessment of the impact of these two types of market process on the functioning of the economy. The simple addition of markets by some common quantitative weight, such as the national income originating in each market, ignores the fact that certain markets, apart from their size, by their strategic location in the economic process are especially important in terms of the economic aims of antitrust policy.[1] The most obvious example is furnished by the markets for capital goods, whose market variables influence investment decisions throughout the economy. We shall discuss the economic significance of different types of markets later in this chapter.

Secondly, we do not attempt to classify individual markets as competitive or monopolistic. Individual markets show varying mixtures of competitive and monopolistic elements; they are more or less competitive rather than all or not-at-all competitive. The point

1. "There is little presumption that an economy which is 40 percent monopolized will be more unstable or inefficient or slower of growth than another economy which is 25 percent monopolized: the industrial distribution and their strength and patterns of behavior are obviously also important variables." G. J. Stigler, *Five Lectures on Economic Problems* (London, 1949), p. 46.

on this continuum which should separate monopoly from competition for public policy purposes is an important substantive issue which we discuss below. In general, the application to individual markets of any criterion we choose requires a fairly thorough industry study and cannot be done solely on the basis of concentration data or other simple statistical materials.

Rather, we aim to provide in two ways a quantitative background for the chapters on policy: first, by an identification of the structurally oligopolistic markets — those which show a small number of large sellers supplying a large part of the output — and second, by an estimate of the size and significance of the sectors of the economy which are exempt from the operation of an antimonopoly policy.

We attach primary significance to the estimates of the size and location in the economy of the structural oligopolistic markets, since these are the ones which at least raise questions for a procompetitive policy, although their actual status can be evaluated only after further study. This requires establishing the size distribution of sellers in each market, a research task of a considerably lower order of complexity than that of identifying monopoly and competition. A summary measurement of the relative size distribution is the concentration ratio, defined as the percentage of total market sales made by a specified number of the largest firms. Individual markets can be classified on the basis of their concentration ratios as either structurally oligopolistic markets, in which the few largest sellers have a significant share of the market; or as unconcentrated markets, in which sales are distributed among many sellers and no small number has a significant share. Both economic theory and experience indicate the likelihood of a monopoly problem in the structurally oligopolistic markets. To be sure, many of these markets may be competitive in behavior, but identification of structural oligopoly gives us a list of those industries which may exhibit monopolistic behavior even though there is no evidence of overt collusion among firms. Such a list provides a basis for inferring the maximum costs and impact of certain types of antitrust policies.

Identification of structurally oligopolistic markets does nothing for the examination of monopoly problems in unconcentrated markets. These are generally problems of business conduct, arising from trade practices, overt collusive agreements, and the like. Their existence and prevalence is demonstrated by both industry studies and litigation, and we do not minimize their importance. In fact, such problems of business conduct are not confined to unconcentrated markets. But these problems are already well recognized in traditional antitrust policy, and both their identification in particular situations and the problems of remedy posed by their existence are relatively simple compared with the problems of monopoly behavior associated with some types of oligopoly structure.

Our second study — the description of the size and location of the exempt sectors — needs little justification. In this survey, we provide some quantitative background for the discussion of the scope of exemptions in Chapter VI.

THE IDENTIFICATION OF STRUCTURALLY OLIGOPOLISTIC MARKETS

The available data permit a reasonable attempt at the identification of structurally oligopolistic markets in two of the four sectors outside the areas of exemption: manufacturing and mining. The other two, trade and service, must be passed by with a nod. Among all these sectors, we attach primary importance to manufacturing. Statistically, it is by far the largest: orginating 32.4 percent of the national income, and employing 27.6 percent of the labor force in 1953.[2] Again these statistical measures understate the importance of the manufacturing sector, for the market organization of the sizable distribution sector is in turn partly a function of the market organization in the manufacturing sector. Furthermore, in an industrial economy, manufacturing has a special role in the dynamics of the economy, for it is in this sector that much of the technological change originates and much of the cyclically important investment decisions are made. Finally, the manufacturing sector may have an indirect nonmarket effect on the norms of business behavior, since it deals with both the distributive and raw materials sectors of the economy.

Beyond the intrinsic economic importance of this sector, manufacturing is the sector in which a procompetitive policy is clearly the dominant public policy, and in which, in the past, application of such a policy has been concentrated. Therefore, information on this sector has a special significance for the discussion of antimonopoly policy. Fortunately, more detailed data are available for this sector than for others.

To identify structurally oligopolistic markets we must make two

2. *Survey of Current Business* (February 1954), pp. 10, S-10 and S-11.

decisions; first, we must set the critical degree of concentration of sales defining a structurally oligopolistic market and, second, we must delimit individual markets. In each decision, the conceptual principle is relatively easy to set forth, while its concrete application must be somewhat arbitrary.

A structurally oligopolistic market is one in which the few largest sellers in the market have a share of the market sufficient to make it likely that they will recognize the interaction of their own behavior and their rivals' response in determining the values of the market variables. Neither economic theory nor experience provides a definite number of firms or a size of market share they must jointly hold for this logic to apply. As our dividing point we have adopted, somewhat arbitrarily, a market share of one third of total market sales for the eight largest sellers, because in the majority of markets with which we are familiar, a smaller number of firms with larger shares of the market generally accompany, to a significant degree, the kind of behavior indicated above. Beyond such a dividing point, the majority of markets with which we are familiar do not appear to function in this fashion.

Within the general classification of structure oligopoly we make a distinction between two subclasses. In what we call Type One structural oligopoly, the first eight firms have at least 50 percent of total market sales and the first twenty firms have at least 75 percent of total market sales. In Type One oligopoly, recognition of interdependence by the leading firms is extremely likely, and the 75 percent share of the first twenty sellers makes it likely that the response of the smaller sellers will not limit the behavior of the larger firms. Type Two structural oligopoly is defined by a market share of 33 percent for the eight largest sellers, with the rest of the market relatively unconcentrated.

The distinguishing feature of this market is the existence of an unconcentrated sector which may constitute a competitive restraint of varying significance on the concentrated firms. Empirical studies of such markets indicate no clear presumption on the importance of an unconcentrated sector in an oligopolistic market, and so this partial oligopolistic market is classified as a separate category within the general classification of concentrated markets.

The economic concept of a market is stated in terms of the behavior of buyers and sellers. Two products belong in the same market if a small change in price (or product) causes a significant diversion in a relatively short time of the buyers' purchases or the sellers' production from one product to another. The quantitative values of the degree and the time dimension of this substitution process which serve to define a market are indicated by gaps in the array of values of these coefficients of substitution as the various combinations of products are grouped together. The substitution process itself is not directly observable, short of an individual study of the functioning of each market. We shall approximate it by two observable factors which are decisive in the buyers' and sellers' response: the geographical extent of the market and the nature of the product itself.

The delineation of actual market boundaries in terms of the product is restricted by the fact that the ultimate source of our data is the United States Census of Manufactures, which publishes data for both manufacturing products, of which there are several thousand, and manufacturing industries, of which there are several hundred.[3] Concentration data for products and industries are usually published by establishments rather than by firms.[4] A census manufacturing industry usually consists of all establishments primarily engaged in the production of members of a given group of related census products, designated by a four-digit code. Therefore, the sales figure for a census industry includes sales of some products which are not primary to the industry and excludes some of the sales of the industry's primary products.

Fortunately for us, data based on the 1954 Census have been published giving the shares of the top four, eight, and twenty firms of the total value of shipments of products primary to each census industry.[5] Firm concentration ratios are also given for the sales of each census product. Creation of economically meaningful markets from data on individual census products typically involves consolidation of numerous products to make a single market, so that considerable accuracy is lost in the computation of market concentration ratios.[6] Therefore, we have chosen to build our markets from four-

3. For a detailed discussion of the criteria used by the Bureau of the Census defining products and industries, see the Bureau's *Standard Industrial Classification Manual*, vol. 1, part I (1945).

4. A census establishment is a single production unit. A large firm is typically composed of many establishments.

5. The data are published in *Concentration in American Industry*, report of the Subcommittee on Antitrust and Monopoly to the Committee on the Judiciary, U.S. Senate, 85 Cong., 1 sess., pursuant to S. Res. 57. Hereafter, this document will be referred to as *Senate Report*.

6. The problem of computing consolidated concentration ratios is discussed in the Methodological Appendix, III.

digit product class groups in order to reduce the aggregation problem. In cases where these four-digit groups are too broad, it is impossible to divide them into economically significant markets. Where they are too narrow, we have grouped them with their close substitutes into consolidated markets. Since the adjustments are all in one direction, the result is a probable understatement of the number of structurally oligopolistic markets.

We have reduced the 440 four-digit product class groups to 191 industries, of which 83 represent combinations of two or more four-digit product classes.[7] Of these, 173 are put forward as economically meaningful markets, while 18 are the inevitable statistical catch-all, a "miscellaneous industry." The number of consolidations is sizable, which reflects a willingness to define markets broadly and accept a low value for the substitution coefficient in separating markets. The breadth of our market definitions is a major reason for defining the concentration ratio of eight firms — 33 percent share as the dividing line for structural oligopoly.

The basic Commerce Department data contain no adjustment for the differing geographic compositions of markets, and hence only in cases where the market is national in scope are these concentration ratios meaningful. Where there are distinct local or regional markets which bind the activities of buyers or sellers, the relevant concentration ratio is the one for each particular local or regional market.

(*a*) *Manufacturing industries with national markets*

National markets have been identified in two ways. In the simplest case, production is concentrated geographically, and thus all sellers are capable of operating in the national market as far as the geographic structure of the industry goes. Less simple cases are identified by a lesser degree of geographical supply concentration and by some evidence that geographic market boundaries are nonexistent or overlapping, and, hence, a significant number of the sellers have the structural possibility of competing on a nationwide basis. Industries which fulfill neither of these criteria are classified as either regional and local or heterogeneous. The last classification indicates a mixed grouping with some products of the industry having a national and others a regional market.[8]

7. Details of industry consolidations as well as computational procedures for the concentration ratios are contained in the Methodological Appendix, III.

8. Methodological Appendix, II, contains an analysis of the classification of industries by extent of the market.

The industries are also classified by size of shipment. This may serve as an index of economic importance in the absence of other information. However, as indicated earlier, any complete assessment of the significance of a market depends on its location in the economic process.

Market Structure

A. Concentrated
  1. Type I, Oligopolies. The first eight firms make 50 percent or more of the shpments and the first twenty make 75 percent or more of the shipments.
  2. Type II, Oligopolies. The first eight firms make 33 percent or more of the shipments, and the first twenty make less than 75 percent of the shipments.

B. Unconcentrated

Size of Industry by Value of Shipments

I. Large, $1,000,000,000 or more
II. Medium large, $500,000,000 to $1,000,000,000
III. Medium, $100,000,000 to $500,000,000
IV. Small, less than $100,000,000

Extent of the Market

1. National — geographically concentrated supply
2. National — geographically unconcentrated supply
3. Local and regional
4. Heterogeneous

The results of this classification scheme for all except the regional and local markets, which will be given a separate analysis in the following section, are shown in Table 1 of the Statistical Appendix. We have included the national concentration ratios for the heterogeneous industries on the following argument. For the products with a national market this figure is meaningful, while for products with a regional market, the actual regional concentration will be much greater than the national figure. Unfortunately it is not feasible to establish the regional concentration product-by-product and region-by-region for these industries. All of the heterogeneous industries have a limited economic meaning since they fall in the "miscellaneous" category, and hence will be separately identified in any summary tabulations.

Table 1. Frequency distribution of manufacturing industries by market structure, extent of market, and size (national and heterogeneous industries)

Markets	No. of industries		Total value of shipments	
A. *National markets*				
1. Concentrated, Type I				
a. Large	12		24,145,557	
b. Medium large	12		8,238,934	
c. Medium	30		9,109,135	
d. Small	4		325,294	
Total, Type I		58		41,818,920
2. Concentrated, Type II				
a. Large	17		54,716,482	
b. Medium large	12		8,773,939	
c. Medium	17		4,999,291	
d. Small	0		0	
Total, Type II		46		68,489,712
Total, concentrated		104		
3. Unconcentrated				
a. Large	20		42,031,980	
b. Medium large	17		12,343,886	
c. Medium	5		1,364,741	
d. Small	1		73,881	
Total, unconcentrated		43		55,814,488
Total, all national markets		147		166,123,120
B. *Heterogeneous markets*				
1. Concentrated, Type I				
a. Large	0		0	
b. Medium large	0		0	
c. Medium	0		0	
d. Small	1		61,241	
Total, Type I		1		61,241
2. Concentrated, Type II				
a. Large	2		5,657,043	
b. Medium large	1		631,133	
c. Medium	0		0	
d. Small	0		0	
Total, Type II		3		6,288,176
Total, concentrated		4		6,349,417
3. Unconcentrated				
a. Large	6		10,210,106	
b. Medium large	6		4,587,365	
c. Medium	1		462,566	
d. Small	0		0	
Total, unconcentrated		13		15,260,037
Total, all heterogeneous markets		17		21,609,454

Table 1. (Continued)

Markets	No. of industries		Total value of shipments	
C. *Total, national and heterogeneous markets*				
a. Large	12		24,145,557	
b. Medium large	12		8,238,934	
c. Medium	30		9,109,135	
d. Small	5		386,535	
Total, Type I		59		41,880,161
2. Concentrated, Type II				
a. Large	19		60,373,525	
b. Medium large	13		9,405,072	
c. Medium	17		4,999,291	
d. Small	0		0	
Total, Type II		49		74,777,888
Total, concentrated		108		116,658,049
3. Unconcentrated				
a. Large	26		52,242,086	
b. Medium large	23		16,931,251	
c. Medium	6		1,827,307	
d. Small	1		73,881	
Total, unconcentrated		56		71,074,525
Total, national and heterogeneous markets		164		187,732,574

Table 1 summarizes the division of industries between concentrated and unconcentrated in terms of both a simple count of industries and a measurement of sales. This indicates that structural oligopoly is the numerically dominant form of market organization in manufacturing. Another summary, in terms of market scope, size, and degree of concentration, is shown in Table 2 of the Statistical Appendix.

However, we have already rejected size as the sole measure of a market's significance, and have stressed the location of a market in the economic process as an additional criterion of importance. The simplest classification of the position of a market is through distinguishing among consumers' nondurables, consumers' durables, industrial input materials for several industries, and investment goods.

The ranking of the relative importance of these types of markets can be best assessed in terms of the policy aims of the preceding chapter, since our objective is significance in terms of an antimonopoly policy. Upon the presumption of the validity of the classical analysis of competition and monopoly, we can consider the organization of the industrial input and investment goods markets as more significant for the first desired market result, competitive resource allocation. In these two markets, the products are sold to other industries, and so affect not only prices but the production decisions and product design of other industries. Hence a monopolistically maintained price for a product such as steel will in turn cause the purchasing industries to alter their production processes and product design in order to minimize the use of the input. The final result then is a widespread change in economic efficiency rather than a simple passing on of a higher price to the consumers. Viewed more broadly and abstractly, departures from a competitive resource allocation in markets located further back in the productive process have an amplified effect through the distortions introduced into the resource allocation of the buying industries.[9]

The consequences of monopoly in consumers' goods markets for resource allocation are confined to the one market and the resulting adjustment is only in the behavior of the consumer. The major effect is in terms of a transfer of income from consumer to producer. Since the producers in turn pass the income on to their employees and shareholders, the changes in income distribution from monopoly are difficult to establish. This is particularly true of a large corporation where the existence of unions, and a relatively changing and widespread stock ownership accompanied by varying dividend policies, creates a very complex process in the division of corporate earnings. Even though we include income distribution as one of our policy objectives, we rank it lower in evaluating the significance of markets because the consequences of monopoly for income distribution are not in one direction. Furthermore, the evaluation of any changes in income distribution cannot be made except on a broad ethical basis.

For the other market results, cyclical stability and dynamic progress, the capital goods markets and material inputs may be likewise more significant than consumers' goods markets, although we attach less weight to these in any event. Almost all theories of the business cycle stress the role of investment and hence the importance of the investment goods industries. In terms of progress, changes in prices of products for material inputs and investment goods industries are more likely to generate the secondary changes in other industries which magnify their impact. Indeed, in the Schumpeterian view of economic history, the major innovations

9. These arguments are developed more fully in I. M. D. Little, *The Price of Fuel* (Oxford, 1953), in the Introduction.

which have induced long waves of economic change are all investment goods or material inputs.[10] However, we recognize that consumer durables may have some of the cyclical and growth significance of the other two and for this reason we have distinguished between consumer durables and nondurables.

We derive from these considerations the following ranking of significance of our four types of industries: investment goods, industrial material inputs for several industries, consumer durables, and consumer nondurables. A sharper distinction can be drawn between the first and last two industries than between the ranking of investment goods and industrial inputs. It should be noted that an industrial input used primarily in one industry, such as cotton yarn, will be classified with the consuming industry, since the preceding arguments do not fully apply to such a product.

Industries have been classified by type through the use of the Leontief input-output table.[11] This table presents the flow of goods in dollar terms between industries and households so that it is easy to distinguish between industries selling directly to the households or to one or two other industries, and those selling to many industries. The former are then divided between consumers' durables and nondurables and the latter between industrial materials and investment goods by the nature of the product. These results have been checked against the general knowledge of the industry's position in the economy.

The results of this classification, industry-by-industry, is contained in an appendix.[12] A summary classification by market type is presented in Table 2.

In general, the evidence points to the conclusion that consumer nondurables are less concentrated than the other three types. Since consumer nondurables rank lowest on our scale of economic significance, it follows that the distribution of industries by size between concentrated and unconcentrated overstates the importance of the unconcentrated industries.

10. The major innovations in the Schumpeterian system are steam power, railroads, electric power, and the automobile. All of these except the automobile are material inputs (power, transportation), but if we trace these innovations further back in the production process, they can be attributed to developments in the investment goods industry such as steam engine and electric generator construction. See J. A. Schumpeter, *Business Cycles* (New York, 1939).

11. See the Methodological Appendix, I, for the procedure used in this classification.

12. See the Methodological Appendix, I.

Table 2. The classification by economic type of the concentrated and unconcentrated industries

Industry size	Concentrated	Unconcentrated
Large		
Consumers' nondurables	11	11
Consumers' durables	4	0
Material inputs	11	8
Investment goods	5	4
Unclassified	0	3
	31	26
Medium large		
Consumers' nondurables	5	11
Consumers' durables	1	2
Material inputs	10	9
Investment goods	8	1
Unclassified	1	0
	25	23
Medium		
Consumers' nondurables	14	1
Consumers' durables	9	2
Material inputs	13	1
Investment goods	10	2
Unclassified	1	0
	47	6
Small		
Consumers' nondurables	1	0
Consumers' durables	1	0
Material inputs	3	1
Investment goods	0	0
Unclassified	0	0
	5	1
Totals, all sizes		
Consumers' nondurables	31	23
Consumers' durables	15	4
Material inputs	37	19
Investment goods	23	7
Unclassified	2	3
	108	56
Totals, by economic types		
All durables	38	11
All nondurables	68	42
All consumers' goods	46	27
All producers' goods	60	26

If we combine the size, number, and economic type of the unconcentrated and concentrated industries, we have the basis for the following conclusion. The manufacturing sector contains a numerical preponderance of structurally oligopolistic markets as we have defined them (even with a size adjustment) which, because of its location in the economic process, has a special importance in the functioning of the American economy. At the same time, this one market type hardly dominated manufacturing, since there is a substantial minority of unconcentrated industries.

(*b*) *Manufacturing industries with regional markets*

Manufacturing industries with regional markets account for somewhat less than 20 percent of all manufacturing sales. The identification of structurally oligopolistic markets among them presents two difficulties: regional markets must be delineated, and then concentration ratios for each computed. The first is difficult because it depends on a fairly detailed analysis of interrelations among buyers and sellers; the second, because there is in general no published size data for firms within the appropriate regional markets. Table 3 of the Statistical Appendix shows the national concentration ratios for the twenty-seven industries with regional markets. These are lower limits of the average regional concentration ratios; only in cases in which each regional market has the same size distribution among the same leading firms will the national ratio be the appropriate figure for structural classification.

It has been possible to examine in further detail only six of the twenty-seven industries, which account for about half of the sales of the whole group: petroleum refining, commercial printing, sawmill and planing mill products, bread and related products, newspapers, and cement. Table 4 of the Statistical Appendix summarizes the available information on these six.

The national ratios lead to the following classifications:

Type of industry	No. of industries	Total value of shipments (millions of dollars)
Type I Oligopoly	5	13,739
Type II Oligopoly	5	3,102
Possible Type II Oligopoly	2	7,005
Unconcentrated	15	26,667

Of the six industries examined in detail, four were classified as unconcentrated on the basis of the national figures; only one, sawmill and planing mill products, remained in this category. One was seen to be Type I oligopoly, one Type II, and one a mixture of Type I, Type II, and unconcentrated submarkets. This suggests that the understatement of the prevalence of structural oligopoly in regional markets caused by using the national ratios as a basis of classification is probably substantial.

All in all, the market structure pattern shown by the regional industries is not too different from that sketched out above for the bulk of manufacturing industries that have national markets.

(*c*) *Mineral industries*

The mineral industries are considerably smaller in size than the manufacturing sectors, originating only 1.6 percent of the national income and employing only 1.46 percent of the labor force.[13] However, since the products of the mineral industries can generally be classified as commonly used industrial inputs, these figures according to our preceding argument, understate the economic significance of this sector. The absence of adequate substitutes for some minerals increases the importance of their market organization, although imports act to offset this in some cases.

The identification of structural oligopoly in the mineral industries is handicapped by the absence of concentration data by firms. This necessitates using establishment data, which ignore the existence of multiplant firms, thereby understating market concentration ratios. Nevertheless, such data may indicate where further research is required by indicating the minimum level of concentration that may exist.

The establishment data are reported for both mines and preparation plants.[14] Since one preparation plant frequently serves several mines or quarries in the same locality, all with common ownership, the plant basis may provide a nearer approximation to firm concentration. However, we make use of both types of data in our analysis.

Our problem of market definition for mineral industries is simplified by the fact that each census industry is defined in terms of a

13. Computed for 1954 from data in *Survey of Current Business* (July 1944).

14. The data are taken from the *Census of Mineral Industries*, 1939 (U.S. Bureau of the Census, Washington, 1941).

single, economically distinct product, so that consolidations are not required. Our procedures for regional classification are the same as described in the Methodological Appendix, II, for manufacturing industries.[15]

The definitions of market structure and size classifications are the same as those for manufacturing, with one exception. The limits of market size have been halved in order to adjust the 1939 shipment data for postwar price changes. This makes the classifications roughly comparable to those used for manufactures in 1954. National concentration ratios for the mineral industries are shown in Table 5 of the Statistical Appendix. Table 3 below provides a summary, showing the number of mineral industries and the value of output by market size classification and by categories of market structure.

More detailed and recent information on a few of the more important mineral industries confirms the classifications made on the basis of the census data. For bituminous coal, the ten largest producers accounted for 24 percent and the hundred largest for 59 percent of the output.[16] In iron ore, the nine largest steel companies owned mines accounting for 41 percent of total production, and controlled by minority ownership, contract, or otherwise, 81 percent of total production.[17] The three largest copper companies account for 60 percent and the nineteen largest, 99 percent of domestic copper output. Imports do not change the picture, because 95 percent of Chilean production, whence come most imports, is owned by the same three largest companies.[18] Lead, zinc, and sulphur are all much more highly concentrated on a company basis than on an establishment basis.[19] Further, market structure in the mineral industries is characterized by the fact that many of the largest producers are integrated across market boundaries, and dominate several markets.[20]

15. We have not used as refined a geographical classification scheme as in the case of manufacturing, dividing the industries between national and regional. Mining is a much smaller sector of the economy, and does not justify as elaborate research as in manufacturing.

16. J. Schmookler, "The Bituminous Coal Industry," in *The Structure of the American Economy*, ed. W. Adams, 1954, p. 78.

17. Federal Trade Commission, *Report on the Control of Iron Ore* (1952).

18. Federal Trade Commission, *Report on the Copper Industry* (1947).

19. See *Metal Statistics* (American Bureau of Metal Statistics, Chicago, 1953).

20. Anaconda, for example, is one of the largest copper, silver, lead, and zinc producers, while Phelps Dodge is a large producer in copper, gold, silver, zinc, and lead. Kennecot, St. Joseph Lead, American Smelting and Refining, and U.S. Smelting and Refining are all important in several metals. See *Metal Statistics*.

Table 3. Summary of mineral industries: number of industries and value of product distributed by extent of market and market structure

Markets	Number of industries	Value of products (thousands of dollars)
A. National markets		
Concentrated markets		
Type I Oligopolies		
Large	0	0
Medium	2	292,507
Small	18	103,323
Total	20	395,830
Type II Oligopolies		
Large	0	0
Medium	1	114,090
Small	1	31,184
Total	2	145,274
Total, Type I and II Oligopolies	22	541,104
Unconcentrated markets		
Large	3	920,462
Medium	0	0
Small	1	12,286
Total	4	932,748
ALL NATIONAL MARKETS	26	1,473,852
B. Regional markets		
Concentrated markets		
Type I Oligopolies		
Large	0	0
Medium	0	0
Small	5	21,457
Total	5	21,457
Type II Oligopolies		
Large	0	0
Medium	0	0
Small	1	9,632
Total	1	9,632
Total, Type I and II Oligopolies	6	31,089
Unconcentrated markets		
Large	0	0
Medium	3	350,121
Small	3	16,017
Total	6	366,138
ALL REGIONAL MARKETS	12	397,227
C. Unclassified		
Large	0	0
Medium	0	0
Small	24	81,901

(d) *Trade, service, and construction*

Trade, service, and construction together constitute a large group of industries whose markets are largely local in character. They account in total for 32.5 percent of national income originated, distributed (in percents) as follows: wholesale trade, 6; retail trade, 11.5; service, 10; and construction, 5. Nearly all the industries in these sectors are ones characterized by very large numbers of enterprises in total. Further, in each metropolitan area, there is also, typically, a large number of enterprises; though in smaller cities and towns this may not be true. But the actual relevant market area, especially for retailing and service, may be quite different from the whole city or metropolitan area. For a food store, it may be a neighborhood of half a mile or so; for the automobile dealer it may even reach outside the metropolitan area. No study has yet been made which would provide a basis for meaningful market-structure categorizations in these areas. As a guess, we can say that the most important distributive trades, especially the food trades, are structurally unconcentrated in the metropolitan areas, the most important service trades likewise; and residential construction, which accounts for over half of all construction, likewise. It is probable that as we move into markets of smaller population size and trades of smaller volume, structural oligopoly at the local market level becomes fairly prevalent. However, the significance of structural oligopoly in terms of policy is far different in these sectors than in manufacturing and mining. Speaking broadly, trade, service, and construction (excluding heavy engineering and specialized activities like tunnel-building) are industries with relatively low entry barriers, whole manufacturing and mining have relatively high ones. Therefore, the traditional view that the local-market industries are essentially competitive in character is probably correct, even though unconcentrated structure is not to be ascribed to them universally.[21]

(e) *Summary*

The implications of our survey for antitrust policy are fairly ob-

21. This comment must be qualified in two ways. First, of course, even within the unconcentrated metropolitan market, the advantages of location lead to differentiation among sellers, and markets are of the large-numbers, monopolistic-competition variety rather than approaching pure competition, as in agriculture. Second, and more important, these markets are subject to many cartel and guild restrictions, some enforced by unions, some by local governments. This is especially true in the service trades and construction, but it also affects some of the retail industries.

vious. If we are correct in our contention that structural oligopoly at least raises questions of an antitrust sort, then these questions are relevant to large and important sectors of the economy. There are more concentrated than unconcentrated industries in manufacturing and mining, they are larger in aggregate size, and they tend to occupy a more important position in the economy. In distribution, service, and construction, the opposite is probably true, but the commodity-producing sectors occupy a more fundamental position. It is clear, then, that the survey shows that a policy orientation that reaches beyond conduct and that goes to the problems of the existence and significance of market power is not aimed at merely marginal or special phenomena, but at phenomena spread widely through the economy.

THE EXEMPT SECTOR

By exempt sector we mean that part of the economy to which antitrust policy does not apply because of legislative exemptions, expressed or implicit. To be sure, this exemption is not complete[22] and in some cases the legislation exempting an industry contains its own antimonopoly provisions. Nevertheless, we can say that the competitive standard applied by regulators is significantly lower than that contained in antitrust laws, so that the exemptions, combined with the operation of the regulatory agencies, give market behavior in these industries a monopoly character of varying degrees and form. The objectives of antitrust policy are either subordinated to other policy goals or sought through direct regulation.

Our purpose in this section is to give a brief, simplified sketch of the size of this sector, its significance, the extent to which competition is limited in each exempt industry, and the market structure of these industries, should the exemptions be modified or removed. In a later chapter we shall examine the public policy rationale of these exemptions.

The major industries which we classify as exempt, as well as their shares of national income, are listed in Table 4. This list is by no means all-inclusive. It excludes minor local public utilities such as cemeteries and rubbish disposal, which are regulated in some states and cities, as well as the smaller natural resource industries, such as Colorado molybdenum, which are subject to state conservation laws. Patents, Webb Pomerene Associations, and retail price maintenance

22. See the discussion in Chapter VII.

represent exemptions so dispersed over the economy that it is difficult to discuss them in the context of a separate exempt sector. The labor market likewise cannot be analyzed by the methods employed for other exempt sectors and hence is also excluded from the following discussion.

The size of the exempt sector relative to the total economy is substantial. As Table 4 indicates, 18.4 percent of national income

Table 4. Percentage of national income originating in sectors exempt from the antitrust laws, 1954

Exempt sector	Percentage of national income	
Agriculture		5.5
Transportation		4.6
Railroads	2.2	
Highway freight carriers	1.3	
Local and highway transportation	0.5	
Water transportation	0.3	
Air transportation (common carrier)	0.2	
Pipeline transportation	0.1	
Local and communication utilities		3.7
Electricity and gas	1.9	
Telephone and telegraph	1.5	
Radio broadcasting and television	0.2	
Local utilities (*n.e.c.*)	0.1	
Commercial banking and insurance		2.5
Commercial banking	1.5	
Insurance	1.0	
Natural resource industries		0.9
Crude oil and natural gas	0.8	
Anthracite coal	0.1	
Total, exempt private industries		17.2
Government enterprise		1.2
Federal	0.8	
State and local	0.4	
TOTAL, EXEMPT SECTOR		18.4

originates in the exempt sector. The presumption in discussions of antitrust policy is that the exempt sector is and will continue to be marginal. At this point, we will not consider to what extent the present size of the exempt sector undermines this assumption. All we wish to emphasize is the obvious point that the exempt sector cannot be dismissed as involving only a few special situations.

Size alone understates the economic importance of many exempt industries. For instance, transportation is a cost to almost all industries, and its price structure determines in large part the spatial organization of the economy. Prices of transportation help determine the boundaries of regional markets, and in this way help to form the market structures of other industries. The importance of electric power, the economy's principal energy input for households and firms, is also greater than its small share of national income would indicate. Commercial banking similarly occupies a strategic position as the major source of short-term credit, as an important segment of the capital market, and as the source of the nation's money supply. Size also understates the importance of insurance companies, which originate only one percent of national income but are a major source of investment funds.

Table 6 of the Statistical Appendix presents in summary form four kinds of information about each of the regulated industries listed: primary regulatory agency, extent and nature of regulation, present market structure, and probable market structure in the absence of regulation. This gives a bird's-eye view of the exempt areas, and serves to point up the existence of two different kinds of rgulation: that applying to industries, the structure of which would be monopoly or concentrated oligopoly in any event, and that applying in otherwise unconcentrated or looser oligopoly structures in which regulation may have the effect of changing the market structure.

III

A Policy for Antitrust Law

In Chapter I we suggested four alternative general goals for antitrust policy. They were (1) limitation of the power of big business; (2) performance (efficiency and progressiveness); (3) "fair dealing"; and (4) protection of competitive processes by limiting market power. For reasons to be set forth in detail hereafter, we select (4) as the most desirable and feasible guide, though willy-nilly and by design, the others will necessarily play some part.

A review of existing antitrust law indicates what to us are some important gaps in coverage. Since the existing law is primarily oriented toward conduct, it does not effectively deal — or at least has not effectively dealt in the past — with undue market power that cannot be associated with bad or unduly restrictive conduct. It seems clear that there now exist significant concentrations of undue market power, some individually held, some collectively "shared" in the sense that the members of the industry behave nonrivalrously for mutual benefit. It also seems clear to us that present law (1) has not been and cannot be fairly construed to cover the mere nonrivalrous actions of members of a noncompetitive industry, i.e., the "parallel" behavior of firms in a classic oligopoly is not "conspiracy"; and (2) may not cover all situations of individual market power that could be attacked without upsetting competitive goals (there is no deficiency here if *Alcoa* and *United Shoe* represent the law on "monopolization").[1] In addition, we believe that the law on conduct should be tightened in several respects if the prevention of undue market power is taken as a central guiding light.

In sum, we are suggesting that the primary goal of antitrust policy be the limitation of undue market power to the extent consist-

1. U.S. v. Aluminum Co. of America, 148 F.2d 416 (C.A. 2, 1945); U.S. v. United Shoe Machinery Co., 110 F. Supp. 295 (D. Mass. 1953).

ent with maintaining desirable levels of economic performance. To carry this out, we propose amendments of the antitrust laws that would (1) enable a direct attack on undue market power without regard to the presence or absence of conspiracy in the legal sense, and (2) severely limit forms of conduct that contribute to, or are likely to contribute to, the creation of undue market power.

THE POLICY GOALS

Almost any policy proposal resolves itself into a statement of a hierarchy of ends, ordered to indicate which should prevail in situations where they conflict. In proposing that the primary goal of antitrust policy be the limitation of market power, we do not make it our sole goal; we also give great weight to the achievement of desirable economic performance. Indeed, in so far as reduction of market power is incompatible with efficiency and progressiveness, we subordinate the first goal to the second. If, for example, the efficient scale of operation in a particular market is so large in relation to the size of the market that efficient firms are so few in number as to make their possession of market power likely,[2] and the reduction of market power cannot be achieved except at the cost of a substantial loss in efficiency, our policy would call for no action against the power itself. But where market power exists and can be reduced without sacrifices in performance, then such action is desirable without reference to the question of how good over-all performance may have been.

The other two of the broad classes of goals — promoting "fair" business conduct and the redistribution of social power between large and small business — occupy a much lower position in our hierarchy of policy aims. We expect that some degree of regulation of business conduct in the interest of "fair dealing" may be necessary. As we have already indicated, the policy of limiting market power will not be pressed to the point of reducing it to negligible dimensions everywhere (and indeed, this is not possible, even if it were viewed as desirable). Thus there may be some case for limiting the way in which residual market power is used. To the extent that some methods of using market power will be controlled on grounds that they are likely to contribute to the perpetuation of market power or to its increase, the area of regulation on pure "fair dealing" grounds

2. A fuller discussion of size, numbers, and market power appears later in this chapter, and there is further discussion in Chapter IV.

will be correspondingly narrowed. But some kinds of conduct which will require such regulation do exist, and where it can be achieved without too high a price in efficiency, we deem it desirable. The following is a brief summary of our recommendations.

Limitation of market power

1. We propose statutory authorization for the reduction of undue market power, whether individually or jointly possessed; this to be done normally by dissolution, divorcement, or divestiture. We would except market power derived from economies of scale, valid patents, or the introduction of new processes, products, or marketing techniques.

2. We suggest, in the alternative, that the program be either (a) a permanent feature of antitrust policy, thus applying both to existing concentrations of market power and to concentrations that may later arise through inadequacies in the law, or in enforcement of the law, concerning conduct; or (b) a program limited to the time required to deal with existing undue concentrations of market power.

3. With respect to either of the above alternatives, we suggest that the policy might be carried out either (a) under a statute in which market power is defined in general terms, requiring a fairly extensive economic inquiry for determination of each case; or (b) under a statute in which market power is more arbitrarily defined, which would facilitate the disposition of cases and more clearly identify the "targets," but could possibly be applied to firms that, in fact, lacked market power.

Limitations on conduct contributing to market power

1. *Mergers.* Particularly if the proposals as to market power are deemed unwise or undesirable, and perhaps in any event, we propose tightening the law on mergers. Some means of making enforcement more effective than it now is seems of paramount importance. We propose, as one step in this direction, a requirement of advance reporting of all mergers involving firms of more than a certain absolute size in assets or more than a certain share of any market in which they operate. We also suggest the possibility of a more arbitrary standard for illegality, in line with the similar suggestion as to market power stated above.

2. *Price-fixing or price-influencing agreements.* Regarding trade

association and similar collective activities, we propose specific statutory prohibition of agreements:

(a) to abide by reported list prices,

(b) to report offers at which no sales are made,

(c) to inform each other of the individual buyers and sellers in all transactions,

(d) to refuse to make reports, submitted to each other, available to buyers or buyers' trade associations,

(e) to submit books and accounts to the inspection of any member of the group or representative thereof; or

(f) to report transactions to each other, or to a representative of the group, within a period of seven days or less after said transactions take place.

3. *Collective refusals to deal.* Apart from those incidentally reresulting from productive joint ventures, we would make collective refusals to deal illegal per se.

4. *Patents and patent licensing.* Proceeding on the basic premise that patentees' realizable rewards can be lowered without significantly reducing the flow of useful inventions and innovations, we propose:

(a) that the patent laws be revised to create a class of "petty" patents, with monopoly rights for five years only, and to raise the standard of invention for seventeen-year patents;

(b) that on restrictive clauses in patent licensing agreements,

(1) price-fixing clauses be made illegal per se,

(2) clauses providing for grant-backs of new patents or exclusive licenses thereunder be made illegal per se,

(3) covenants not to contest patent validity be invalid in any licensing agreement containing restrictions in addition to a uniform royalty provision,

(4) cross-licensing and pooling agreements contain no restrictions beyond that for a uniform royalty charge on each patent from all licensees (except that the owner may restrict the use), and

(5) all licensing agreement be registered with the Federal Trade Commission (but not made public);

(c) that Section 7 of the Clayton Act be revised to cover acquisitions of patents from individuals as well as from corporations.

5. *Price discrimination.* We propose that the Robinson-Patman Act be repealed, in favor of a statute dealing separately with (a)

price discrimination directed against competing sellers and (b) price discrimination that harms particular buyers. In each case, we would make some substantive changes in the existing law. In both cases, we would liberalize the "cost" defense and specifically exclude from the law all geographic price discrimination that is accounted for entirely by differences in transportation cost.

Procedural and related recommendations

1. We propose that criminal penalties be limited to the so-called per se offenses.

2. We propose that treble damages also be limited to the per se offenses; that no private suit be maintainable under a market power statutory provision; and that judgment under the market power provision would not constitute prima facie proof of anything under Section 5 of the Clayton Act.

3. We suggest the creation of a special court for adjudicating monopoly cases and other Sherman Act cases in which divestiture is part of the relief sought. For an extended program against undue market power, we propose a special court, with the prosecuting function placed in the hands of a new administrative agency. We also propose certain procedural steps designed to clarify and speed the trial of economic issues of fact.

Our reasons for giving primary emphasis to the fourth of the general goals of policy stated above and for making the above recommendations are partly positive and partly negative. Our positive reasons rest ultimately on a value judgment. The most important aspect of the competitive process is that it is self-controlling with regard to private economic power.[3] For all the important qualifications and limitations of the doctrine of the invisible hand which modern economic analysis has produced, that doctrine remains the basic political justification for an enterprise economy in which major economic decisions are compelled and coordinated through the market. It is the fact that the competitive market *compels* the results of its processes which is the ultimate defense against the demand that economic decisions be made or supervised by politically responsible authorities. Without such market compulsion, that de-

3. But not, of course, self-maintaining (see Chapter I). Nor is this meant to deny the existence of problems regarding the stability of the market economy in the aggregate, which we exclude from our particular discussion.

mand appears ultimately irresistible in a society committed to representative government. It is our preference for the kind of autonomy in economic life which a market-organized society makes possible that forms the particular judgment we make.

Our negative reasons are more objective, and less subject to dogmatic acceptance or rejection. In essence, they amount to the proposition that the alternative standards present definitional and administrative problems of such magnitude that consistent and sensible enforcement would be well-nigh impossible. While similar difficulties would attend the carrying out of a market power standard, we conclude that they would be much less severe. Moreover, we believe it is possible to formulate arbitrary tests designed to reduce administrative problems under a market power standard with considerably more confidence in the results than if similar steps were taken in order to carry out the other designated goals.

We now turn to a detailed discussion of the workability of policy standards that we substantially reject.

STANDARDS OTHER THAN MARKET POWER

Limitation of big business power

We would discard the general limiting of big business power as an independent goal of antitrust policy. Some change in the size distribution of firms will be a by-product of the limitation of market power. To the extent that general business power rests on market power, the limitations of one will correspondingly limit the other. Any antitrust policy, if vigorously prosecuted, that goes beyond the regulation of conduct represents (or reflects) some limitation on the general social and political power of big business. An attempt to press the restraint of big business beyond these results, which are incidental to the pursuit of other aims, would be so costly in terms of other goals that we rule it out as a desirable policy.

Two paths might be taken in pursuit of the goal of limiting the power of big business: first, direct control of large firms along the lines of the regulation of public utilities; second, radical reformation of the existing size distribution of business firms, plus continued controls on the absolute size of business firms. The first of these involves the abandonment of competition as a general policy and its replacement by pervasive detailed regulation, a course we reject without pausing to belabor the point. The second possibility, drastic dissolution and divestiture of existing large firms together with some control on the growth of firms, appears as an element in some discussions of antitrust policy.[4] But if such a policy is to achieve significant results in changing the size distribution of business firms, its costs in terms of desirable economic performance would be tremendous, both immediately and in the long run. Suppose, for example, we imposed a one-plant, one-firm limitation on the size of businesses. In manufacturing, about 60 percent of total output is produced by multiestablishment firms; in many industries the figure is 75 percent or more.[5] The 32,000 manufacturing establishments of the multiplant firms were operated by some 8000 firms.[6] To carry out a one-plant, one-firm, policy within any short period would require measures on a heroic scale. If completed in a decade, the program would require the reorganization of an average of at least 800 manufacturing firms alone per year. This seems hardly possible, except at great cost in administrative resources and with a substantial reduction in the efficiency of the firms undergoing reorganization. And more reorganizations would be required in mining, distribution, and other sectors. Even after transition costs were past history, considerable economies of personnel management, selling, production, scheduling, and research would be sacrificed by a strict one-plant, one-firm rule, and total output correspondingly reduced.

We have used the one-plant, one-firm rule as the most drastic reorganization scheme that is in any sense feasible, and it seems clear that it is hardly a practicable proposal. But it is doubtful that any considerably less drastic proposal would make a significant step toward the policy goal in question — limiting the influence of large business. Suppose, for example, the 1000 largest manufacturing en-

4. Proposals of this sort rarely appear explicitly in academic literature. There is is what Keynes has called an underworld literature which carries these views, ranging from T. K. Quinn's *Giant Business, Threat to Democracy* (N.Y., 1953) to F. Raymond's *The Limitist.* (N.Y., 1957) "Respectable" academic discussions which contain in weaker or stronger form undertones of the same position include the writings of Walter Adams, Corwin Edwards, and the late Henry Simons.

5. See 1954 *Census of Manufactures,* vol. I, ch. IV.

6. See Census Bulletin CS-1, 1954, *Company Statistics,* table B, p. vii, for the number of companies primarily engaged in manufacturing; and the 1954 *Census of Manufactures,* vol. I ch. IV, for the number of manufacturing establishments they operated. In addition to these manufacturing establishments, the 8000 multiunit companies operated about twice as many nonmanufacturing establishments of all kinds, including central offices, auxilliaries, sales branches, and sales offices, which have been ignored in the discussion that follows.

terprises[7] were drastically reorganized so that each was split into at least ten parts, and the larger ones were split into enough fragments so that no resulting fragment had assets of over $25 million.[8] The result would be to add some 10,000 firms to the manufacturing sector, ranging in asset size from roughly $1 to $25 million. This can be compared with the 330,000 firms now in manufacturing, of which about 10,000 to 12,000 are now in the $1 to $25 million asset size range, and perhaps 500 are now larger than $25 million. Similar operations in the other parts of the market-controlled sectors — trade, service, construction, and mining — would lead to even less impressive results, since these areas have smaller firms, on the average, than manufacturing, and very large firms are less important in them than in manufacturing.[9] Altogether, given a total business pop-

7. See the FTC list published in 1951. Here again we use manufacturing as our example, both because figures are available and because it is the most important sector of the economy in which the problems for antitrust policy associated with very large firms are significant.

8. The proposed division would not be practicable in just this form, since the creation of firms within the size limit would involve the division of plants in the petroleum, chemical, primary metal industries, and probably in some others. The more than tenfold division would apply to the 49 corporations in the list with assets of over $250 million. In the five years since the list was published, the largest firms on it have grown considerably in asset size, along with the general growth of output and the substantial rise in prices. *Fortune* published a list of large industrial corporations (July 1955), which appears roughly comparable, although it excludes nonpublicly held corporations such as Ford, some of which are on the FTC list. That list contains 76 corporations with assets of over $250 million; and 19 of these had assets of over 1 billion compared with 11 on the FTC list. These 19 increased their aggregate assets by about 60 percent; this comparison is unreliable, since the exact basis of the *Fortune* compilation in terms of subsidiaries, etc., is not known.

9. On January 1, 1952, the manufacturing population was some 330,000 firms. Of these, 110,000 were corporations. In 1947, the most recent year for which data are available, 75 percent of all the firms and 48 percent of the corporations had fewer than 20 employees (*Survey of Current Business*, April 1955, pp. 14–20). The Statistics of Income, Pt. II, for 1955 gives 130,000 as the total number of corporate income tax returns in manufacturing, of which 124,000 had balance sheets. The following distribution is by total asset size of those with balance sheets:

Total asset size	No. of returns
$100 million or more	247
$50–$100 million	201
$10–$50 million	1,446
$5–$10 million	1,511
$1–$5 million	10,400
$500 thousand to $1 million	9,900
$250–$500 thousand	15,200
$100–$250 thousand	26,100
$50–$100 thousand	19,600
Under $50 thousand	39,400

ulation (excluding farms) of some 4 million firms, of which about 3.6 million are in the market-controlled sectors, the kind of changes sketched above would make little difference in the relative importance of small proprietorships on the Jeffersonian model and large bureaucratized enterprises with hired managers and absentee owners. Yet such a program is as drastic a reorganization of large business, en masse, as we can conceive would ever be carried out. This is not to say that the program would make no difference to the economic importance of large firms or to the functioning of markets, but as we have already stated, it would go little beyond our other policy proposals in changing the distribution of power between large and small business.

Performance

To give performance more importance than we would give it in our market power standard is an appealing alternative policy, and one which always has supporters. The logic of this view is clear: progress and efficiency are the two great historical achievements of

---

These are returns rather than corporations, and exceed the number of corporate enterprises, since most returns are filed on a nonconsolidated basis. Thus the large corporation with many subsidiaries files many returns. Most of this over-reporting is concentrated in the first three size classes. The FTC list of the 1000 largest manufacturing corporations gives the following distribution for these classes:

Total assets	Number		
$100 million or more	138		
$50–$100 million	123	Total assets	Number
$10–$50 million	661	$25–$50 million	207
		$10–$25 million	454

In the other sectors, the number of firms and the proportion with fewer than 20 employees in 1947 was:

Sector	Thousands of firms 1952	Percent with fewer than 20 employees, 1947
Mining	38	n.a.
Construction	394	94
Wholesale Trade	276	93
Retail Trade	1937	98
Services	735	n.a.
Total, above, and manufacturing		3608
Finance		332
Transportation and Public Utilities		181
Total		513
Grand Total All Industries		4121

Source. Survey of Current Business (April 1955), pp. 14–20

American industry; the simple and obvious aim of public policy in matters of industrial organization should be to promote more progress and efficiency. The central question in the application of antitrust policy — unfair practices aside — then becomes: is the subject firm progressive and efficient? If so, it should be free from legal attack or control; if not, it should be open to such action. Our own standard would give an important place to the evaluation of the efficiency aspects of performance; the central point of difference between it and the performance alternative is thus the place of progressiveness.

Let us consider the implications of making progressiveness the main content of the standard by which the compliance of business firms with the public policy of the antitrust laws is measured. Any decision to intervene in the affairs of a firm on antitrust grounds — whether by proscribing or prescribing aspects of its conduct, or by altering its structure and its situation — is then based on the determination that the alteration will lead to better results than those in the pre-existing situation. Further, if any notion of liability and compliance with law is involved, it must be assumed that this or some similar alteration, had it been made before the period for which the results of the firm's operations are examined, would have led to superior results — more progress — than actually took place.

This is a peculiarly difficult proposition to establish either directly or by deduction from the kind of evidence that is available. In general, the available evidence will show in fact what progress has been achieved by the firm over some past period, in terms of decreased costs, new products, new applications for old products, increased outputs; and what resources have been devoted to the achievement of these results, in terms of expenditures on research and development, investments in new plant, new resources of supply, new channels of distribution, market research, sales engineering, and the like. Some of this information will be available in fairly exact terms, such as measures of input reductions per unit of output, or dollar expenditures on research or plant expansion. Some may be much less precise, such as evaluations of the degree to which new products are superior to old, especially in the case of consumer goods; but even in this case usable information will not be lacking. What will be lacking is any basis for deciding whether the firm's performance was good or bad in light of its opportunities. The record may reveal that output has grown ten times in the period under study; it will not reveal whether or not output could have grown fifteen times if price policy had been different or if more vigorous efforts had been made in product development, in foreign marketing, or in cost reduction. The record may show that expenditures of money and of the time of trained men on research and development were large and continuous, and that the decrease of inputs per unit of output as well as the flow of new and improved products were great; it will not in general show whether returns per dollars or per professional man-hour were high or low, or would have been higher or lower had the situation or conduct of the firm been different than it in fact was. True, there may be exceptional situations in which the spectacular quality of the results overwhelms question, or in which the almost total lack of effort speaks for itself. Yet even in such cases the problem is not completely solved. Would a big research effort in the poorly performing industry pay for itself? Could the excellent performer have bettered even its own spectacular record if it had operated under different market conditions?

Our inability to get the evidence which is needed to answer such questions has three causes. First, it is almost always impossible to find comparable firms or groups of firms differing only in respect to the features of industrial organization under question, but similar in respect to technology, markets, and the various aspects of what might be called objective research opportunities whose performance on the score of progressiveness can be compared. Frequently, firms in the same industry are jointly involved in the noncompetitive situation which raises the problem of policy: they are cooperating oligopolists, they are all members of the closed patent pool, etc.; thus the performance of some does not furnish a standard by which the performance of others can be measured. Nor do the smaller firms in the market — those which might be complainants rather than defendants in antitrust proceedings — generally offer a useful standard by which progressiveness can be measured. They frequently specialize in supplying some segment of the market, and thus are not faced with the same range of problems and possibilities as their rivals. Further, the hindrances placed in their way by the existence of their larger rivals may be the essence of the situation in question. Again, the question is not, did firm A produce more progress per unit of resources than firm Y over the past period, given the actual situation, but rather, did firm A produce more progress per unit of resources than firm Y would have, if the market relations between A and Y were different from what in fact they have been?

Second, we rarely can make up for the lack of objective comparisons by the use of the informed judgment of disinterested experts. This is so not because expert opinion is lacking, but because it is rarely available except from those who have actually made the decisions whose consequences are being evaluated. This is especially the case in respect to research and development activity and to the creation and commercialization of new products. The outsider can hardly be expected to possess the kind of information either about the particular applications of technology to the problems of the firm, or about the market and financial situation of the firm that is a part of a decision to attempt one development and reject another, to spend parsimoniously in one case and generously in another. The insider who assisted in forming the decisions under review can hardly be disinterested. What appeared to him as sensible choices in the light of available knowledge at the time he made them will almost inevitably appear so again on review, leaving aside any interested motives he may have in defending the actions of the firm with which he is associated.[10]

Third, economic analysis does not provide us with a conceptual framework within which the facts of particular examples of more or less progressiveness can be fitted.[11] Nor do we have a large tested body of empirical information showing how particular results in progressiveness were associated with other aspects of performance and with market structure, which could in part substitute for a theoretical framework of analysis.

All the problems of dealing with progressiveness in isolation remain if we try to make a combined evaluation of both progressiveness and efficiency.[12] To them a new one is added: the relative weights to be given progressiveness and efficiency and the treatment of the interrelations between them in arriving at a combined score. Again, we lack an analytical framework to guide us on this

10. For concrete examples of these problems, see C. Kaysen, *United States v. United Shoe Machinery Corporation* (1956).

11. See above, for examples of some of the conceptual difficulties in evaluating progressiveness.

12. We neglect other aspects of performance as less important, and unnecessary to the argument. Similar problems arise in evaluating selling costs, but of lesser complexity.

point. We shall indicate our general views on this subject in the subsequent discussion of a market power standard. We merely point out here that while general views may suffice for the purpose of drawing broad policy conclusions, they are extraordinarily difficult to apply to particular markets.

"Fair dealing"

"Fair dealing" as a standard of business conduct is now and historically has been an important element of antitrust law.[13] Why should it not become the central goal of antitrust policy? To answer this question, we must pause to see what content can be given to the term.[14] Our own policy proposal involves fair dealing in two senses. First, in so far as fairness is defined to mean the character transactions would have if they took place in competitive markets, our policy, by aiming at the achievement of more competitive markets, would create fairer transactions as a by-product. Second, we have proposed that some specifically defined kinds of unfair conduct be forbidden, in the light of inevitable limitations on achieving completely competitive markets. If fairness is to be given a more central position than this, it must mean either: (1) that every transaction (or set of transactions) should be scrutinized to see how closely it corresponds to what would have resulted had the transaction in question been carried on under competitive conditions: (2) that some notion of "proportionately equal" treatment, in the light of the circumstances, becomes the standard of fairness; or (3) that what recommends itself to the conscience of the business community as fair becomes the standard.

On analysis, the utility of either (1) or (3) as a guide to administration is doubtful. The latter fails because there is in fact no agreement in the business community on what is fair in just those situations which create the need for public regulation. Potential complainants and potential respondents are divided on what actions recommend themselves to their consciences as honest competitive methods: the discount house and the "fair-trading" appliance

13. As pointed out in Chapter I, it is probably correct to assert that the interests in "fair" and "free" competition (the latter term carrying the sense of no special restraints imposed on particular competitors, especially by government) are the major interests which antitrust law historically has sought to protect. The importation into the law of an abstract community interest in economic efficiency, and in competition as such, apart from particular instances of unfair competitive practices is, according to some, a novelty and a novelty of doubtful value.

14. See Chapter I above.

dealer share no sense of what is fair in price policy. The first guide, what would result under competitive conditions, will fail to provide a usable administrative guide in one of two ways. In application it will either resolve itself into an analysis of whether competition does or does not prevail in the required degree, and a judgment of fairness accordingly, or it will turn into an effort by the administrators of policy to predict the outcomes of market processes, both actual and hypothetical, and to evaluate the fairness of a situation in accordance with its predicted outcome. In the first case, fairness as such has simply disappeared as an independent policy goal, and we are essentially back to our proposed market power standard. In the second, the application of the standard becomes impossible. If, to take an earlier example, the administrator of policy is charged with deciding whether or not the competition of discount houses with full-service, high mark-up dealers is fair or unfair, he must forecast whether, in a competitive market, the new type of outlet would or would not make substantial inroads on the business of the old. In part, he could rely on judgments of whether the market is or is not now competitive, and we would be back to the first case. This might not suffice, in which instance he would be forced to base his decision on just the kind of reading of the future that those in the market are usually unable to do with any unanimity though their business success and even their livelihoods are at stake. This is a burden which cannot wisely be imposed on the agents of the law. The results would inevitably be arbitrary and capricious as well as economically harmful in efficiency terms whenever a bad guess led to the suppression, as unfair, of that which would in time prove to be a successful and superior new way of doing business. The situation implied in this example is neither extreme nor atypical, and many of the important problems will arise in a similar context.

Thus we are thrust back to (2) — the notion of equal treatment for those in similar positions — as the content to be given to fairness when it is applied in practice. This is in fact the kind of standard which has guided the application of the Robinson-Patman Act as a standard of fair competition in pricing and related matters; and as the history of that act illustrates, it presents its own dilemmas. The administrator must strike a balance between two courses. The first is to consider every case as a different set of circumstances which defines its own standard of fairness, and thus prescribes conduct in detail (assuming, against all reason, that this would be feasible in terms of administrative resources). The second is to make so broad a classification of what constitutes similar circumstances and thus demands similar treatment, as to put severe and costly limitations on the flexibility of business decision. To take an example of this dilemma, in rationing a basic material in short supply, how can "fair conduct" be determined? If suppliers allow price to rise to the point where markets are cleared, perhaps they are safe from criticism. But if some buyers have long-term contracts at lower prices, may not those who are forced to buy at the high spot price complain that they are being squeezed? And if long-term contracts are available only for large amounts, are small buyers' complaints justified? Yet if rationing takes place on the basis of past purchases rather than market price, competition among the consumers is hindered, and the efficient growing purchaser may be held back in favor of the larger declining one.

The application of a standard of fairness defined in terms of equal treatment thus leads either to high efficiency costs, if broad rules are laid down as to what constitute similar circumstances, or to a large measure of substitution of detailed regulation of particular transactions for market competition, if each set of circumstances is scrutinized to provide its own standard of fairness. Thus, none of our three alternative definitions of fairness provides a policy standard that is both administratively feasible and free of high costs in terms of efficiency.

LIMITATIONS OF MARKET POWER: DEFINITIONS, ANALYSIS, AND PROBLEMS

We have stated that our primary policy goal is one of curbing undue market power, whether individually or jointly possessed, to the extent consistent with the achievement of desirable economic performance. We would therefore make no direct attempt to eliminate market power derived from economies of scale, valid patents, or the introduction of new processes, products, or marketing techniques, nor would we impose the remedy of dissolution where for these or other limited reasons the performance costs would be too great. In addition, we recognize the need for considerable regulation of the conduct of firms, to control attempts to achieve or maintain market power, to control practices that are likely to create or maintain such power, and to control the use of such power that our policy would deem "reasonable."

Having disposed of alternative policy goals on the principal ground that they pose definitional and hence administrative problems of a quite unmanageable nature, we wish to repeat at the outset of this discussion that a market power standard is by no means immune to difficulties on this score. Indeed, one of the purposes of our discussion is to point out just what, and how serious, those difficulties are; and the existence of these difficulties, though we believe them much less severe than those inherent in alternative policy aims, leads us eventually to consider the desirability of adopting some arbitrary tests of "market power," and of limiting any direct program against undue market power to a fixed period of time.

Market performance, market structure, and market power

Our interest in the operation of markets[15] involves two elements: certain specified results, which we have called desirable economic performance, especially those of efficiency and progressiveness; and the character of the market processes themselves, in particular the scope of decision for the firms in it, and the extent to which the market compels the particular performance actually observed.

Antitrust policy, however, cannot operate directly either on performance or on processes: we cannot conceive of an effective order which says, be efficient, or, be competitive. Rather, policy operates directly on market structure and on firm conduct in order to affect processes and performance. "Market structure" we use to mean those conditions external to the firm which are relatively permanent or which change only slowly, and which affect, if they do not determine, the way the firm operates. Such features of a market as the numbers of buyers and sellers, the techniques of production and marketing, the geographic distribution of production and demand, the character of demand for the product, are all elements of market structure. "Conduct" comprises aspects of the market which are the result of specific decisions of firms and which are, at least conceivably, alterable in relatively short periods of time. Patent-pooling arrangements, the use of exclusive dealerships, basing point pricing formulas, are examples of market conduct. Crudely put, conduct is subject to alteration by injunction; change in structure requires some more drastic reorganization measures of the dissolution, divestiture,

15. We have used the term "market" without definition. Briefly, it is a group of buyers and sellers who, respectively, seek each other out as sources of supply and as customers or potentially could do so with respect to a group of products which are close substitutes. We will elaborate on this definition in Chapter IV.

and divorcement type. But this is a crude distinction, and the line between what is called structure and what is called conduct is not always an easy one to draw. In particular markets, there is an intimate association between certain lines of conduct and certain structural features of the market which makes a sharp separation artificial. Thus in a market with a very small number of sellers and closely similar products, such as the cigarette market, the phenomenon of price leadership typical of such markets may be classified as "conduct," or viewed simply as a correlate of the structural features of small numbers and closely similar products. Application of the policy criterion would lead to the classification of price leadership under structure since, in this situation, it would be impossible to alter it merely by injunction.[16] Conversely, we can think of examples of conduct which, when persisted in, alter structure. Thus a policy of exclusive dealing maintained by many firms in a particular market may over time limit the kind of distributors who are able to carry the product in question, and thus make this aspect of market structure different than it would have been without the exclusive distribution policy. Thus it is not useful to attempt to maintain too rigid a distinction between structure and conduct; structure in a broad sense can be taken to include both structure proper and conduct. In this broad sense, the structure of a market, from the point of view of a particular firm, comprises the circumstances external to that firm which condition its decisions, including the characteristic conduct of other firms in the market.

Ideally, we should like to make a complete analytical chain from market structure (including conduct) to processes to performance. We would then be able both to deduce present performance from observation of present structure, and to predict what alterations in performance would result from particular changes in structure. Further, we would be able to say to what extent any observed pattern of performance was compelled by the structure of the market, and to what extent it was the result of policy choices by firms, which could well have been other than they were. The theoretical model of the perfectly competitive market provides an example of such a one-to-one correspondence of structure, processes, and performance. In practice, our analytic apparatus is inadequate to the task of providing such correlations in the study of actual markets, and the prospects of speedy improvement in it are not bright. We can

16. See discussion of collusion and parallel action, Chapter IV.

neither predict market performance from market structure, nor can we tell from structure alone how competitive the processes of the market are. A major consequence of the gaps in our knowledge is that our conclusions about the functioning of any concrete market depend on the joint study of both structure and performance. We cannot determine what structure is without examining certain aspects of performance. Our problem then is to trace out the underlying structure both by direct observation and by inference from the behavior of certain performance variables in the known circumstances of the past.

Thus, for example, a conclusion that barriers to entry in some markets are high may be based in part on an examination of the size of the smallest efficient production unit, the nature of distribution channels, the existence of a closed patent pool, etc. In part, however, it will rest on the observation of continued high profits and nonprice rationing of output among customers in periods of high demand. In general, we would not be able to draw a confident conclusion on this point on the structural evidence alone, but would require confirmation from past performance consistent with our inference on structural evidence. Each thorough industry study does something to close the gap in our knowledge of the associations between structure and performance, but their number is still far too few.[17]

Our inability to predict performance from structure is not the only serious gap in our knowledge. We are only somewhat better off in predicting the relations between the various individual aspects (or dimensions) of performance, and the ultimate results, in terms of the whole economy, which we view as desirable. Efficiency and progressiveness are the results we seek that are closely related to the functioning of markets.[18] We can define efficiency with some precision, and characterize the dimensions of performance which measure its various aspects in detail. The same cannot be said of progressiveness: we lack both a standard against which the observed measures of progress can be tested and knowledge of the relations between measures of progressiveness and measures of efficiency. Ideally, a

17. For evidence of certain kinds of structure-performance associations see J. S. Bain, "Relation of Profit Rate to Industry Concentration, American Manufacturing, 1936–40," *Quarterly Journal of Economics* (August 1951), Workable Competition in Oligopoly," *American Economic Review* (May 1950), and *Barriers to New Competition* (1956).

18. See Chapter I.

standard of performance for any particular performance dimension should reflect the relation of that aspect of performance to the achievement of both efficiency and progressiveness. Thus, for example, a standard of profit performance should depend not only on the result of efficiency, which by itself requires that the long-run profit in excess of the supply price of capital and entrepreneurship be zero, but also on the result of progressiveness, which conceivably might call for higher profits in any industry deemed capable of innovating. In practice, though, our knowledge does not permit us to discuss what the profit standard should in fact be, if progressiveness as well as efficiency are taken into consideration. We may be able to say something about profits in a particular industry, in the context of a detailed examination of that industry, but we lack the basis in either theory or experience for making any generalized statements about profit standards which reflect the relation of profits to all the desirable results we seek to achieve.

The consequence of our ignorance is that performance standards fall into two classes: those concerned with the efficiency aspects of performance, which derive from the competitive model and are mutually interrelated in definite ways; and those concerned with progressiveness and other aspects of performance, which rest on no corresponding theoretical structure. The functioning of any market must be tested against these two classes of performance standards separately, and then some *ad hoc* evaluation of the possible consistency or inconsistency between them must be made, since a general statement of their relationship cannot be made.

(1) *Efficiency aspects of performance.* The efficiency aspects of performance divide, in turn, into three classes: relations between prices and costs; relations among output, capacity, and demand; and technical efficiency.

(a) *Prices and costs.* Price-cost relations are measured for individual firms, and they refer to average behavior over a long period. Ideally, we are looking for information on the behavior of prices with respect to long-run average costs; averages of prices and costs over a period long enough to include at least one complete business cycle, and preferably several cycles, serve as an approximation to this ideal.[19] In conditions of stationary demand, with output con-

19. For most industries with which we are concerned, long-run average costs are equal to long-run marginal costs (neglecting sunk costs, usually very small), and thus we can speak of average costs throughout. For some, this will not be true, be-

stant, on the average, price should approximate cost, including some measure of normal profit. Where demand and output are declining in the long run, prices should fall short of costs as long as output is declining faster than productive capacity. Since capacity can be adjusted only slowly, over the average, prices for products with declining demands should fall short of long-run average costs (including normal profits). With long-run rising demand and with output continually pressing on capacity, price should on the average exceed cost (including normal profits).

For the single-product firm, average profits are a fairly good measure of long-run price-cost relations. Average profit should be in the neighborhood of normal profit when output is constant over the long run, below it with declining output, and above it with rising output. Normal profit is defined as the long-run supply price of capital. While no exact measurement of it exists, it can be approximated in several ways. First, the bond-interest rate on first-grade industrial bonds, plus an allowance for the extra riskiness of returns to equity capital, appropriate to the character of the industry (e.g., high for an industry like steel with sharply fluctuating cyclical fortunes, low for an industry like bread baking in which fluctuations are much less), is one good approximation. Second, the historical average returns for firms in competitive industries over long periods can serve as another approximation.[20] Both the measure of normal profits and the profit averages for firms and groups of firms will be sufficiently crude so that no fine determinations of "correct" price-cost relations can be made. If normal profits are of the magnitude of, say, 6 to 8 percent on invested capital, an average profit rate of 9 percent over ten years could not be identified as supernormal with any confidence, but one of 12 percent could.[21]

---

cause of rising supply prices for some scarce factor, say, a mineral raw material. Then long-run marginal cost will be greater than long-run average cost, and it is the former which should be compared with price.

20. To be sure, this raises the problem of identifying "competitive industries," independently of profits. While this is not entirely easy, some industries have sufficiently large numbers, and sufficiently easy entry, to be identified on structural grounds alone as competitive with a high degree of confidence.

21. We do not discuss the difficult index-number problems that often arise in measuring profits in period of rapidly changing price levels. In general, it can be said that they are soluble to a degree, but where they arise, the roughness of our approximations is further increased. Another aspect of the problem of profit measurement is conceptual: not everything which the corporate books show as profits should be counted as such; some profit items are rents in the economic sense, and in the case of mineral production or the exploitation of water power sites, it is necessary to make some allowance for these rents in order to judge the profit figures.

For the more typical case of the multiproduct firm, average total profits are not a satisfactory measure of price-cost relations, since high price-cost margins on some products might be counterbalanced by low margins on others, making for an average not different from the level of normal profits. It is thus necessary to have some measure of price-cost margins for each product, or for each major product line, and to apply the appropriate tests to each separately. This is the more necessary in that the development of demand for different product lines may differ, and thus the appropriate profit rates. Where demand is stable, the price-cost margins should, on the average, be the same among various products and product lines. Persistent departure from such equality — interproduct price discrimination — is a symptom of inefficient performance. The costs referred to, here as elsewhere in this discussion, are long-run average costs. In the long run, the costs of producing individual items in most product combinations are separable, in the sense that combinations of products in different proportions would have different costs, and thus the average cost of producing the given volume of each product in the particular combination can be calculated. Cases of true long-run joint costs, where two or more products are produced in fixed proportions, are very rare: where they exist, price-cost margins on the separate products cannot meaningfully be defined. In most industrial multiproduct firms, however, what may first appear as joint overhead costs of producing several products are in fact common costs but not joint costs, since the products can usually be produced in differing proportions, sometimes by varying the production processes used, and thus price-cost margins for the separate products can be defined.

The competitive model, which defines economic efficiency, tells us that prices should equal costs, product by product, in long-run equilibrium. Translated into observational terms, when demand is stationary, substantial departures from price-cost equality, on the average of a period of years, indicate the existence of noncompetitive performance. When demand is growing, we expect excess profits or margins. Stated crudely, we can say that these are of the appropriate order of magnitude if (1) the excess profits do not persist when the expansion of capacity and output ceases or (2), where growth is continuous, the excess profits are of the order of the rate of growth of capacity.[22] If either of these conditions is violated, then

22. This second standard is a rough one, at best. It is derived from simple gen-

we can conclude that price-cost behavior differs from efficient behavior as defined by the competitive model.

In conditions of long-run declining demand, we would expect prices to fall below costs, including normal profits. In general, the magnitude of the gap depends on the character of fixed plant and on the relative importance of short-run variable and short-run fixed costs in the cost structure of firms in the industry in question. As long as output declines faster than capacity, losses should persist. If capacity is very rapidly adjustable (low fixed costs), then price may equal, or nearly equal, average costs even with declining demand.

We have set forth a standard of price-cost relationships that applies to long-run behavior, as measured by average values of the relevant variables over fairly long periods of time. This standard tells us nothing about price-cost relations in the short run. In particular, two kinds of situations may lead to substantial short-run departure from the price-cost relations described above without indicating inefficient performance as we define it. First, in industries with large amounts of specialized fixed capital and highly variable demand, we do not expect prices to equal short-run marginal costs at all times, fluctuating violently as demand fluctuates. Rather, over the cycle prices may fluctuate much less than short-run marginal (or short-run average variable) costs, and still maintain appropriate long-run relations.[23] Second, in industries where the firm typically produces many products, and product lines are rapidly changing, it would not in general be the case that price-cost margins would be the same among all products and product lines. Rather, newer products, lacking imitators by competitive firms, would tend to show higher margins than better established ones. But in the long run these would tend to wear away with competition, and margins on established products would tend to equality.[24]

eralizations of competitive models, under somewhat restrictive assumptions, from stationary conditions to conditions of steady growth. Another way of looking at "normal" profit is to identify it with the average rate of growth of the whole economy, plus an appropriate risk premium; then industries with higher than average rates of growth, maintained over long periods, might be expected to show higher profit rates.

23. In a competitive model, price would always equal short-run marginal cost. But this is efficient only when exit and entry are really free and quick. In practice, in industries of the kind described, such as steel, price fluctuations of the short-run competitive kind might be disequilibrating in the long run, and, at best, would make no contribution to long-run adjustment.

24. The relation of innovation to profits and the model of competitive behavior is difficult to state in any but very broad terms. In general, the first successful use of

(b) *Output, capacity, and demand.* The second set of performance dimensions relevant to efficiency are the relations among output, capacity, and demand. An efficiently functioning industry shows no excess capacity at the cyclical (or cyclical-seasonal) peaks in production. In measuring excess capacity, allowance must be made for the existence of obsolete equipment, kept for stand-by purposes, which is occasionally brought into use at seasonal peaks in demand but is not regularly utilized. Again, we are interested in long-run excess capacity, and the appropriate measurement is an average over several peak periods. Excess capacity is compatible with efficiency if it is accompanied by losses, and by declines in capacity which tend to reduce the excess. In local or regional market industries where there have been regional shifts in demand (e.g., cement or gypsum), excess capacity and losses in some regions may be observed along with profits and growing capacity in others, consistent with economic efficiency. But persistent excess capacity not accompanied by losses is a mark of inefficiency and of undue market power.

Excess capacity is usually a phenomenon of declining demand. The corresponding problem in situations of rising demand is the expansion of capacity to meet growths in demand. Persistent lags of capacity behind demand, indicated either by nonprice "rationing" of output at demand peaks or by sudden spurts in prices at periods of high demand, show a maladaptation of capacity to demand. In examining the relation of capacity to demand in any particular in-

---

an innovation leads to supernormal profits for the user firm; in time, imitation and rival innovations compete away the profits. By and large, innovation is not a costless happy accident but the result of an outlay of resources in research, development, and promotion. In the long run, then, it might be expected that the profits of successful innovation would be pressed by competition down to just covering the costs of innovation, including those of unsuccessful developments. But there are many features of the process of innovation which make it difficult to apply this standard of rewards and costs with any rigor or precision. Much innovative activity is overhead, and covers a wide variety of products, and the results of particular efforts are unpredictable so that correspondence between costs and returns for any particular range of products with the resource inputs and successes among firms is often far from close: a costly innovation may fail, a relatively simple modification of it may succeed.

The lags between first innovator and rival innovators and imitators are variable; in some cases profits are quickly worn away, in others they persist over a long period of time. Finally, the particular incidence of effective restraints on imitation and rival innovation furnished by the patent laws is highly variable, so that a judgment of the extent to which supernormal profit can be viewed as the "rent" of a legal license is difficult. Yet with all these difficulties, some judgment on an *ad hoc* basis in any particular situation can be made as the relation between costs and returns in innovative activity, and particularly wide discrepancies detected.

dustry, allowance must be made for the time taken to build new plants and, where it exists, for any unusual variability of demand.

(c) *Technical efficiency.* The requirements of technical efficiency are three: production must be by efficient methods ("on" the cost curve), in plants of efficient scale, and at efficient locations. The first point is largely an engineering matter, but it also means that firms should show no obvious internal inefficiencies in terms of knowledge of costs, accounting procedures, and the like. The second point is also primarily a matter of engineering judgment, but in judging the appropriateness of plant scales, allowance must be made for lags in the adaptation of new techniques, and for the persistence of production in existing plants of old design even in competitive conditions, so long as variable costs are recovered. Similarly, in judging the efficiency of plant location, shifts in demand and the persistence of production at existing locations must be taken into account. Both judgments — that of efficient scale and that of efficient location — thus are applicable rather to new or recently built plants than to the whole industry, especially in situations where demand and technology are both changing rapidly.

When these three sets of conditions are met, production is efficient in the sense that no reorganization of inputs would lead to greater outputs from the given bundle of resources. The equilibrium of the competitive model, in which all industries are perfectly competitive, is efficient in this sense, and it is of course for this reason that we deduce the efficiency conditions from it. In practice, of course, we cannot observe industries in equilibrium. But we can observe the extent to which changes in external circumstances are met by responses moving toward equilibrium, and whether or not these movements are rapid or relatively slow. Such observations can lead us to a judgment on whether or not industry performance is efficient.[25]

25. A fourth condition of efficiency also deserves mention: the equality of private and social costs and private and social benefits. If some real costs of production are not borne by the producing firm, and if some real benefits of production can be enjoyed without payment, then the money costs and returns of the firm, which guide the allocation of resources, do not record the appropriate signals. But the equality of private and social costs, especially in the areas relevant to our study, is not a major problem. Where it exists, as in crude oil production, it reflects inappropriate property institutions, and therefore cannot usually be remedied by change in the degree of competition.

To look at the same problem another way, it is only if property institutions are such that there is a substantial equality of private and social costs and benefits that a price mechanism operating through private profit-maximizing enterprises will lead

(2) *Other aspects of performance.* The second group of performance dimensions include progressiveness and selling costs. What they have in common is the purely negative attribute that we have no ideal standard against which to measure them in the same way that we can measure efficiency against the standards provided by the competitive model. In discussing them, we can add little to what we have already said.

Progressiveness, the more important of the two, includes the introduction of new end-products, and the introduction of new techniques of production which reduce costs, so that a given bundle of inputs yields more outputs than it could previously. Observed progress in reduction of costs and creation of new goods is not difficult to record. It is, however, difficult to measure in any comparative or analytical sense. We know that relatively new technologies — those of oil, chemicals, electronics — appear to provide more scope both for the development of new products and for cost reduction than relatively mature technologies — those of meat packing, textile production, garment manufacture. But sometimes a revolutionary enough discovery turns an "old" into a "new" technology, and the boundaries between them are to a large degree arbitrary. Further, it is not clear to what extent we are trying to measure "absolute" progressiveness, to what extent progressiveness in relation to the opportunities offered.[26] In general, we can say that the more progressiveness, the better, but even this may not always be true. While the addition of new products to a previous range of choice unequivocally makes consumers no worse off, the same cannot be said if new products displace old. When a new product becomes "fashionable," and a corresponding old product ceases to be offered, consumers may or may not be better off. Cost reduction presents no such paradox; any cost-reducing innovation is worth what it saves, and no more than this will knowingly be expended in achieving it.[27]

---

to efficiency. Where there are wide divergences between costs and benefits to particular individuals or firms and to the community at large, there is a general case for nonbusiness operation as, for example, in the provision of sanitation or education. Thus we are carried outside the sphere of markets competitively allocated, which we have marked off as the area of our investigation in Chapter I.

26. To the extent that we think in terms of how well a market is functioning in relation to some ideal, it is the latter measure which is appropriate. On what is perhaps a more pragmatic view, if we seek simply for what is bad enough to be worth trying to improve, both elements enter.

27. The addition of new products and a concomitant subtraction of old ones is not an entirely imaginary situation: the model changes in the automobile industry

While we can talk in abstract terms about the relation of the costs of innovation to the returns from it, in a fashion similar to the general notion of the equalization of costs and returns by market processes, we can find little concrete guidance for the analysis of innovation in practice. This is in part because of possibly remediable ignorance, in part because of deeper difficulties which we have already indicated above.

The appropriateness of expenditures on selling and promotion is the other aspect of performance in this class. We seek to determine whether an industry, or some of the firms in it, spends "too much" resources in this way. Although we cannot define "too much," we are not entirely without some guide lines. In the first place, resource expenditure on pure deception or misinformation can clearly be called wasteful. However, much advertising and other selling effort conveys no information at all, strictly speaking, and it is not possible to determine whether this is wasteful in the same sense. "It is better" is a phrase with no specific content, but whether or not the expenditure of resources on repeating it in print or on the air waves is useful, it cannot be called deceptive. Secondly, promotional expenditures by rival sellers which are mutually self-canceling, so that the demand curves of the sellers are the same after the expenditures as they would have been without them, can also be termed clearly wasteful. But it is difficult to determine which expenditures are self-canceling in this respect, and which do alter the pattern of relative demands.

In conceptual terms, we can analyze the results of sales promotion efforts into three components: the provision of "useful information," the test of which, conceptually, is that buyers would be willing to pay for it, if it was provided and priced separately rather than tied to the goods promoted; the influencing of tastes, usually in nonrational ways, so that the ultimate pattern of tastes is different than it would be in the absence of all sales promotion efforts except those of the first class; and, finally, the purely mutually stultifying efforts of rival sellers, whose net effects are zero. But in

present some elements of this situation. Or, to take another example, consider a discriminating monopolist who spends all his excess revenues (over what a group of competitors otherwise similar would earn) on product development. The competitors would have less to show in the way of new products. But is the monopolist, unrestrained, producing too much progress in some sense? Again, this is not an entirely imaginary situation; the United Shoe Machinery Corporation's policies showed something of this sort.

general we have no way of dividing the effects of specific sales promotion activities according to this scheme. Chesterfield advertising may be canceled by Lucky Strike advertising, but together they may increase the demand for cigarettes relative to that for liquor or food. If this is so, the separation of the third class of effects from the second is difficult. Since consumer tastes are essentially nonrational, we cannot logically apply purely rational criteria — that is, "usefulness, in the sense defined above — to make a division between what is wasteful and what is not. Even misinformation may be effective in changing consumer tastes; if we define it as wasteful, it is rather on the ground that if the consumer knew the truth he would reject the influence of the promotional effort, but this is perhaps an overly rational assumption about actual behavior.

Another possible analytic standard is provided by the notion of the "competitive" amount of sales promotion, which would occur in a particular market if all firms spent money on sales promotion along profit-maximizing lines, if there were no barriers to entry into the market, and if there were no economies of scale of sales promotion, so that large expenditures by particular existing sellers could not create entry barriers for potential rivals or force out those who fell behind in the race.[28] But again we cannot translate this standard into observational terms which permit us to apply it to a particular industry.

All in all, with respect to both progressiveness and excessive selling costs, we are left with some general guides, and the task of applying them, *ad hoc,* to particular industries in the light of such information as appears relevant.[29]

28. This corresponds roughly to the Chamberlin model of an industry of large numbers, with product differentiation and free entry. See E. H. Chamberlin, *Monopolistic Competition,* Chapters IV, V. The essence of free entry is that the sales promotion efforts of any particular firm must be capable of fairly close imitation by other firms, although pure copying may be barred. But just what "fairly close imitation" is cannot be specified in the abstract.

29. There is a third aspect of performance of much less significance which also falls in this class: the adequacy or superfluity of product variety. In part, this is an efficiency problem, and the production of too much product variety, in the sense of producing products for which prices do not cover costs, is covered by the efficiency criterion. On the other hand, the problem of insufficient product variety is not. The nonproduction of a potentially remunerative product cannot generally be detected: it is really an aspect of progressiveness, and of the introduction of new products. In the competitive model, all products whose costs could be covered by their prices would be produced. Conceivably some products could be produced under discriminatory pricing whose costs would not be covered under simple competitive pricing. Traditionally, the need for discriminatory pricing to cover costs has been viewed as an indicator of the need for government regulation, since some degree of monopoly

(3) *Structure.* When we turn from performance to structure, we can be briefer without being less clear. The structure of a market, broadly defined, consists of those stable features of the environment of a business firm which determine or condition the firm's decisions. They are more or less stable, in the sense that in any short-run period, the structure can be viewed as given, although in the long-run market structures do change.[30] In examining market structure, we seek ultimately to determine whether or not the structure is such as to compel or conduce to competition by the firms in the market, where competition means, as we have several times said, both certain kinds of economic results and a certain kind of process which leads to them. Since the markets of experience do not show any simple one-to-one correspondence between a single structural configuration and the processes and results of the market, such as characterizes the perfectly competitive market model, our examination of structure is inevitably incomplete in its answer to the question. But we can say something about whether particular aspects of a given market structure, in the context of the other aspects of that structure, probably do or do not conduce to competition in the market.[31]

The major elements of market structure can be divided into five classes: (1) the breadth of the market and the character of demand, (2) the number and size distribution of sellers and buyers, (3) the conditions of entry for new sellers and expansion for existing sellers, (4) the character and importance of product differentiation, and (5) the degree of independence of action among sellers and buyers.

The first element of market structure involves the delimitation of

---

is necessary for the successful practice of discrimination. We do not think that much more can usefully be said on this point.

30. We can identify market structure with the underlying forces that shape the factor-supply and market-demand curves facing the firm. In the competitive model, with the profit-maximizing firm which cannot influence the markets in which it deals, the market-demand and factor-supply situations determine the decisions of the firm. More realistically, the power of many firms to exercise some influence, at least in the short run, on the markets in which they operate, and the inadequacy of strict profit maximization as a rule of behavior for the business firm in the face of decisions with consequences reaching into the uncertain future, leave a considerable area for firm "strategy." Thus we speak of market structure conditioning rather than determining the behavior of the firm.

31. The context is all important. J. M. Clark's pioneer essay on workable competition pointed out that once a market fails to conform to the structure of the competitive model in some respects, its conformity in others may or may not be conducive to competition. See "Towards A Concept of Workable Competition," *American Economic Review* (June 1940).

the market and the cataloguing of the major characteristics of the demand for what is traded in it. Delimitation of the market involves tracing out the geographic area and the group of products within which sellers' offers are substitutes for each other in meeting the demands of buyers.[32] In examining the geographic and product boundaries of the market, it is necessary to consider both how they are drawn under the present price and transport cost regime, and how they have fluctuated and would fluctuate with changes in prices (including the prices of the relevant substitutes) and in transport costs. The economic character of the product — durable, semi-durable, perishable, consumers' good, producers' good, and the time pattern of demand — the character of seasonal and cyclical fluctuations, its long-term growth, stability, or decline, are the most important attributes of demand to be examined.

The number and relative size distribution of both sellers and buyers — their market shares — both currently and over time form the next major element of market structure. In general, numbers and size distribution on the selling side can be summarized into one of four patterns: large numbers and no relatively large firms — *atomistic structure;* a small number (less than twenty) of firms supplying 75 percent of the market, with no one supplying more than 10–15 percent and a fringe of smaller firms supplying the rest — *loose oligopoly;* a very small number (eight or fewer) firms supplying 50 percent of the market, with the largest firm having a 20 percent or higher share, and with or without a fringe of small suppliers — *tight oligopoly;* and a single large firm supplying 60 percent or more of the market, with no other single seller supplying a significant proportion of the demand — *dominant firm,* or *partial monopoly.* A similar classification can be applied to the buying side. Relative size distributions must be viewed in the perspective of time: the structural element we seek is the average situation over a long period rather than that existing at any particular moment. Of course, persistent changes in market shares are also important, and any movement toward greater or less concentration as well as the average picture of the whole period of study must be taken into account.

The third element of market structure on our list is the set of conditions affecting the entry of new sellers into the market and the expansion of existing sellers. In part these overlap, in part they are

32. Some of the technical problems of doing this and the kind of information needed are discussed further in Chapter IV.

distinct. The first of the conditions affecting entry is the optimum scale of the plant and firm in relation to the size of the market, and the actual scales of existing sellers in comparison with the optimum. Entry is usually difficult where the optimum scale is relatively large, the cost disadvantages of suboptimal scale are significant, and existing sellers are at optimal scale. Large absolute optimum size (as well as large size relative to the market) adds to the difficulty of entry because of the large capital requirement for an optimum firm or plant.[33] These conditions are also important in respect to the expansion of existing firms, although optimum plant size may be more important and optimum firm size less important than in the case of new entrants.

Barriers preventing free access to technology are a second important class of conditions affecting entry and the expansion of existing firms. Patents are one form such barriers take, and such patent practices as the freedom of licensing, the existence of pools, and the like, as well as the intrinsic importance of the patented technology, determine how high these barriers are and how they operate with respect to existing and new firms in the market. But patents are not the only kind of barriers to technology. Secret know-how or "corners" on scarce trained personnel may be equally important. Third, access to factor supplies may not be possible on equal terms to established firms and new entrants, or to all established firms. The pattern of ownership of scarce factors — mineral deposits, naturally favorable sites, and the like — is important in this respect. Where such factors are tied to some existing firms, would-be entrants and other existing firms may not be able to buy as much of the resource as they want at any price. In general, the labor market does not present similar features, but in special instances it might, such as in the case of specially skilled or talented persons mentioned above. Every new firm — as opposed to a new entrant into a particular market which is an established firm in some other market — finds it usually has access to capital on less favorable terms than its established rivals. This is partly because new firms are usually small, and capital is available more cheaply to large than to small enterprises, partly because newness itself is a disadvantage in the eyes of suppliers, since it is associated with a higher risk of failure than prevails for similar "seasoned" firms. Markets for fabricated inputs may show

33. Both the rising supply price or rationing of capital and risk factors make entry on an absolutely large scale more difficult than on a smaller one.

customary supplier-buyer relations, or long-term supply contracts, which put newcomers at a disadvantage. Access to markets, like access to factor supplies, may not be available on equal terms to new entrants and existing sellers, or to all existing sellers. The character of distribution channels, the existence of forward integration into distribution, the existence of quasi-integration through such practices as exclusive dealerships, requirements contracts, long-term leases, and the like, all determine how the new entrant will fare in disposing of his product. Similarly, where expansion of sales means expansion of distribution outlets, some of the same circumstances will bear on the ability of existing sellers to expand. In general, the organization of the buying market is an important feature of market structure for the selling market.

The fourth element of market structure is the character of product differentiation — advertising, selling costs, promotional efforts, design variation, etc. — and its importance in the market. Logically, this might be seen as another element in the conditions of entry, but it is important enough to warrant distinction. The existence of important product differentiation, with "loyal" customers of particular sellers who view the products of other sellers as poor substitutes, usually involves many elements: product variation, heavy advertising expenses, other heavy selling expenses. Where these exist they make entry for a new firm difficult in that it must overcome the established good will of existing sellers. Since this good will is a function not only of the current outlays of existing firms on selling and advertising, but of the sum of such outlays over many years, the magnitude of the new entrant's handicap can be considerable, and may be overcome only after an unprofitable period of years — an investment in creating good will. Where product differentiation is important, the whole character of entry may change, in that the would-be entrant can offer only a rather different product than existing sellers. In the extreme, the publisher of a new weekly picture magazine, for example, would not be selling the same product as *Life* or *Look,* in the sense that the new steel producer would be selling the same product as U.S. Steel or Bethlehem.

Finally, the degree of independence of action of existing sellers in the market is an important element of market structure. The existence of collusive agreements, trade association arrangements for price reporting, pricing formulas, market sharing arrangements, all come under this head. So does the existence of a well-defined system of price leadership, or other observable nonindependent action, even though it is not crystallized in institutional form.

As we have repeatedly warned, it is not generally possible to evaluate the significance of individual elements of market structure, taken alone, for particular markets. But we can broadly, and with exceptions, distinguish what is likely to be more and what is likely to be less conducive to competition, on the average. The broader the market, the less important product differentiation and promotional efforts, and the more independence of action among sellers and buyers both, the more will the market structure probably be one which is conducive to competition.

(4) *Market power.* As a result of this long excursion into the meaning of market performance and market structure, we are now in a position to define market power more fully than we have heretofore. A firm possesses market power when it can behave persistently in a manner different from the behavior that a competitive market would enforce on a firm facing otherwise similar cost and demand conditions. When the "can" in this definition is emphasized, we see that the concept of market power is basically a structural concept. We ask, does the market permit or constrain firms to behave in such-and-such a way, or not? But, although the concept is one of structure, we do not rely on the examination of the elements of market structure alone in making judgments about market power. Because of our inability to correlate structure and performance with precision, we look at performance directly, taking what the firm's performance has been as the best evidence of what it can be. Since we are interested in the future as well as in the past, we look at structure as well as performance, in order to correlate as well as we can the observed performance with the observable features of market structure, and thus be able to predict the probable relation of future to past performance. Further, since we are interested in antitrust policy, and action of antitrust type operates immediately on conduct and structure and only indirectly on performance, the correlation of performance with structure is a necessary step in the application of antitrust policy to concrete cases. Only the efficiency dimensions of performance can be evaluated in terms of the competitive standard, and thus an examination of the efficiency dimensions of performance can tell us whether or not performance has been consistent with the absence of market power. Thus an examination of whether or not a firm has market power involves an

examination of both the market structure in which it operates and the efficiency dimensions of its performance.

Our definition of market power, strictly construed, is consistent with a notion of "unexercised market power," which would exist when a firm could, but did not, behave differently than would a firm in an otherwise similar competitive market. Logically the existence of unexercised market power is inconsistent with profit maximization. A firm which had the power to increase its long-run price-cost margins, for example, and did not do so would be sacrificing income it could earn; the same would be true for other dimensions of performance. However, we cannot rely on firms engaging in profit-maximizing behavior even where it is well defined, and this is not always the case,[34] so we may say that the existence of unexercised market power is a real possibility. To detect it, however, we would be forced to rely on structural information alone since, by hypothesis, it would not be reflected in past performance. In general, then, we may say that unexercised market power is not readily detectible, though in specific circumstances the structure of a particular market might point so strongly to the existence of market power that we might be willing to infer that it exists unexercised even in the absence of noncompetitive performance. In practice, the problem is unlikely to arise, since most firms with market power wish to benefit from it in some way.[35]

We have spoken so far of the market power of a firm in the singular. This is strictly appropriate only for markets with dominant firms — monopolies or partial monopolies. In the more typical market structures of oligopoly, market power is possessed not by one but by a group of firms and is dependent on the mutual interrelations of their behavior. In such situations, we can speak loosely of

34. For example, there may be a question as to which is the profit-maximizing policy: to leave margins lower and discourage entry, or to raise them and run the risk of lowering future income by increasing competition. No single answer can be given to this question even if the probabilities were known; the answer depends on the relative utility attached to present and future receipts of income expected with varying degrees of probability.

35. It is worth emphasizing that "concealed" market power, in any other sense than unexercised power, cannot exist. If the potential for noncompetitive behavior is taken advantage of, and where it exists it almost always is, it will produce a pattern of behavior which indicates its existence, although that pattern may not include high profits or other obvious benefits to the firm. If the power is unused, it is foregone. Another way of stating this same point is to remark that the exercise of market power, where it exists, is merely "good business" under the circumstances, and does not imply any predatory or unethical practice, though it may in particular cases include them.

the market power of a particular firm in the market, but we must do so with the realization that this is shorthand for a situation in which market power is the collective attribute of a number of firms whose several actions have certain interrelations, and that, strictly speaking, one firm alone might not possess the power.[36]

In the long run, the maintenance of market power, whether by a single firm or by a group, implies the existence of significant barriers to entry into the market by new sellers. Without such barriers, the attempt to exercise power would in general attract new sellers, whether the attempt took the form of maintaining high price-cost margins, either in general or for particular products, or of rationing output in periods of high demand without raising prices. But the converse proposition is not true; the existence of substantial barriers to entry in a particular market may not lead to the possession of market power by any of the sellers in it. The behavior of existing sellers may be such as to leave none with significant power. In most cases, it is also a condition of a firm's possession of market power that it be one of the major sellers in a structurally oligopolistic market — that it have a small number of important competitors and a relatively large share of its market, or else, of course, that it be a dominant firm. There are exceptions: markets of atomistic structure in which overt agreements and restrictive practices function effectively enough to limit competition persistently. But they are not frequent; typically, the successful cartel is in a small — rather than a large — numbers market. Oligopoly structure, like blockaded entry, is not a sufficient condition for the existence of market power, nor is a combination of the two. As we have already indicated, we cannot in general state sufficient conditions applicable to all markets.

(5) *Unreasonable market power.* Our primary policy goal is the limitation of market power, not its entire abolition. We recognize that it is impossible to reduce to zero the market power of firms in most markets: economies of scale limit the possible number of efficient sellers in many markets; the facts of geography and transport costs limit the size of many markets; advertising, other kinds of promotional effort, and consumer desires for product variety are real and permanent and thus product differentiation cannot be

36. This point is developed in detail in Chapter IV. We may add here that when we speak of "collective attributes" we do not say that the firms are necessarily concerting their actions through an overt agreement, but merely that the power of any one of them is a function of the actions of all of them, in the context of the structure of the market.

wished away; the advantages of established sellers over newcomers are persistent and often significant; and there are inevitable limitations on entrepreneurial knowledge, on entrepreneurial rationality, and on factor mobility which can lead to significant imperfections in particular markets. Our standard of limitation, then, must leave us content with some positive quantum of power in most markets. Let us call what we will accept a "reasonable degree of market power," and what we judge exceeds that, "unreasonable market power." We can then phrase our goal as the abolition of "unreasonable market power."

In defining unreasonable market power, we look to two different kinds of criteria: one of magnitude and one of source. We certainly wish to draw some lower limit to the degree of market power which is worth noticing; and we must recognize that some kinds of market power may not be avoidable, except at costs — say in efficiency — which we are not prepared to pay.

Any market power which is persistent we deem sufficiently great in magnitude to warrant notice. Persistent we define in terms of a period of at least a decade — long enough to reflect behavior over more than one cycle, not long enough so that underlying conditions of demand and technology will typically show radical changes. But since we have already defined market power so as to incorporate the notion of persistence,[37] we can dispense with repetition, and say that any market power which is perceptible is of great enough magnitude to be worthy of notice.

Market power resting on certain bases we consider "reasonable," because we think it either undesirable or impossible to eliminate them. First, where economies of scale are such that only a very small number of efficient sellers can survive in a market, a substantial degree of market power in these sellers may be inevitable. It could be reduced only at the cost of producing at higher costs in inefficiently small units; this price we do not desire to pay.[38] In small markets and geographically segmented markets, this limitation may be of considerable importance. Second, where market power rests solely on barriers to entry arising from the legal use of basic patents, it is likewise to be considered reasonable. The policy of the antitrust law must be accommodated with the policy of the patent law: this

37. See preceding discussion.

38. We have already indicated in Chapter I that this proviso will not make our policy a nullity. In most markets, much less concentration than now exists is compatible with efficient scale of operation.

is a minimum accommodation.[39] This exception is probably not of great quantitative importance. Typically, market power which involves patent barriers to entry rests on patent pooling, licensing arrangements, and other practices, and further barriers than those provided by patents alone. But some examples which would come under it can be found, for example, nylon during the life of the basic patents. We speak of basic patents because effective market power could not rest solely on patent protection of relatively minor features of technology; where no important technical improvements are involved, the market power must be supported by other means, and thus falls without the exception. Third, where market power rests on the introduction of new processes, products, or marketing techniques, it also falls within the exception of reasonableness. Again, although this is probably a quantitatively unimportant category of exceptions, examples can be found. One kind is the production of a superior product, not based on patented technology, which other firms simply fail to imitate. The skilled or fortunate producer may then achieve persistently high margins over costs which are not competed away by his rivals, and thus show market power as we have defined it. Perhaps *Life* or *Look* or the *Saturday Evening Post* exemplifies this in some degree in the field of weekly magazines. Of the three bases of market power which we consider reasonable, only the first — economies of scale such as permit only few efficient firms in the market — is likely to be of substantial quantitative importance in practice.

If we wish to eliminate unreasonable market power, we must in general move toward less concentrated markets in which there are more sellers with smaller shares. An increase in the number of competitors and a decrease in the relative market positions of the larger of them is usually a sufficient condition for the reduction of market power in any market. The maximum increase in numbers consistent with efficiency represents the practicable limit to the reduction of market power. But though an increase in numbers and a decrease in concentration is usually a sufficient condition for making markets more competitive, it is not generally a necessary one. In many markets, practices of one kind or another — price reporting arrangements, patent pools, exclusive dealing contracts, etc., — are indispensable buttresses to the power of leading firms; without them, a

39. A detailed discussion of problems in patent and antitrust law appears in Chapter V.

sharp reduction in that power would take place over time. Even so, it is clear that a policy of eliminating unreasonable market power will involve a much more widespread use of dissolution and divestiture remedies than has been the case in the past. Up till now, these were measures of last resort, to be used only when no other remedy which promised *any* relief appeared practicable, and, even then, more often in the case of defendants whose offenses had been aggravated by predatory conduct or conspiracy. Under the proposed policy, programs for reducing the relative size of firms large in particular markets will occupy a preferred position, to be invoked, in general, unless other remedies promise to do a thorough job.

But this preferred status requires one important qualification: dissolution or divestitures are not to be carried out at any substantial cost in terms of economic performance. The first implication of this proviso is that the size of existing plants sets a lower limit to any dissolution proposal, even where they are bigger than the size needed to achieve minimum costs. The obvious costs involved in the division of any existing technical unit preclude such measures. Second, the plan of divestiture must contemplate the creation of viable firms with reasonable prospect for survival. Third, any absolute advantages of existing units must be taken into account in reorganizing market structures: the specific advantages that are peculiar to existing firms should not be cast away without consideration. In particular, though the progressiveness dimensions of performance play no part in evaluating the existence of market power or its reasonableness, no change in market structures which will significantly lower the level of performance in this respect should be made. Here again our interest in limiting market power is controlled by our interest in securing desirable economic performance. Considerations of fairness may further limit the scope of desirable reorganizations of market structure. Since the interests of customers, suppliers, and smaller competitors must be taken into account to some extent,[40] at least the speed with which any going market arrangements can be changed will be limited.

The result of considering the costs of reducing market power as well as its reasonableness is to make possible, at least logically, a

40. The imperative here is pragmatic. Any administrative agent which enforces the proposed policy will in fact be forced to listen to at least some of the parties affected by reorganization proposals other than the subject (defendant) firms, and thus to take account of their interests to a greater or lesser extent.

situation in which we condemn a firm as possessing unreasonable market power, and yet are unwilling to take measures to reduce it. In practice, again, this should not prove an important problem: partly because business practices are frequently important elements in noncompetitive market structures, and these can usually be changed without losses in performance; partly because, typically, the largest firms in the larger markets are multiplant firms well beyond the optimum firm size, and operating many optimum-sized plants.

Moreover, with respect both to claims that market power is "reasonable" in terms of defined exceptions, and to claims that structural reorganization would entail substantial performance losses, we would place the burden of proof on the defendants. In short, we would resolve doubts in favor of reducing market power rather than maintaining performance. One reason for this is a practical one — the relevant information is in defendants' hands or can be more readily obtained by them than by the government. The other reason is an unprovable but plausible judgment that reduction of market power is more likely to improve performance than to worsen it, an assumption we shall shortly examine more thoroughly.

We have deliberately avoided the phrase "workable competition" up to this point because it has been used in a wide variety of meanings since it was originally coined by J. M. Clark.[41] There is one sense of workable competition in which it is used to label an idea essentially the same as the idea we have propounded under the name of "no unreasonable market power." This identifies markets as workably competitive when they cannot be made more so, consistent with the requirements of efficiency and the recognition of the realities of consumer preference and geography. That this state is labeled competitive implies a judgment of fact that the limitations do not preclude the existence of competitive markets. An alternative judgment on this issue might be that many markets are not only unimprovable but also unworkably competitive, in the sense that the minimum market power which can be attained is a very high minimum. Such a judgment would lead to a quite different view of what,

41. *American Economic Review* (June 1940). For some of the meanings, see E. S. Mason, "The Current Status of the Monopoly Problem in the United States," *Harvard Law Review* (1949); C. D. Edwards, *Maintaining Competition* (1949); M. A. Adelman, "Effective Competition and the Anti-Trust Laws," *Harvard Law Review* (1948); C. E. Griffin, *An Economic Approach to Anti-Trust Problems* (1951); W. Adams, "The Rule of Reason: Workable Competition or Workable Monopoly," *Yale Law Journal* (1954).

if anything, antitrust policy should try to do. We have already argued that this alternative view is not correct, and applies at most to a few markets.

There is, however, another version of workable competition which represents something quite different. This involves an over-all evaluation of market performance, usually with heavy weight given to progressiveness. Where the score is low, the market and the firms operating in it are not viewed as competitive and some change is considered in order; where it is high, the market is workably competitive. Competition is thus identified with desirable economic results, and competition as a process is accorded little or no weight. This view is radically different from our own, and one which we consider to be an undesirable policy standard.[42] To summarize our prior discussion, we view any over-all evaluation of performance as impossible and therefore delusive as a basic standard of what workable competition is.

Power versus performance: How much conflict?

In our proposed standard of policy we have given primacy to the limitation of market power over the promotion of desirable economic performance. We limit the possible loss in performance that might be caused by its application in particular situations by subjecting reductions in market power to the proviso that they should sacrifice neither efficient scale nor progressiveness. However, our allocation of the burden of proof in justifying market power as reasonable or rejecting reorganization proposals as too costly is such as to resolve doubts in favor of reducing power, rather than in maintaining performance. Can we say how important the conflict between the two kinds of goals is in fact?

The limitation of market power may conflict with the achievement of desirable performance in two ways. Since the progressiveness dimension of performance is not taken directly into account either in defining unreasonable market power or in seeking to reduce it where it exists, there might be a direct conflict between reducing

42. The first view of workable competition is found in the work of Mason, Adelman, and Edwards cited above. The second is found in Griffin, and also in A. D. H. Kaplan, *Big Enterprise in a Competitive System* (1954), and in the 1952 report of the Business Advisory Council to the Secretary of Commerce, entitled *Effective Competition*. This characterization is broad: Mason and Adelman on the one hand and Edwards on the other do not agree on what kind of evidence is relevant to discovering whether competition is workable, nor are Griffin's views those of Kaplan's.

market power and achieving a high rate of technical progress. The efficiency dimensions of performance do enter directly into the definition of market power, and thus a similar direct conflict is not possible. Nonetheless, indirect conflict may be even more important. Efficiency and progressiveness both depend ultimately on vigorous entrepreneurship, which constantly seeks to better existing methods and push business to the utmost pitch of efficiency. Competitive market structures themselves will not produce the substance of competition if all entrepreneurs are slackly content with the quiet life and traditional ways.[43] Conceivably, a policy of reducing market power could have serious unfavorable repercussions on the motivations of entrepreneurs and, thus, indirectly on economic efficiency and progressiveness. We examine these two possibilities in turn, noting that in both cases we will be better furnished with speculation than with well-grounded empirical knowledge.

The idea that monopoly in some degree might be an important prerequisite of a high rate of progressiveness was first formulated by Schumpeter, for whom it was one aspect of his general theory of the "perennial gale of creative destruction" which was at the heart of the capitalist process. His central notion was that some degree of market power provided both the finance and the "breathing space" which made possible the risky investments in innovation, and also provided the rewards, the big prizes in the lottery, which were necessary to stimulate others to innovate.[44] These ideas have been repeated — if not improved — in the recent literature of the "new competition."[45] In general, it is not unfair to say that the writings cited contain more assertions than they do evidence, but together with other evidence they do provide some basis for the belief that there may be substantial economies of scale involved in the process of research, development, and promotion of new products and processes. These arise from several causes. First, uncertainty about the way in which the results of particular research endeavors will prove to be useful means

43. The competitive model assumes away this problem, because it assumes perpetual striving after maximum profits. In actual markets, managerial ignorance and inertia are important sources of inefficiency. It is, of course, one of the virtues of a competitive market that it does not permit some entrepreneurs to be lazy: if some are vigorously pursuing profits, the rest will be forced to follow. "The greatest of all monopoly profits is a quiet life."

44. See *Capitalism, Socialism and Democracy* (1942), chapter VIII. See also E. S. Mason, "Schumpeter on Monopoly and the Large Firm," in *Schumpeter, Social Scientist*, ed. S. Harris (1951).

45. ee A. D. H. Kaplan, *Big Enterprise in a Competitive System;* and D. Lilienthal, *Big Business, A New Era* (N. Y., 1953).

that the firm which produces a wider rather than a narrower range of products will be able to profit from more of the results of its research efforts. Second, since research is a slow process with long-deferred yields, and a research organization must operate fairly steadily to be good, it cannot readily be expanded and contracted. This points to advantages for a firm large enough to be able to finance research at a reasonably steady level and with enough confidence in its own future to be willing to invest in slowly maturing projects. Third, the benefits of exchange of ideas and experience and of pooling men with different types of training and temperaments, given the necessary restrictions of commercial secrecy which keep such an exchange within the firm, point to some minimum size for an effective research unit. Fourth, equipment requirements in some kinds of research are heavy, and in themselves lead to need for substantial scale.

Further, it is clear, aside from these arguments, that the atomistic firm of the competitive swarm might have neither incentive nor ability to invest in research. Incentive would be lacking because of the high turnover of firms, which would make any individual firm loth to spend on benefits which might come too late for it to reap and which, in many cases, may be quickly copied by all rivals without cost to them. Ability might be lacking simply because funds for speculative investments of this type might not readily be provided by outside investors, and the profits of the atomistic competitor would be too meager to do the job. In areas such as the chemical, oil, and electronic industries, for example, where large investments and current outlays are required for research, organized research might disappear under atomistic conditions.

But neither this argument, nor the probably correct conclusions on the existence of some economies of scale in research and development activities, is helpful in settling our problem. Since we are talking only in terms of business units at least as large as those necessary for efficient production and distribution, the problems of competitive atomism are irrelevant. In crude terms, our problem is to distinguish between the ability of the $500 million to $5 billion firms to contribute to a high rate of progress, and that of the $50 million to $500 million firms.[46] Firms which are big enough to be technically and

46. These figures are very crude, but they may be used as a broad indication of the size ranges involved in our policy proposal. Further, of course, we measure size relative to particular markets; the firm may become large without growing very large relative to particular markets, though it is not now characteristic of giant firms.

managerially efficient in most of the oligopolistic industries are big enough to fall outside the area of obvious disability in research and development; whether they are as efficient as their bigger brothers is not shown by presently available evidence.

On the other hand, competition is clearly a stimulus to innovation. It is precisely when old products made by old processes yield only meager returns that the economic stimulus to discover new products or cheaper processes is strongest.[47] Thus reduction of market power may not impair the capacity for innovation, and it will certainly increase the incentive to it.[48] Further, not all innovation is the fruit of large-scale organized research and development effort. Much of it takes place in industries where such activity is minimal, and flows from the work of the engineer, the skilled foreman, and the factory superintendent. Here the effects of competition on incentive may be far more important than the effects of high and secure profits in contributing to the finance of industrial research.[49]

This discussion is necessarily inconclusive, since the fundamental information we require for an adequate discussion is lacking. But it hardly justifies the anticipation of a widespread and serious direct conflict between the reduction of market power and the maintenance of a high rate of progress, given the exceptions to the main direction of policy which are available whenever such conflict can be demonstrated.

Our second possible conflict is more serious. If energetic enforcement of a policy designed to limit market power produces a significant diminution of the vigor of entrepreneurship, the policy will not

47. Two good studies of innovation and invention in particular industries make this point clear. See W. R. Maclaurin, *Innovation and Invention in the Radio Industry* (New York, 1949), and A. A. Bright, Jr., *The Electric Lamp Industry* (New York, 1949). For innovation under conditions of monopoly, see C. Kaysen, *United States v. United Shoe Machinery Corporation* (1956).

48. Again, the irrelevance of the purely competitive model to this problem is worth noting. Even without strong patent protection, the innovator gets an important head start over imitators which, together with his existing good will, protects him from complete and quick competition.

49. The rapid expansion of industrial research activity has been recent, and greatly stimulated by World War II and the continued spending of the Defense Department thereafter. Total expenditures on industrial research in the U.S. rose from $900 million in 1941 to nearly $10 billion currently. About half the total is currently financed by the federal government. The electrical, aircraft, and chemical industries accounted for about 55 percent of the total expenditures. See the B.L.S. pamphlet, *Scientific Research and Development in American Industry*. The average rate of growth of productivity in all manufacturing has been fairly constant at about 3.5 percent per year over a long period of time, though fluctuating from year to year. See G. J. Stigler, *Trends in Output and Employment* (New York, 1947).

be worth while. After all, we wish to achieve our results without great costs in terms of desirable economic performance and if we cannot, we must abandon the proposed policy. The essential danger arises from the fact that an attack on market power that relies heavily on dissolution and divestiture is an attack on achieved growth, and may be viewed as a threat against further growth. In our economy, growth is the badge of entrepreneurial success, and the achievement of growth is an important stimulus to entrepreneurial effort. Any limitation of growth may thus have wide repercussions on the general efficiency of enterprise far beyond the firms directly affected by particular antitrust proceedings.

It is clear that the proposed policy will limit certain kinds of growth, and — as seen by those on the receiving end of the policy — it will penalize growth achieved in the past. Any firm which is large relative to some market in which it operates or any large firm which is growing substantially relative to some market in which it operates will certainly be open to scrutiny and perhaps to action under the antitrust law. Some firms will be dissolved or lose part of their holdings because they are large relative to the markets in which they operate. While the policy involves no limitations on the absolute size of firms, as distinguished from their relative size in particular markets, it will close certain routes of growth — such as merger — to firms that are already very large.[50]

Other kinds of growth possibilities will remain open, however. A firm which grows in absolute size by diversification purely through internal growth without mergers, and does so without becoming large relative to any market, will not come within the scope of the ban on unreasonable market power. But typically, the large firm today, though diversified, is fairly heavily concentrated in a few markets in which it does occupy a relatively large position.[51] At the very least, therefore, our proposal will require some shift in past growth patterns if continued growth is to be attained. Further, by increasing the degree of competition, it will tend to make growth somewhat more difficult. In general, the most important limitation on the size of firms is the limitation on their growth imposed by the "crowding" of other firms competing for customers. The stronger the competition, the more stringent the limitations on growth, espe-

50. See discussion on mergers, Chapter IV.

51. The only good evidence on this point is an out-of-date TNEC Monograph No. 27, *The Structure of Industry*, part VI, "The Product Structures of Large Corporations." This uses data from the 1937 *Census of Manufactures*.

cially on growth at a rate faster than the growth of total demand. Despite this, however, we are not inclined to consider as probable the danger that a significant decline in entrepreneurial vigor will be the consequence of our policy proposal. Our view rests in part on what we consider relevant, though indirect, evidence from recent economic history, in part on more speculative grounds. The New Deal and Fair Deal, apart from their verbal thrusts at the power and prestige of "big business," imposed many substantial limitations on the freedom of business decision, especially in labor relations and financial policy. The verbal reaction was pained and eloquent. But there is no convincing evidence that the vigor of business effort was in any way impaired. Recovery from the depression may have been slow, but there is little indication that a more sympathetic administration would have revived business any faster.[52]

More specifically, the level and structure of individual and corporate income taxes in the past two decades increasingly has been such as to diminish greatly the financial rewards of business activity, especially relative to those of lower-income occupations. A group of recent studies of the effects of taxation on business incentives fails to show any general loss of incentive or any over-all reduction of the quantity or quality of business effort.[53] High taxes have had two important kinds of effects on business effort and on business investment. First, taxation lowered financial capacity: had there been more income after taxes, there would, in the period studied, have been more investment. Second, where the impact of taxation changed the relative balance of costs and rewards in different situations or activities, just the kind of marginal adjustments in resource flow occurred that might have been expected.[54] But over-all qualitative effects in business performance were not apparent.

52. True, it may be that the processes reducing incentives move at so slow a pace as to be visible only in retrospect. Every restraint on business, every diminuation of the social esteem and the monetary rewards accorded business activity, contribute to the process of decline, but the pace remains glacial. These assertions have been made by Schumpeter and others, but they remain assertions and can be met only by counter-assertions. There are no visible signs of a general decline in business vigor; nor have there been any in the whole postwar period.

53. See J. K. Butters, "Taxation, Incentives, and Financial Capacity" in Papers and Proceedings of the American Economic Association, *American Economic Review* (May 1954). Butters summarizes the studies of the group at Harvard Business School; see the individual volumes he cites, especially T. Sanders, *The Effect of Taxation on Executives* (Boston, 1951).

54. Thus, for example, high tax rates on marginal current income led to growth of executive pension and retirement pay plans, which in turn tended to diminish executive mobility, since, with high marginal tax rates, the cost of recompensing an

The Public Utility Holding Company Act[55] and the experience of the electric power industry under Section 11 of it provide an example which is perhaps closer to our problem than that of the effects of taxes. Section 11, the so-called death-sentence clause, provided for the simplification of corporate structures in holding companies and the limitation of their holdings to a single integrated system. There were 2917 companies subject to the Act; as of June 1953, 812 companies with assets of about $11 billion had been subject to reorganization proceedings. Most of these were in 21 major holding company systems; the reorganization of 12 of which involved major litigation over a long period of time. Yet the vigor of growth of the power industry was no less in the past 18 years than in the 18 years preceding. During the whole period the industry has been one of the most rapidly growing in the whole economy, marked by large investment programs and continuous improvements in a technology.[56] Neither the vehement ideological battle which preceded the passage of the Act nor the extensive and bitterly fought litigation which followed it affected the management performance of the industry, as far as can be seen.

The weight of these examples is arguable. It may be said that taxation has always been with us, and the impact of a change in taxes is not to be compared with that of a public policy which seeks out individual business firms and directs their reorganization or prevents their growth. The growth of demand for power during the whole period of the industry's existence has been so great as to blanket all incentive effects of the sort we are considering. The New and Fair Deals are too broad a category of experiences to be used for comparative purposes. Nonetheless, we think them relevant. What they seem to us to show is the general hardiness of entrepreneurship in American business and its survival without visible damage through a variety of unpleasant experiences.

The motivations which conduce to effective entrepreneurship and management are apparently built deep into American society. They do not operate merely at the level of visible economic rewards,

---

executive for the loss of retirement benefits consequent on a move would be very high. This in turn might diminish over-all productivity, because it hindered the optimum distribution of men among executive jobs, though the quantitative magnitude of this effect was not observable.

55. 49 Stat. 803, 812, 813.

56. See J. M. Gould, *Output and Productivity in the Electric and Gas Utilities* (N.Y., 1946).

or even at the level of current symbols of business achievement in terms of size and growth. Rather they stem from the whole structure of American society — its emphasis on occupational achievement, its drive toward universal egalitarianism, its great geographical and occupational mobility, the relative unimportance of family ties.[57] Radical changes in fundamental aspects of the social structure would be prerequisite to a significant change in the efforts of American businessmen toward effective management and entrepreneurship. That the scope of our own policy proposals is more modest need hardly be said.

All in all, we consider it unlikely that the negative effects of the proposed policy on good economic performance will reach significantly beyond the specific firms that are brought within its reach. When its impact on them in this respect promises to be serious, it would be taken into account.

The regulation of conduct

Our program of limiting market power would require some regulation of business conduct as well as the reshaping of situations of market power. Regulation of business conduct would be of two kinds: that which rests basically on market power criteria and that which rests basically on criteria of fairness.

Our goal dictates the regulation of business conduct which may lead to an increase in market power, or contribute to its maintenance, where it has in fact produced that effect or where it has a strong probability of so doing. In other words, we would, as under present law, seek to control actual or incipient restraints on competition. Some kinds of conduct are two-sided in that they have important business justifications other than their potentially restrictive effects, and their potentially restrictive effects vary with the market context in which they occur. Regulation of such conduct requires fairly complete investigation of the market situation in which it occurs, though it may not be necessary to have as complete an investigation as is required for a proposal aimed at reorganizing market structure. Conduct which falls into this category includes mergers, requirements contracts, exclusive dealing arrangements, and patent licensing and pooling arrangements. Another class of

57. See F. X. Sutton, "Achievement Norms and the Motivations of Entrepreneurs," in *Entrepreneurship and Economic Growth*, papers presented at a conference in Cambridge, Mass., November 1954.

conduct comprises practices whose sole or major aim is restraint of competition, and which are probably harmful whatever the market context in which they appear. Such practices can be regulated by per se rules without the necessity for an examination of their actual effects in particular circumstances.[58]

Typically, neither the direct attack on market power nor the control of business conduct on market power criteria will reduce market power to zero. Indeed, in many markets the economic limitations on reorganization which we mentioned will result in the persistence of significant degrees of power in some firms. Thus some scope will remain for the regulation of the exercise of residual power in terms of fairness. The nonoppressive use of power in business transactions, as they are viewed by the weaker participants in them, is the substantive aim of policy in such situations. One class of examples arises where buyers or sellers in national markets deal with sellers or buyers in narrower regional or local markets. The power of any particular buyer, let us say, in the national market may be small, or it may be reduced to the minimum. Yet, in regard to the transactions with a particular local, market supplier, the national buyer may possess great bargaining power. This reflects essentially the imperfection of the market and the immobility of the local supplier. The bargaining power of the buyer is measured by the costs to the seller of getting in touch with other customers whom he has never served, or otherwise spending resources to dispose of his output through different channels, as well as the risk that he may fail to sell as much in this way as he has sold to his big customer in the past. Ultimately, the buyer can pay the seller as little as he is willing to take and still remain in business as a supplier. From an economic point of view, the full exploitation of the seller by the buyer, through payment of the lowest possible price at which he will continue to serve, represents an appropriation by the more powerful firm of rents which might otherwise accrue to the less powerful one. This appropriation is possible with little or no impact on efficiency or on market structure because of the imperfections of the market and the immobility of the entrepreneur in the local firm. The prevention of such exploitation is thus not an aspect of promoting the competitive process but rather an end in itself, given the inevitable limitations on factor mobility and information in nearly every market, no matter how competitive.

58. See Chapters IV and V for discussion of these two classes of practices.

Another class of examples to which the same observations apply is furnished by situations in which large firms operate as partial suppliers of capital to small firms which are their customers, through leasing expensive capital equipment or sites to them, as in the case of relations between gasoline refiners and service stations. The prevalence of capital rationing, and the risks involved in cutting loose from existing sources of capital, tie particular customers closely to their supplier in a way which creates much opportunity for exploitation. This opportunity is relatively invariant, within wide margins, with varying degrees of competition in the supplying market.

Possibilities of this sort provide an important rationale for statutes like the Robinson-Patman Act, independently of the effects of the practices it forbids on competition. To be sure, in concrete cases it is not always possible to draw a firm line between what is done on grounds of fairness and what is done on grounds of preventing the incipient development of market power. Some practices are both unfair and contributory to the growth of market power. Analytically, however, the separation is worth making.

How significant would the changes be?

The standard of unreasonable market power we have defined is in terms a standard of business situation rather than of business. conduct. In this respect, it differs from what has traditionally been a major element in the policy of the antitrust laws throughout their history — the element of intent or fault.[59] The Sherman Act is a criminal statute, and it is to be expected that it should ban some kind of conduct which conceivably the offender could have eschewed. It is hardly in the spirit of our legal tradition to apply criminal sanctions to some one because of a situation in which he finds himself willy-nilly. In form then, the change we propose is a serious one, and indeed we would abandon criminal sanctions as a method of enforcing it. Is the change equally serious in substance? In light of the exceptions which we allow as for "reasonable" market power, it might appear that we exempt those who find market power innocently thrust upon them and hence are merely saying the same thing the law now says but in different words. We believe the proposal would be more than that.

59. See, for example, the definition of monopolization given in the *Report of the Attorney General's National Committee Study of the Anti-Trust Laws* (1955), pp. 43–56, especially p. 55, where monopolization is described as monopoly power plus an element of deliberateness.

Application of our proposed policy, with the reduction of market power as a central goal, would result in four significant changes in the present policy of the law. First, the direct regulation of conduct would be guided by the goal of limiting limitation of market power; practices would be viewed primarily, though not entirely, in terms of their effect in creating or maintaining market power. This would result in a shift of attention by the agencies of enforcement from the history of individual commercial transactions, viewed as evidence of illegal intent, to a stronger focus on the economic functioning of the market, the role of particular firms in it, and the possibilities of improving its function. Such a shift would contribute to a more rational selection of cases for action by enforcement agencies, and a more meaningful trial of issues in the adjudication process.

Second, the relation between judgments on market power and evaluations of market performance in the administration of the law would be defined in entirely different terms than it now is. As our quick survey in Chapter I of the important recent cases shows, it is difficult to state in any specific way the relative importance now attached to judgments on structure and judgments on performance. The cases point to a situation in which the original trier of fact will have considerable latitude in assigning weights to these two sorts of judgments, both in respect to finding liability and prescribing remedies. In the nature of the situation, there can be little reliance on precedent to guide the trier within the scope of his discretion. Defendants will always press a performance standard; our previous discussion indicates the difficulties the trier will have in assessing their claims. Thus the present pattern of decisions points to a considerable variation in the standards of decision from case to case, whenever something more than conspiracy in the crude sense and conduct traditionally deemed predatory are involved—in other words, in the typical big case involving counts under both Section 1 and Section 2 of the Sherman Act. Such variation can be avoided either by rejecting the new elements which have entered into the administration of the antitrust law and returning to earlier standards in which conduct and intent were central, or by pressing on to define the ways in which finding market power and evaluations of market performance should enter into determinations in antitrust law. Our proposal goes in the latter direction.

Third, certain kinds of noncompetitive oligopoly situations now lie without the reach of the law. Where a very small number of rival sellers sell somewhat different products, or highly specialized and complex products, so that price identity is difficult to define, and their noncompetitive conduct manifests itself in no overt market division scheme, pricing formula, or the like, their conduct probably is not subject to the present law.

On a standard of intent, or deliberateness, it is difficult to find such conduct illegal, consistently with the usual meaning of the terms intent and deliberate.[60] To be sure, intent can be read to mean that any firm with market power intends to have it and use it, and therefore any firm with market power violates Section 2 of the Sherman Act. But this is a strained construction, and projection of the rationale of cases like *Alcoa* and *Tobacco* to sustain it appears unwarranted. Our standard would cover situations of this kind.

Fourth, remedy proposals involving structural reorganization of firms — dissolution, divestiture, and divorcement — would occupy a much larger place in antitrust policy than they do now. There would be many situations in which the maintenance of market power depended heavily on patterns of conduct, and thus market power could be limited without reorganizing firms. But in many situations of tight oligopoly, significant reduction of the power of the dominant firms demands an increase in numbers and decrease in concentration. In such cases, and in the case of dominant firms, the presumption would be in favor of reorganization remedies.

The first change would be felt throughout the whole area of application of antitrust policy. The second would be important in the typically big cases involving charges under both Sections 1 and 2 of the Sherman Act. The third and fourth differences in policy would be of somewhat narrower application, but the area to which they apply is one of great importance. An indication of the scope of their potential relevance is given by the extent of tight oligopolies shown

60. The relevant example is the cigarette market. In *American Tobacco*, the behavior of the major producers was found illegal under Section 2 of the Sherman Act, but on the theory that there had been a conspiracy among them. If we dismiss the jury's finding of conspiracy as erroneous (See Nicholls, *Price Policies in the Cigarette Industry*, especially chapter XIV, XX, XXIV), we find that the behavior that was condemned was indeed thrust upon the defendants, given the market structure and the desire to maximize profits. A more pointed example would occur in a market of similar concentration with sellers offering somewhat different products, and simply failing to invade each other's product lines and price aggressively. The impossibility of finding conspiracy on the *Tobacco* model in this situation would probably leave it outside the reach of the law as it is now interpreted.

in Chapter II above; they constituted about one third the number of all national-market manufacturing industries, and accounted for about 25 percent of the value of output of all such industries.[61]

POLICY ALTERNATIVES AND VALUE PERSPECTIVES

The framework of factual judgments and value assumptions within which we have outlined our policy proposal is not an inexorably compelling one. Competition as a process valued for its own sake may be deemed much less important than we have indicated, desirable economic performance, much more. The possible significance of conflicts between reducing market power and maintaining good performance could be viewed as greater than we have viewed it, without doing violence to such evidence as there is. The political aim of revising the balance between large and small business could be deemed worth achieving even at great costs in efficiency and progressiveness. From such changed premises, quite different conclusions would naturally emerge on what antitrust policy should be.

But even within the broad framework we have laid out, policy conclusions of a rather different sort than our own are possible, given some changes in emphasis in dealing with the admittedly incomplete evidence, some changes in the willingness to act or not to act when the outcome is in doubt, and some small changes in the ultimate value premises. It seems worth while to indicate sketchily what changes in the view of the situation underlying the policy problem lead to what kind of changes in policy recommendations.

The first element of a different view would be doubt that the possible conflicts between reducing market power and maintaining good performance are adequately treated by our limiting provisos on efficiency and progressiveness. The second is doubt about the confidence with which incentive repercussions of a policy making free use of dissolution remedies can be safely put to one side. The third is the assignment of a higher implicit weight to the importance of progressiveness wherever doubts as to the probable impact of policy measures on progressiveness arise. Our own proposal resolves such doubts in favor of the primary aim of reducing market power; to resolve them the other way, in favor of maintaining progressiveness, is not a very long step. Finally, somewhat less confidence in

61. See Chapter II, Table 1. This may be a somewhat too broad definition of the probable area of application of these aspects of our policy. A narrower one is given by the 41 industries in which the first 8 firms had over 75 percent of the output. See the Statistical Appendix, S.A. Table 1.

the objectivity of the standards by which judgments of market power can be made, coupled with a greater confidence in the ability of administrators to determine what kinds of conduct maintain or increase market power in particular situations, forms the fourth element in the alternative view. The broad outlines remain the same: competitive processes are valued as ends in themselves; both the difficulty and the undesirability of relying heavily on performance alone are recognized; fairness as such apart from competition is given no great weight; no effort is made to use antitrust policy as a lever for altering the balance between large and small enterprise in the society as a whole.

On the basis of this alternative view, with its important differences in detail within the same broad framework, it may be appropriate to come to quite a different set of policy recommendations. The use of dissolution, divorcement, and divestiture remedies may be left as it now is, or even diminished below the present level, on grounds of the possible adverse effects on incentives. The central technique of policy would become the control of conduct, with a view to preventing any kinds of practices which sustain or increase market power. In particular, fairly stringent limitations on mergers would occupy a central place in policy. While market power standards would provide the basis for regulating conduct, no attempt would be made to deal directly with existing concentrations of market power. Rather, we would rely on the restraint on mergers and the control of other kinds of restrictive conduct, and on time and new developments, to diminish gradually the importance of existing market power. When we say that conduct would be regulated on market power standards, we do not deny scope for per se rules against certain practices. We merely mean that the central question to be asked about any practice, whether viewed in general, from a per se approach, or viewed in the context of a particular market situation, is: how does it contribute to sustaining or increasing market power; rather than: is it fair, or is it reasonable.

It is clear that a policy of this latter type has certain advantages in administrative simplicity over our own proposal to limit market power directly. In the first place, it is closer to the traditional standard of antitrust policy, with its emphasis on fair conduct and intent. Continuity in policy is always an advantage, if it can be achieved. Second, from the point of view of business firms, it is a policy that is easier to comply with. Since it leaves present situations alone and addresses itself to future conduct, the duties of business firms under it are somewhat clearer than under the market power standard. The increase in clarity should not be exaggerated, however, since the necessity for interpreting the propriety of some practices in the light of the market situation gives rise to just the same sort of difficulties in application as does a market power standard. Enforcement will be somewhat easier, since less detailed investigation and less lengthy proceedings will in general prove necessary to justify orders forbidding or modifying business practices than would be required to justify orders reorganizing business firms.

Yet, despite these advantages, there is something to be said against this line of policy in addition to the reassertion of our previously stated position on the fundamental issues involved. First, the rigorous control of conduct is not without its own problems. To the extent that existing concentrations of market power are important, this control must be detailed and pervasive. A policy which will inevitably be administered with fluctuating vigor and resources may achieve more by moving in large, discrete steps to change market structures when it moves, than by vainly trying to maintain continuous pressure on conduct. Second, as we have just pointed out, the difficulties of evaluating the context of conduct may be little less than those of coming to an over-all conclusion on market power, so that the advantages in this direction are small, in comparison to the considerably lessened effectiveness. Significantly, the difficulties are most serious in the area which would bear the brunt of the alternative approach, namely, that of mergers. Finally and most important, there is the prevalence of existing oligopoly situations in which the leading firms already possess considerable market power. Many of these are impervious to the regulation of conduct, and even without further mergers, dominant firms in such markets will tend to grow at least as fast as the markets in which they sell, if not faster. In many markets, the great advantages associated with an entrenched position assure this. The fact that in the past such firms have tended to grow with their markets, and to maintain their relative positions even after they ceased to grow significantly by merger, bears this out.[62] Thus the alternative policy will tend to leave an important part of the area of tight oligopoly markets untouched. These reasons,

62. See J. F. Weston, *The Role of Mergers in the Growth of Large Firms* (Los Angeles, 1953).

in addition to our more fundamental views on the nature of the policy problem, convince us of the superior virtues of our own proposals. Nevertheless, we do not think that they need be universally convincing. Thus we will continue to refer to possible applications of the alternative policy view to some of the specific problems of policy that we examine in the two following chapters.

There are two other alternatives that deserve consideration. One is suggested by our prediction, in setting forth the demerits of reliance on regulation of conduct, that significant concentrations of undue market power are likely to persist unless dealt with directly. Could not this objection be met by a program limited to the clearing up of existing concentrations of power, without making it a permanent feature of antitrust law? This would mean a statute, somewhat like the Public Utility Holding Company Act, empowering an administrative agency to enforce the structural reorganization of firms or groups of firms possessing undue market power, all such proceedings to be commenced within a specified period of years. To make the program manageable and to promote the most efficient use of enforcement resources, a statute would impose more or less arbitrary cutoffs on the size and significance of industries potentially subject to reorganization, so that no more than, say, thirty or so industries would be affected.

There is much to be said for this alternative. The prospects for success of strengthened laws against conduct would be substantially improved if projected on a clean slate, i.e., if existing noncompetitive situations were reorganized along more competitive lines. Such a program, if effectively carried out, would drastically reduce the burden on enforcement agencies of policing the conduct of firms with market power. Moreover, if there is any tendency for the power of existing powerful firms to cumulate, that contribution to the woes of enforcement agencies would also be removed.

In addition, a limited program would minimize whatever disincentive effects would attend a permanent prohibition on unreasonable market program. To be sure, businessmen may fear a repeat performance or an extension of the policy, but it seems unlikely that such fears would have the impact on business behavior and decisions that a permanent statute allegedly would. Finally, the setting of a time limit would probably result in more rapid deconcentration of existing industries and a more consistent enforcement program —

assuming that the time limit is long enough and the funds are large enough to enable the enforcement agency to proceed against all subject to the law (which may well be a hazardous assumption).

Nevertheless, some obvious questions can be raised. A limited program would suffice if tightened laws on conduct would preserve competition in the reorganized markets, and if they would insure that significant concentrations of unreasonable market power would not develop and persist in other and new industries in the future. We cannot be highly confident, or even confident, that this would be true, principally because of serious doubts that enforcement is likely to be adequately sustained. Moreover, to speculate further on the subject of incentives, it is at least possible that a concentrated program of deconcentration would be far more disruptive than a prolonged but piecemeal approach. However, while inclined toward making dissolution of unreasonable market power a permanent feature of antitrust law, we are not disposed to reject a limited program as an obviously undesirable alternative.

The last alternative we wish to consider is in fact not an alternative to those previously discussed, but an approach that is applicable to each of them. As is manifest, an accurate determination of the existence of "market power," or of the probable effects of a merger, will ordinarily require an economic investigation of considerable depth. Moreover, the guides to judgment, even on the basis of extensive economic facts, are something less than precise and certain. We wish neither to magnify nor to underestimate the uncertainties these difficulties would create and the burdens they may impose on enforcement agencies, be they administrative bodies or courts. But to the extent they do or would exist, they could be curbed by importing into the pertinent statute some more or less arbitrary presumptions on the basis of which the appropriate determinations would be either guided or compelled. For example, it might be provided in a statute directed against unreasonable market power that:

> "Market power shall be conclusively presumed where, for five years or more, one company has accounted for 50 percent or more of annual sales in the market, or four or fewer companies have accounted for 80 percent of such sales."

Where the specified facts were found, the adjudicating body would be able to turn, without having to make an exhaustive economic analysis of the industry, to the question of whether the presumed market power fell within any of the law's exceptions, and to the question of the appropriate relief. To use another example, it might be provided as part of an antimerger statute that:

> "Adverse effects on competition shall be presumed whenever a company that for five years or more has accounted for 20 percent or more of annual sales in a market acquires any competitor in that market, unless such competitor is insolvent or in obviously declining circumstances."

The appropriateness of these or similar arbitrary determinations depends on the probable validity of either of the following two conclusions: (1) there is a rational connection between the stated facts and the presumed result, so that the result is likely to be in fact correct in the vast majority or instances; or, at the least, (2) even if the result is likely to be correct only in a bare majority of — or even fewer — cases, the application of the law to those cases where the presumption is not in fact true will cause no social harm, or will cause harm that is largely outweighed by gain in effective enforcement.

Such conclusions are not easy to come to. We certainly could not come to the first conclusion with regard to the antimerger provision given above; we would be less reluctant to come to the second. As for the presumption on market power, we would be reluctant to come to the first, and cautiously optimistic about the second.

But even assuming that the suggested arbitrary tests are plausible, their plausibility rests almost entirely on the fact that they require a definition of markets, and a careful definition of markets — as *Cellophane* shows in approach if not in result — requires in many cases an examination of much the same economic evidence that is pertinent to a determination of whether or not market power exists, or is likely to be enhanced by a merger. In short, the certainty contributed by these arbitrary tests is to a substantial extent delusive. What this means is that the closer a test approaches to certainty, where economic regulation is involved, the less certain it is that the test is either reasonable or unlikely to cause substantial harm.

IV

The Policy Applied: Size, Integration, and Mergers, and the Proposed Policy

We have defined broadly a revised antitrust policy which has as its central aim the elimination and prevention of unreasonable market power. To specify more concretely what this policy is, we shall examine its application in some detail to six major problem areas of industrial organization: size; integration; merger; collusion, tie-ins, exclusive dealing arrangements and other practices presumptively bad per se; patents; and price discrimination. With respect to each, we ask what the nature of the problem is, how the law deals with it presently, and what changes are desirable in the light of proposed policy goals. We treat the first three problems, as well as briefly discussing joint ventures, in the present chapter, and the other three in Chapter V.

SIZE

The nature of the problem

The existence of large firms is central to nearly every problem in antitrust policy in our economy. Firm size can be defined in two different ways: absolutely, in terms of total assets, total sales, or total employment; or relatively, in relation to some market or markets in which the firm operates. The second definition makes size something which is closely related to market power, and thus brings it directly within the focus of a policy aimed at limiting market power. On the other hand, there need be no close relation between absolute size and market power: small firms may have large market power because they are large relative to their rivals in the market. But in fact the size and product structure of firms in the industrial sector of the economy is such that there is a fairly high correlation between absolute and relative size. Most absolutely big firms are also big in relation to at least some of the markets in which they operate. In this section, we will treat size chiefly in its relative sense, adding at the end of the discussion a few observations on the relation of size in an absolute sense to competition.

Size as market share has an obvious relation to market power. In general, it can be said that a large market share, held either by a single firm or by a small number of firms acting jointly, is a necessary condition for the existence of substantial market power in a market. The exception to this is the case of the successful, well-functioning cartel in a market with large numbers and no dominant firms; but this exception is more apparent than real, since it is difficult for a cartel to operate successfully in such a situation unless it has an extramarket device for controlling entry — either governmental power, or the use of union coercion.[1] This necessary condition is not, in general, a sufficient condition. Also, whether one or several firms are involved, there must be some barriers to entry — either created by the policy of the firms or arising from the technical, institutional, and legal environment of the market — which make possible the continued exercise of market power without a drastic loss of market share and profit in the long run. Further, when several firms rather than one are involved, the conditions which make for joint action by all, rather than for rivalrous individual action, must be present.

The first requisite to dealing with relative size is to measure it: this means properly delimiting the market and getting a usable measure of the market share of the dominant firms or firm. While the delimitation of a market in terms of products and of geographic and time dimensions is not an easy task, it need not be one beyond the powers of the policy administrator, on the basis of evidence which is mainly the ordinary result of business operations. In product terms, it involves defining the range of products other than those physically identical to the output of the firm(s) in question which are close substitutes for that output from the point of view of consumers, both at current prices and over a range of prices including

1. It is conceivable that there might be a large number situation in which, nonetheless, entry of further sellers is technologically impossible — a sort of large-numbers St. Louis Terminal case. But it is hard to find an actual example of this.

the historical range of price fluctuation, and which are produced at comparable costs.[2] In the geographic dimension, the geographic structure of supplier-customer relations must be traced out. Products with high transport costs frequently have markets much narrower than the whole of the United States, and different regional markets often contain different competitors with varying market shares in them.[3] The time dimension is relevant to the determination of both the product and the geographic limits of the market. In general, elasticities of both supply and demand increase with time, and some specification of the time period with respect to which the defined market relationships are presumed to hold is always needed. What is usually relevant is neither the very short period, in which only existing buyers and sellers can operate, nor the very long period, in which new technologies, new price structures, and new transportation patterns may enter to make any current material obsolete. Crudely put, some idea of market relations which have held five years in the past and which may be expected to hold for five years in the future is appropriate.[4]

Once the market has been defined, the measurement of market share is usually a straightforward computation. Sometimes, however, it may present difficulties. In the *United Shoe* case, for example, two problems arose in defining market share: should stock or flow measures be used, since under the leasing system United owned machines currently in factories as well as the increment of machines newly leased each year? What was the right weighting system to be used

2. This last is an important point, frequently neglected in discussions of interindustry competition. The monopolist of a product with some near substitutes at prices considerably higher than his production costs has a choice of having a high price-cost margin and a low "market share" in the combined market, defined by his outputs and that of the substitutes at the high price, or a much higher market share and a low-price cost margin, since at the lower price, many of the higher price products would cease to be substitutes. Failure to deal with this point was the major error in the reasoning of Judge Leahy in the Du Pont case (Cellophane). See Stocking and Mueller, "The Cellophane Case and the New Competition," *American Economic Review* (1954). It was ably discussed as long ago as 1916 by Judge Hand in the Corn Products case, 234 Fed. 964 at 975–977.

3. The Columbia Steel case is an example both of the difficulties of defining a regional submarket and the feasibility of dealing with these difficulties once the attention of the trier and the parties is directed to them. What was actually done in defining the market was a crude but usable approximation; a far better job could have been done on the basis of the defendant's records, if the trier or the government had raised the right questions.

4. We would, however, be inclined to presume that existing relations will hold for the future in the absence of convincing proof that, e.g., new substitutes or new competitors will upset them.

for measuring the aggregate market share from the market shares of some hundreds of individual machines? In the *IBM* case another difficult problem arose in that IBM's share plus that of its rivals did not necessarily add up to 100 percent. In general, IBM's rivals, such as National Cash Register Co., provide computing devices which require much more clerical labor to operate than do the competing IBM devices. IBM's revenue plus National Cash revenue (both adjusted to a sales basis) then falls short of the revenue IBM would receive if its machines displaced those of National Cash, since part of the new revenue IBM would receive now goes to clerks as salaries, rather than to the rival seller. These examples show not only that there are difficulties in measuring market shares, but that they can be solved.

It is safe to say that the data ordinarily generated by the operations of the business — in some cases supplemented by information about firms which would not be parties to an antitrust suit as conducted under present law, or by special market surveys made for the proceeding — used in the light of a reasonable degree of economic knowledge, could always provide usable market definitions and usable estimates of the market share of a firm or group of firms. Neither the volume and difficulty of access of the materials involved, nor the analytical sophistication required to deal with them would, we believe, be disproportionate in terms of the substantive importance of the policy.

Market share having been determined, the basic problem of moving from an estimate of market share to a judgment on market power arises. We have already discussed this problem at length in Chapter III, but a few further remarks on it may be in order. In the simplest case, say that of the single large firm with more than 35 percent of the market, with no rivals larger than a tenth its size, the problem turns primarily around the conditions determining the ability of existing rivals to expand and new producers to enter.[5] The undoubted short-run power of the large firm in this situation, when the industry is operating at full capacity, would extend over a substantial period only if its rivals could not expand their outputs at costs at all comparable with its costs, and new firms could not enter

5. This is not to say that a firm with 35 percent market share and no significant rivals generally possesses any considerable market power. But this situation might well be used as a presumptive boundary, to mark off what warrants further investigation from what does not. To justify the initiation of a trial or other formal procedures, much more would be required.

at comparable costs. As we have already indicated, judgment on the questions would depend on an examination of both the cost situations, factor supply conditions, and practices of the industry — in short, market structure — and the actual price, profit, investment history of the large firm and the whole industry — in short, the efficiency aspects of market performance. A larger market share of the dominant firm without rivals of substantial size would strengthen the presumption that the firm has large market power, but it would in no way change the kind of questions which would require study before this conclusion would be fully justified.

For the single large firm, the problem of determining market power can proceed in a relatively straightforward manner along the lines examined in Chapter III. Difficulties multiply, however, in the more typical situation of structural oligopoly — a small number of large firms with a large combined market share.[6] In practice, single-firm monopolies or near monopolies are rare; the problem of market power typically arises in markets characterized by structural oligopoly. Nickel, incandescent electric light bulbs, and shoe machinery are the only examples of near monopoly that come to mind; none of the manufacturing "markets" defined along industry lines in Chapter II showed examples of the dominant firm without significant rivals.

The primary problem in the oligopoly situation becomes one of determining the relations among the existing large sellers: are they behaving in such a way as to create jointly shared market power, or are they behaving rivalrously in such a way as to prevent any one from enjoying any significant degree of market power for more than the very short run? This is the question traditionally discussed under the heading of "parallel action," of whether the firms are implicitly or explicitly colluding to increase their joint profits. "Parallel action" is a misleading phrase, which at best is usefully applicable to price policy and not always there. The substance of the problem is whether the rival firms are acting so as to limit each other's market power, or whether they are acting so as to maintain a situation of

6. In Chapter II the criterion of eight firms with 33 percent or higher market share was used as a criterion of structural oligopoly on the market definitions there available. But those were really industry, not market, definitions, and took only rudimentary account of geographic fragmentation of markets. For markets defined more precisely, perhaps a criterion of eight firms with a market share of 50 percent, fifteen with a market share of 80 percent, might be a useable presumptive boundary. The usual concentration ratio defined in terms of the first four sellers appears inadequate; *vide* steel, petroleum, rayon.

considerable market power, exercised by all of them jointly. The essence of the problem is not, Is there parallel action; but rather, Is there anticompetitive action?

In general, anticompetitive action in an oligopolistic market is action which leads toward joint profit maximization for the oligopolists as a group. There may be market sharing, with or without price leadership; rivalrous effort may be directed to product variation and promotional efforts which create barriers to entry and at the same time permit high profit margins; there may be rationing of consumers and limitation of new investment in the face of rising demand. Joint action may appear in obvious forms of overt collusion, and thus be easy to detect; it may appear in forms which can be apprehended only by a thorough analysis of the market. Some market features are conducive to joint action — slowly growing or declining demand, large cyclical fluctuations in demand, relatively stable technology, standardized products, high seller concentration and low buyer concentration. Others promote competitive behavior such that no firm possesses significant power — rapidly increasing demand, rapidly changing techniques and frequent product innovation, differences in costs among rival sellers, high concentration among buyers. But in general we will need to make a direct examination of the efficiency dimensions of performance — price-cost relations, output-capacity relations, capacity-demand relations, technical efficiency — as well as examining structure to see whether or not it is conducive to joint action.

It is important to note that we cannot discuss the problem only in terms of the intent of the sellers in the market, as evidenced by their choice of policies from among all possible market policies which they could have in the particular context.[7] There are market structures that leave sellers no policy short of joint maximization that would be tolerable or justifiable in business terms — the cigarette market, for example. There may be market structures in which a wide range of rivalrous or coordinated action among the sellers would be compatible with positive profits — the titanium pigments market, for example. On our view of policy, this does not justify the conclusion that cigarette sellers are not and titanium oxide sellers are liable under a monopolization complaint, because the former had market power thrust upon them, so to speak, while the latter chose

7. This might be termed the standard of conduct that is "no more restrictive than necessary," in the context of the market situation.

joint action (with collusion) in a situation in which they could possibly have chosen otherwise. Since we address ourselves to situation and effects rather than to conduct and intent, we view both groups of firms as equally liable, assuming that unreasonable market power was present in both situations.

How the law now deals with size

A brief statement of how antitrust law now deals with relative size would indicate that, as such, the law does nothing with it. Brief statements are necessarily misleading ones; our statement can be expanded to say that the law has not proscribed large relative size unless:

(1) it is associated with predatory conduct; or,

(2) in an oligopoly situation, it becomes the basis of a conspiracy charge, the evidentiary support for which is largely a showing of parallel action; or

(3) large size, along with some kind of conduct, shows that the single large firm is monopolizing or has monopolized in the sense of Section 2 of the Sherman Act.

As in 1920, so today, "mere size is no offense." [8]

Under the present law, the problem of the large firm (or firms) is one which involves either Section 2 or both Sections 1 and 2 of the Sherman Act. The classic single-firm monopoly cases — the "old" *Standard Oil* case (1911), the "old" *American Tobacco* case (1911), the *Corn Products Refining* case (1916), the *Harvester* (1914) and *DuPont* (Powder) (1911) cases[9] — revolved about an intent to monopolize, revealed by mergers, conspiracy, and a wide-ranging variety of practices aimed clearly at driving out competitors, often involving fraud and bad faith and sometimes verging on coercion, as well as by the success of the practices in most of the cases. The limits of this doctrine were shown in the old *Shoe Machinery Case* (1918), and the *Steel Case* (1920), in which the dominant firm, verging on monopoly in the first case, occupying over 50 percent of

8. U.S. v. U.S. Steel Corp., 251 U.S. 417 (1920).

9. Although all of these involved conspiracy charges as well as charges of monopolizing. U.S. v. American Tobacco Co., 221 U.S. 106 (1911); Standard Oil Co. of New Jersey v. U.S., 221 U.S. 1 (1911); U.S. v. Corn Products Refining Co., 234 Fed. 964 (S.D.N.Y. 1916); U.S. v. International Harvester Co., 214 Fed. 987 (D. Minn. 1914); U.S. v. E. I. du Pont de Nemours, 188 Fed. 127 (D. Del. 1911).

the market in the second, was found clear of liability because free of illegal intent to monopolize.[10]

The single-firm cases in which monopolizing has been found under the "New Sherman Act" are two: *Alcoa* and *United Shoe Machinery*.[11] The *Alcoa* opinion, embodying the proposition that no monopolist monopolizes unconscious of what he is doing, and resting the finding of monopolizing on the fact that Alcoa "embraced every opportunity" for expansion, thus foreclosing opportunities otherwise open to potential rivals, goes very far in the direction of making large relative size (over 60 percent but not necessarily as much as 90 percent of the market) illegal. But an extension of the logic of the opinion to a different fact situation by another court appears unlikely. First, the actual position of Alcoa, as near monopolist (except for secondary and small imports) for a period of twenty-five years after expiry of the basic patents on which its original monopoly rested, is unlikely to be repeated. Second, the appellate court was faced with a set of findings by the original court which ran contrary to its own sense of the facts. An *Alcoa* decision based on the finding that Alcoa's conduct in respect to power contracts, bauxite sites, and the Duke transaction at Saguenay was exclusionary, would hardly have been surprising. Even in the wide scope of Sherman Act decisions, Judge Hand's interpretation of monopolizing seems too broad a piece of legislation to be generally applied.

The *Shoe* case tells another story. It does not go so far in the direction of forbidding large relative size as such. Rather it strikes down size when it is buttressed by conduct less competitive than possible. United's practices took United's market power out of the class of "thrust-upon" exceptions, assuming that we view the 1918 Supreme Court's erroneous approval of the mergers which created United as the equivalent of a legal license. Again, the ease with which this standard can be transferred to other cases is questionable. Not every single-firm monopoly has an origin legally protected from scrutiny by the trial court; without this, *United Shoe* might have been another *DuPont Powder* or *International Harvester* case. Further, the identification of practices not dictated by the circumstances

10. U.S. v. United Shoe Machinery Co., 247 U.S. 32 (1918); U.S. v. U.S. Steel Corp., 251 U.S. 417 (1920).

11. U.S. Aluminum Co. of America, 148 F.2d 416 (C.A. 2, 1945); U.S. v. United Shoe Machinery Co., 110 F. Supp. 295 (D. Mass. 1953).

of the market, and more restrictive of competition than feasible alternatives open to the firm, cannot always be made with the clarity that the special circumstances of United's leasing system made possible.

The cases offer even less support for a doctrine of illegal power than they do for one of illegal monopoly power.[12] The argument that some such doctrine exists is based on the parallel action cases, chiefly the "new" *Tobacco* case (1946) and the *Paramount* case (1948), to a lesser extent the *Interstate Circuit* case (1939) and the *Cement* (basing point) case (1948).[13] In all of these, the Court found a conspiracy in violation of Section 1 or Sections 1 and 2 of the Sherman Act. In every case evidence of parallel action by defendant firms in an industry with an oligopolistic structure played an important role in the finding of conspiracy. Not even in the *Tobacco* case, however, can it be said that the finding of conspiracy rested only on evidence of parallel action; the jury found collusion, although the evidence on which it based that conclusion is not readily apparent.[14] In every one some evidence of communication, direct or indirect, more or less recent, appeared as additional evidence of the conspiracy. In the *Paramount* case, action was not only parallel but exclusionary, and its exclusionary effect was dependent on the fact that it was jointly taken by all the defendants. Even the *Tobacco* case cannot be read to say that parallel price policies and parallel policies in some other respects — practices in respect to setting up and attending tobacco auctions — by a small group of firms with a very large market share are in themselves illegal. Parallel action was used as evidence from which was inferred — rightly or wrongly — a collusive agreement directed both at pricing policy and at the exclusion of the ten-cent brands. Once the collusive arrangement was inferred, the finding of Sections 1 and 2 violations involved no legal novelty.

More recent cases give no further support to the proposition that parallel action, without more, is conclusive evidence of conspiracy in small numbers markets. *Theatre Enterprises v. Paramount Film Distribution Corp.*[15] (1954) shows that parallel conduct can be justified

12. Compare Rostow, "The New Sherman Act: A Positive Instrument of Progress," *University of Chicago Law Review* (1947), 14:567; and Bowman, "Towards Less Monopoly," *University of Pennsylvania Law Review* (1953).

13. American Tobacco Co. v. U.S., 328 U.S. 781 (1946); U.S. v. Paramount Pictures, Inc., 334 U.S. 131 (1948); Interstate Circuit, Inc. v. U.S., 306 U.S. 208 (1939); FTC v. Cement Institute, 333 U.S. 683 (1948).

14. See the excellent analysis in Nicholls, *Price Policies in the Cigarette Industry*.

15. 348 U.S. 537 (1954).

as the product of independent responses to similar circumstances by firms in the same market. *C-O-Two Fire Equipment Co.*[16] (1952) shows that parallel action, along with much else, is useful as evidence in establishing a conspiracy. In general, the more faithful the parallelism, the larger the numbers involved, the more complex the changes through which parallelism has persisted, the greater the number of market variables which have shown parallel behavior, the less easy will it be for the trier to believe that he is witnessing the independent responses of several firms to the same market situation; and therefore the more persuasive will parallel action alone be as evidence on which a finding of overt collusion (conspiracy) can be made. More than this, however, we cannot say.

The kind of remedies courts apply in monopolization cases are as important an element of the present law on size as the standards of liability on which they make judgments. In general, remedies involving reorganization of defendant firms — divestiture, divorcement, and dissolution — are not now widely used. The government asked for some measure of dissolution or divestiture in *National Lead*, *Alcoa*, *Paramount*, and *United Shoe*, all recent cases involving tight oligopolies or dominant firms. *Tobacco* was brought as a criminal case, and thus no issue of remedy of this type arose. Only in *Paramount* was there divestiture — granted on appeal after it was refused by the district court. The basis of what on remand became the district court order divorcing exhibition from production-distribution was twofold: the remedy originally proposed by the district court, competitive bidding for films on an individual basis by exhibitors, would be unworkable; and the integration of exhibition with production-distribution was a necessary link in the collusive ties among the major defendants. In *Alcoa* and *Shoe*, government-proposed dissolution proposals were rejected by the respective district courts on the ground, among others, that they were infeasible. This was clearly a correct judgment of the proposal in *Shoe*, and probably a correct one of that in *Alcoa*, though in both cases it appears possible that a feasible proposal could have been put forward. In *National Lead*, the Supreme Court rejected the government's appeal from the district court's refusal to order dissolution, observing that no showing had been made that four firms would be better than two, or six better than four.

Other recent cases in which divestiture remedies have been or-

16. 197 F.2d 489 (C.A. 9, 1952), cert. denied, 334 U.S. 892.

dered have followed somewhat the pattern of the "old" divestiture cases: *Standard Oil* (1911), *American Tobacco* (1911), *International Harvester* (consent, 1912). These include *Crescent, Schine,* and *Besser.*[17] In *Crescent,* the several corporate defendants were ordered to sell their holdings of each other's stock, the individual defendants had to choose which among the corporations they would hold stock in and manage, on the grounds that these intercorporate ownership relations were part of the means of a conspiracy among the several corporations. In *Schine,* the Supreme Court asked the district court, on remand, to rationalize its divestiture order either in terms of a theory of illegal acquisition *or* in terms of what was necessary to dissipate the illegal situation. Both of these cases may be viewed broadly as indicating some simpler notion of reducing the market power of the defendant exhibitor chains in their respective regional markets, and the actual results would be consistent with this interpretation, but the language of the opinions does not say this. Besser was ordered to give up its stock in a competitor which it had covertly acquired, on the ground that this was part of a campaign of monopolization. In all these cases, coercion and predatory practices played some role, and divestiture was related to the existence of bad conduct in this sense. *Griffith,* on the other hand, seems to go further, although the opinion is not entirely clear.

Defects of the present law

The principal defect of present antitrust law is its inability to cope with market power created by jointly acting oligopolists. Only when joint action takes the form of parallelism sufficiently striking and detailed so that it will support an inference of overt collusion, and directed toward such objects — price fixing, or the exclusion of rivals from the market — as bring collusive action within the ban of an illegal conspiracy to monopolize or restrain trade, do oligopolists now fall within the reach of the law. In the absence of a detailed market-by-market survey of business conduct, it is impossible to say with any precision how much is or is not reachable, but we believe it is safe to say that a considerable number of industrial markets exist in which oligopolists, acting jointly, possess substantial degrees of market power, which they exercise without engaging in conduct violating the Sherman Act.

17. U.S. v. Crescent Amusement Co., 323 U.S. 173 (1944); Schine Chain Theatres v. U.S., 334 U.S. 110 (1948); Besser Mfg. Co. v. U.S., 343 U.S. 444 (1952).

While we are inclined to think that present law on individual monopolization is largely satisfactory, and while the single-firm monopolist does not present an important problem of market power in many markets today, the uncertainties of the law in defining what "monopolizing" conduct is may act to restrain efficient performance by large firms which are not now possessors of putatively illegal market shares. General Motors and Alcoa, for example, may fear to lower prices and expand capacity, even though they may be (and are widely believed to be) more efficient than their rivals, for fear that such action will lead to large increases in their market shares and subsequently to liability as monopolizers under Section 2. In such a situation, the law frustrates itself, for it results neither in efficient performance nor in compulsion by the market.

Finally, remedy orders in cases involving large firms which singly or jointly dominate particular markets frequently fail to make structural changes through dissolution, divorcement, and divestiture. The caution of courts in applying what are considered drastic remedies is natural, given both the vagueness of the standard of liability and the tremendous area of discretion in making remedies, not in any way limited or guided by the legislation. But this does not mean that the limited reliance on these remedies is satisfactory, or that the legislation should not be revised to encourage their further use.

What is to be done?

(1) *Liability.* To make the law serve the aims of our policy proposal, an unreasonable degree of market power as such must be made illegal.[18] While not all unreasonable market power can be attacked directly through reorganization remedies because of problems of transition costs and feasibility raised by such measures,[19] a new standard of liability should be framed directly in terms of market power. The prohibition must apply to power jointly exercised by a group of oligopolists, whether or not collusion as now defined by law is present, as well as to the power of the single dominant firms. This change in the law is sufficiently far-reaching so that it would be necessary to embody it in new legislation. Neither the language and history of the Sherman Act, nor the recent cases we have examined above, gives a sound basis for expecting or asking

18. See Chapter III for our definition of an unreasonable degree of market power.
19. See Chapter II.

for a judicial reinterpretation of the present law along the lines proposed.

In addition to the change in substantive scope that would result, the proposed change would have a considerable impact on the presentation of cases. Problems of intent, coercion, etc., would recede to the role of minor features in a proceeding which would typically center on an analysis of market structure and of those aspects of market performance which are relevant to a judgment on market power. Under these circumstances, it may be that the present enforcement system, relying largely on the courts, is inappropriate. Perhaps what comes into the court could be a much more clearly organized analysis of the market, most of which will be stipulated, and the court proceeding proper could be confined to a hearing on the disputed points of evidence and on the significance of the whole picture of the market. These matters remain to be explored in the part of this study devoted to the embodiment of the proposed policy in law and the creation of appropriate machinery to administer it.

Any administrative machinery will operate to some degree within the framework of the adversary process. Within this framework, we envision a proceeding under the market power standard as taking the following form. The enforcing agency — prosecuting attorney or administrative body — will be required to show that the firms (or firm) under examination possess market power, as we have defined it, by:

(1) delimiting the market in which the firms operate and by describing the characteristics of the demand which they meet;

(2) establishing the average market share of the group and the individual firms over the period under study, and noting any trends in market shares;

(3) examining the conditions of entry into the market, the conditions of expansion of output for firms other than the respondents, and the actual history of entry and nonentry;

(4) where a group of firms is involved, showing that the market is such that they do in fact act jointly to exercise market power, rather than in such a way as to limit each other's power.

(5) testing the conclusions of (1) through (4) against the relevant dimensions of performance: price-cost margins, in the aggregate and for separate products and submarkets; output-capacity relations; capacity-demand relations; technical efficiency. While the

information examined under (1) through (4) may indicate the absence of market power, it cannot, alone, demonstrate its existence in the usual case.

All these matters can be dealt with on the basis of materials usually found in business records, although they may frequently involve analyses of these materials not ordinarily made in the course of business. Problems in weighing evidence will of course arise, conflicting opinions will be offered as to the meaning to be attached to particular figures, but all the problems are soluble to a practically useful degree of precision.[20] Respondents may, of course, rebut any of the evidence offered by the government. It is possible to hope that the items under (1) and (2) can be agreed on by the parties, or at least reduced to a few sharp conceptual issues. Similarly, the actual performance data under (5) could be agreed on, leaving to dispute their significance and the evidence under (3) and (4).

The government, having made a case for the existence of market power, will have met its initial burden and made a prima facie case for liability under the market power standard. It will then fall to the respondents to show that their market power is reasonable, under the exceptions provided for in our standard: economies of scale, patents, and the introduction of new products, processes, or techniques.[21] Since respondents bear the burden of proving the reasonableness of their market power where it exists, any doubts and insufficiencies of evidence will tell against them, just as doubts and insufficiencies in the proof of the existence of market power will be resolved against the government.

(2) *Remedies.* The substantive effects of our proposed change in the law depend as much on what kinds of remedy orders the new law leads to as on the change in the standard of liability itself. The logic of our policy goal, as we have argued in Chapter III, calls for a widespread application of dissolution remedies, on the ground that an increase in numbers and reduction of concentration is the surest

20. The substantiation of these assertions may be found in the records of the *Shoe Machinery*, *Cellophane* (Du Pont), and *Investment Bankers* cases — though more in the offerings of defendants than in those of the government. The possibilities of reducing the length of the proceedings is discussed in Chapter VIII. For an example of a very thorough analysis of market structure and the efficiency aspects of market performance without benefit of the detailed access to corporate records provided in an antitrust proceeding, see J. S. Bain, *The Pacific Coast Petroleum Industry*, parts I and II (Berkeley, 1944, 1945).

21. See above, Chapter III.

and most durable way of reducing market power. Thus, in most situations where the administrator of the law made a finding of unreasonable market power, the presumptive remedy would be the reduction in the size of the largest firms by divestiture and dissolution, within the limits of the rule against breaking up existing plants. There would be exceptions. First, our policy of not splitting up existing firms to the point of sacrificing demonstrable economies of scale would place limits on the amount of dissolution. It is worth noting that, typically, evidence relevant to the assertion of the reasonableness of existing market power would also be relevant to the determination of what these limits were. Second, there would be cases in which market power rested clearly on practices — say the existence of a closed patent pool, with territorial and product divisions. Here, if market concentration were not high, dissolution would appear unnecessary. Third, there may be cases in which the respondents could show that because of special circumstances, not relating to economies of scale, dissolution would result in a permanent loss of substantial economies. Fourth, it may be difficult to create new firms that would have a reasonable chance of survival. For example, one of the plants of a two-plant firm may be inefficient or badly located and thus incapable of effective competition as an independent unit.

Reorganization remedies, when applied, would not be limited to horizontal dissolution — splitting firms up into several smaller replicas with similar activities. In particular situations, vertical divestiture might be just as important or more important. Where market power rested on backward integration over scarce raw material resources or bottleneck transport facilities, this might be the case. Again, where distribution outlets were foreclosed by integration, vertical divestiture plus injunctions against achieving the effect of integration through exclusive dealing or other contractual devices might be indicated. In all these cases, a determination of liability which centered around defining the degree and sources of market power would produce the information on the basis of which appropriate remedy arrangements could be devised.

We base our presumption in favor of dissolution on the proposition that changing a tight oligopoly market into a looser one, or a market dominated by a single seller into one in which several large firms operate by reorganizing the larger firms in the market, will in fact change the market sufficiently so that the degree of market power exercised by the (still) relatively few large firms will be greatly reduced. Put crudely, the proposition is that the market with ten moderately large and thirty small firms will be much more competitive than the same one would be with four very large firms and thirty small ones. We also assume that the limits of reorganization we have suggested above will not be such as to prevent any effective program of increasing numbers from being put into effect.

Both experience — such as it is — and logic support the first proposition: the looser the oligopoly structure, the less market power any individual firm or the group as a whole exercises. Although evidence is scant, loose oligopoly industries such as oil refining and rayon appear to show more competitive behavior by the large firms than do tight ones such as cigarettes and flat glass. In general, joint action by oligopolists without the operation of an explicit cartel depends on the symmetry of their interests. Small numbers make it likely that each firm will serve a similar segment of the whole market. The larger the number, the greater is the likely diversity among firms: in costs, in the part of the market which they serve, in the range of products offered, in the kind and volume of expenditures devoted to innovation, in the expectations of executives concerning future changes in cost and demand. These diversities in turn increase the probability that some of the firms in the oligopoly group will find independent action rather than joint action advantageous, and so make less likely a pattern of action which approaches joint profit maximization. To be sure, factors other than the size and character of the rival firms are important in determining the way an oligopolistic market functions — the nature of the product, the technological maturity of the industry, the rate of growth of demand, the cyclical stability of demand, are all important. But within the framework defined by a given set of values of these variables, the larger the number of rival sellers and the smaller the relative size of the largest few, the more likely will it be that no firm and no group exercises much market power.

Further, the same reasons which make independent action rather than joint action more likely in a loose than in a tight oligopoly situation make it less likely that a well-functioning cartel can operate. In general, the larger the number of firms and the less important the relative position of the leading ones, the more is required in the way of machinery of information, communication, and enforcement to make an explicit agreement work. Given the illegality of such agreements, only those with a minimum of organized machinery can be expected to function undetected. Thus not only joint action based on "oligopolistic rationality," but also joint action based on an overt agreement, is less likely in practice the larger the numbers and the smaller the size of the leading firms in the market.

Finally, when the relative size (and thus the absolute size) of the largest sellers in a market is reduced, the entry barrier for new firms is, in general, also reduced. This arises from the fact that a significant element of the entry barrier is the superior liquid resources of existing firms in relation to most new ones; this puts the new entrant at a disadvantage in any "war" situation, price or otherwise, which existing sellers might initiate as a response to his entry. Given the fact that liquid funds are not freely available at the going price to the new entrant (or indeed, to any firm), the larger the absolute size of existing sellers, the greater is this disparity, and the greater this dimension of the risks associated with entry.

Our second assumption is that reorganization remedies can achieve significant changes in concentration within our stated limitations: no sacrifice of economies of scale or of substantial efficiencies unique to the firm, and the requirement that new firms created by divestiture have reasonable chance for survival. A well-buttressed conclusion on this point would require knowledge not now available, and unlikely to become available soon — unless as a by-product of our proposed policy. We simply cannot show in any detail, for example, what scale economies are available to the *firm* in the relevant size range. But the available evidence which we reviewed briefly in Chapter I is consistent with our assumption that they are not widespread.[22]

Similarly, we doubt — to the point of perhaps striking it as a defense — that there would be many cases where dissolution of a

22. One problem of economies of scale is somewhat perplexing — that of the real capital costs of large versus smaller firms. In general, larger firms can secure capital on more favorable terms. Some of this differential reflects their greater stability of earnings, in part associated with market power; some of it reflects the fact that they are on the average older and thus better established and more seasoned risks in the eyes of lenders than smaller firms. Thus there is a mixture of real social economies and private advantages which is difficult to disentangle. Further, most of the advantages of scale in this respect apply further down the scale than the range of "large" (crudely $50 to $500 million assets) to "giant" (crudely $500 million to $5 billion assets), which is the crucial range for much of our policy proposal. Finally, to the extent that the real savings in capital cost exist, they are advantages of absolute size, rather than size relative to a particular market, and thus could be available to sufficently diversified large firms with no market power.

firm would cause a permanent substantial loss of economies. We reject completely the argument — sometimes implicit and sometimes explicit in discussions of size and efficiency — that the only really scarce resource is managerial talent. The argument is that large firms exist because of the superior talents of their managers, and that any obstacles placed in the way of their continued expansion will only lead to the substitution of inferior for superior management, with the consequent waste of resources.[23] The argument has no support in any evidence. If the advantages of the "superior" management are cost advantages in production and distribution, there is no evidence to support their widespread existence. That some firms are more efficient than others is clear; but that these differences are large and relatively permanent does not seem to be the case. If the advantages are to be seen in "superior" decisions with regard to market strategy, rather than in more efficiency in day-to-day operations, the whole argument takes on a question-begging character. Market power is justified on the grounds of the superior ability of the dominant firm to exercise its market power to its own advantage. In other words, antitrust policy should aim to punish those firms holding market power who do not use it to the full advantage of their stockholders. But once a market departs substantially from competitive conditions, the test of management wisdom in terms of "results" from the stockholders' viewpoint is hardly a test of economic efficiency.

The third limitation on reorganization remedies — that firms must be created that have a reasonable chance of survival — may be of considerable consequence. In this respect, the easily attained feasibility of reorganizations under the Public Utility Holding Company Act, where each new independent company was a "natural monopoly," can give little comfort. We would suppose it to be the rule rather than the exception that there will be at least some variations in efficiency among the plants of a multiplant firm, and, in the case of a firm producing many products, varying degrees of specialization among plants that may have at least some bearing on their respective fates as independent firms. However, we believe that in most cases these factors, while making the formulation of a feasible plan more difficult and perhaps reducing the number of new firms

23. We have already pointed out in Chapter I that acceptance of it is really incompatible with belief in either the possibility or the desirability of a competitive economy.

that can be created, would not prevent reorganization altogether. To a substantial extent, the burden of a comparatively inefficient plant will be reflected in, and lifted by, a comparatively low capitalization of the new firm inheriting such assets.

(3) *Injunctive remedies.* Even if reorganization remedies become typical in market power cases, as here proposed, injunctive remedies directed toward conduct will still occupy an important place in the administration of the law in cases in which market power is the primary issue. First of all, the limits to reorganization remedies will be of sufficient importance in some cases so that there may still be reason to control the conduct of the respondent firms. Such control will be directed toward two goals: the abolition of practices which contributed to the maintenance of market power by the respondents, and secondarily, to proscribing unfair or exploitative conduct. The first aim may also be important even when there has been a dissolution remedy; some restraint for a period of years on the practices of the successor firms may be necessary to get the full benefits of dissolution in the reduction of market power. For example, in a situation in which patents had played an important role in buttressing the power of a large firm, a remedy might include both dissolution and an injunction directed to the successor firms forbidding exclusive cross-licensing of patents among them. Secondly, there will always be situations in which structural remedies are impossible; for example, the situation of the old St. Louis Terminal Railroad Co., in which the only remedy possible was an injunction opening access to the facilities on equal terms to all.[24]

(4) *Administrative feasibility.* How feasible are our proposals for market power liability and for widespread use of reorganization remedies? It may be that they strain the capacities of an administrative system dependent on the attorney general and the courts, and that any serious effort to put them into practice would require a different procedure for producing remedy orders than that now operating. But some general comments can be offered here without discussing the problem of suitable administrative machinery, which we take up in a later chapter. The change in the standard of liability would effect an important change in the kind of information produced in and by the enforcement process. Respondent firms, in attempting to show that their market power was reasonable, would

24. See Gamco v. Providence Fruit and Produce Bldg., 194 F.2d 484 (C.A.1, 1952), for a modern instance.

necessarily assemble and discuss most of the information relevant to a judgment on how much dissolution was feasible, if any. To be sure, important problems of evaluation on which respondents' judgments would differ from those offered by the government would remain. In general, respondents' judgments on such matters would be based on closer knowledge and greater *expertise* than those offered by the other side, though they could hardly claim to be disinterested. But even this problem is not insuperable. Once respondents knew that they were bound to suffer some amount of reorganization, they would have a substantial interest in presenting some feasible plan, although not perhaps the most drastic feasible plan. As representatives of their stockholders, the managements of respondent firms would be concerned to see that any reorganization proposals put into effect did in fact create viable successor firms, so that their stockholders were not disadvantaged unnecessarily. This interest, plus the criticism by the other side inherent in the adversary proceedings, would prevent the offer of impractical plans or the failure to offer any at all on the part of respondents. For this process to work, however, a minimum condition is that the level of knowledge in the relevant areas of economics and industrial engineering available to the government in such proceedings be far higher than it is now in the typical presentation of an antitrust case.

We recognize that judgment on the existence of illegal market power will not always be obvious, and that judgment on the appropriateness of specified remedies may be even less often obvious. Lengthy proceedings are likely to be the rule, but we believe that the probable gains of such a program justify both the uncertainties and the costs.

INTEGRATION

Nature of the problem

Integration is a broad term, which denotes the combination in one firm of activities carried on (either currently or historically) in several separate firms. We can distinguish three types of integration: horizontal, vertical, and conglomerate. Horizontal integration is the union of several establishments engaged in the same activity under one central office. It raises no problems not discussed in the previous section on *Size*, or the following one on *Mergers*. Vertical integration is the combination in one enterprise of establishments related as customers and suppliers. From the point of view of an existing enterprise, vertical integration can involve either extension backward, to include its sources of supply; forward, to include its outlets; or both. Vertical integration may be complete, when the whole supply source or outlet system is within the enterprise; or partial, when some outside purchasing and selling (relative to the stage to which we refer) still takes place. We shall concern ourselves in the present discussion with vertical integration. Conglomerate integration is any that is neither vertical nor horizontal. For example, the ownership by General Motors of the Ethyl Corporation (in part) is an example of conglomerate integration. Conglomerate integration raises certain problems of nonhorizontal size, i.e., size other than market power, which we have referred to briefly above and will discuss further below.

Vertical integration, viewed either statically as an aspect of market structure or in dynamic terms as a path of firm growth, presents a variety of problems for competitive policy. In general, vertical integration in competitive markets would exist wherever there were real economies of transfer within the firm rather than through the market. Sometimes these economies are technical, as in the case of the integrated steel plant, and the integration leads to an alteration of the structure of the plant as well as the firm. Sometimes the economies are planning and marketing economies, as in the case of meat-packing branch houses, and only firm structure reflects the change. But vertical integration may also exist in situations where it offers no social gains, and is related to the achievement, maintenance, spread, or exploitation of market power.

In the first place, vertical integration raises again the problems of nonhorizontal size. In general, entry into a vertically integrated industry is more difficult than would be entry into one of its component horizontal stages, at least by the amount of the extra capital costs. Where the integration of existing firms is complete rather than partial, a would-be entrant may have no opportunity to enter at one horizontal stage, because no supplying (or buying) market exists to serve him (or which he could serve). In some cases, this must be accepted as a consequence of large efficient scale, just as large horizontal size must be accepted. In others, the integration may exist chiefly because of its importance as an entry-limiting device as, for example, in the integration of distribution and first-run exhibition in movies.

Secondly, vertical integration converts what in its absence would be variable costs into fixed costs by substituting investment in fixed equipment for current outlays on purchases. This undoubtedly has important effects on price policy, in particular in oligopolistic industries with wide cyclical fluctuations in demand. The nature of these effects is not uniform, but depends on the particular market structure in which they occur.

More important to antitrust policy are the possible effects of vertical integration as source and carrier of market power. Vertical integration backward over limited raw material supplies or forward over limited market outlets may provide either the basic sources of the market power of the firm or important buttresses to it. For example, the maintenance of the monopoly position of Alcoa, in the period after the expiration of its basic patents, was aided greatly by its purchase of bauxite mining companies in Europe, and its policy of acquiring leases on power sites in advance of their development and use. Together, these greatly increased the barriers to the entry of would-be rivals. Similarly, the backward integration of steel firms into ore production and the lack of any real market in ore make more difficult the entry of new steel producers. Examples of forward integration over limited distributive outlets are not so striking, since entry into distribution is generally easy.

Even more drastic are the entry-limiting effects of integration backward or forward over a regulatory boundary which separates a sphere of legal monopoly from the competitive area. Thus the position of the Western Electric Company as by far the dominant manufacturer of telephone equipment arises from the fact that it is the supplier subsidiary of American Telephone and Telegraph Co., the legal monopolist of local telephone service in most of the country and of all long-distance service. Similarly, the integration of Pullman car manufacturing with Pullman car operation, when the latter was tied to the railroads by a series of long-term contracts, amounted to the same thing, even though the Pullman Company did not hold a formal legal franchise. The monopolist customer, by preferring to deal with his integrated supplier, simply forecloses the market to competitors.

Neither a franchise nor a limited raw material supply is necessary to spread market power by integrating. Firms possessing significant market power at one stage in a production chain can, by integrating backward or forward, spread that power to lower and higher stages.

Their ability to do so is limited both by their power in the "primary" market and by the conditions of entry in the market into which they integrate. In general, if that market is fairly competitive, and entry into it is free, there will be little advantage to integration by the powerful firm. However, a firm's "primary" position may be so strong that it can control entry or exclude competitors at its new level by a "squeeze" or by refusal to deal. The existence of some market power in supplying and purchasing markets, however, makes backward and forward integration attractive by promising the capture of monopoly rents by the integrating firms. Where the relative power of the firm in the primary market is greater than that of firms in the supplying or buying markets, integration leads to the spread of market dominance into them. Even if the market power in the buying or supplying market is only that which comes from product differentiation and brand preference, this may present sufficient prospects of gain to justify integration; especially since the spread to a further market of the integrating firm's dominance may enable it to enhance the degree of differentiation in the market which it enters.

Finally, vertical integration offers opportunities for the use of market power not available to firms operating in a single-stage market. Both price and nonprice discriminations are made possible by vertical integration, especially partial vertical integration in which a firm is both supplier and competitor of other firms, or both customer and competitor. By narrowing the margin between the price at which it supplies its one-stage rivals and the price at which it sells the product with which their output competes, it can limit their profits, their growth, and even drive them out of business. Such price squeezes existed in the aluminum industry in the relations between Alcoa, as ingot supplier and as seller of sheet, and the nonintegrated sheet rollers. They existed in the oil industry when pipe line subsidiaries of the oil companies were charging very high tariffs. By rationing the supplies of nonintegrated customers, or by simply refusing to deal with them, the same results can be brought about, although they do not involve price discriminations.

Similarly, vertical integration in some directions combined with sales of semifinished products in others may offer opportunities for price discrimination which the one-stage producer could not achieve, even though his market power was great. Thus, for example, if the demand for aluminum ingot for casting was relatively inelastic, and for sheet and wire relatively elastic, Alcoa by integrating into sheet and wire production and supplying ingot to foundries could segregate the two markets, and in effect achieve different real prices in them. This would be impossible for an unintegrated seller of ingot.

All these examples of the spread, increase, or maintenance of market power by vertical integration involve the existence of horizontal market power at some stage of the integrated enterprise. Where this is entirely absent, vertical integration cannot create it.[25]

The present law

Integration in itself is not now prohibited by the antitrust laws. Whenever integrated firms have been subject to legal attack, the attack has been on the presence and abuse of market power by the integrated firm, perhaps in ways available only to integrated firms, but not on integration as such. The theory has been offered that integration per se is illegal since it excludes all other firms from supplying the integrating firm (or from buying from it), but it is completely without warrant in the cases. Only two recent cases involve this proposition in any degree: *U.S. v. Yellow Cab* and *U.S. v. Columbia Steel.*[26] In the former, in the original decision on the pleadings, some element of monopoly in at least two local cab markets was present. The exclusionary character of the integration, therefore, turned on the monopolization of the local markets for the purchase of cabs by monopolizing taxicab service therein. On the second round, when the case was tried on the merits, no monopoly was found and the case was dismissed. In *Columbia Steel* the government did advance a per se argument, but it was squarely rejected by the majority of the Court, which went on to find that at neither the rolling level (Columbia) nor the fabricating level (Consolidated) did the acquisition confer significant market power on the U.S. Steel Co. in the western market.

U.S. v. Paramount and *U.S. v. Pullman* are two recent cases in which vertical dissolution, separating defendants into successors operating independently at different stages of production, was a major part of the remedy order.[27] Both were cases in which market

25. We defer to later sections our discussion of quasi integration by means of requirements contracts and similar arrangements (Practices and per se rules), and vertical integration by merger (Mergers).

26. *Yellow Cab,* 332 U.S. 218 (1947) on the pleadings; *Columbia Steel,* 334 U.S. 495 (1948).

27. U.S. v. Paramount Pictures, Inc. 85 F. Supp. 881 (S.D.N.Y. 1949). U.S. v. Pullman Co., 50 F. Supp. 123 (E.D. Pa. 1943); *aff'd per curiam,* 330 U.S. 806 (1947).

power at one stage led to the exercise of market power at other stages because of vertical integration. In *Paramount*, it was power at the first-run exhibition level which reinforced power at the distribution level; this in turn enabled the defendants to exploit effectively their control of distribution to subsequent-run exhibitors. In *Pullman*, the operating company's dominance of the service business, based on long-term contracts with the railroads, was used to achieve a near-monopoly of Pullman car manufacture for its subsidiary, Pullman–Standard. Since vertical integration was in each case a buttress to horizontal market power, the remedial decrees properly ordered some measure of vertical dissolution. The complaint against Western Electric (1949), on grounds of monopoly based on the Western Electric–ATT integration (see above), would have justified a vertical dissolution remedy on the same grounds. But nothing in these cases can support a view that integration as such is now illegal, or even dubiously legal.

Modifications in the present law

Since the vices of integration always arise out of a connection between integration and horizontal market power, there is no need for law which applies to integration per se. Where our policy directed at limiting market power succeeds, no further concern for integration is necessary. Thus the present state of the law in this area is, speaking broadly, satisfactory.

This broad approval deserves further qualification or amplification on two points. The first is with regard to the kind of situation presented by the *Western Electric* case. Integration across the competitive-regulatory boundary should be prohibited, both because it may spread monopoly from the regulated area to the unregulated one, and because it complicates the tasks of regulation when some of the activities and costs of the regulated enterprises are outside the scrutiny of the regulator. But it is not clear that antitrust suits with dissolution remedies as a goal are the best means of enforcing such a prohibition. Perhaps direct prohibitions in the legislation defining the enterprises subject to regulation is a more desirable route.

Second, in light of the exceptions to and limitations on our suggested approach to limiting market power, the policy would fall far short of reducing it to negligible dimensions in all areas. What is to be done where substantial residual market power is left in the hands of a firm that is vertically integrated into other markets? One course is that marked out before. We proposed that where substantial market power must be left intact, it may be appropriate to formulate injunctive remedies designed to limit its growth, to foster new competition, and to prevent the exploitation or overpowering of other firms. The same general guides could be followed in regulating by injunction the practices of a vertically integrated firm.

However, the problems of formulating and supervising a decree of this sort become peculiarly difficult in the context of vertical integration. The *Alcoa* case illustrates the dangers that an injunctive decree would seek to forestall. A vertically integrated firm with a high degree of control over the supply of a raw material can "squeeze" its competitors in the fabricating markets by raising the raw material price or by simply diverting supplies from them to its own fabricating facilities. In other words, the threat is that market power in one market can be extended to another. Presumably, therefore, injunctive safeguards must regulate the pricing and distribution policies of the defendant firm. This comes close to a public utility kind of regulation (see *United Shoe*[28]), and it is extremely difficult to define limitations that are both satisfactory in a policy sense and easily enforceable.

The power to exert a price squeeze, for example, could be curbed by providing that the integrated firms' fabricating operations must show a profit with raw material invoiced to fabricating facilities at the firm's price to others. But this simple formulation may go both too far and not far enough. It goes too far if, because of a fall in demand for fabricated products, fabrication facilities generally are operating at a loss. It does not go far enough in that a bare profit — which complies with the hypothetical decree — is below a normal profit necessary to keep independent competitors in business. The difficulties attendant upon any attempt to cure these defects by specifying a "normal" profit are sufficiently obvious that they need not be elaborated here.

Similar if not more serious problems are encountered in attempting to forestall a supply squeeze by injunctive decree. It is easy enough to specify a crude rationing formula, e.g., that the integrated firm must offer at least "x" percent of its total raw material output to independents. But unless regularly revised (and on what basis?), this could quickly become an uneconomic market-division arrange-

28. U.S. v. United Shoe Machinery Co., 110 F. Supp. 295, 349 (D. Mass. 1953).

ment, unduly curbing the growth of the more efficient companies (which may include the integrated firm itself).

One possible solution to the price squeeze is to require that the integrated firm make comparable profits on the investment in each of its operations. This is simply another way of saying "no price discrimination," an injunction which the court in *United Shoe,*[29] in a multiproduct context, refused to direct. If attainable, it would reduce a firm's profits on the "monopolized" level to those obtained on the "competitive" level—a result akin to the basic theory of public utility regulation, but considerably divergent from the variety of price discrimination that utility regulation in practice permits.

It is not at all clear, however, that this result could always be achieved even by a company that in good faith gives it a try. There may be divergences in profit rates because of honest miscalculations of future costs and demands. Moreover, if the "monopolized" commodity, e.g., a basic raw material, is in short supply, there is no way of equalizing profits except (1) by pricing the raw material so low that demand exceeds supply, and the supply must be rationed, again requiring some method of "fair allocation"; or (2) by expanding production, which takes time. These matters aside, the result of "no price discrimination" does not as such seem too unreasonable to us, though it may be called harsh and a deprivation of the logical fruits of a "monopoly" that itself may have been deemed reasonable. Viewed as a device to contain "monopoly" within that monopoly's own ground, it is in a real sense simply an application of the rationale of the patent tie-in cases. Moreover, an injunction of this kind may well persuade a firm to spin off its less profitable facilities, i.e., to voluntarily "disintegrate," which would put an end to the dangers the decree was intended to check.

But if vertical divestiture is feasible, under the standards applicable to horizontal dissolution, we believe it should be enforced at the outset against a firm whose dominant market power at one stage cannot be eliminated. There will be at least some cases where horizontal dissolution is not feasible but where vertical dismemberment is, and the superiority of such relief to injunctive remedies—even for the victim—warrants that it be used.

If vertical divestiture is not feasible, we believe that injunctive decrees, despite their difficulties, should be tried rather than leaving the firm to proceed as it will. We would have hopes that the diffi-

29. U.S. v. United Shoe Machinery Co., 110 F. Supp. 295, 349 (D. Mass. 1953).

culties are more theoretical than real, that what constitutes "compliance" could be sensed if not precisely explained, that most firms will make an honest effort to comply, and that those who may be reluctant will do so out of fear that an exasperated court might otherwise find that divestiture is indeed "possible." Vague as the injunction against price-squeezes may have been in the *Alcoa* case, the company seemed quite able to avoid such tactics after the decree took effect.

MERGERS

Nature of the problem

The importance of past mergers in creating the present size distribution of industrial firms is well known, and we have already referred to it. The history of merger movements shows clearly that mergers have been one of the major routes by which large firms achieved dominant positions in their markets. It is clear that some policy which prevents or limits mergers is of central importance in a procompetitive program. To be sure, we could wait for mergers to occur and deal with their consequences, when necessary, along the lines already suggested, but the wastefulness of a procedure which first allows merger and then, after a lengthy and costly proceeding, severs what has been joined, hardly needs laboring.

The problem lies rather in the other direction. If mergers have been the royal road to monopoly and oligopoly in the past, why not simply forbid them altogether? We must begin, therefore, by considering the important reasons for mergers other than the achievement of dominant size and the elimination of competition. From the standpoint of ownership and management in the small or moderate-sized firm which is frequently the acquired firm in a merger, several important motives for selling can be discerned. First, there is often a lack of management succession when present executives reach retirement age, or die without trained successors. Second, a retiring owner-manager may prefer a more diversified investment portfolio than that represented by his own business; this may be especially important in respect to building an estate. Third, there is the difference between the capital-gains tax and the income tax, which may stimulate the retention of earnings rather than their withdrawal as dividends, and the subsequent sale of the business so built-up for the capital gain. All these reasons make the maintenance of some market for going businesses an important part of the incentives to the owner-manager to build up and run a business. Forbidding all mergers would reduce significantly the rewards of the entrepreneur in just the area where individual entrepreneurship is still important.

From the viewpoint of buyers — acquiring firms in mergers — we can see another set of reasons. When, as in the period immediately after World War II, stocks are selling below book values and well below replacement costs of fixed capital, mergers become a cheap way of expanding capacity. The loss-carry-forward provisions of the corporation income tax law provide a stimulus to the acquisition of unprofitable firms in order to reduce the tax liabilities of the acquirer. Other special circumstances, including allocations and price controls, stimulate mergers by allowing acquirers to secure quotas for scarce raw materials or licenses to produce high-margin products. But aside from such special circumstances, whenever a firm wishes to enter a new market, to produce a new product, to use a new technique, a merger may provide a low-risk method of doing so, compared with extending its own organization and activities in the appropriate way. By acquiring a going concern, the firm avoids the costly process of getting acquainted with new techniques, products, and markets, and all the risks and expenses involved in creating a new organization to carry on unfamiliar activities. The possibility of entering new markets by merger may lower entry barriers significantly: entry via merger may be followed up by expansion of capacity and output; without the merger possibility, the entry may not occur at all. By lowering risk barriers to entry, mergers may make for more competition.

From the standpoint of both buyers and sellers, mergers may promote efficiency. Where the appropriate scale of operations or degree of integration of the firm changes, mergers may provide the most economical method of reshaping the structures of existing firms to the new cost conditions.[30] Similarly, where a particular line of activity is declining, the acquisition of firms engaged in it by firms in expanding markets may be the most economical way to salvage the assets of the declining firms, providing a much greater social as well as private transfer-value than could be achieved if the organi-

30. Note that this argument applies to firms, not plants. In general, mergers do not directly result in changes in the scale of plants.

zation were destroyed and the capital assets sold in the second-hand market.

The special circumstances which stimulate mergers in order to acquire quotas, licenses, and transferrable tax offsets may be ignored as inappropriate to determining policy because they simply involve transfers of income rather than changes in real costs or outputs and because some of them are undesirable in themselves — e.g., the tax incentives to acquiring deficit firms. The desirability of the kind of arbitraging which takes place in the capital market when divergences between stock prices and replacement values of assets stimulate mergers may be assigned a relatively low weight as a factor in policy. But the other reasons for mergers cannot be similarly dismissed in formulating antitrust policy with respect to mergers.

Our problem then is to gain the advantages of prohibiting mergers which serve to increase market power, yet to do so with as little effect as possible on the market for business assets, or on the availability of the merger as a method of entry in markets that are new for the merging firm, or on the possibilities of increasing efficiency through mergers.

The present law

Section 7 of the Clayton Act, as amended in 1950, is relatively untested as of this writing. Only six decisions have been handed down that give any substantial guides to probable interpretation: the decision of the Supreme Court in the *DuPont-GM* case; the decisions of the District Court and of the Court of Appeals in the *American Crystal Sugar* case; the District Court decision in the *Bethlehem* case; and the FTC opinions in *Pillsbury* and *Crown Zellerbach.*[31]

The primary issue is the kind of proof that will be deemed sufficient to establish the probability of a "substantial lessening of competition" or a "tendency to monopoly." In this respect the legislative history of the 1950 amendment is not particularly enlightening, to say the least. It was clearly intended that less need be shown in a Section 7 proceeding than would be required to strike down a

31. U.S. v. E. I du Pont de Nemours & Co., 353 U.S. 586 (1957); American Crystal Sugar Co. v. Cuban-American Sugar Co., 152 F. Supp. 387 (S.D.N.Y., 1957), 259 F.2d 324 (C.A. 2, 1958). *In re* Pillsbury Mills, FTC Docket No. 6000 (Dec. 28, 1953); *In re* Crown Zellerbach, FTC Docket No. 6180 (Jan. 3, 1958); U.S. v. Bethlehem Steel Corp., 168 F. Supp. 576 (S.D.N.Y., 1958).

merger under the Sherman Act. At the same time, the committee reports accepted the proposition, set forth in the *International Shoe* case,[32] that a probability of substantial harm, not a mere possibility, must be shown. It is difficult to reconcile these two positions, since an informal judgment as to future probabilities would seem to demand an inquiry of as broad a range, if not as penetrating a depth, as is required in establishing past effects.

One way out of this corner is to decide that the requisite probability of harm shall be conclusively presumed on the basis of certain specified showings. *Standard Stations*,[33] a Section 3 case, is the classic example of this approach, holding that exclusive-requirements contracts are illegal whenever they foreclose "a substantial share of the line of commerce affected." Whether such an approach may be called a compromise of the two positions taken in the legislative reports, or is instead an abandonment of any serious effort to determine actual probabilities, depends on whether the selected conclusive presumption makes sense for the generality of cases. Be that as it may with regard to Section 3 — is a "quantitative share" test, or variant thereof, to be applied here?

DuPont-GM clearly says that it is in so far as vertical acquisitions are concerned. "Foreclosures" of a substantial share of the "relevant market" by vertical acquisition will receive the same treatment as foreclosure by exclusive contracts. Moreover, unless *DuPont-GM* is *sui generis* because of the large size of the companies involved, the "relevant market" will be narrowly defined; no *Cellophane* refinements will be pertinent in a Section 7 vertical merger proceeding.

It is not certain, however, that the Court would similarly dispose of horizontal mergers. There is an argument that the two kinds of mergers are distinguishable. For one thing, a "foreclosure" test is literally inapplicable to horizontal mergers; per se, such a merger forecloses neither competing sellers from access to buyers, nor buyers from access to those sellers. The direct quantitative impact of a vertical merger is missing. It may be reasonable to decide that a conclusive presumption of probable harm shall apply to a merger of two competitors who are both "quantitatively substantial" in their market, or to any more than *de minimis* acquisition by an already powerful firm, but the justification is much more involved than that supporting the apparent rule on vertical mergers.

32. International Shoe Co. v. FTC, 280 U.S. 291 (1930).
33. Standard Oil Co. of Calif. v. U.S., 337 U.S. 293 (1949).

Indeed, none of the other decisions cited above — all horizontal merger cases — goes so far. In *Pillsbury*, the Trade Commission flatly rejected a "quantitative share test," and in *Crown Zellerbach*, though faced with quantitative shares that seemingly would have fully warranted striking down the merger without more, it examined such other considerations as freedom of entry before reaching a conclusion of illegality. In *Crystal Sugar*, the District Court relied more on the fact that the merging companies were both active price-cutters in an industry tending to price stability, and on unique circumstances precluding new entry or relative growth by existing firms, than on quantitative shares, and the Court of Appeals seemed to approve this "qualitative" test. *Bethlehem* comes closest to a quantitative share test, but other considerations seemed to be relied on in part.

Nevertheless, there is little indication that an unbounded economic inquiry as to the probable effects of a horizontal merger will be either demanded or permitted, at least by the courts. Even under the *Pillsbury* opinion, it seems unlikely that there will be a generally effective defense — apart from the "failing company" exception — to a showing that (1) the merging companies aggregate, say, 25 percent of their market; (2) past mergers within the industry have contributed to a growing concentration; and (3) new entry is difficult or unlikely. A survey of the cases brought by the enforcement agencies, to date, tends to indicate that they are proceeding more or less on this assumption.[34]

No light whatever can be shed on the probable status of "conglomerate" mergers, which the committee reports on the 1950 amendment indicated were to be covered by revised Section 7. We are inclined to believe that few if any true conglomerate merger cases — entirely devoid of both vertical and horizontal aspects — will be brought, if for no other reason than that standards of illegality seem wholly elusive. Most mergers that crudely appear to be conglomerate will prove to have vertical or horizontal elements or both if the markets involved are carefully analyzed and defined. The Hazel Atlas, Continental Can merger, for example, is "conglomerate" only on the assumption that cans and bottles are completely noncompetitive.

34. See Markham, "Merger Policy Under the New Section 7: A Six Year Appraisal," *Virginia Law Review* (1957), 43:489.

How should the law be interpreted?

The key question in any interpretation of Section 7 is, What meaning shall be given to the characterizing phrase "the effect of such acquisition may be substantially to lessen competition, or tend to create a monopoly?" It is this phrase which defines the mergers Section 7 forbids.

In order to carry out the logic of our policy goal — the limitation of market power — we would propose initially that any merger which appears likely to create market power (as we have defined it) where none existed before, or to increase pre-existing market power, should be banned by the law. Since the test applies to market power which will or will not be present in a future situation, it must necessarily be couched in terms of probabilities. What is outlawed are mergers which have a substantial probability of creating the undesirable effects, not those which conceivably might do so. For purely horizontal mergers, or for what might be called the horizontal elements in a merger — involving firms which compete in the same market — both the creation and enhancement of market power must be considered. For vertical mergers, or vertical elements in a merger, only the enhancement or extension of market power is relevant, since a nonhorizontal merger cannot create such power where it did not exist before. But it can, through the leverage effects of firms in one market on those in another to which they stand in the relation of supplier or customer, enhance existing power, or enable it to be applied in a new market.

If our general test were to be taken strictly, the government would in general be required to offer proof similar to that which would be relevant in a market power proceeding, as discussed in the first section of this chapter. In a horizontal merger case, the government would have to show either that the acquiring firm already has market power, which the acquisition would detectably enhance, or that market power would probably result from the merger. In a vertical merger case, the government would need to show existing market power, plus a probability that it would be extended into the new field or enhanced by the acquisition (such as the acquisition of a source of raw material that is in short supply). But in so far as the proof concerns future probabilities rather than presenting existing facts, it would differ in some respects from that appropriate to a market power proceeding. In particular, much more reliance would have to be placed on structural evidence, since behavioral evidence would normally be available only for the market as it has existed in the past. At best, therefore, a strict application of the market power approach to mergers would involve some resort to presumptions if the antimerger program were to be at all feasible administratively.

We are inclined to go even farther, certainly if our market power proposal were deemed unwise, and even if it were duly incorporated into law. Even in the latter event, prophylactic proceedings are manifestly superior to ones designed to cure. We would therefore tend to accept in general the pattern that the current law has either taken or seems likely to take, as summarized above. We need not take a position on whether such interpretations of Section 7 are appropriate as the law now stands; if not, we would make the necessary amendments.

To be somewhat more specific, we would establish the following propositions as bench marks:

1. *Vertical mergers.* An acquisition of a relatively substantial customer or supplier by a firm with 20 percent of its primary market is prima facie illegal.

2. *Horizontal mergers.* (a) Any acquisition of a competitor by a firm with 20 percent or more of its market is prima facie illegal. (b) Any merger of competitors who together constitute 20 percent or more of a market is prima facie illegal.

3. A merger prima facie illegal can be justified only by convincing proof that (a) the acquired company is in failing or obviously declining circumstances, or (b) the acquisition will yield substantial economies of scale or economies in resource utilization that cannot be effected feasibly in any other way (e.g., internal expansion or the acquisition of assets from other than a competitor, customer, or supplier).

The criteria of prima facie illegality would not, of course, preclude the government from establishing probable ill effects from mergers involving firms of smaller relative size. Severe limitations on entry, the fact that the acquired company has been an active influence on prices — these and other factors would warrant a finding of illegality on the basis of fairly small market shares.

This brings us to the critical problem of market definition. We believe that the presumptions set forth above require that fairly close attention be paid to definition of markets. In general, we would not apply *Cellophane:* at the least, for example, we would require that defendants urging a broad definition of a product be required to prove convincingly that physically distinct substitutes are comparable in all significant respects, production costs included.[35] On the other hand, we question the casual approach to market definition in *DuPont-GM*. Where producers can and do produce several products interchangeably, the capacity currently devoted to one of those products understates the amount that should fairly be deemed to be "in" the market.[36] Without a minimally reasonable definition of markets, criteria based on quantitative shares become whimsy.

Does this mean that antimerger cases would again turn into unduly prolonged economic investigations? We must concede that where the market problem is complex — either in the product or geographical dimension — the issues cannot be readily resolved. But, as pointed out before, we think that satisfactory evidence is usually available in business records, and that with proper focus it can be gathered and presented without inordinate delay. Moreover, there are many mergers, perhaps most, where the market problem is not much of a problem, and here the cases can be quickly disposed of, if indeed — in the light of the certainty — they would come up at all.

We have made no recommendations concerning "conglomerate" mergers, and we are inclined to make none. The only leverage in a merger of this kind is the leverage of money. Many firms without significant market power have plenty of money. There is no apparent reason for letting them make conglomerate acquisitions, and at the same time rule that a firm with market power cannot. We are not prepared to say that it is reasonable to cut the latter off from any acquisitions. In view of the comparatively stringent ban on vertical or horizontal acquisitions by firms with market power, it would seem a reasonable concession to the advantages of mergers as entry-facilitating devices, and to the importance of a strong market for assets, to permit conglomerate acquisitions for everyone, perhaps

35. However, we do not mean to preclude a showing by the government that a merger of producers of distinctive substitutes may substantially lessen competition. The Hazel Atlas, Continental Can merger is allegedly such a case.

36. This point was recognized in U.S. v. Columbia Steel Co., 334 U.S. 495, 510–11 (1948).

barring some extreme cases where adverse effects are obvious or the concentration of wealth is huge, e.g., AT&T and U.S. Steel.

The reasoning behind our comparatively hard position on mergers, in addition to considerations already raised, is that any expansion of a firm by merger is less competitive in its effects than would be the corresponding expansion made by new investment. This is obvious: new investment adds to supply and capacity; the merger does not immediately, though it may lead to such addition in the long run. To be sure, closing the merger route may shut off expansion by a particular firm, but this is not necessarily undesirable. If expansion by merger is a response to an anticipated increase in demand in the market of the acquired firm, the prevention of the merger may delay the expansion of the acquiring firm, but it need not ultimately prevent it. If it does prevent expansion, it will do so only because, in the interval of delay, other firms have seized the opportunity first, in which case there is no social loss. If the anticipation is correct, and the profit opportunity exists, it will be met in a way which will lead to greater capacity and ultimately to a more competitive structure of the expanding market if both the would-be acquirer invested to expand, and the potential acquisition or others did likewise, rather than if the merger took place. The anticompetitive effects of horizontal merger in situations of expanding demand where one of the firms or the combination has market power hardly need be argued.

If the market of the acquired firm is not expanding, why the merger, unless the anticompetitive effect is substantial? Conceivably, a merger may permit the achievement of economies of scale (presumably managerial rather than plant economies), but it would be rare that these would be of sufficient magnitude to justify a merger in a stationary market. In a declining market, there would be no reason for an outside firm to acquire a going business, as such. In general, mergers of firms with each other in a declining market would probably fail to confer market power on the merged firm, and thus escape the ban of the law. However, exceptions to this statement are possible in circumstances where one or two existing firms may make a positive profit, although no newcomers would find it worth while to enter.

In any event, in most markets the ban on mergers would extend only to some of the sellers. Many would be free to merge in any nonhorizontal way, since they would have no market power. Those with market power could make conglomerate acquisitions except in rare cases. Many horizontal mergers would also be legal, since they would create no power. The question of whether the assets and the capital-raising ability of the firms not forbidden to engage in merger activities would be large enough, in relation to the assets and capital-raising power of the firms which did come under the ban, so that a well functioning market for business assets would continue to operate, is not one we can answer precisely. We know that in recent merger movements, acquiring firms have been large firms in terms of asset size, but we simply cannot say what proportion of these have been firms with sufficient market power to be prevented from making the acquisition they made by our proposed law. It is likely that in certain fields — basic metals, chemicals, and machinery — the proposed policy would weaken significantly the demand side of the market for businesses, since many of the large firms in these markets have considerable market power, and acquisitions by them would be likely to come under the ban of the law as we think it should be interpreted.

Joint ventures — a special problem

A special problem not covered by the foregoing discussion is the joint venture, which may be viewed as a form of quasi merger. By joint venture we mean to include only joint participation in the creation of a new producing organization; we exclude joint purchase of existing assets, which analytically differs little from the merger question. Because of many complications, we shall not offer a blueprint, but largely confine ourselves to a general assessment of the problem as we see it.

There are two important kinds of joint ventures for which substantial economic justification can be offered: the joint venture formed to share unusual risks that would not be undertaken by any single firm; and the joint venture which enables the participants to achieve economies of scale in the performance of certain functions — such as research and development — which are most efficiently carried on by units much larger than could be supported by any individual firm. Nevertheless, there are obvious dangers in joint ventures; they may gain substantial power in one or more markets and either threaten or achieve monopoly. Moreover, cooperation in the joint venture may, either necessarily or because of the temptations bred by close association, lead to a reduction of competition among the participating firms in other respects.

There has been surprisingly little law on joint ventures as such. Joint ventures were one of several features in some of the international cartel cases — such as *GE, ICI, Minnesota Mining,* and *Timken* — where they went down as parts of illegal schemes.[37] But few clear guide lines on the status of joint ventures, divorced from collateral illegal activities, have ever appeared. We think it is safe to assume that they are not illegal per se any more than mergers are (see *Columbia Steel*). Moreover, our reading of *Terminal Railway* and *Associated Press*[38] — which are joint venture cases in a real sense — leads us to conclude that even the joint venture with monopoly power is not illegal as such, whenever it appears that an organization of such size is necessary to achieve substantial economies. We assume that similar protection would be accorded joint ventures in risky fields on a showing that, but for the venture, no entry would take place. On the other hand, *Terminal* and *AP* also indicate that the activities of a joint venture possessing undue market power will be subject to varying degrees of judicial control, of a public utility type. The *Terminal* decree, for example, required that outsiders be allowed to invest in the company, or obtain its services, on nondiscriminatory terms. *AP* was enjoined from discriminating against applicants for membership on the ground that they competed with existing members.

Generally speaking, we agree with what the sketchy existing law on joint ventures seems to indicate. Like any other combination or conspiracy in restraint of trade, a joint venture should be condemned on proof of a specific intent to use it as a vehicle for eliminating competition or on proof that it has been so used. And, parenthetically, any collateral restrictive agreements among the joint venturers, not intrinsic to the venture itself, should be treated on their own merits whether or not the venture itself is deemed legitimate. In the absence of proof of invidious intent, the problem is one of assessing potential advantages and disadvantages in joint ven-

37. U.S. v. General Electric Co., 82 F. Supp. 753 (D.N.J. 1949); U.S. v. Imperial Chemical Industries, Ltd., 100 F. Supp. 504 (S.D.N.Y. 1951); U.S. v. Minnesota Mining & Mfg. Co., 92 F. Supp. 947 (D. Mass. 1950); U.S. v. Timken Roller Bearing Co., 83 F. Supp. 284 (N.D. Ohio 1949), modified & affirmed, 341 U.S. 593 (1951).

38. U.S. v. Terminal R. R. Assn., 224 U.S. 383 (1912); Associated Press v. U.S., 326 U.S. 1 (1945).

tures from the point of view of public interest, and in determining what characteristics of joint ventures are likely to produce a balance one way or the other.

The potential risks can be briefly stated. One is that the price, output, and other decisions of the joint venturers — for themselves and for the venture — may be so intrinsically interrelated that they will differ substantially from those that would be made if the venture were independently owned — a risk most likely where the joint venture produces the same goods as do the joint venturers. Another risk is that cooperation in the joint venture will spill over into collateral restrictive behavior among the joint venturers, simply as a matter of close association. Finally, there is the risk that substantial market power in one market may be used to create similar power in others.

The potential benefits of joint ventures, as already indicated, are the creation of new capacity in the face of unusual risks and the greater utilization of economies of scale. And in any event, the joint venture, unlike a merger, adds to productive economic activity.

The seriousness of the risks in joint ventures depends principally on four considerations: (1) whether the joint venture possesses or threatens to possess substantial market power; (2) whether the joint venturers, individually or collectively, possess such power; (3) whether the joint venturers are competitors; and (4) whether the product of the joint venture is closely related — horizontally or vertically — to those produced by the joint venturers.

We would draw the line between the presumptively lawful and the presumptively unlawful joint venture on the basis of the seriousness of the risks in light of the above considerations. Following this approach, we would deem the following joint ventures to be presumptively lawful:

(a) any case in which neither the joint venture, nor its participants (individually or collectively), nor the venture plus participants, has substantial market power; and

(b) any case in which there is no close relation between the product of the venture and any of the products of the participants.

In the first, where there is no substantial market power, the price and output decisions of both the venture and its co-owners would by definition be governed largely by market forces, and the possibilities of intrinsic interrelationships and of effective collateral collaboration would be too small to warrant questioning the joint venture itself, even assuming identical products and that the co-owners are competitors. In the second, jointness creates no additional risk of market power spreading from one market to another, apart from the pooling of financial resources; and there would be no risk of interrelated price and output decisions as between the venture and the joint venturers. The only additional risk would be that of collateral agreements where the joint venturers are competitors. But given the potential benefits of the ventures, we do not think this warrants treating the conglomerate joint venture any differently than the conglomerate merger.

There are probably some other cases that ought to be considered presumptively lawful on similar grounds. One, for example, is the case where the joint venturers are competitors, have substantial market power, and have created a jointly owned company for producing a material which they purchase and use in their own production, but the joint venture lacks market power, and the material is sold to many other industries as well, so that the joint venturers do not have substantial *buying* power. But the following cases, among others, should be treated as presumptively unlawful:

(1) where the venture and the co-owners sell in the same market, and one or the other has substantial market power;

(2) where the co-owners are competitors, the products are vertically related, and either the group or the venture has substantial market power in dealing with competitors of the other.

The important and much more difficult question is what defenses should be permitted to overcome a prima facie case of illegality. Existing law seems to require a double-barreled defense, that substantial economies were achieved or inordinate risks shared, *and* that the venture was in some sense necessary to meet these estimable aims. With this, we generally agree. However, necessity can be variously defined. There are at least two possible meanings: (1) that the venture is the only way in which the participants could themselves achieve the economies or undertake the risks; or (2), a more demanding test, that the joint venture with *those* participants is the only effective way in which the goals could have been or can be reached. There is much to be said for the more demanding test. The public interest is satisfied if economies are utilized and risks taken. The only public interest in the identity of those who serve as vehicles for such progress is in making sure that the development comes in as competitive a way as possible, and it is on this very point that the joint venture deemed prima-facie illegal scores badly.

With regard to the joint venture that itself possesses market power, it could be argued that if economies of scale and the taking of risks are to be protected, then the market power that goes with them will exist in any event, and there is no warrant in penalizing the particular form used. With this we disagree in what may be the most likely cases, namely, those we would treat as presumptively unlawful. We would so treat them for precisely the reason that the joint ownership poses threats to competition that independent ownership would not — in the horizontal case, the threat that the market power of the venture will be enhanced by cooperation of and among the joint venturers; in the vertical case, the threat that market power at one stage will create or enhance market power at another.

The most serious objection to the harsher test is that it imposes a heavy, if not impossible, burden of proof on defendants. Where economies are substantial and obvious, for example, how could defendants prove that the opportunities would not have been seized in due time if the joint venturers had not done so? Possibly in some situations it could be shown that the opportunities were known for a considerable period of time without anyone attempting to grasp them. Arguably, this should suffice. The speed with which economies are effected is certainly of consequence to the public interest. On the other hand, it may be advantageous in the long run to sacrifice some speed for the sake of more competitive forms of utilization. The difficulty is that there are no present informational resources and perhaps no likely resources whereby the factual probabilities in this respect could be assessed. It might be surmised that the joint venture to share risks is more likely to stem from necessity in the more demanding sense than the joint venture to achieve economies of scale. That is our hunch, but it is only a hunch.

We therefore sympathize with the courts who have not gone so far as to insist on the more demanding version of necessity described above. Yet we are also inclined toward that test, at least where economies of scale are the defense; we are inclined to run the risk that some economies may be sacrificed or delayed.[39] However,

39. Compare the Court's statement in *Terminal* that if the injunctive decree failed to protect outsiders, the court would consider divestiture as the only feasible alternative, loss of economies or no.

we would confine this approach to domestic joint ventures, since foreign ventures take place in a context where a different balance between the interest in "competition" and the interest in seizure of opportunities may well be appropriate. Finally, we agree with the position taken in *Terminal* and *Associated Press*, that even where the joint ownership and the venture is deemed to be lawful in itself, despite the existence of substantial market power, it is appropriate to impose whatever restrictions are necessary to insure that the power is not abusively used.

Mergers and dissolution

The interpretation of Section 7 of the Clayton Act that we propose and the vigorous application of dissolution remedies in market power cases are to some extent substitutes for each other. If a very rigorous control over mergers is maintained, the need for dissolution proceedings is less. One possible view of our whole policy proposal is to emphasize the close control of mergers and leave the use of dissolution remedies where it is now. The prospective nature of merger restrictions deprives them of the disincentive effect that dissolutions, viewed as punishments for success, appear to have to some. Thus those who accept the diagnosis presented in Chapter III but value efficiency more, who are less concerned with power, and who see the growth of the whole economy as a force which works to reduce entrenched positions of power over time, might well espouse an even more stringent interpretation of Section 7 than we have proposed, and simply abandon the use of reorganization remedies. We have reviewed this position in Chapter III, and simply refer back to it at this time.

V

The Policy Applied: Practices and Per Se Rules, Patents, and Price Discrimination

PRACTICES AND PER SE RULES

The logic of per se rules

In the application of the antitrust laws, certain kinds of business conduct have come to be viewed as illegal per se, independently of any examination of their effects in the particular case or of the circumstances which led to them. The gains of per se rules in terms of administrative simplicity are great since they are relatively clear, they are self-enforcing to a much greater extent than prohibitions which depend on the evaluation of effects in complex market conditions, and they therefore lessen the volume of proceedings necessary to achieve a given level of enforcement. Any actual proceeding is relatively simple, since it involves only the identification of the illegal conduct and the proof that it occurred. The investigations into market situations and market results characteristic of other antitrust proceedings are unnecessary.

The administrative logic of a per se rule requires that it fulfill two conditions. First, it must be addressed to business conduct rather than to a market situation, since the judgment of illegality without examination of circumstances and effects is fair only when what is illegal is voluntary conduct by a firm, which it could have avoided. Second, the class of practices (or line of conduct) which is forbidden must be readily identifiable. Both the firm acting in the market and the administering tribunal should be able to decide without difficulty, in a high proportion of the situations which are likely to arise, whether or not particular conduct is in the forbidden class. To be sure, there will always be borderline cases in which conduct may not be clearly forbidden or clearly lawful; what is necessary is that the border area be a small part of the total territory encompassed by the law.

The substantive justification of a per se rule must rest on the fact or assumption that the gains from forbidding the specified conduct far outweigh the losses. The magnitude of this difference, plus the administrative gains, must be enough to justify the element of arbitrariness which is always involved. This requires, first, that the harmful effects of the practice be significant; and second, either that they depend to a great enough extent on the outlawed practice so that they cannot be easily achieved in other ways, or that such ways can be anticipated and also be forestalled by per se rules. If these conditions are met, then one of three further conditions must be met:

(1) The condemned practice is always harmful, whatever the circumstances of its use. In our context, this means that the practice can serve only to lessen competition, that it always does lessen competition, and that it has no other justification.

(2) The practice is sometimes harmful and sometimes neutral, but never contributes positively to the working of the market. A practice may be harmful when it achieves its intended effects and neutral if it fails; in either event it has no beneficial effects which cannot be achieved without the practice.

(3) The practice is sometimes harmful, sometimes neutral, and sometimes beneficial, but the aggregate of harm in situations in which it is harmful far outweighs the aggregate of benefit in situations in which it makes a beneficial contribution to the working of the market. Or alternatively, there are both harmful and beneficial aspects of the practice in a particular situation and these vary from situation to situation; but in the aggregate of all situations, harm far outweighs benefit. The difference between aggregate harm and aggregate benefit must be so great that the cost of distinguishing harmful and beneficial situations by an examination of the relevant circumstances is not worth incurring. In general, the first of these three conditions is never met; it is the second and the third — especially the third — which are practically relevant.

Our problem is thus to see whether or not there are practices which satisfy these criteria and so should be made illegal per se. By the very fact that we are dealing with practices — that is, conduct — the appropriate remedy is always the injunctive remedy:

cessation of the practice. Indeed, an alternative necessary test for a per se rule (but not a sufficient one) is that what it forbids can be remedied effectively by an injunction or a cease-and-desist order.

In addition, we shall deal with certain practices, such as tying arrangements and exclusive requirements contracts, that may not be subject to a per se rule in the strict sense, but have been or might be declared illegal on the basis of minimal factual showings that fall considerably short of establishing actual and substantial harm in any particular case. We shall use much the same criteria as those stated above in determining whether these "nearly" per se rules are appropriate to the practices involved.

Practices now illegal per se or nearly so

The law as currently applied defines or appears to define several practices as per se violations under Section 1 of the Sherman Act. They are agreements to fix prices or divide markets, concerted refusals to deal, and agreements tying the sale of one product to the sale or purchase of another.

The *Madison Oil* case has become the classic statement of the per se rule against price fixing and market sharing, and it is clear that any explicit agreement to fix prices or share markets will be condemned.[1] If anything is left of *Appalachian Coals*[2] in this respect, it is a limited protection to joint selling activities that make some acceptable contribution to improving competition (e.g., by eliminating erroneous indications of available supply) without conferring market power. A large volume of criminal cases in which defendants plead *nolo* and civil complaints in which they consent to cease and desist testify to the certainty of the rule whenever evidence of explicit agreement can be shown. The courts have had more difficulty identifying price-fixing in the absence of an explicit agreement. Trade associations, in addition to a host of other activities, often have price-reporting and cost comparison schemes. When identified as "in effect" price-fixing arrangements, price reporting schemes have been struck down, as in *American Column and Lumber, American Linseed Oil,* and *Sugar Institute.*[3] But schemes with many ele-

1. U.S. v. Socony-Vacuum Oil Co., 310 U.S. 150 (1940).
2. Appalachian Coals, Inc. v. U.S., 288 U.S. 344 (1933).
3. American Column and Lumber Co. v. U.S., 257 U.S. 377 (1921); U.S. v. American Linseed Oil Co., 262 U.S. 371 (1923); Sugar Institute v. U.S. 297 U.S. 553 (1936).

ments similar to these have been found not to be price-fixing arrangements in *Maple Flooring, First Cement,* and *Tag Institute.*[4] Perhaps the first two of these may be dismissed as being based on defective pleadings or as clearly erroneous, and unlikely to be followed again; but the third cannot be readily so classed.

Parallel action as evidence of agreement also raises questions for the applications of the per se rule. But it appears safe to state that no per se violation has ever been found or is likely to be found merely on the basis of parallel price changes among several firms. Parallel price changes by a large number of firms will almost inevitably require such a machinery of intercommunication that evidence of agreement will be plentiful. Even an industry of small numbers will typically require agreement of some kind on such matters as transport charges, "extras," and the like. While *Theatre Enterprises* leaves the possibility open,[5] we doubt that mere parallel price behavior would suffice to establish agreement in those situations where, by proof or by obvious appearances, the hypothesis of rational individual decision in the light of known market facts is equally plausible.

Like price-fixing, concerted refusals to deal — boycotts — also appear to be illegal per se. The Supreme Court said as much by way of dicta in *Columbia Steel* and *Times-Picayune;*[6] and while susceptible to other interpretations, the earlier decisions, cumulatively if not individually, pointed in that direction. Nevertheless there are some uncertainties in this area, and some evidence, as in *Cleveland Insurance Board,*[7] that lower courts are hesitant to follow a per se rule until faced with a direct holding from above. The uncertainties seem to involve both matters of definition and matters of substance. Is it a "concerted refusal to deal" for the American Medical Association to exclude chiropractors from membership? If it is, it certainly should not be deemed illegal per se and in all likelihood would not be; but the more likely result is that such exclusion would not be deemed a concerted refusal to deal. On the other hand, if the AMA conditions membership on agreement to abide by certain

4. Maple Flooring Mfrs. Ass'n. v. U.S., 268 U.S. 563 (1925); Cement Mfrs. Protective Ass'n. v. U.S., 268 U.S. 588 (1925); Tag Mfrs. Institute v. FTC, 174 F.2d 452 (C.A. 1, 1949).

5. Theatre Enterprises, Inc. v. Paramount Film Distributing Co., 346 U.S. 537 (1954).

6. U.S. v. Columbia Steel Co., 334 U.S. 495 (1948); Times-Picayune Pub. Co. v. U.S., 345 U.S. 594 (1953).

7. U.S. v. Insurance Board of Cleveland, 144 F. Supp. 684 (N.D. Ohio 1956).

rules, and one of those rules is a refusal to patronize hospitals that admit the patients of chiropractors, there is clearly a concerted refusal to deal and the per se issue is inescapable. Here, we surmise that the Supreme Court dicta would become a holding, and that the per se rule would apply. Another problem is that presented by what we might term an economically "necessary" productive joint venture — an enterprise which is feasible only through joint participation — which we believe fairly describes *Associated Press.*[8] The exclusion of others from a necessary joint venture — by closed membership and by refusing to sell the products to them — would seem to be a "collective refusal to deal" but not one that is likely to be held illegal without some showing of dominance, threatened dominance, or undue advantage. Taken as a whole, the *Associated Press* opinion seems to go no further.

For all practical purposes, tie-in contracts also fall within the select category of practices that are illegal per se. To be sure, *Northern Pacific*[9] stops short of saying so, but it might as well have said so. The Court had held in *International Salt*[10] that it was "unreasonable, per se, to foreclose competitors from any substantial market." While the tying product was a patented machine, which might have implied that *Salt* was to be limited to patent or other "monopoly" cases, it was noted in *Standard Stations,*[11] discussing *Salt,* that there was no showing that equivalent machines were unobtainable and no showing of what proportion of the machine business defendants held. In *Times-Picayune,* after reviewing the cases, the Court stated that a tie-in contract was illegal under Section 1 of the Sherman Act if both a "monopolistic" position in the market for the tying product, and coverage of a substantial (dollar) amount of commerce in the tied product, were shown.[12] But it was evident, before *Northern Pacific,* that "monopolistic" position was very loosely defined, as shown by *Salt* and by *Paramount Pictures,*[13] where a patent and a copyright respectively were presumed to convey it. Thus, the words "dominance" and "monopolistic position" required nothing more than "sufficient economic power to impose an appreciable restraint on free competition in the tied product." [14] This would seem to be

8. Associated Press v. U.S., 326 U.S. 1 (1945).
9. Northern Pac. Ry. Co. v. U.S., 356 U.S. 1 (1958).
10. International Salt Co. v. U.S., 332 U.S. 392 (1947).
11. Standard Oil of Calif. v. U.S., 337 U.S. 293 (1949).
12. Times-Picayune Pub. Co. v. U.S., 345 U.S. 594, 608–609 (1953).
13. U.S. v. Paramount Pictures, Inc., 334 U.S. 131 (1948).
14. 356 U.S. 1, 11 (1958).

shown by the existence of the contract itself, covering a substantial amount of commerce. Since *Times-Picayune* stated that tie-ins were illegal under Section 3 of the Clayton Act on a showing *either* of "monopolistic position" or "quantitative substantiality," the tests under the Sherman and Clayton Acts are virtually the same.

In addition to tie-ins, Section 3 of the Clayton Act covers other kinds of exclusive dealing arrangements, including requirements contracts. The statute outlaws these practices "where the effect . . . may be to substantially lessen competition or tend to create a monopoly." The question is the interpretation to be given this clause.

The law on requirements contracts and other types of exclusive arrangements is less settled than that on tie-ins. *Standard Stations* held such contracts to be illegal under Section 3 whenever they "foreclosed a substantial share of the line of commerce affected." At its harshest, this is a somewhat friendlier test than that applied to tie-ins, since it requires proof of a substantial share of a relevant market, in percentage terms, rather than mere substantial dollar volume. But *Standard Stations* is obscure on two important issues of interpretation; and subsequent decisions, particularly the opinions in *FTC v. Motion Picture Advertising,*[15] leave some doubt that the test of illegality will in all cases be as simple as it appeared to be. The obscurities concern the meaning of foreclosure and the extent to which, if any, it is possible to argue in any particular case that a "requirements" contract for a short term is simply the normal economic unit of sale for the market involved. Standard's "foreclosure" of dealers was foreclosure of competitors only to the extent that competitors could not, by securing other or new dealers, obtain comparable access to the consuming market. Moreover, most of the contracts were terminable at the end of six months of any contract year, so that the period of foreclosure was arguably too brief to constitute any substantial restraint on competing producers. The facts would probably have warranted the result reached since (as the Court surmised in a footnote) good dealer locations are limited, and other factors made it difficult for dealers to change from one supplier to another or indicated that six months was a longer term than economic needs would dictate. But the Court's failure to deal fully with these issues left some doubt that they were to be given any consideration.

The Federal Trade Commission has taken a different course,

15. FTC v. Motion Picture Advertising Service Co., 344 U.S. 392 (1953).

erroneously assuming that a *Standard Stations* footnote discussion on the comparative abilities of courts and agencies to deal with complex economic questions entitled it to do so.[16] The Commission has indicated that it would look to a considerable range of facts beyond "quantitative share" before holding requirements contracts illegal. However, there has been no case so far in which the Commission has upheld contracts that would have fallen under the *Standard Stations* test.

In general, it seems fair to conclude that there are still some doubts about giving exclusive dealing arrangements and requirements contracts (a particular form of exclusive dealing) the kind of treatment so confidently given tie-ins.

Problems of the present law, proposed modifications

We can best discuss the problems raised by the law as now interpreted, and examine suggestions for change, by first considering separately the problems of identifying the practices to which per se rules are or should be applicable, and then justifying the application of such rules.

Problems of identification arise chiefly in the area of price-fixing agreements. While explicit price-fixing agreements, provable by documentary evidence or the parole testimony of participants, offer no problems, there are other important practices of this nature which do. Is parallel price action, without more, price-fixing? Is the parallel practice of basing-point pricing, or of universal freight equalization, without more, price-fixing? Does it become price-fixing whenever it involves some collusive action, e.g., the use of a common freight rate book, or the like? Are trade association price-reporting systems and uniform cost accounting schemes price-fixing agreements?

As we have already indicated, we reject the identification of parallel pricing as a kind of price-fixing agreement, or as invariably offering a firm basis, in itself, for an inference that an agreement underlies it. Price parallelism can result from nonconcerted action by sellers of a standard product in a small-numbers market, and therefore a determination of whether or not an agreement exists requires an investigation of the functioning of the market. Basing-point pricing, including universal freight equalization, also cannot be identified as the result of price-fixing arrangements, if by basing-

16. *In re* Maico Co., Inc., FTC Docket No. 5822 (Dec. 2, 1953); relying on Standard Oil of Calif. v. U.S., 337 U.S. 293, 310 n.13 (1949).

point pricing we mean uniform delivered prices at consuming points, and the practice of freight absorption by sellers. These practices can arise by parallel responses of individual sellers to the market situation, where sellers are few and are spread geographically, product is standard, and shipping costs significant. Usually, basing-point systems in practice do involve some measure of agreement: agreement on a freight-rate book which provides a uniform method of calculating delivered prices; agreement, where the product is complex and comes in a variety of grades, sizes, etc., on a price structure relating the price of each variety to some standard price — such as the "extra book" in steel; agreement to calculate delivered prices only on the basis of rail transport; agreement not to sell f.o.b. mill, or to do so only at a premium over the mill base price; and so forth.

The law at present has treated agreements to maintain a basing-point pricing system as illegal under Section 1 of the Sherman Act, or as unfair methods of competition under Section 5 of the Federal Trade Commission Act,[17] on the theory that they are agreements to fix prices. While collusive use of basing-point pricing should be outlawed, some difficulty arises in determining when delivered pricing and freight absorption involve collusion. What is required is an analysis of how the price and transport pattern actually works: whether, for example, the use of all-rail-freight and a rate book reflects merely the lack of other available means of transport and of savings of labor in computing freight costs, or whether it involves an agreed refusal to ship by alternative means and the use of the freight-rate book to effect the agreement.

Trade association price-reporting activities present a second identification problem. These activities have as their ostensible purpose the dissemination of market information in order that the participating sellers can make more rational price and output decisions. By making available to their members the record of transactions in the market, the association reporting system contributes to a more perfectly functioning market. Beyond the ostensible purpose, there may also be use of the reporting system as the vehicle of a price-fixing arrangement. Can the legitimate price-reporting system be distinguished in any simple way from the one which operates as a price-fixing scheme, or is it necessary to undertake a detailed examination of the effects of any system before pronouncing judgment on it? The major cases suggest that so far the courts have been unable to find

17. We here ignore the Robinson-Patman aspects of basing point pricing.

a formula. What distinguishes *Maple Flooring, Tag Institute,* and *Cement Manufacturers Protective Assn.* from *American Column & Lumber, American Linseed,* and *Sugar Institute* cannot easily be described.

Yet the difficulties of drawing an appropriate line are not insuperable. They arise in large part from the application of false analogies in analyzing the effects of price-reporting systems. In general, the kind of markets in which trade association price-reporting schemes operate are imperfect and, though they contain large numbers of sellers and buyers, they involve significant elements of oligopoly, at least in the short run. These elements arise because geographic and product subdivision of markets tends to create subgroups of sellers whose price and output decisions react more immediately on each other than on the market as a whole. Disseminating as much information as possible as rapidly as possible is usually justified by analogies to organized auction markets, where competition is nearly perfect.[18] But in markets where oligopolistic elements are present, some ignorance and uncertainty about the behavior of rivals is an important competitive element in the market, since it prevents "rational" oligopolistic calculation leading to joint maximization of profits. In the trade association situation, dissemination of too much information too promptly is possible; where it takes place, it facilitates noncompetitive price maintenance and output restriction. Criteria which distinguish undesirable price-reporting systems from those which cannot, on their face, be condemned are as follows:

(1) agreements to abide by reported list prices;

(2) reporting of offers, even though sales are not made at the offered price;

(3) identification of individual buyers and sellers in every transaction;

(4) refusal to make reports available to buyers, including buyers' trade associations;

(5) opening competitors' books to each other;

(6) reporting transactions and disseminating information without some lag.

18. The prevalence of speculative elements in the auction markets, in which, in general, buyers and sellers both hold stocks which are substantial in relation to the current inflow of new goods into the market, marks another important point on which the analogy breaks down. But it would take us far afield to discuss this point thoroughly.

A price-reporting system which contains none of these objectionable features can still perform useful functions in making the market more perfect, but it cannot serve as an effective price-fixing vehicle. The undesirability of (1) and (4) needs little comment. Nor does (2); in connection with (3) it may be the chief means of using the reporting system as a vehicle for bringing pressure against individual sellers and buyers. As for (5), though a reporting agency may wish to audit the books of members, there is no reason why competitors should have full knowledge of the business transactions of their rivals unless it is to check on their adherence to a price-fixing scheme. The reason for (6) is that some delay in reporting is an important safeguard to impose on any scheme: the shorter the reporting lag, the more useful becomes the information as a means of disciplining individual buyers and sellers, and reminding everyone of the folly of "chiseling." It is difficult to specify in general terms what an adequate lag is, but it would seem that the two-day lag between transaction and report on all off-list sales which the Tag Institute tried to achieve was too short. Perhaps a weekly report should mark the boundary of what is suspicious. The most important single point is (3); if market information is all the reporting system provides, it will function sufficiently well by providing figures for groups of suppliers and customers, subdivided finely by product and region, but not so as to identify individual transactions.

The presence of any of these features should serve to condemn a price-reporting plan as a price-fixing scheme, and thus be illegal per se. This is not to say that a price-reporting scheme lacking them cannot have some effect on the market, but rather that the likelihood that it can do so is sufficiently small so that it is worth while to give such schemes the protection afforded by requiring the government to bear the burden of showing an undesirable effect.

There are three additional price-fixing identification problems that arise, two of which appear usually in a trade association context: agreements to standardize products, the dissemination of cost-accounting methods, and joint selling or buying agencies. The first is a troublesome one, inasmuch as standardization in most cases is likely to have desirable consequences and at the same time reduce the uncertainties that play a competitive role in a small-numbers market. We are inclined to conclude that standardization of sizes, grades, qualities, and the like should be treated as presumptively lawful in itself; that further evidence of intent to eliminate competition, as appeared in connection with the agreement to eliminate sales of "seconds" in *Standard Sanitary*,[19] must be shown in order to identify the standardization as being part of a price-fixing scheme. We, of course, exclude from such protection any agreements on price differentials for various standardized grades as being wholly unnecessary to standardization itself, and simply a species of price-fixing.

The dissemination of cost-accounting methods can sometimes be a vehicle for price-fixing. When a trade association cost-accounting scheme is an invitation to uniform mark-ups over raw material and labor costs to determine total manufacturing cost, and uniform mark-ups over cost to determine "proper" selling prices, it should be classed as a price-fixing scheme. But the publication of distributions of mark-ups, or distributions of ratios of overhead to variable costs is not in itself objectionable, and should not fall within the classification of price-fixing agreements.

Our final problem of identification in the price-fixing area is that of the joint selling agency, such as was found in *Appalachian Coals*, or its counterpart, the joint buying agency. The problem is akin to, if not a part of, the problem of joint ventures. We do not think joint selling or buying agencies may properly be condemned as price-fixing agreements and hence illegal per se, because they may in some circumstances achieve legitimate economies wholly unrelated to any adverse effects on competition, and because, in consequence, an intent to enhance prices (in the case of the joint selling agency) or depress prices (in the case of the joint buying agency) cannot be generally inferred. Joint selling agencies may merely achieve "economies of scale" in distribution, i.e., reduction of unit selling costs, that individual producers — though themselves large enough to effect economies of scale in production — could not achieve. Similarly, joint buying agencies can often effect economies, through quantity purchasing and unified warehousing, that are unavailable to buyers purchasing individually.

Any restraint of competition from the activities of the joint agency largely depends on exclusivity. For example, a joint selling agency without a commitment by members to sell through it alone could not raise price by restricting supply, since members would tend to sell outside the agency, shading the agency's high price. It is possible that legitimate economies could be achieved, and the in-

19. Standard Sanitary Mfg. Co. v. U.S., 226 U.S. 20 (1912).

herent dangers of cooperative action avoided, by nonexclusive arrangements; that is, if the joint agency is indeed able to effect economies, it might draw the business of its respective members without compulsion. If this were true, a simple test could be applied — the exclusive agency is illegal per se; the nonexclusive agency, per se, is not.

However, we have some doubts that this assumption is correct. A joint buying agency, for example, can achieve the economies of quantity purchasing only if it has enough committed orders to make up a "quantity," or at the least if it has reasonable assurance that members will buy the quantities purchased. A cooperative commitment may be necessary at least to get the agency operating. Similar commitments may be necessary to make a joint selling agency effective. Perhaps these doubts are unwarranted; perhaps, if economies are available in mass purchasing or mass selling, new firms will hazard the starting-up risks and fill the void. But we have suggested a market power approach to joint ventures and are not inclined to single out joint selling and buying agencies for harsher treatment. Thus, in the absence of evidence of intent to reduce price competition or of actual effects on price that are unrelated to cost savings, the test would be whether the joint selling agency has the power to enhance prices by restricting supply, whether the joint buying agency has the power to depress prices by withholding demand. This is substantially the test of *Appalachian Coals,* disregarding the question as to whether it was correctly applied to the facts of that case. If the exclusive joint agency is found to possess such power, it would be held illegal in the absence of a clear showing that there are substantial economies which cannot be achieved by a nonexclusive agency or by independent firms.

We deliberately exclude as a defense any notions of "countervailing power." We proceed on the assumption that unreasonable market power on the selling or buying side will be reduced to minimal proportions. And as for remaining legitimate market power, we take the general position that it should either be regulated or should be entitled to at least one fruit — the right to charge a "monopoly" price.

We turn now to tie-in arrangements, which also present problems of identification. For example, the distinction between a tying arrangement and an exclusive dealing arrangement may be difficult to draw. After all, an exclusive dealing arrangement ties the purchase of some units to the purchase of others, the purchase of one product to the purchase of another. But the tying arrangement can usually be distinguished as involving a tied product or products, and a different product or products to which they are specifically tied. In the typical case the product to which the tie is made is patented, or monopolized, or the object of high consumer preference, and it is precisely the use of the market power conferred by this position to increase sales of the tied product which is objectionable. Another kind of difficulty of identification can arise where there is no explicit prohibitory agreement which enforces the tie, but only a large price difference between the tied and the separate purchases. Thus, for example, the motion picture distributors contended that block booking was merely "wholesaling" and did not involve any element of tying. No hard and fast rule can be laid down; where the price differences are sufficiently great, the arrangement can be identified as a tie-in, as in the block booking situation and the *United Shoe Machinery* case under the Clayton Act;[20] if not, then the only problem that arises is one of price discrimination.

Exclusive dealing arrangements and requirements contracts present no great problems of identification, since they usually involve express agreements which show their character on their face.

Having identified the practices we might wish to forbid without an inquiry into their effects in each particular situation, can we justify so treating them? We can with respect to price-fixing agreements, agreements to maintain a basing-point system, concerted refusals to deal, and tying arrangements. With respect to exclusive dealing agreements and requirements contracts, we cannot.

The appropriateness of a per se rule against price-fixing agreements, including trade association price-reporting schemes which fall within the defined category, is usually argued in terms of the second of our three justifications. Whenever such agreements are effective, they limit competition in an undesirable way. When they are ineffective — which they frequently are because they do not embrace a large enough share of the market, or are not backed up by a sufficiently powerful enforcement mechanism, or do not provide for effective control over entry — they do no positive good. Therefore, everything is gained and nothing lost by outlawing them, whatever their effect. This argument is sound in the main, but requires some elaboration.

20. United Shoe Machinery Co. v. U.S., 258 U.S. 451 (1922).

A standard defense of price-fixing is that there may be too much competition in some situations, such as in a declining industry, and that an agreement limiting price-cutting may be beneficial. We shall discuss this matter at some length in Chapter VI. For the moment, we briefly dispose of this defense on two grounds. First, the declining industry usually shows too much competition because it draws heavily on the supply of some immobile factor, which does not withdraw from the industry in the face of decreasing relative rewards. Where the immobile factor is capital, the price mechanism should function through a sequence of losses and, if necessary, bankruptcies to revalue capital downwards to a level where there are no longer losses; and price-fixing only impedes the working of this process. In practice though, the immobile factor is more frequently labor (mining, agriculture), and the price system often seems inadequate to bring about an appropriate amount of movement. Neither competition without price-fixing, nor price-fixing, solves the problem. In fact, price-fixing may tend to make it worse by actually drawing increased resources into the industry, as has in fact happened more than once in the past. Second, the problems presented by a declining industry or by a highly cyclical industry are not appropriately solved by private business decision released from the check of competition, but require some responsible governmental control, with legislative sanction. If competition is to be suppressed, it should be done only with some degree of public control.

Our proposed ban on certain trade association reporting practices may involve giving up some kinds of market information which would be useful and yet, in some circumstances, would not produce any anticompetitive effects. Yet it appears worth while to be on the safe side, since the gains from getting more market information than our proposed rules permit are small, but the widening possibilities of using the reporting systems for restrictive purposes are great.

Where a basing-point pricing system involves explicit agreement, it too should fall within the price-fixing rule. Generally, basing-point and similar price structures arise in an oligopoly market. They facilitate, though they may not cause, a pattern of price leadership which contributes to high price-cost margins and other noncompetitive behavior. Some kind of basing-point system, involving frequent uniformity of delivered price at a consuming locality and price discrimination via freight absorption, may be inevitable in these markets. Yet the difference in the effectiveness with which the system functions to promote price leadership, and to maintain prices in periods of falling demand, will vary greatly between a situation in which there is agreement to use the system and to follow the base-prices of the leader, and one in which such agreement is lacking. In particular, where alternative cheaper means of transport, such as trucks and waterways, exist, but their use as bases for quoting delivered prices is avoided by agreement, the elimination of such agreement will create the kind of uncertainties which promote price changes when demand changes, and will reduce the effectiveness of the leadership arrangement in maintaining profitable margins in the face of declining demand. It is sometimes argued that some degree of price leadership is necessary to prevent price-cutting so drastic as to endanger the long-run stability of the industry. This has never been tested in practice; analysis of the proposition suggests that oligopolistic rationality, even without the support of an agreed basing-point mechanism, will prevent price cuts so deep as to threaten the whole industry with bankruptcy in periods of cyclically declining demand. On this basis, it could be concluded that no harm is incurred by preventing the perfected basing-point system that rests on explicit agreement. If agreement is deemed necessary, the terms should be subject to public control.

Agreements to boycott are sometimes defended on the grounds that their objectives are reasonable: e.g., that they are necessary to maintain the plane of competition, by boycotting unethical firms. This was the argument in *Fashion Originators' Guild* [21] where the aim of the boycott was to prevent piracy of uncopyrighted dress designs by refusing to supply them with the originals produced by the guild members. Though a particular situation may call for some remedy, the boycott seems a dangerous one. For every legitimate example there are fifty in which the unethical seller is subject to boycott for "chiseling" on prices, or for dealing through unauthorized channels, short-cutting wholesalers or jobbers, and the like. The anticompetitive effect of the boycott in such cases is clear; indeed it is the chief weapon which the price-fixing association can use to force its suppliers or customers to punish those who break the agreement. Thus, though a per se rule against boycotts may prevent their use to remedy some abuses, the facility with which they are used for anticompetitive purposes and the infrequency of other occasions on which they are used suggest that the costs of the rule will be far

21. Fashion Originators' Guild of America, Inc. v. FTC, 312 U.S. 457 (1941).

outbalanced by the gains. Moreover, where recognized abuse exists, correction should depend on legislative sanction; or should be carried out under the power of the Federal Trade Commission to attack unfair methods of competition or to promote voluntary observance of fair methods through trade practice conferences.

The last practice which we would subject to a per se rule is a tie-in arrangement. Statically viewed, every tie-in can be translated into a price discrimination, since we can always conceive a pair of relative prices which would result in the same pattern of transactions in the tied and tying goods as does the tie-in arrangement: presumably, this pattern is different from that which competitive dealing in the tied good would create. Like price discrimination, tying implies some market power on the part of the seller practicing it. Without such power, the buyer would not take the tied pair of goods unless he were willing to do so on exactly the terms of the tying arrangement. The power frequently arises because of legal monopoly enjoyed by the seller in the tying good — a patent or a copyright — but it need not. Some power in the market for the tying good will suffice, whatever its basis.

If the only effects of tie-ins were those of price discrimination, we could not justify our per se ban. But viewed in dynamic terms, tie-ins have effects which go beyond the effects of comparable price discriminations, and lack justifications which price discriminations may have. A tie-in always operates to raise the barriers to entry in the market of the tied good to the level of those in the market for the tying good: the seller who would supply the one, can do so only if he can also supply the other, since he must be able to displace the whole package which the tying seller offers. Developing a substitute for the tying product may be very difficult, if not impossible. Thus tying tends to spread market power into markets where it would not otherwise exist: for example, few firms are prepared to supply machines like those of IBM, whereas many may be prepared to supply punch cards.[22] On the other side of the argument, price discriminations may have a variety of justifications; the most general one is

22. While theoretically the impact on entry may be achieved by price discrimination, it is much more difficult to do so in practice. Thus IBM, to pursue the example, could have sold cards under costs, and priced machines so that the package remained (on the average) as costly. But it is much more likely that some other card producer would have the capital, know-how, etc., to compete, than that anyone else would get into the machine business. Again, with a patented item, the same point holds.

that price competition in imperfect markets almost always involves some element of price discrimination as a necessary ingredient. Can we offer any similar justifications for tying arrangements?

Looking at situations in which such arrangements have been accepted or commended by the courts, we see cases like *Pick v. General Motors,* and *General Talking Pictures v. American Tel. & Tel.*[23] In both cases, the issue was whether a tie-in could be justified on grounds of the need to use seller-supplied parts or auxiliary equipment in order to protect the functioning of the seller's main product. In *Pick,* the court found this was justified; in *General Talking Pictures,* that it might have been in the past, but was not at the time of the suit. But in either case, the same end could have been achieved without an absolute tie. In *Pick,* the use of GM repair parts by Chevrolet dealers could have been enforced during the warranty period as a condition of the warranty.

There seems to be little substance in the argument which the court accepted that the tie was justified past the warranty period because defective repairs would reflect on GM rather than on the dealer making them. Given the widespread use of nondealer repair services by GM and other car buyers on the one side, and the possible advertising advantages to the dealer of certifying that he used genuine parts on the other, there seems no basis for extending the tie past the warranty period. In *General Talking Pictures,* which turned around the use by motion picture theaters of AT&T auxiliary equipment with the newly introduced AT&T (Western Electric) sound equipment, AT&T's defense was that the equipment was novel and that performance could not be insured without the use of the complete system, since rival auxiliaries were not up to standard. The actual proviso did not specify that AT&T equipment should be used exclusively, but rather that it must be used only with equipment of equal quality, the determination to be made by AT&T; clearly the effect was little different from an exclusive-use contract. The court found this requirement had been justified by conditions in the trade at an earlier period, but was no longer justified in 1937 at the time of the suit. But the same protection could have been achieved had AT&T given a performance warranty or a repair contract on favorable terms, conditioned on the use of AT&T equipment exclusively.

23. Pick Mfg. Co. v. General Motors Corp., 80 F.2d 641 (C.A. 7, 1935), *aff'd per curiam,* 299 U.S. 3 (1936); General Talking Pictures v. American Tel. and Tel. et al., 18 F. Supp. 650 (D.C. Del. 1937).

If the technical state of rival equipment justified adherence to the conditions, buyers would do so; if not, they would at their own risk pursue another course when it appeared advantageous. The proposed substitute for the tie-in would be, in effect, a cost-justified price difference in the repair contract, assuming that AT&T could in fact justify its repair bills as lower for theaters using its equipment exclusively. These examples show that the desirable results achieved by these tying arrangements were not in fact dependent on them, but could be achieved in other ways. This is true in general. Therefore, a flat rule against tying arrangements, regardless of whether or not they serve a useful purpose, appears justified. We would modify it only by a requirement that a not insignificant volume of commerce be involved in order to exclude random small transactions of no consequence.

Turning to requirements contracts and other exclusive dealing arrangements, a strict per se rule of illegality cannot be justified. The opinion in *Standard Stations* suggested reasons why. A requirements contract may provide substantial gains in certainty and ability to plan forward, for both buyer and seller, in a market in which supplies or demands fluctuate unpredictably and widely. This is especially true when relations across the market are such that those on one side can aggregate the orders or offers of those on the other, and so average out their fluctuations. Thus, in canning, for example, the demands of an individual canner or of a group of canners in a small supply area may fluctuate widely with fluctuations in crops. Over the market as a whole, fluctuations may be much less. Requirements contracts may give canners security and protect them from the necessity of bidding in a high spot market in the case of bumper crops, while giving can manufacturers a much better basis for output planning than would exist in their absence. Yet the same contract may have effects on entry and pricing that are undesirable. The extent of these anticompetitive effects depends on such factors as the term of the contract, the price mechanism it involves, the extent to which all buyers and sellers in the market use similar contracts, and the structure of the market on both the buying and selling sides. Any attempt to set off advantages against disadvantages, and to compare the terms of the contracts with what is needed to provide the advantages demonstrated, involves an examination of the circumstances which give rise to contracts and their actual effects in operation.

Similarly, economic justifications can be given for exclusive dealing contracts. They may contribute to the creation and effectiveness of distribution outlets; in some cases, dealer loyalty to a particular seller's product may contribute to the vigor of competition — but only provided that the exclusive arrangements do not impede competitors' access to the ultimate consuming market.

We believe these considerations — and that of effective enforcement — would best be accommodated by applying the *Standard Stations* test, "foreclosure of a substantial share of the line of commerce affected," with two provisos that may or may not have been implied by the Court in that case. The two provisos both concern the meaning of "foreclosure." First, the term of a requirements contract may be sufficiently short that it may fairly be called the appropriate unit of sale for the industry concerned. If so, it should no more be deemed to foreclose competitors than would any sale, since competitors have regular and repeated opportunity to make the next "sale" to the buyer. Second, exclusive arrangements with dealers, as opposed to ultimate consumers, constitute foreclosure only if competing producers cannot obtain other dealers with comparable access to the consuming market, or can do so only at relatively great expense.

With these provisos, we think *Standard Stations* is a reasonable disposition of the problem; on balance, the adverse effects of significant foreclosure are likely to outweigh by a considerable margin the benefits to the economy of exclusive arrangements which have a foreclosure effect.

PATENTS

The nature of the problem

The correct location of the disputed boundary between the monopoly which is granted by the patent law and the competition which is enforced by the antitrust law is a difficult and important problem of antitrust policy, and any respectable policy proposal must attempt to resurvey the boundary, if not relocate it. On the one hand, it has been our policy to grant the patentee a right to exclude others from the use of his invention for a term of years in order to encourage invention; on the other, we observe that patents have effects on the structure of industry which can fairly be said to go beyond the proper scope of specific monopolies on particular inventions. The problem in broad terms is: how do we compromise between the goal of encouraging invention and that of preventing the patent grant from becoming the support of extensive and entrenched positions of market power?

This problem can be discussed at six levels (at least):

(1) *Patent office procedure.* How are patents issued; what time lags occur between application and issue; what are interference procedures; what are the incentives to grant rather than to withhold patents in the patent office and the consequent conflict between patent office and court standards of patentability; and so forth.

(2) *The standard of patentability, taking the court decisions and patent office grants together.* Do we grant patents too freely; could we raise the standard of patentability without materially reducing the flow of invention and innovation?

(3) *Practices of patentees.* To what extent are patents licensed, cross-licensed, pooled, and on what terms? How do various terms and conditions affect the impact of patents on market structure?

(4) *Patent accumulation.* Does the fact that large numbers of patents are held by a single assignee make the system function in a way different from what was intended? Should accumulations built up by patent acquisitions and exclusive licenses be treated differently than accumulations resting on the inventive work of a firm's own laboratory?

(5) *The interactions of patents and other aspects of market power.* To what extent are problems which we tend to view as patent problems really due to the existence of firms with substantial market power otherwise based? To what extent, conversely, does a particular set of market structures make the patent system superfluous by providing in other ways the protection from competition which it is the purpose of the patent to offer?

(6) *The incentive to invent and innovate and the patent system.* Over-all, does the whole complex of institutions, including the patent system, within which invention and innovation take place result in overcompensating inventors and innovators, so that we could receive the same flow of their output with lower rewards to them? Or does it result in underpayments, so that we are depriving ourselves of a flow of innovations which it would be worth paying more to get?

Of this list, we shall discuss chiefly (3), (4), and (5); we shall make some suggestions on (2), and comment very briefly on (1) and (6). The basic problem is the last one: a logical discussion of the others involves some appraisal, implicit or explicit, of the answer to this question. Yet information on the basis of which a well-grounded answer could be given is lacking, and it is far from clear just how it could be provided even with extensive research. We can, however, make a few observations on certain aspects of the problem.

First, since the marginal cost of using new knowledge once it is available is zero, we can say, in the abstract, that a patent system inevitably tends to restrict the use of new techniques more than would be desirable, assuming we could find some other acceptable basis on which invention and innovation could be paid for. Government bounties as well as government-financed research, with results made freely available to all, are both practicable methods of insuring a supply of invention and innovation; the difficulty is that they involve so wide a departure from a system of private property and private enterprise or raise such vexing problems of standards of evaluation (and in turn of fair and impartial administration), that we are not prepared to espouse them.[24]

Second, if it is true that in recent years the courts have curbed the innovators' reward by raising the standards of patentability and by narrowing the rights of the patentee against infringers, licensees, etc., we might speculate that the previous supply price of invention and innovation was more than covered by the rewards offered, since there has been no corresponding visible decline in invention or innovation. We might then be inclined to suspect that the rewards offered at present still exceed the supply price.

Third, whether or not one cares to accept at face value either of these quite shaky speculations, we may say that the most striking characteristic of the present system is its inflexibility. Every patent grants the same rights as every other; every patentee is entitled to all he can get in the market on the basis of these rights. Perhaps reforms which increased the flexibility of the reward, without changing its gross level, might improve the functioning of the system. It is important to note, however, that most proposals for increasing flexibility also involve a reduction in the average or aggregate reward, since they do not call for an increase in what the most deserving patentee now gets from his grant, but only some downward adjustment of what possibly less deserving ones get. Some proposals of this type will be advanced below. While they aim at reducing

24. Note, however, that we have relied on one, in part, in the atomic energy field, and on the other almost entirely in agriculture.

rewards presently available on some patents, in total their effect would be to lower the aggregate rewards the patent system now enables patentees to achieve. Thus we are implicitly accepting the proposition that we can lower rewards without significantly reducing the flow of invention and innovation. What needs emphasis here is that the mechanism of the market is so imperfect in paying to each innovation its supply price, because of the great uncertainties involved, that to a considerable extent the supply in any particular field depends on rewards in general: innovation is a lottery, and it is the high prizes that count. We may well be able to reduce the level of the high prizes, or eliminate some prizes, without necessarily reducing participation.

We wish to say nothing in detail about patent office procedures and practices because the problems lie outside the scope of our discussion. The patent office has been criticized for delay and for its low standard of patentability in relation to the standards enforced by the courts. Both failings are important: the first because delay often results in an extension of the effective period over which a patent excludes others; the second because the disparity between what the patent office grants and what the courts will enforce puts great weight on the relative ability of disputants in patent matters to bear the large costs and delays of litigation. A patent is a license to sue: where the outcome is uncertain and the trial costly, the large patentee can in practice enforce claims against weaker rivals which the courts would be unlikely to support. The remedy for both these weaknesses lies in giving the patent office more resources, so that more and abler examiners could work more carefully and with less delay. This should be possible. At worst, the fees for patents could well be raised substantially to cover part of the increased costs. If any tax on patent holdings, along the lines explored below, were adopted, the receipts therefrom could be used for the same purpose.

In examining the practices of patentees in respect to licensing, pools, and the like, we look for two kinds of undesirable effects. First, to what extent do particular practices make it possible for the patentee to secure a monopoly which extends beyond the terms of the grant, so that he can exclude rivals from a field far wider than that defined by his patented invention? Second, to what extent do particular practices create a situation such that, at the expiry of the patent, competition by outsiders is made impossible, so that the patent in effect becomes a perpetual license? In asking these questions, we again note that if we conclude, first, that practices having such effects are widespread, and second, that they should be prevented because they are beyond the protection of the patent law, we are in effect recommending that the aggregate rewards to patentees be reduced.

On the first point, the most important kinds of practices with undesirable effects are those which use patents as a vehicle for cartel arrangements extending to the whole output of an industry, whether patented or unpatented. The *Gypsum*, *Masonite*, and *Hartford-Empire* cases exemplify such practices.[25] Their common feature is to attach to licenses under a patent or group of patents a set of price-fixing and market-sharing agreements; and to use these licenses, which are held by all the major producers in the industry, as the legal basis for a tight cartel. The agreements typically provide that no licensee shall challenge the validity of the patents under which he is licensed, that each shall open his books to the patentee in order that royalties may be computed; and they carry various restrictions on the price, production, and marketing policies of the licensee. Since the agreement prevents challenge to the validity or scope of the patent by those who, in its absence, would be most interested and able to do so, the cartel can be organized around a "paper patent" which, in fact, might assert no valid or important claim. A second class of devices for extending the scope and force of a patent are tying devices of various sorts. We have already discussed these above.

The most important patent practices which result in extension of the life of the monopoly far beyond the life of the patent grant also involve more than one firm. They include the closed patent pool, the exclusive cross-licensing agreement, and the grant-back provision tied to a cross-licensing agreement. All, in one way or another, create a closed group of firms which share in an advancing technology; if the group is originally made up of large firms in the industry, or the technology which they hold in common is of substantial importance, the market in which they operate will increasingly be closed to other firms. An arrangement which combines the vices of all three practices is the joint patent holding company, created by a group of actual or potential rivals to develop new technology in a

25. U.S. v. U.S. Gypsum Co., 333 U.S. 364 (1948) and 340 U.S. 76 (1950); U.S. v. Masonite Corp., 316 U.S. 265 (1942); U.S. v. Hartford-Empire Co., 323 U.S. 386 and 324 U.S. 570 (1945).

field in which they hold complementary or competing patents. The Radio Corporation of America was organized as a result of a patent stalemate between General Electric, Westinghouse, and AT&T in the new radio field. The new company started off with 2000 patents, and its creators, by a division of fields agreement, blocked off the most important possible source of future competition — their own. RCA was in an excellent position to dominate the radio field through patents, as GE did the incandescent light field; and would have had it not been for antitrust action, which separated RCA from GE and Westinghouse and allowed them to re-enter the field.

Yet, unlike the use of patents to organize cartels, the cross-licensing and pooling arrangements arise out of a social need and serve some purpose other than promoting monopoly. Patents on complementary technology, each part of which is useless without the other, are frequent. Some arrangements by which the whole technology can be practiced are required. Patent pools can be similarly beneficial; they are simply wider cross-licensing agreements in which several firms are involved. Grant-back provisions are more dubious, particularly those requiring the licensee to assign all his improvement patents to the licensor, or to grant the licensor exclusive licenses thereunder. The former tends either to perpetuate the monopoly of the basic patent holder or to discourage innovations by the licensee, whose efforts will simply continue his dependence on the licensor. The latter is little less restrictive, since it confines the use of the developing technology to the two parties to the license. The licensor of the original patent or patents may have a legitimate interest in insuring access to improvements; indeed, the public interest may be served by compelling the licensing of those improvements. But these private and public interests would be fully protected by a provision requiring the licensee to grant back a nonexclusive license on any related future patents he obtains.

Patent accumulation raises some fundamental problems in the relation of the patent system to competition. A large number of patents tends to turn into something much larger than the sum of its parts. Even if no particular patent in a large accumulation is of great importance or wide scope, the mere number tends to create great barriers for other firms trying to produce and sell in the market. At every point, they find some patent held by the firm with a large accumulation, which tends to increase heavily the problem of "inventing around" the technology of the accumulating firm or otherwise engaging in effective technological competition. Moreover, the firm with large patent holdings in a given field becomes the inevitable market for inventions in the field made by firms outside it or by individual inventors. Typically such inventions cannot be practiced without being combined with patented technology under the control of the large patent holder. This puts the outside inventor at a disadvantage in bargaining over licenses, royalties, etc., and usually induces him to assign his patent or grant an exclusive license to the already dominant patentee. Thus large accumulations tend to snowball once they reach a certain size, provided there are no other equally large ones against which their holders must compete. Further, the nature of modern technology and the organization of modern industrial research permit the holder of large numbers of patents to design his research policy so as to fashion a patent blanket over an area of technology, even if acquisitions of inventions from outsiders are not important. The firm can explore as many alternative channels to the same functional result as possible, and patent everything that is possible. The costs and risks of patent litigation further enhance the oppressive effects of a large accumulation of patents. When a new firm or a new product appears on the market, the large holder will almost always find some patent among its many which the newcomer can be charged with infringing. Rather than undergo ordeal by trial, the newcomer may agree to take a license under restrictive conditions, or may decide to sell out and withdraw.

Patent practices and market power interact in both directions. Pre-existing market power, whether or not based on patents, makes the use of patents as exclusionary or cartelizing devices more effective. The problem of patent accumulations is most serious in the hands of a dominant firm without large rivals. The closed pool and the cross-licensing agreement are most important in industries which are structurally oligopolistic, and in which other entry barriers are already high. On the other hand, it is precisely in these same situations that the importance of the patent incentive may be relatively small, since so many other restrictions on competition already exist that it is less necessary to have the patent restriction in order to stimulate invention and innovation. Were market power not based on patents reduced to the minimum possible, the significance of patents as aids to monopoly would fall greatly, while the importance of the patent as incentive might increase.

Historically, perhaps the most important kind of interaction between patents and more generally based market power has been the use of the monopoly period under the patent to build up a position of market power with other bases, so that after the expiration of the patent, other firms cannot enter even though the technology is open to them. The most striking example of this is provided by the history of Alcoa; the more so that there have been no major changes in technology since 1911, when the Bradley patent expired. The problem of persistent market power also appears in industries of very rapidly developing technology. There, firms replace patents with more patents; the technology of old patents is obsolete by the time they expire, and firms not in the technological race at an early stage may find entry difficult thereafter. But this is an effect which is inevitably under a patent system; a "pure patent effect" not dependent on market power arising from nonpatent sources.

In the tight oligopoly market, the closed patent pool may serve both to organize the market and limit interfirm competition, and to exclude possible entrants who would alter the structure from tight to loose oligopoly, e.g., the *Hartford-Empire* case. By contrast, in a loose oligopoly situation, the importance of patent restraints is likely to be much less. In the oil industry, for example, there has been little patent barrier to entry. This arises in part because the development of technology has been to some extent in the hands of specialist firms which construct oil refineries, such as M.W. Kellog Co. and the Houdry Process Company. In part, it arises because the relatively loose structure of the market, the wide geographical variations in prices and costs, have permitted a competitive fringe to operate at least in some parts of the market. It is conceivable that a closed refining patents pool, in the absence of the construction corporations, could serve as an instrument to organize the industry into a tight cartel; but the existence of the competitive fringe and the smaller majors helps to explain why the refinery construction companies operate and why a closed pool was not organized. Even a tight oligopoly, however, may show vigorous technological competition when there are no patent pools or other arrangements between the rivals limiting their technological independence. Thus, for example, Westinghouse and Otis are the only manufacturers in the high-speed elevator field. Westinghouse entered the field in the mid 1920's, breaking Otis' monopoly and leading to a lively technological race. By contrast, the patent arrangements by which GE dominated the electric lamp industry prevented Westinghouse from taking any independent technical initiative there, though it undoubtedly had the resources to do so. Even this cursory examination suggests that the problem presented by accumulation of patents tends to diminish, the less the market is dominated by a single firm or by a small group of large firms acting together.

The present state of the law

The antitrust laws now forbid certain of the practices examined above, in most of the circumstances in which they occur, but ignore others.

Restrictive licensing agreements, especially those that fix the price at which the licensee must sell, limit his output, limit his market area, and the like, have been held illegal whenever they involved all or most of the producers selling in the same market. More precisely, whenever the courts find that a patent licensing arrangement among a group of competing firms is the basis for a price-fixing or market-sharing agreement, the arrangement is struck down. *Hartford-Empire, Gypsum, Masonite,* and *Line Material* all exemplify this proposition; *U.S. v. New Wrinkle* (1952) is a recent application of it.[26] But the old *GE* case (1926) which held that a price-fixing restriction in a license to manufacture and sell was "reasonably adapted to secure pecuniary reward for the patentee's monopoly" has not been overruled, although the issue has never really been squarely presented.[27] While it is true that conspiracy is not so obtrusively present in the single license case, the result may well be the same as in the plural license case if the one licensee is the only other important producer. Should such a case arise, it is hard to believe that the Court would find the reasoning of the old *GE* case a usable precedent. Similar difficulties arise in considering license restrictions on the use to which the patent may be put. It is a fair guess to say that whenever restrictive arrangements of any complexity are involved in licensing arrangement among a group of firms, the courts will find an illegal agreement. But single restrictions, especially as to individual licensees, are still valid. Thus in *Turner Glass v. Hartford Empire,*[28] the 7th Circuit found valid a restriction limiting Turner's use of Hartford's patented bottle-mak-

26. U.S. v. Hartford-Empire Co., 323 U.S. 386 and 324 U.S. 570 (1945); U.S. v. Line Material Co., 333 U.S. 287 (1948); U.S. v. New Wrinkle, 342 U.S. 371 (1952).
27. U.S. v. General Electric Co., 272 U.S. 476 (1926).
28. 173 F.2d 49 (C.A. 7, 1949).

ing machinery to certain types of glassware; in *Atlas Imperial Diesel Engine Co. v. Lanova Corp.*,[29] the District Court of Delaware upheld a provision restricting the use of a patented product to motors of more than 1000 cubic inch displacement.

As we have already noted in the previous section, tying arrangements in which patent licenses are conditioned on the purchase from the licensor of unpatented materials, or on the licensing of other patents, are virtually illegal per se.

Cross-licensing arrangements in which there has been an element of complementarity (reasonableness) and which have not involved price-fixing conspiracies were held valid in the *Cracking* case.[30] In the *Transwrap*[31] case the Court held that a license involving a grant-back clause was not illegal per se; in the *Cellophane* case,[32] the District Court also found nothing wrong with a similar arrangement contained in the DuPont license to Sylvania. The status of agreements not to contest is doubtful. In general, the licensee is estopped from contesting the validity of the patent under which he takes a license, whether or not he contracts expressly to refrain from so doing. However, if the license contains a price-fixing clause which would be illegal under the Sherman Act in the absence of a *valid* patent, then the licensee may contest, even if an express clause against it is part of the license. A series of recent cases from *Sola Electric v. Jefferson* to *McGregor v. Westinghouse* and *Katzinger v. Chicago Metallic Mfg.* all repeat this proposition, usually over strong dissent.[33] If we can view this proposition as established, then no cartel agreement hung on a patent license can be protected by a no-contesting clause against the break away of one or more members, a clearly desirable result.

Patent accumulation, without more, is not illegal. Though the District Court in the new GE lamp case found that GE had "monopolized patents" in violation of Section 2 of the Sherman Act, the finding was novel and it is by no means clear that such a determination would be sustained in a higher court. In *Hazeltine*[34] the Supreme Court said, somewhat gratuitously, that the mere accumula-

29. 79 F. Supp. 1002 (D. Del. 1948).
30. Standard Oil Co. (Indiana) v. U.S., 283 U.S. 163 (1931).
31. Transparent-Wrap Mach. Corp., v. Stokes & Smith Co., 329 U.S. 637 (1947).
32. U.S. v. E. I. du Pont de Nemours & Co., 118 F. Supp. 41 (D. Del. 1953).
33. 317 U.S. 173 (1942); 329 U.S. 402 (1947); 329 U.S. 394 (1947).
34. Automatic Radio Mfg. Co. v. Hazeltine Research, Inc., 339 U.S. 827, 834 (1950).

tion of patents, no matter how far it reached, was not a violation of the antitrust laws. Since the results of the GE case could have been reached on other grounds, the significance of the finding is not great. This case, like the *Hartford-Empire* case, presented a situation where the accumulation of patents was part of a much broader pattern of agreements aimed at monopolizing and thus well within the conventional definition of what the patent law does not protect. In the *United Shoe* case the court refused to find that the patent accumulation was illegal when requested to do so by the government.[35] It did find that the accumulation of patents played a minor part in contributing to the maintenance of a dominant market position which was illegal, but other practices, especially leasing, were more important in this respect. On the other hand, that case is significant because the defense contention that the leases were valid exercises of defendant's patents was rejected; in the first *Shoe* case, it had been accepted. *Hughes Tool Co. v. Ford*[36] is another example of an attempt to justify a leasing arrangement on the basis of the lessor's patents; again, the court found that the leasing was intended to exclude competition and had done so, and was therefore not justified on the basis of the patent.

In *General Electric,*[37] the fact that acquisitions had played an important part in building up GE's patent holdings in lamps, bases, and lamp-making machinery helped the Court to its conclusions. Acquisition underlines specific intent. But if we have argued correctly above on the snowballing effect of large accumulations, acquisitions may not reflect any specific intent to monopolize, but may stem merely from position. At the minimum, some distinction would undoubtedly be drawn between a dominant position based largely on acquisitions, and acquisitions which themselves flow from the dominant position of the acquiring firm. Even if patent accumulation as such cannot be attacked under the law, especially when the patents are largely the result of the firm's own research, in a variety of cases in which Section 2 liability has been found on other grounds, and in which defendants are large holders of patents, some form of reasonable-royalty compulsory licensing has been part of the remedy order. The courts were persuaded that patents helped to contribute

35. U.S. v. United Shoe Machinery Co., 110 F. Supp. 295 (D. Mass. 1953).
36. 114 F. Supp. 525 (D. Okla. 1953).
37. U.S. v. General Electric Co., 82 F. Supp. 753, 816 (D. N.J. 1949).

to the market power of the firms in question, and thus some lessening of their power to do so appeared appropriate.

Possible reforms

We assume, as before, that no grand changes in the whole design of the patent system are contemplated, that the basic features of the existing patent system — including some degree of exclusion and the rights to license, assign, and charge other than uniform royalties — are retained. Within this framework, what kinds of change in the patent system and in the boundary of the area it protects from the competition which the antitrust laws enforce are feasible and desirable?

First, we agree with the implicit position of the courts that the patent office is applying far too loose a standard of patentability for the grant of a seventeen-year monopoly. There are a good many reasons for the persistence of the gap between the patent office and the courts, but two seem to be of primary importance — the administrative burden of careful investigation of the prior art, et cetera, and the tendency, in the event of doubt, to believe that ingenuity should be rewarded rather than turned away with nothing. It is difficult to overcome these pressures by mere admonishment, statutory or judicial, although we would approve a revision of the law and do approve the more demanding position of the courts. As a possibly more fruitful and, to prospective inventors, a clearly more palatable approach, we suggest that a new class of petty patents be created, which would run for, say, five years, to be granted for inventions of minor importance. Petty patents would be granted either to applicants who requested them, or to applicants for full patents when there was substantial doubt as to the novelty and scope of the claimed invention. The standard of investigation in the patent office, which is effectively the standard of invention on which patents are granted, could be fairly low for petty patents. This would make it easier to raise the standards in the case of major patents, running as they now do for seventeen years. The search of the existing art, the testing of the meaning of various claims against what the invention discloses, and so on could be carried on at a much more intensive level than they now are.

We realize that this proposal, in practice, might cause more trouble than it was worth. It would add to the mystical issue of patentability the problem of drawing a line between two kinds of patentability. Moreover, unless statutory standards could be spelled out with less vagueness than they now are, applicants might — at the outset at least — tend to shoot earnestly for the big patent in almost every case. But we believe that the availability of a consolation prize would both make it easier for the patent office to stop short on inventions lacking in apparent significance — to put the burden on the applicant, so to speak — and at the same time persuade many inventors to grasp for the more certain lesser reward than for the doubtful large one.

If the proposal tended to work out in this way, the advantages would be several. First, the power of firms to use trivial inventions, either singly or in groups, as the basis of restrictive arrangements would be greatly diminished by the short life of the grant. Second, patents would not be sought on many trivial inventions since the defensive reasons for so doing would be greatly weaker than they now are. Third, accumulations of patents would have a significance more nearly related to their aggregate importance: an accumulation of petty patents would be much less effective as an exclusionary device than the same accumulation is now, when each grant runs for seventeen years. Fourth, if by this and other means the level of patentable invention as defined by the patent office can be made to correspond more closely to the level of patentable invention as defined in the courts, some of the ways in which the present system works to the disadvantage of the small firm and to the advantage of the large one will be changed. The large cost of litigation and the great difficulty of predicting its outcome will no longer weigh so heavily as it does now.

Turning to matters more directly germane to antitrust policy, we would impose more severe limitations on restrictive licensing practices than the law now imposes. First, we fully support the courts' position that a covenant not to contest the validity of a patent is ineffective against a licensee when the license contains restrictions which, but for a valid patent, would violate the antitrust laws. Second, we are in full accord with the decisions against price-fixing restrictions in industry-wide and near industry-wide licensing agreements, but we would go further. There is an element of paradox in trying to put these cases together with the *General Electric* case of 1926, if the effort to reconcile is simply on the basis that price-fixing in one license is all right but in multiple licenses is not. Presumably, the justification for permitting price-fixing is along these lines — it is reasonable for the patentee to protect the profits from his own manufacture of the patented product. The licensing of others tends to spread the technology and insure more competitive conditions when the patent runs out, and such licensing may preserve competitors from extinction in those cases where the patent is so significant that the patentee, by keeping it to himself, could monopolize the field. But this justification is just as applicable to multiple as to single licensing. The significant distinction between the two is the practical consideration that, generally speaking, the greater the number of licenses, the more likely it is that licenses are being accepted for price-fixing advantages than for the intrinsic merits of the patent.

There are ways of determining, or trying to determine, which of these two purposes — price-fixing or self-preservation — has probably motivated the arrangements.[38] Perhaps this would be a desirable way of dealing with price-fixing provisions in patent licenses. One can conceive of cases where a price-fixing restriction would be the only effective way, short of no licensing at all, in which a small firm patent-holder could protect its manufacturing operations against a large rival. But we would be inclined to cut the knot by overruling *General Electric,* and making a price-fixing provision in a patent license illegal per se. The patentee would still have the not inconsiderable power of collecting royalties and of setting the royalty rate high enough to provide a substantial buffer. In some cases, of course, the inability to utilize a price-fixing clause may lead the patentee to refuse to license altogether. But this need not prove undesirable; it may well promote technological competition by threatened competitors and greater advances than would otherwise take place.

These same considerations, plus additional ones, also lead us to the position that licenses conditioned on grant-backs to the licensor of improvement patents, or exclusive licenses thereunder, should be flatly outlawed. A grant-back of nonexclusive licenses is adequate protection for the patentee.

Next, we believe it would be desirable to limit cross-licensing and pooling arrangements to agreements providing uniform royalties on each patent from all licensees (not, of course, uniform among

38. See Furth, "Price-Restrictive Patent Licenses Under the Sherman Act" *Harvard Law Review* (1958), 71:815.

different patents in the pool or cross-licensing arrangement) with one exception: patentees would be permitted to restrict the use of pooled or cross-licensed patents to a limited field. For example, an automobile firm may wish to put into an auto patent pool a patent it holds on synthetic leather upholstery, restricting licensees to use it in auto manufacture only and licensing the patent to furniture manufacturers, say, on quite a different basis. The argument for the exception is that the degree of royalty discrimination it allows is consistent with the general purpose of the patent law to allow the patentee to get as much revenue from the patent as he can, while it does not lead to the same kind of exclusionary effects which other restrictive licensing agreements have. The main proposal rests on two grounds. First, where the pressure for cross-licensing and pooling is strong, as in blocking situations, the proposed limitation on the character of agreements will not inhibit cross-licensing. Second, there will be situations in which cross-licensing agreements at uniform royalty rates, without output or price restrictions and the like, will not appear attractive to patentees. These are likely to be precisely the situations in which elements of competitiveness in the separate technologies are great enough so that independent development along parallel lines of competing technologies will probably take place in the absence of cross-licensing. Further, of course, prohibition of this sort will be much simpler administratively than a case-by-case scrutiny of every cross-licensing arrangement to see whether the restrictions, if any, are counterbalanced by the advantages of joining complementary patents.

Another desirable reform in the area of patent practices is the registration of licensing agreements. Some government agency — presumably the Patent Office but possibly the Federal Trade Commission — should be informed of the provisions of every patent assignment and license agreement, and this information should be secured in such a way as would make it competent evidence of the patent practices in question in any antitrust proceeding. Whether or not, apart from judicial or administrative proceedings, the information should be publicly available is a difficult question. On the one side, the natural desire of both patentee and licensee is to keep the terms of the agreement private; publication may impair the strategic position of either party in subsequent bargains. Thus the provision might act as a general deterrent to licensing. On the other, it might be argued that the use made and the rewards secured on a government franchise should be public; and even that every patentee should report annually on the sales and income of patented articles, so that the publicity requirement would extend beyond those who licensed patents. On balance, the argument against publicity appears to outweigh the argument for it.

We see no reason why accumulation of patents by acquisition should not be treated as a Sherman Act offense whenever the purpose or effect of the acquisition is to create or maintain a position of dominance. Should anything more be done? Some diminution in the power of firms to build up dominant patent aggregations will be achieved by the creation of a class of petty patents, as proposed. It is possible to go much further by treating patents as "assets" under Section 7 of the Clayton Act, and applying the proposed standard of interpretation to the acquisition of patents, patent applications, and inventions by large firms, and interpreting both assignments and exclusive licenses as acquisitions. Complete coverage would require revision of the law, which now speaks of the acquisition by one corporation of the assets of another, since patents frequently are acquired from individual inventors as well. If this were done, the effect would be to forbid a firm with significant market power from acquiring patents either by assignment or exclusive license (but with no bar to acquiring the right to practice patented art by *nonexclusive* license); and to prevent any patent acquisitions on a scale large enough to give the acquirer market power where he had none before. Under this standard, for example, United Shoe would have been barred from acquiring the Little patents on what became the Littleway process for making women's shoes. This, the most important patent acquisition since United's original formation, put into United's hands a new process for shoe-making and the machines adapted to it. The process was important enough so that it is reasonable to believe others would have developed it, without the United acquisition, and thus have provided significant competition with respect to a good part of the market.

The major problem posed by such a policy is the effect it would have on the market for inventions and patents. Most of the incentive for research and development work by independent inventors and laboratories is provided by the existence of a market for patents; our suggested proposal would not exclude important potential customers altogether, since it would permit nonexclusive licensing to anyone; but it would certainly weaken the market to some extent.

However, if our broader policy against market power were adopted and were effective, the relative importance of the Section 7 limitation on patent acquisition would decline. To the extent that dissolution and other devices reduces the role of firms with large market power in the industrial economy, firms not prohibited from acquiring patents would constitute a much larger relative share of the market than they would if the proposed Section 7 standard were in effect now.

Two further proposals to deal with patent aggregations deserve examination, though both of them appear to create difficulties which might well outweigh their merits, taken in the context of the whole policy proposal. The first is for a cumulative tax on patents, rising with the number of patents held by an individual, and levied at a higher annual rate for each year over the life of the patent.[39] The purpose of this would be to discourage the holding of patents on second-best methods, or on devices which might prove useful for defensive or harassing purposes in patent bargaining, and by so much deter the building up of large patent accumulations. The disadvantage of this proposal is that it would penalize the firm with holdings in many different technologies, corresponding to its activities in many different markets, as heavily as it would the firm with the same accumulation of patents in one area of technology. To the extent that size divorced from market power is not under attack, this is an undesirable result. If we make the rate of progression of the tax steep enough to have a significant effect on patent holdings at all, this is a serious objection. It is also true that the proposed tax would treat patents acquired by purchase in the same way as those which result from the research efforts of the patentee's employees. This may be viewed as a deterrent to large-scale research efforts; but since the rewards from successful invention would be great relative to the tax, the magnitude of this effect would likely be small.

The second proposal is the creation of a limited system of compulsory licensing at reasonable royalties. The limited system we propose would allow a complaining firm to sue for a license on a seventeen-year patent held by another, provided either that the patent had not been used for a period of five years from its effective date, or that the patentee was limiting its use in a way which was contrary to the public interest. In addition, the complainant would

39. Germany had a tax on patents which rose over time, but it was not graduated according to the size of patent holdings.

be required to show that he had negotiated in good faith for a license, and had made a reasonable offer of royalties. If the plaintiff met his burden, the court would award a license, at a royalty it found to be reasonable after hearing evidence on the patentee's research expenditures, proportion of successful developments, and the like.[40] In any case in which the patent was not used by the patentee — presumably because it covered a second-best alternative — it would be sufficient for the plaintiff to show that he intended to practice the invention, either in a commercial process of manufacture or by embodying it in a commercial product. Failure to practice the invention after a reasonable period would cause the license to lapse. When the patentee was using the patent, the plaintiff's burden would be much heavier. He would be required to show that, at prices including a reasonable reward for invention and innovation, there was a substantial unsatisfied demand for the patented product or process, which the patentee refused to meet. Blocking patents would not come within the scope of the proposal, since real complementarity provides an incentive for cross-licensing, and, in its absence, competitive invention rather than cross-licensing is desirable. Only nonexclusive licenses would be awarded by the court; but the award of a license on a particular patent to one plaintiff would form no precedent on which a second plaintiff would be entitled to another license. Since the award of the first license would change the situation, a second plaintiff would face a trial of the issues *de novo*.

The great virtue of this proposal is the flexibility it would give to the patent system. By limiting compulsory licensing to situations in which the patentee can be shown to be acting against the public interest — and often against his own interest in that he underestimates the long-term elasticity of demand for the new product — the uniform reduction of incentives implicit in ordinary compulsory licensing proposals would be avoided. By allowing courts to vary royalties as well as grants of licenses, a further element of flexibility would be introduced. The great drawback of the proposal is the burden of new litigation it would impose on the district courts; and the detailed supervision of patent practices it implies. This burden may be small if the mere existence of the right to sue results in the private settlement of all but a small fraction of requests to license.

40. We hasten to point out that it is virtually impossible to set forth satisfactory standards for determining a "reasonable" royalty. Apparently the job gets done in antitrust decrees, and in a workable manner, but it is hard to tell how or why.

Even with these favorable limitations, the administrative costs of the proposal appear high, and would indicate the desirability of limiting compulsory licensing to cases of nonuse. Moreover, if our broader policy proposals were carried out, the dimensions of the problem of patent accumulation would be very greatly reduced. The problem now takes its most serious form where market dominance and patent accumulation combine to reinforce each other. If a program of limiting market power is carried through, then the limited compulsory licensing scheme should not be introduced. But if such a program is considered infeasible, or if it is put into effect at a very slow pace, with reliance placed chiefly on the growth of the economy and severe limitations on mergers, then the licensing scheme would have a place in the armory of antitrust weapons.

To summarize, we suggest six revisions in the present patent law in the direction of limiting the permanent anticompetitive effects of the patent grant. Five of them are suggested firmly: the creation of petty patents; prohibition of price-fixing in patent licenses; prohibition of cross-licensing and patent pooling arrangements which embody more than licenses at uniform royalties in each field to which the licenses apply; prohibition of licenses conditioned on grant-backs of future patents or of exclusive licenses; and the application of proposed Section 7 standards to patent acquisitions. One proposal is suggested more tentatively, to be adopted only in the event our main proposals for reducing market power quickly are not — the institution of a limited system of compulsory licensing. Taken together, these reforms certainly reduce the aggregate rewards which patent holders will be able to earn from their patents. Some of the changes can be viewed as correcting abuses, some as changing the system. But from the point of view of present patentees, there is no real difference, in that their effects all point in the same direction. But we have decided, more implicitly than explicitly, and certainly without any detailed examination of evidence, which does not exist, that the reforms proposed will reduce significantly the extent to which the patent system results in the creation of positions of enduring market power extending beyond the scope of the patent grant, without at the same time reducing the rewards to invention and innovation below their long-run supply price and so reducing their flow. Perhaps the best basis for optimism in this respect is the fact that the lottery elements in the process of invention and innovation bulk so large that the long shots should still look enticing.

PRICE DISCRIMINATION

The nature of the problem and the dilemmas of present policy

Price discrimination occurs whenever goods are sold at prices which differ from each other by more than long-run average costs. It can appear in various forms: the same good is sold at different prices; different goods with different costs are sold at the same price; two goods are sold at prices that differ by more than costs. Usually the term is applied to situations involving the comparison of price-cost relations of a single seller, although logically it need not be so confined. We shall use it in this narrower sense; thus, when the comparison involves several goods, they will be related goods in the sense of being produced by a single seller. Again, the use of the term in discussions of public policy is usually limited to situations which involve only one good, or to situations in which several goods can be viewed as a single one plus additional services or facilities, and the markets in which they are sold are related. But the logic of the definition applies equally well in the case of two dissimilar outputs of the same producer, sold in different markets. If the margin over average cost is different for Chevrolets than for Cadillacs, this is price discrimination no different from that which occurs if the margin over average costs is different for Chevrolet convertibles sold in Chicago than for the same cars sold in Detroit.

Viewed statically, price discrimination is a sign of resource misallocation, indicating too much output of the low-priced and too little output of the high-priced goods, or too much sale in the low-priced and too little sale in the high-priced market.[41] In dynamic terms, the significance of price discrimination is more complex. In imperfect markets, especially those with important oligopoly elements, price discrimination is often an indispensable element of

41. In certain cases, such as that of efficient quantity discrimination in which marginal price for every buyer equals marginal cost, no resource misallocation arises. But even here there are income transfers among buyers, and from buyers to sellers: unless average price equals average cost for every buyer. The only situations in which even a crude approach to efficient discrimination (in this sense) is made are in public utility industries, where declining long-run average cost curves provide an argument for such pricing systems.

price competition. Oligopolists may be willing to test the market by discriminatory price cuts, which they hope to keep secret for at least some time, when they are unwilling to make general changes in prices to which their rivals will immediately react. In such market, periods of "chiseling"—discriminatory price concessions—almost always precede downward price changes. Price discrimination is also an important predatory tactic, useful in the achievement and maintenance of market power. The large firm with widespread operations and a large product line can drive out rivals by selective price-cutting, by product or geographically, without correspondingly lowering its margins in general. Price discrimination or the power of the large firm to practice price discrimination—charging low prices in the areas of the market in which other barriers to entry are least—also acts as a deterrent to entry. Further, the practice of price discrimination may simply represent a device by which the dominant firm increases its profits at the expense of small customers and suppliers, even though it does not attempt to change their positions in the market.

Some degree of market power is always necessary for a firm to practice price discrimination. The firm may possess merely the small degree of market power conferred by customer inertia and the time-lag of the spread of price information among buyers. If so, the discrimination it practices must be equally transient. Sporadic discrimination of this type exists in every imperfect market. The possession of substantial market power permits continued price discrimination. Conversely, the persistence of discriminatory prices, especially where price differences are large relative to cost differences, is a symptom of the possession of substantial market power by the discriminating seller.

The problem of policy is to strike down discrimination as a predatory practice and as exploitation of market power, yet at the same time to allow discrimination to function as part of the mechanism of price competition. Is it a soluble problem?

The present effort at solution is embodied in the Robinson-Patman Act. The main features of the Act are:

(1) Definition of discrimination as a price difference, or non-proportional difference in services, facilities, or things of value furnished along with goods in a sale.

(2) Prohibition of price discrimination whenever its effect is to lessen competition or to injure, destroy, or prevent competition with any person competing with either the seller, the buyer, or customers of either of them. Prohibition of discrimination in services, facilities, etc., is not so qualified.

(3) Allowing price differentials which make due allowance for cost differentials.

(4) Allowing the justification of price discriminations where proved necessary to meet the equally low lawful price of a competitor, or the justification of discrimination in facilities, services, etc., as necessary to meet the similar offers of a competitor.

In addition, there are other provisions, of which the most important to our purpose are the quantity-limits clause and the prohibition of brokerage payments by a seller to a buyer or buyer's agent.

In its language, legislative history, and application, the Act has run into three important dilemmas. First, its basic purpose has not been clear: it points in two directions. One is the suppression of discrimination as an anticompetitive practice; the other, the protection of small individual firms from price disadvantages in their transactions in the market. As we have noted, these two purposes, in practice, have no necessary correlation.

The second dilemma is that it has concentrated its attention on price differences rather than on price discrimination. True, Sections 2(d) and 2(e) reach out to encompass nonprice discriminations of certain types. But under the Act as a whole it is difficult to deal with the kind of discrimination which arises when prices are the same in the face of cost differences. Where this arises under basing-point and similar geographic price systems, the Commission probably could — but more recently does not — define "price" to mean mill net yield, and so find discrimination though buyers' prices are the same at various locations. But in other situations this is not the case: the manufacturer who sells at the same price in trainload lots and in cases may be violating the prescriptions of common sense, but he is not violating the Robinson-Patman Act. The dilemma may be an inevitable one. The identification of discrimination in the absence of price differences would represent an overwhelming administrative problem even in relation to that presented by the Act now. A similar problem is presented by the price differences among similar commodities of different grade and quality; the common kind of discrimination in which mark-ups differ among different products sold by the same producer lies beyond the Act's reach. Again, this appears inevitable. A third kind of omission, not equally inevitable, is that the Act as now framed reaches only sellers' discrimination, as by different selling prices. Though Section 2(f) makes the knowing receipt of discriminations by the buyer illegal, it still refers to sellers' discriminations. Yet there are situations outside the reach of the law in which buyers pay different prices to different sellers of the same merchandise. The most important of these arise in connection with the supply activities of large merchandisers like Sears-Roebuck, or Macy's.

Finally, and perhaps most important, the Act creates an administrative dilemma of formidable proportions: on the one side, the Commission must set a standard which is enforceable, which requires some precision; on the other, it must pay some attention to practicalities, which requires some looseness and discretion. The most difficult area in which this dilemma arises is that of cost justification. The Commission has been heavily criticized for imposing standards of precision, detail, and timeliness on cost justifications of a kind that in effect make almost any cost justification impossible. Yet the alternative, to give the Commission discretion to consider "reasonable approximations" to "probable costs," rather than requiring actual records of costs incurred in the precise transactions under scrutiny, would create a broad but ill-defined area of discretion and tend to encourage widespread disregard of the statute. The difficulties of defining what constitutes meeting of competition in "good faith" are also formidable. How much knowledge of the circumstances surrounding other sellers' prices must a seller have in order to act in good faith?

As the Act has been administered, the Commission has probably leaned to the side of protecting individual competitors, even at the expense of diminishing market competition, although any conclusion of this kind would be hard to establish. The strongest critics of the Act see in it nothing more than a device for price maintenance, and a guarantee of the positions of high-cost sellers. But even if this is extreme — and some recent decisions of the courts and the Commission would indicate that it is — there can be no question that the dilemmas are real, and that the Commission has had little success in resolving them.

Recommendations

To some degree, the above dilemmas are inescapable in any statute purporting to deal with price discrimination. One answer would be to dispense with any specific statute altogether, and leave the matter to regulation under the Sherman Act; but at least some of the dilemmas are bound to reappear there unless price discrimination is to be immunized entirely, a result which makes no sense to us. We believe that limitations on price discrimination are a proper part of any antitrust policy, even the broadened policy we have outlined herein. There will always remain a considerable number of firms with substantial market power under any policy that is kept within reasonable bounds. Moreover, there will always be situations in which the power of a seller with respect to particular buyers (or a buyer with respect to particular sellers) is great, even though the seller's general market power is small. These cases occur because of the imperfections in most markets, and the different geographical scope of sellers' and buyers' markets. For example, Standard of Indiana's power in the mid-continent market might be weak, its power in the Detroit local area relatively strong, and its power with respect to particular Detroit service stations who had been selling Stanolind gas for some time even stronger. Whenever a particular buyer must incur significant costs to transfer his patronage from his supplier to another, whether by reason of location, or ignorance of the market, or dependence on special facilities or services offered by the supplier, the supplier may be in a position to discriminate against that buyer up to the extent of his transfer costs, even though the supplier's general market position is weak.

Moreover, though significant market power would remain under any reasonable antitrust program, a broadened attack on market power would materially reduce not only the frequency of anticompetitive or oppressive price discrimination, but also the frequency of those situations in which price discrimination performs a dynamic competitive role. Thus, we could protect "fair dealing" values with considerably less sacrifice than rigorous enforcement of the Robinson-Patman Act would now entail.

Nevertheless, the existing statute is unsatisfactory in many respects, and while the difficulties and dilemmas cannot be fully resolved, we believe they could be considerably reduced. We would abandon the present act and, in starting afresh, give separate treatment to price discrimination adversely affecting competition among sellers, on the one hand, and price discrimination that harms particular buyers, on the other.

A good argument could be made for dispensing with any particularized treatment of price discrimination which is, or is intended to be, a device for excluding competing sellers. If "predatory" price discrimination was not an offense under the Sherman Act when the original Clayton Act was passed, it certainly would be now in its more egregious forms — as an unlawful "attempt to monopolize." Moreover, there is some doubt that price discrimination of this kind is a common phenomenon. But there are difficulties in leaving the matter to be dealt with under Section 2 of the Sherman Act only. Definition of the offense is sufficiently uncertain so that Section 2 could be interpreted to cover either too little or too much. It would cover little if limited to the firm with monopoly power in one or more markets since invidious price discrimination can be carried on with considerably less than monopoly power. On the other hand, Section 2 would cover far too much if the courts equated all discriminatory price-cutting with an illegal "intent" to monopolize.

We would therefore be inclined to give the matter specific treatment, and suggest a statutory provision along the following lines. We use statutory language not for the purpose of indicating precisely what should be enacted, but to indicate as clearly as we can the kind of "anticompetitive" price discrimination that should be proscribed.

(1) It shall be unlawful for a seller to undercut, persistently or frequently, the prices of competitors in one or more substantial markets whenever:

(a) he does not, with reasonable promptness, make corresponding price reductions in other substantial markets; and

(b) the reduced prices are significantly less than the prices charged in other substantial markets; and

(c) the price differences substantially exceed amounts which were in good faith reasonably estimated to be the probable savings in making the lower-priced sales; and

(d) the probable effect has been or will be to lessen competition or tend to create a monopoly in any substantial market; such effect to be conclusively presumed where the seller is large in one or more of the higher-price markets, and where total sales in such market or markets are a large part of the total sales in all the markets in which the seller does business.

(2) In determining whether or not price differences exist, due regard shall be given to services or facilities furnished by the seller to various buyers; provided, however, that differences in price or net price that are entirely accounted for by differences in transportation cost shall not be subject to Section (1).

(3) On a showing of substantial price differences unrelated to differences in transportation cost, the burden shall be on defendant to show that the differences did not exceed a good faith reasonable estimate of probable savings.

(4) Only competing sellers may bring a private action for alleged violations of Section (1).

A statute along these lines would not cover isolated, sporadic price discrimination, because such discrimination is not likely to be significant and is likely in many cases to represent simply the first stage of a general price reduction. The proposal does not cover discriminatory low prices that merely meet the prices of competitors, since the meeting of competition is far more likely to be a defensive than a predatory tactic. We do not mean to suggest, however, that the "meeting" of prices may not be evidence of a price-fixing conspiracy in violation of the Sherman Act. Further, the proposal excludes the kind of geographic price discrimination that is inherent whenever a firm sells widely a product that involves significant shipping costs. On balance, we can see no good reason for discouraging this kind of market interpenetration, which serves as a check on monopolistic pricing and on undue price increases in local or regional markets.

Two other features deserve comment. First, we retain an economic definition of price discrimination by taking into account cost savings; this is essential if a proscription of price discrimination is to make any sense at all. At the same time, we would couch the "defense" in terms of good faith estimates rather than accounting niceties, in order to provide some flexibility for business pricing decisions and in order to make the defense one that is available in fact. Second, the presumption as to adverse effect — where the seller is large in some markets and where those markets are large — is designed both to exclude and include. It is intended to exclude the case of a producer who is strong only in a small local market, and who is attempting to expand against larger competitors in other markets. It is designed to include, by lightening the burden of proof in such cases, the seller who probably has market power in important markets.

We now turn to the problem of price discrimination that has no probable adverse effect on competition among sellers, but that does harm particular buyers who are in competition with other (larger) buyers paying lower prices. Again, we shall state our proposal in statute form, but without implying that any law incorporating the approach must so read:

(1) It shall be unlawful for a buyer to make a purchase, or for a seller to make a sale, on the condition or agreement that the seller will not offer equally favorable prices or terms of sale to another buyer.

(2) It shall be unlawful for a buyer to receive, or for a seller to grant, frequently or for a period of more than one year or for two successive contract periods, prices or terms of sale which he has reason to know are more favorable than those received for goods of like grade and quality from the seller by a competitor of such buyer who buys and takes delivery in substantially the same quantities and by substantially the same methods, or who is denied an opportunity so to buy and take delivery.

(3) It shall be unlawful for a buyer, who buys and takes delivery in substantially different quantities or by substantially different methods than a competing buyer of goods of like grade and quality, to receive, or for a seller to grant, frequently or for a period of more than one year or for two successive contract periods, an allowance, rebate, or discount which he has reason to know exceeds the amount which could have been estimated in good faith by the buyer and the seller to be the probable saving to the seller attributable to such differences in quantities or methods of sale or delivery. If the buyer performs functions or operations which the seller performs for buyers who do not receive the allowance, rebate, or discount, the cost to the buyer of performing such functions or operations may be the basis, in a proceeding against the buyer, for estimating such probable saving; *provided,* however, that nothing in sections (1), (2), or (3) shall preclude a seller from absorbing transportation cost in excess of what the buyer would pay in pur-

chasing from a competing seller, or preclude a buyer from accepting delivery on such terms.

(4) On a prima-facie showing in any proceeding under section (2) or (3) that the buyer received more favorable prices or terms, the defendant shall have the burden of proving good faith belief that the buyer was not being favored or, under section (3), that the amount of the allowance, rebate, or discount did not exceed a good faith estimate of probable savings to the seller.

(5) It shall be a defense to any proceeding under section (2) or (3) that the lower price or more favorable terms matched an equally low competitive offer which the buyer or seller knew or had clear reason to believe was nondiscriminatory.

(6) Private actions under sections (1), (2), and (3) may be brought only by injured buyers. Damages shall be limited to actual damages, except that in the absence of proof of damages of greater amount, damages shall be presumed to be the amount of the discrimination.

The above proposal would narrow the existing law in some respects, and broaden it in others. First, only persistent discrimination would be illegal. Second, more liberal scope would be granted for a "cost savings" defense. Third, the "meeting competition" defense would be restricted specifically to situations in which the seller clearly had reason to believe that the competing offer was nondiscriminatory. No discriminatory competing offer will suffice even though conceivably legal. Fourth, treble damages would be eliminated, but the plaintiff would recover at least the excess that he paid.

Each of these changes seems to have merit, and, together, to give a reasonable amount of protection to small buyers without inordinate losses to competitive pricing. Moreover, we believe that such revisions would reduce the administrative difficulties under present law, and, on balance, reduce its scope.

We wish to comment further on only one point — the "meeting competition" defense. The proposed statute would be considerably simplified if this defense were eliminated entirely. Moreover, the defense, strictly speaking, is irrelevant to the protection of "fair dealing," the basic purpose of any such law. However, as suggested by the Supreme Court in the first *Standard of Indiana*[42] opinion,

42. Standard Oil Co. v. FTC, 340 U.S. 231 (1951).

where in fact the favored buyer has received a low nondiscriminatory offer from a competing seller, the seller who meets that offer with a discriminatory price cut is injuring the disfavored buyers no more than they would be injured anyway. Thus, in such circumstances — at least in theory — there would be little point in prohibiting the discrimination. We conclude that it would be a reasonable compromise to allow the defense, but to impose a stiff burden of proof.

VI

Exceptions to Competitive Policy: Regulation and Exemption

Basic though the protection of competition may be to American economic policy, it is obvious that legislative exceptions cover significant areas of the nation's economy. Most major agricultural commodities are produced and sold under price support programs. Varying degrees of public regulation are imposed on transportation, electric power, gas, broadcasting, crude oil production, and other industries. Statutes protect collective bargaining by labor, and resale price maintenance in the field of distribution.

Each of these areas presents a veritable thicket of problems, both of analysis and of public policy. We lack the space to plunge deeply into any one of them. Instead, we are primarily concerned with the economic justifications for exceptions to competitive policy, and with the kinds of regulation or exemption that have been or might be adopted to best carry out selected policy aims.

The discussion will be divided into the following two parts: the reasons for regulating or exempting private economic activity, and a brief discussion of selected regulatory or exempt areas and the policies therein pursued.

REASONS FOR REGULATION OR EXEMPTION

For clarity of analysis, it is important to distinguish among the following three kinds of situations that may make departures from antitrust policy either necessary or desirable:

(a) Situations in which competition, as a practical matter, cannot exist or survive for long, and in which, therefore, an unregulated market will not produce competitive results.

(b) Situations in which active competition exists, but where, because of imperfections in the market, competition does not produce one or more competitive results.

(c) Situations in which competition exists, or could exist, and has produced or may be expected to produce competitive results, but where in light of other policy considerations competitive results are unsatisfactory in one or more respects.

We draw these distinctions because they suggest different kinds of regulatory approaches to meet the different problems they pose. Of course, there is no intrinsic reason why more than one situation might not be found in the same industry. (That is, we may find an industry which is inherently noncompetitive but where competitive results, even though obtainable through regulation, would not be a preferred policy goal anyway.) However, neither is there any intrinsic reason why two situations should always be found together. The necessity of regulating an inherently noncompetitive industry does not of itself require the abandonment of competitive goals. Putting it another way: the reasons that support regulation do not necessarily justify a particular kind of regulation or a particular set of regulatory aims.

There is a related point. The fact that some regulation is necessary does not mean that extensive regulation is necessary. To cite an example that will be treated more fully later — the need for safety regulations in air commerce does not necessarily require restrictions on freedom of entry. Moreover, regulation can easily expand beyond the scope appropriate to the conditions that first produced it, and often for reasons quite unrelated to those originally deemed pertinent. The new reasons may be sufficient to justify the extended reach, but intelligent policy-making requires that they be treated on their own merits. "Logical" extensions of regulation are not always logical. Similarly, the conditions that first produced regulation may well change to the point that regulation should be reduced or drastically revised.

We shall not discuss in detail the reasons why competitive results may properly be altered to serve other policy ends. National defense, fiscal policy, plain humanity, and other considerations often dictate intervention in competitive processes. The resolution of competing policies is essentially a qualitative political decision involving a wide range of complex considerations, and with some exceptions we do not wish to state our views in this context.

However, we do want to go into the first two situations described above — the inherently noncompetitive market, and the competitive market that fails to produce competitive results — in order to pinpoint just what it is that accurately identifies them; for regulation is often mistakenly imposed for "failure" of competition in situations where competition is not failing at all.

Inherently noncompetitive markets

Natural monopoly. In the economic sense, natural monopoly is monopoly resulting from economies of scale, a relationship between the size of the market and the size of the most efficient firm such that one firm of efficient size can produce all or more than the market can take at a remunerative price, and can continually expand its capacity at less cost than that of a new firm entering the business. In this situation, competition may exist for a time but only until bankruptcy or merger leaves the field to one firm; in a meaningful sense, competition here is self-destructive.

As noted, economies of scale is a relative concept. Natural monopoly may exist in a market as large as the entire country, as seems probably the case in the telephone industry. In the past, high transportation costs created many local natural monopolies which have since been largely eradicated. In today's underdeveloped countries there are many markets so thin that industries which are highly competitive in more industrialized countries are natural monopolies there. In the United States and similar countries, however, few industries now fall in the natural monopoly category. The list of significant industries of this type is largely exhausted by the telephone industry; distribution of power, gas, and water; electric power production (in most areas); and railroads (in some).[1]

"Natural monopoly" is traditionally the classic case for extensive regulation of the price, service, investment, and other management decisions of the industry concerned. There is no a priori reason why such regulation should not be aimed at securing approximately competitive results: prices at a level yielding a return on investment which is comparable, taking into account diverse risk factors, to current rates in the capital market; no discrimination in prices and services, so that each consumer pays prices proportional to costs; discontinuance of services that do not yield an appropriate rate of return; efficiency of operations; and progressiveness in low-

1. There are disturbing indications that newspaper publishing is approaching this unhappy state in many cities and towns.

ering costs and developing better services. Yet the aim, however well-directed, may well miss the mark.

It is particularly difficult for regulation to ensure efficiency and progressiveness because the bench marks supplied by competitive firms in comparable positions are typically absent. Of course, the regulatory commission supervising the operations of a local electric power company can look at the record of other power companies; and publicly-owned generating and distributing systems may be set up as yardsticks. It seems clear, for example, that TVA, whatever else may be said for or against it, taught pessimistic private utility operators that the elasticity of demand for power, and the consequent possibilities of cheaper production, were considerably greater than they had thought. But the situation of other utilities usually differs in significant respects, at least to the point that the regulatory commission, if it is of such a mind, may have great difficulty in establishing the existence of inefficiency or unprogressiveness with any degree of certainty.

As for nondiscriminatory pricing, it is extremely difficult in many instances to determine whether a particular pattern of prices is discriminatory or not. At the minimum, a well-developed system of cost-accounting is required, and the allocation of joint costs is bound to be arbitrary to some degree. Even apart from these difficulties, price discrimination has been an accepted feature of most regulatory schemes. In some circumstances this may have economic justification. Where demand for a utility's services is declining — because of the growth of competing goods or services in some of its markets, migration of population or industry, etc. — the point may be reached at which no level of nondiscriminatory prices would cover total costs; here the choice is between letting the utility go out of existence once its plant is worn out, with loss of service to those who are willing to pay for it, and charging discriminatory prices — highly remunerative prices to those who will pay, and "competitive" prices (making some but comparatively little contribution to overhead) to those who will pay no more. Similarly, price discrimination may be justified even though compensatory nondiscriminatory pricing is possible, in situations where the business obtained from "lower price" customers makes some contribution to overhead costs and thus permits lower prices to the "high price" customers than they would otherwise have to pay to obtain continued services. Finally, price discrimination may be justified as a method of effecting "external" economies, in situations where social costs exceed private costs. For example, the social costs of coal-burning furnaces (in air pollution, etc.) may make it desirable to set low rates for electricity and gas.

However, two cautionary comments should be made regarding all except the "external economies" case. First, the economic justification for price discrimination in such cases rests on the existence in fact of economies of scale. That is, the situation must be such that a reduction in size of fixed plant and equipment to a capacity appropriate to the reduced (or "high price") demand would raise the total cost of service to the point that even higher prices would have to be charged than if present size were kept and discriminatory prices maintained. Second, the economic justification supports only those prices that make some return over variable costs; it does not extend to prices that cause an actual operating loss and thus increase rather than decrease the burdens on the higher price customers.

Finally, the economic justification for a particular pattern of discriminatory prices does not necessarily apply to the patterns of discriminatory prices actually permitted by utility regulatory commissions. Actual patterns frequently reflect other than economic considerations. We hasten to add, however, that no invidious implications are intended by this classification. The noneconomic considerations may justifiably be deemed decisive. We merely insist that they be recognized for what they are.

Natural oligopoly. We repeat here for purposes of completeness what has previously been pointed out and more thoroughly discussed, namely, that economies of scale may produce noncompetitive market structures well short of single-firm monopoly. The market may be able to accommodate more than one company of optimum size, but not enough to produce satisfactory levels of competitive behavior. As we have stated, it seems reasonably certain that most of the many few-firm industries in this country are not natural oligopolies in the true sense of the phrase; the firms in such industries are much larger than is necessary for lowest costs, and the markets could take a correspondingly large number of firms of smallest efficient size. For reasons earlier set forth, we think reorganization of such markets is preferable to regulating them.

For the remaining true oligopolies, some form of regulation of behavior may prove desirable, but as a general proposition we are inclined to believe that full-scale regulation of the public utility type is likely to be unprofitable. The mere existence of several firms gives some latitude for rivalry, for a degree of competition. Performance may be less satisfactory than what active competition would ensure, and yet still be equal to or better than what could be hoped for from extensive regulation, particularly if antitrust law is rigorously applied against restrictive conduct.

Competitive markets that fail to produce competitive results

An industry may be competitive in both a structural and some behavioral senses and yet fail to achieve one or more of the expected competitive results.

We note at the outset that this does not describe the situation in which a "countervailing power" thesis is said to apply. The argument for permitting or creating economic units with countervailing power obviously contemplates the existence of other units whose power is to be offset, i.e., the absence of competitive conditions. Nor does it necessarily describe a situation in which arguments for "parity" or "equalizing the terms of trade" are relevant. Prices and incomes in one area may well fall in relation to prices and incomes in others. This may be due to the fact that competition governs prices and incomes in the area whose relative position is worsened, while monopolistic elements characterize the other areas, but if so it would be more appropriate to place the blame on the monopoly elements, not on competition. Or it may simply be due to changes in the pattern of demand against the interests of the declining group, in which event the results are what one would expect from the competitive process. Where resource and income allocation are distorted by the existence of monopoly elements in some segments of the economy, we believe that the better approach would be to eradicate or minimize the monopoly elements, not encourage additional monopoly elements in other sectors.

We also note that general arguments have been made that progressiveness in products and techniques cannot be achieved in purely competitive situations, that the lure of monopoly profits is essential to progress. We have considered this position in earlier chapters, and there is no reason to repeat that discussion here. We recognize that there may be some validity in the thesis. Just as social costs may exceed private costs in many situations (e.g., industrial pollution of streams), so the net social benefits of innovations may exceed the net private benefits to innovators unless the private rewards are enhanced by bounty or by some degree of monopoly. But we disagree with the policy implications of the argument if the implications are that existing monopoly elements should be sanctioned or given further protection. We see no indication that there is too little monopoly in the American economy; the patent laws seem to provide ample, if not inordinate, rewards for new developments. The seeming lack of progressiveness of some allegedly competitive industries — such as building construction — is often attributable to the fact that the industries are in fact hobbled by monopolistic restraints. In others, claims of unprogressiveness have been made, but they do not seem to be wholly convincing. The principal difficulty, which we have previously adverted to, is that of determining what the relevant standard of progressiveness is in the face of substantial ignorance of what the opportunities for progress are.

Setting these general contentions aside, it is certainly true that imperfections of one sort or another *may* prevent the achievement of competitive results in a substantially competitive industry. For example, producers or consumers may be ignorant of some of their alternatives, and hence make choices they otherwise would not make. Presumably, the remedy in such a case is to set up informational organizations to transmit market and related information, a legitimate and helpful function that government bureaus and trade associations often perform. But we are primarily concerned with two categories that are most commonly used to justify interference with competitive processes — ruinous competition and conservation — since it is in these areas that the reasons for intervention continue to be most commonly misused.

Ruinous competition. In most instances, apart from natural monopoly situations, ruinous competition simply reflects a commitment to the industry of factors of production in excess of current demand. Usually excess capacity is thought of in the investment sense, i.e., excess fixed factors like plant and equipment. Ruinous competition may well be prolonged in an industry characterized by a fairly high ratio of fixed to variable costs. Given slack demand, or overexpansion of capacity, the incremental cost of production may fall far below total unit cost. Fixed factors are not being fully utilized; they can be more fully utilized at little or no extra cost, and thus the cost of higher output is only the cost of those factors (labor, materials, etc.) needed in additional amounts. In a competitive industry, this generates strong pressures toward price cutting, and price may be expected to fall to incremental cost. As price drops below the incremental cost of less efficient producers, their capacity will be withdrawn from production. But if inefficient capacity is relatively small, or the excess capacity relatively great, prices may settle at a level unprofitable to all or most producers and persist there for fairly long periods of time, until all excess capacity is worn out or withdrawn. In short, the losses may be severe and the process of adjustment a long, painful one.

Nevertheless, this does not necessarily mean that government intervention, or protected self-help by private agreement, is economically justified or good public policy. A changing economic system is always in the process of making some kinds of capacity redundant, and in a competitive economy losses resulting from excess capacity are, of course, a means of conveying information that such excess capacity exists. Losses are the mechanism by which the economy's resources are redirected into more wanted pursuits, and if competitive allocation of resources is accepted as a desirable general welfare goal, interference with the process should have some justification beyond the mere fact that an industry is sick.

The kind of intervention usually demanded is that which is likely not to cure the situation but rather to insure that it will persist much longer than it otherwise would. What is usually sought is price support, by public authority or by authorized private agreement, and production quotas are often necessary to make the price support effective. It may be that not even these steps will improve the affected industry's lot — if demand for the product concerned is highly elastic, a raising of price may well make the industry's losses more acute than before. This is likely to be the case where the decline in demand has been caused by the rise of competitive substitutes, as has happened to railroads, coal, and a host of less significant industries. But to the extent that price-fixing restores the profits or cuts the losses of the industry's producers, cure of the basic problem — excess capacity — is simply postponed, and meanwhile resources are being uneconomically used from an over-all standpoint. Again, we do not contend that it would in all cases be unreasonable to slow down the readjustment process, to assuage the pains; we merely point out that the economic price should be recognized in any policy calculation, and we also suggest what is obvious, namely, that intervention to protect the incomes of one group makes it extremely difficult to resist the demands of others.

We believe the same comments apply to some forms of intervention other than price support, such as direct action to retire inefficient capacity at a rate faster than would normally occur. It seems clear that abnormally fast retirement of capacity is also economically wasteful — the fact that utilization of capital equipment will yield some return over variable costs at going prices indicates it should be used. Forced retirement, however, might in some situations be preferable to protected survival by price support, as it would tend to concentrate production in the more efficient plants.

There are conceivable economic justifications for intervening in an excess-capacity situation even on the general premise of seeking long-run competitive results. Excess capacity may exist for a variety of reasons — seasonal swings, cyclical ups and downs, or permanent overcapacity because of overbuilding or shifts in demand. We have been discussing excess capacity in the latter sense. Where the overcapacity is short run, the costs of scrapping and then rebuilding, or of shutting down and then reopening, could conceivably be large enough so that some protection of incomes to forestall scrapping or shutting down would be economically worth while to the economy. However, it would seem probable that in seasonal variations such considerations would be adequately taken into account in entrepreneurial decisions. As for cyclical variations, all or most industries tend to be afflicted at the same time, and it is difficult to imagine a feasible method of subsidizing them all; moreover, governmental fiscal policy — tax reduction and spending — seems clearly the more appropriate vehicle for dealing with the problem.

There is one other sick industry problem to be commented upon. We have been discussing destructive competition caused by excess capital investment. Prolonged general losses in an industry may be due not only to overinvestment, which keeps fixed factors in use even though total costs are not recovered, but also to immobility of variable factors, which keeps them employed in the same use at returns which decline with the decline in price. This has happened from time to time with specialized labor, usually where technological changes have rendered skills obsolete; with labor in certain geographical areas; and in agriculture, where, in addition to excess capacity in the investment sense, farmers apparently will persist in their occupation despite substantial reductions in money income.

Nevertheless, while such circumstances may raise political and social problems of greater magnitude than those caused by overinvestment, the economic analytical aspects are much the same. Price supports for agricultural crops seem clearly inadequate as a long-run cure for excess farm production. Putting a floor under wages in depressed industries involves the same problems as product price control. If the derived demand for labor is highly elastic, wage fixing may reduce the total wage bill; even if inelastic, unemployment will be somewhat greater unless "share the work" plans are evolved through agreement. If wage stabilization is effected without work sharing, the relocation of labor may be accelerated, which may be a net benefit; but since this kind of policy would be more painful than what it replaced, it is highly unlikely that it would be followed. A greater wage bill, and greater individual wages through work sharing, would ameliorate conditions, of course, but as in the case of price-fixing in an overcapacity situation, it postpones eventual solution of the basic difficulty at some economic cost to the economy as a whole. Direct measures to speed relocation — such as government financial assistance, job retraining, stimulation of new industry by public power developments, and the like — would be a more satisfactory cure and probably a less costly one in the end.

Conservation. Intervention in the competitive process has often been based on a claimed need to conserve natural resources. Here, too, it is important to recognize just why it is that the resources should be conserved.

One might distinguish between conservation of resources that are irretrievably exhausted in use, and conservation of resources that can, but need not, be irretrievably lost in use or that can be used in a way that increases the cost of restoration. We believe, however, that the analytical problems are much the same.

Land and timber resources fall in the latter category, and the problem here is a potential, and ofttimes actual, deviation between the time horizons of the users and what may fairly be said to be the proper time horizons needed to achieve economically optimal rates and methods of use. Thus, intervention to promote soil and timber conservation techniques may often be classed as intervention to achieve competitive results. However, just as with natural resources exhausted by use, intervention here requires assumptions, or predictions, as to what future demands will be. The desirable level of soil conservation expenditures will vary with predictions as to how much land will be needed, and how badly, years hence. This in turn requires predictions concerning the likely rate of progress in farming technology, population growth, changes in food consumption patterns, and the like. Waste of land or of timber resources is always waste in an engineering or technical sense, but it may not be economic waste. Fertilizers, irrigation, and other expenses incurred to maintain the fertility of farm land would constitute economic waste if the land later became redundant. Of course, revision of exploitative patterns may reduce waste in both an engineering sense and an economic sense where currently estimated future use is as high or higher than at present; and conceivably, because of ignorance, revision may reduce current economic waste, where producers are unaware that their net yields would be increased by changed methods.

Similar comments may be made about such exhaustible resources as crude oil. Intervention to change exploitative patterns may eliminate waste in the engineering and economic sense, short run as well as long run, as compulsory unitization of oil fields quite apparently would do. On the other hand, methods of oil field exploitation designed to extract the maximum amount of oil may well involve excessive opportunity costs — either in terms of resources or of too great a dislocation of time preferences (rate of use over time). And intervention to slow down the rate of use, while it may be economically justifiable in terms of calculations of the social optimum rate of use, requires assumptions or predictions as the basis for such calculation. Needless to say, such predictions and calculations need not be precise, but the following considerations, at the least, would be pertinent: (1) likelihood of further discoveries; (2) importance of the resource to the economy, e.g., iron ore; (3) availability from other areas and at what cost; (4) likely availability of substitutes and likely cost of such substitutes.

It seems to us that as a practical matter the decision to slow down the rate of use can rarely if ever be made on purely economic grounds. The time preferences of consumers cannot really be determined accurately, and in any event, they are probably not independent of the producing and selling patterns of the industry — a change in the level of output, for example, may shift the scale of time preferences. Thus, the "social optimum" rate of use is almost certain to be a political calculation in the sense that someone other than consumers is deciding what is best for them or for the country as a whole. Typically, policy considerations in addition to what consumers, as consumers, would prefer are taken into account.

We do not contend that such other considerations could not properly be called decisive in any given situation, but since the economic justification for intervention in the name of conservation is a cloudy one, we are disposed to caution. "Conservation" is too easily used as a cloak for outright economic protectionism, for restricting competition so that producers can obtain greater than competitive returns. There is no inevitable relationship between conservation of producers' incomes and conservation of scarce resources.

Moreover, assuming that a slowdown in use is deemed appropriate, there are better and worse ways of achieving it. The rate of use can be curtailed either by curtailing demand or by curtailing the offered supply in any one year. Demand might be curtailed generally, by rationing, or specifically, by prohibiting certain uses outright; it might be curtailed indirectly by excise taxation, or, using gasoline as an example, by regulations limiting the horsepower of pleasure automobiles. Similarly, supply might be curtailed directly, by prorationing, or indirectly, by a severance tax. There is no one answer as to the preferred choice among these various means, for different policy considerations, and different conditions, would lead to different choices. We do say that one method — prorationing of supply — is least likely to be desirable economically, largely for practical reasons. Almost certainly, prorationing will be done not on the basis of efficiency considerations but on the basis of giving each producer a share that, while probably leaving him sullen, will not leave him rebellious.

COMMENTS ON SPECIFIC AREAS

The following discussion, necessarily, is more declaratory of our views than of reasons in support of them. While it is an attempt to apply the foregoing analysis to certain present problems, that analysis gave no serious consideration to the kinds of noneconomic policy considerations that might well override economic considerations in any specific instance. In short, the following discussion rests heavily on our own assessment of competing interests. We readily concede that different balances might not unreasonably be struck.

One other general point should be made. Substantial alteration of existing regulatory and exemption patterns would of course materially affect existing interests. Such interests have no "vested" legal rights in whatever benefits the existing patterns afford; nor should the likelihood of damage to such interests be deemed to preclude changes of substantial advantage to the national interest. Nevertheless, we think it appropriate, in those situations where immediate substantial changes would drastically impair values resting on the status quo, to provide for a more gradual transition wherever gradualism is feasible, in order that adversely affected interests may have time to make adjustments in the light of prospective changes in their circumstances.

Railroads and trucking

In the 1930's the rapidly developing trucking industry was able to undercut railroad transportation charges on many items, usually where the margin between railroad charges and costs was particularly wide. High margins were usually found among high-value low-bulk goods, but also occurred among bulky products such as steel and cement on certain hauls. The imposition of regulation on the trucking industry was at least partly motivated by the desire to minimize the truckers' downward impact on price. To the extent that regulation today keeps minimum trucking rates on some goods above the amount that would yield the truckers their full cost plus a normal return, shippers of other goods by rail are in effect being subsidized by those shippers who, absent regulation, could ship more cheaply by truck.

The problem, in short, is that the erosion of rail transport monopoly in shipment of many goods has made a great part of the discriminatory rail pricing system untenable without control of the pricing by competing forms of transportation. Government regulation prevents the normal results of the growth of competition and decline of monopoly, namely, a reshuffling of business among railroads and other movers in accordance with relative efficiencies. The price is paid in inequities and economic waste.

We recognize that the pressures which have given rise to the existing pattern of regulation would not cease to exist if the pattern were drastically revised, and that they may be sufficiently strong that some accommodation would have to be made in other ways. Nevertheless, we agree with those who contend that the present pattern is a highly inefficient way of making an accommodation.

We agree that trucking should be freed of rate regulation to the maximum extent possible, in order that its particular superiorities may be taken full advantage of. The setting of minimum trucking rates has been defended on three principal grounds: (1) that it is necessary to the survival of the railroads; (2) that it is necessary to prevent destructive competition among truckers themselves; and (3) that it is necessary to promote safety standards, which truckers would allegedly sacrifice if pressed too hard by competition in rates. None of these contentions seems convincing. Safety standards can be effectively maintained by direct regulations, backed by sanctions that can be made as severe as necessary to insure compliance. And with possible minor exceptions, the economic conditions for destructive competition simply do not exist in the trucking industry.

As for the impact on the railroads, several comments can be and have been made. First, it seems highly unlikely that the full impact of truck competition would render all or even most railroad hauling unprofitable. It may well make a substantial part of existing railroad facilities and equipment redundant in the sense that the facilities and equipment will not return their investment cost; pending the using up of such capital, the railroad operations may be unprofitable over-all. But after the readjustment period, there would seem to be room for profitable railroad operation with facilities (and overhead) reduced to accord with the reduced volume of traffic. Second, if survival of threatened railroad services is deemed essential — for reasons of national defense or otherwise — direct subsidies of the essential services would be a less costly way of doing it than would the present method of protected inefficiencies. Direct subsidies, moreover, would seem to be more equitable and appropriate — particularly where maintenance of service is deemed to be required by the national interest — than the indirect subsidies paid by particular users who are deprived of the cheap transportation competition would give them.

There may well be hidden costs in the discontinuance of rail service. Cessation of commuter trains, for example, would increase the already appalling traffic problems that plague metropolitan areas. Even increases in fares may divert substantial numbers of commuters to undesirable use of their own cars. In either case a direct subsidy, derived from tax revenues, might well be appropriate. But to repeat — such a subsidy is preferable to a form of regulation that preserves high revenues in parts of the railroad's system by immobilizing the competition which the railroad faces there.

The question of hidden costs suggests a further measure with regard to trucking. It seems quite possible, if not probable, that the taxes paid by trucks for use of the highways do not approach their share of the costs of building and maintaining them, and that they should pay their proper share if their costs are to reflect the true cost of trucking. The difficulty, of course, is in determining what the trucker's share of highway cost should be; some evidence can be obtained as to the respective contribution of trucks and passenger cars to highway wear-and-tear, but allocation of original cost is for the most part arbitrary.

Finally, if trucking were to be freed of rate regulation, what about the railroads? Certainly maximum rate regulation should be kept in effect, as a check on exploitation of transportation markets that the railroads still substantially monopolize. Should railroads be free to lower their prices at will in the face of competition from trucks? It seems to us that some minimum rate regulation would have to be maintained even though not imposed on trucks. The railroads, with a broader scale of operations (in both products and geography), possess a power of price discrimination that truckers, competing among themselves, usually lack. Thus there is a real possibility that the railroads, completely free to reduce prices, might indulge in selective predatory price-cutting in the strict sense, i.e., charging prices below variable costs in order to drive truckers out of business, and then raising prices later. This would be an uneconomic result, and even though potential re-entry of truckers would limit the railroads' power to raise prices unduly, the result would still be an uneconomic use of resources and probably a great deal of instability as well.

Thus, we believe that any proposed reduction of rail freight charges should be subject to suspension on a showing that the proposed new rate would be less than the variable costs of rendering the service. Theoretically, it would be desirable to impose a higher limit; a price that covers only variable costs does not reflect true costs of service. But the practical problems of determining allocable overhead costs in any reasonable time, if ever, seem so insurmountable that no administrable standard other than the one just suggested seems possible. However, the aim could be furthered in two ways: (1) by close regulation of maximum rail charges in the monopolized areas, so as to limit the financial ability of the railroads to set prices in competitive areas that yield very little over variable costs; and (2) by establishing a rule that new low rates cannot subsequently be raised without a showing of increased costs, so that the railroads would not lower their rates unless the rates would be advantageous for the long run. The latter would still leave the railroads free to lower their rates almost to variable costs to make profitable use of existing excess capacity until worn out, but this is the "competitive" result anyway.

Airlines

As with trucking, we are inclined to believe that the regulation of airlines is far more extensive than is now justified. At the outset of regulation, some control over entry may have been necessary in order to administer the airmail subsidy. The original system of competitive bidding open to all broke down in the late '30's, when some lines offered to carry mail free in the hope that they could preempt the routes and make up their losses with future subsidies. Moreover, while the Civil Aeronautics Act contemplated considerable reliance on competition, control over entry was provided for in the obvious belief that unrestricted competition might not assure the sound development of air transportation in the public interest.

Yet there is some reason for concluding that the present regulatory scheme was never actually justified by the desire to promote the development of air transport. As one student has put it:

> The Government, like other purchasers of air transport service, has always stood to gain by the most efficient possible performance of subsidized service, which in turn could only result from the maximum of free competition consistent with the mechanics of subsidization. Moreover, there is little doubt that a support program not involving a virtual guarantee of individual carrier profits could have been developed at any time in the past; that such a program could have been a more effective way of accomplishing any really justifiable policy of promotion; and that one of the main points in its favor would have been the greater scope for competition which it would have permitted. There are many types of promotional program whose administration does not involve any restriction on the competitive activity of the subsidized firms. Among these are tax remission, Government financing of essential research, free or below-cost airways, and other devices whose cost does not increase with the number or capacity of firms participating in the subsidized activity. Some other forms of promotion, such as direct payments to carriers, do necessitate some limitation on the number of firms subsidized at any given

time, but not only do not rule out but require for maximum effectiveness a periodic opportunity for review of commitments to particular firms and possible replacement by others. No promotional program justifies protection of the revenues of subsidized firms from unsubsidized competition.[2]

It certainly cannot be said that the CAB has altogether neglected competition. It has insured that the growth of air travel should be accompanied by a larger number of airlines serving any given route, and the degree of competition in the sale of specific air transport services had undoubtedly increased. Since the most reliable estimates of future air transport demands show continuing great increases, a continuation of this policy would insure more competition. Nevertheless, in eighteen years of administering the Civil Aeronautics Act, the Board has not certified a single new domestic trunk line, and has permitted mergers which substantially reduced the number of "grandfather" carriers. The important innovation of coach service was introduced by nonscheduled carriers in the teeth of bitter opposition by the scheduled airlines and a lukewarm or hostile attitude of the CAB. To be sure, the concern for the grandfather carriers was probably warranted by the legislative history of the Act. Congress was clearly concerned with minimizing the subsidy payments to carriers, and was willing to restrict competition accordingly. But subsidies have practically disappeared, and at least this reason for restricting competition no longer seems present.

The other reasons for continuing control over entry closely parallel those advanced for limiting competition in trucking. They are these: (1) protection of revenues on profitable routes is necessary to recompense for losses on other routes; (2) limitation of entry is necessary to preserve safety standards in air transportation; and (3) service would decline because airlines under the pressure of competition would abandon regular schedules. None of these arguments persuade us. Regarding the third, as the above cited authority has concluded, it appears that competitive pressures in the air transport field work toward rather than away from greater regularity of service because that is what the market demands.[3] As

2. Lucile Sheppard Keyes, "A Reconsideration of Federal Control of Entry into Air Transportation," *Journal of Air Law & Commerce*, vol. 22, no. 2 (1955); reprinted in *Materials Relative to Competition in the Regulated Civil Aviation Industry*, pp. 219, 221 (1956), 84 Cong., 2 sess., Senate Select Committee on Small Business.

3. Keyes in Senate Select Committee on Small Business publication cited above, p. 223.

for the first two reasons, much the same comments can be made as were made above concerning regulation of trucking.

We see no reason why users of air transport service on profitable routes should be compelled to subsidize less profitable or unprofitable routes by being deprived of competitive rates. If air transportation should be made available to all sections of the country, regardless of profitability, the scheme should be subsidized from general revenues, not by particular groups of travelers or shippers.

Nor do we see why limitations on competitive entry are necessary to preserve safety standards. Continued certification can be made dependent on compliance with specific safety regulations. The threat of decertification would seem to be effective enough to induce such compliance.

The present and prospective conditions of air transportation, particularly the prospect of steadily growing demand, indicate to us that reliance on reasonably free competition would not be misplaced. Such a policy may reasonably be expected to lead to more rapid growth and progress than the past regulatory scheme has produced.

Crude oil production

We are not entirely convinced that conservation of crude oil, in the sense of spreading out the rate of use over time, is a clear necessity. At least, we are not convinced that a radical reduction of the rate of use that would exist under unrestricted competitive conditions is required. Oil and oil products are obviously of vital importance to the economy — to motor transportation, to various industries, and to national defense. Yet exhaustion of domestic sources will still take many years; and we apparently have vast reserves of oil-bearing shale and coal from which oil products can be derived at costs that are not prohibitive and that are likely to decline as technology improves.

It may be quite reasonable to take a much more pessimistic view. But even if we did and a clear case for conservation was made out, it seems clear that the present program is an inadequate and highly inefficient way of going about it. The actual workings of the prorationing program make it at least doubtful that conservation is indeed the principal goal. State prorationing quotas are apparently determined on the basis of running estimates of demand for oil products at going prices; price-maintenance rather than any independent calculation of appropriate rates of use seems to be the principal aim. Of course, restrictions on output, though based on the aim of price maintenance, at the same time do conserve oil in the sense that rate of use is slowed down, but there is no evidence whatsoever that the rate of use achieved by these restrictions is an appropriate one or that an appropriate rate is even sought.

Moreover, if conservation were indeed the goal of state and national oil policy, there are some obvious steps that would have been taken but have not. Compulsory unitization of oil fields to eliminate wastes in drilling and loss of oil and gas is long overdue. Imports of crude oil and oil products would be encouraged rather than discouraged, particularly when imports could come in at considerably less than the going domestic prices. Needless to say, free importation would seriously undercut if not demolish the price maintenance features of prorationing, but this by no means compels the conclusion — if conservation is truly the goal — that importation should be sacrificed and price maintenance saved.

It is claimed that price maintenance, by increasing the profitability of crude oil operations, serves the interests of conservation in two ways: (1) high prices encourage maximum extraction from declining fields, and (2) high prices stimulate greater expenditures in exploration for new sources of supply. We suppose that this is true. Nevertheless, there are other ways, besides price maintenance, of stimulating maximum recovery from existing fields and the discovery of new ones. Owners of high-cost fields could be subsidized — directly by payment or indirectly by tax concessions — or the fields could be taken over and managed by the government. Direct subsidies could also be used to stimulate exploration (if, indeed, depletion allowances are not enough — or too much). These devices seem superior to price maintenance, from an economic standpoint, even without reference to the high desirability of imports; with such reference, there seems to us to be little question. With latent domestic production kept high, for the purposes of national defense, there is everything to gain and nothing to lose from relying on low-cost foreign sources to as great an extent, and for as long a time, as possible.

To the extent that a price rise, or price maintenance, would be effective, we believe that the imposition of high severance taxes (perhaps graduated to insure continued extraction, and avoidance of loss, in high-cost fields) would be a more satisfactory device, both economically and administratively. We recognize that the pressures now put on the rationing authorities would be transferred to the legislatures in the drafting of tax legislation; and that the allocative patterns of production might well not be substantially different from what they are now. But there would in any event be more room for competitive pressures than exist under a prorationing program.

Actually, however, if use is to be curbed, any program directed at increasing the price of crude oil seems likely to be inadequate. Ultimate increases in the price of refined products are likely to be greatest on those uses for which there are no present substitutes, and where, for this reason, the cut-back in use is not likely to be large. Moreover, from the standpoint of conservation policy, it would seem wiser to curb the uses for which substitutes are available, not those for which petroleum products are unique. There may be exceptions — it is questionable, for example, whether much would be lost in reducing the consumption of gasoline by limiting the horsepower of passenger cars. But generally speaking, direct prohibition or curtailments of specific uses would seem to be the most appropriate way of slowing down the rate of exhaustion of crude oil reserves. There is no doubt that sudden institution of direct controls would be painful — the costs to the individual business or consumer of converting over to other fuels may be heavy. To minimize these losses to committed interests, the policy might be gradually imposed, e.g., by allowing time for the using up of existing oil-burning equipment.

These alternative measures, of course, constitute interference with competition. We conclude, however, that they would either involve less costly interference with competition, or more efficiently carry out a policy of conservation, or both, than does the existing system of regulation.

Organized labor[4]

We start with the premise that protection of collective bargaining, in the general sense, is a well-entrenched and justifiable feature of public policy. Even though the conditions that once warranted the active promotion of labor organization may have substantially

4. This section draws heavily on Mason, "Labor Monopoly and All That," in *Economic Concentration and the Monopoly Problem* (1957), pp. 196–220; and Cox, "Labor and the Antitrust Laws — A Preliminary Analysis," *Univ. of Pennsylvania Law Review* (1955), 104:252.

changed in most areas and most industries in the country, collective bargaining still serves important values that cannot easily be served in other ways. Employers may in fact be totally unable to exploit their employees: the employers may sell in intensely competitive markets, and their employees may have many alternative sources of work, so that wages are in fact determined by the impersonal forces of the market. Yet this is not universally true, to say the least, and even if it were, the employer might still appear to be determining his employees' wages unilaterally, and the employees would believe they were victimized by inequality of bargaining power. Union organization and collective bargaining produce a feeling of security that would be real and important even though the economic benefits actually derived were of little or no consequence.

Moreover, collective bargaining can contribute substantially to the goals usually identified with competition. Producers are frequently ignorant of the full range of cost-reducing methods that are available to them. Upward pressure on wage rates may goad employers into finding more efficient ways of running their business. Union pressure and the pressure of competitors need be no different in this respect.

Yet a "conflict of some magnitude between the values of collective bargaining and the values of competition seems inescapable."[5] Labor unions are obviously monopolists with varying degrees of monopoly power. There are intrinsic limitations, again of varying force, that may limit their ability to exploit the power as fully as a rational monopolist would. Ordinarily, for example, a union cannot drive the wage rate to a point that would maximize the total wage bill because substantial unemployment of its members would be the result; and devotion to the principle of "equal pay for equal work" precludes any extensive wage discrimination. Nevertheless, the use of union power in the self-interest of members may damage the legitimate interests of other groups in the economy in much the same way as does the use of monopoly power for the self-interest of business firms. Continuous pressure for wage increases in a situation of full employment may contribute heavily to inflation and require extensive monetary and fiscal countermeasures or even wage-price controls. Setting this problem aside, which we do on the hopeful excuse that it is beyond our present subject,

5. Mason, p. 209.

it is clear that restrictive union activity, whether or not agreement with employers is involved, may directly harm other industries in particular and consumers in general.

In the attempt to resolve competing policy considerations in the area of clash, some practices can probably be found which all but the strongest partisans would agree should be condemned, and some which should clearly be permitted. Some practices may seriously damage the competitive process without adding much to a union's ability to obtain its ends; others may do little damage to competition (in addition to the "damage" inherent in collective sale of labor services) and yet materially contribute to union welfare. Yet many practices of substantial consequence do not fall in these happy categories. A practice that seriously alters competitive results will often be one that would measurably improve the position of the union and union members indulging in it. Here, limitations on union activities will be limitations on the economic benefits that organized workers can secure. In other words, the usual goals of unionization and collective bargaining — higher wages, lower hours, better working conditions, and greater job security — are acceptable goals only in an abstract sense. Unless labor activities are to be completely untrammeled — unless the policy of protecting collective labor effort will always override the policy of protecting competitive processes and goals — these goals cannot be used as a test of what is permissible and what is not. The decision to prohibit or limit a particular practice is a decision that economic benefits, though promoted by the practice, cannot be obtained in that way.

This also highlights a difficulty that afflicts antitrust policy generally, that of differentiating between the good and the bad in a way that is both clear and effective. A test couched in terms of ends is unsatisfactory in this light, as we have just indicated — a particular practice may raise wages and seriously interfere with competition at the same time. For much the same reason, "intent" is likely to prove unserviceable, as the obvious consequences of a particular kind of activity are "intended" at least in the legal objective sense, and hence intent is multiple. Nor do we think that "primary intent" resolves the difficulty, since the primary intent of restrictive practices may well be to gain economic benefits and yet the adverse impact on competition may be too serious to warrant their being permitted.

Finally, we see no ready general formula that is likely to provide a suitable differentiation between acceptable and nonacceptable restraints, regardless of the conditions in which they are used. The guiding principle of "restraints on commercial competition" sketched out in the *Apex Hosiery* case was never amplified because of *Hutcheson*.[6] There are those who recommend that it be restored and given a chance for case-by-case development. The position is not an untenable one, particularly if enforcement were confined solely to civil injunctive suits by the government, but it at least requires the assumption that labor needs no more assistance in its efforts to organize nonunionized firms or industries than that provided by the prohibitions against employer interferences. Even *Apex*, for example, did not overturn the earlier antitrust decisions that had outlawed "secondary" boycotts of products produced by nonunion labor; these were deemed to be "restraints on commercial competition." Organizational strikes at nonunionized factories were saved, but certainly in the past this was a weapon that often proved inadequate, and the more potent boycott was perhaps the only effective organizing device left. We might concede that even without *Hutcheson*, enlightened interpretation of the "commercial restraint" test would have led to reversal of the earlier cases, on the ground that the restraint of product competition resulting from a boycott was merely an incidental or indirect consequence of the legitimate purpose of "eliminating that part of such competition which is based on differences in labor standards." But there are other complexities that make it difficult if not impossible to separate the product from the labor market, and make it difficult if not impossible to proscribe certain restraints that affect both markets without making explicit or implicit policy decisions for which the general test provides no guide. Boycotts of new products, such as prefabricated items in the construction industry, and resistance to the introduction of labor-saving machinery are obvious examples.

We believe that despite the difficulties of drafting clear and effective rules in this area, the policy decisions should be made by Congress in as detailed a way as is feasible, and that the role of the courts should be correspondingly minimized. We would start with the position of *Hutcheson* case, as modified by *Allen Bradley*,[7]

6. Apex Hosiery Co. v. Leader, 310 U.S. 469 (1940); U.S. v. Hutcheson, 312 U.S. 219 (1941).
7. Allen Bradley Co. v. Local Union 3, IBEW, 325 U.S. 797 (1945).

that collective labor activities for the purpose of raising wages, shortening hours, gaining more work, etc., are immune from the antitrust laws unless joined with collective business action to fix prices, limit output, boycott competing products, and the like. We would then proscribe by legislation those activities which on balance are thought to have too great an economic or social cost. It seems clear that such individual legislative policy decisions will need to be re-evaluated as conditions change, and that they will depend heavily on the effectiveness of other statutory policies designed to protect legitimate labor interests in other ways. Restraints once protected in order to promote the growth of unionization and collective bargaining may no longer be worthy of exemption because the harm is still substantial and the contribution to labor now less necessary. Similarly, restraints designed to protect against loss of jobs are rendered less necessary by steps to maintain a full employment economy and to relocate workers in new jobs.

For lack of competence in this complex area, we offer no specific recommendations. But we are generally inclined to believe that the current strength of organized labor, the widespread recognition of organizing and collective bargaining rights, the growth of unemployment compensation, and the near certainty that no political party will again permit extensive unemployment to continue for long, all justify a sterner approach to restrictive labor practices than once might have been appropriate. This is not to say necessarily, however, that the current limitations on union activity, as incorporated in the Taft-Hartley Act, do not go far enough, though we would be inclined to strengthen the prohibition of secondary boycotts. Nor do we believe, with respect to the principal issues of this antitrust study, that union restrictions on competition are of such serious moment that the significance of a strengthened antitrust program against business restraints is substantially undermined.

Resale price maintenance

We agree with the majority of the Attorney General's Committee to Study the Antitrust Laws that the Miller-Tydings and McGuire Acts should be repealed, substantially for the reasons set forth in the Committee's report, and for other economic and policy reasons that have been too well and often set forth to be repeated here.

Granted that complete removal of resale price maintenance, which has already been shredded by adverse court decisions in many states, would mean some reduction in the opportunities for profitable small business operations, we simply take the view that such a loss is not comparable to the gains to the economy and consumers generally from free competition in distribution.

One further comment: strengthened antitrust programs along the lines we have suggested would create additional business opportunities which monopolistic elements now foreclose. These opportunities, by and large, would lie in areas other than those now populated by small distribution units, and their utilization would call on different talents. But it may fairly be said that we need have less concern for the opportunities now sheltered by resale price maintenance if other entrepreneurial opportunities are increased.

VII

Other Public Policies and the Structure and Functioning of Markets

Direct regulation and the enforcement of the antitrust laws are not the only ways in which government affects the structure and functioning of markets. Other public policies, the impact of government as a purchaser (or sometimes as a seller) on markets in which it appears, and taxation, all have consequences which are or may be important for the way markets operate. In this chapter we shall examine in summary fashion the most important of these activities, their effects as they currently operate, and possible changes which might lead to more desirable results from the viewpoint of the goals of procompetitive policy. Any consideration of possible changes must, of course, recognize that the policies in question are primarily directed to other goals, and therefore that policy change may not be possible without a different resolution of conflicts among competing policy goals. We restrict our examination to the activities of the federal government, chiefly for reasons of space.[1] As a consequence we ignore the effect of a good deal of state and local activity in licensing, zoning, health, and the like, which often severely restricts entry into certain trades, and sometimes results in price-fixing as well. These effects occur chiefly in local market trades, especially

1. The restriction has some other justifications. The federal government is, of course, far more important than all other governmental units in the reach of its policies. As an economic unit, it outweighs the combined total of all other government units about 2 to 1: total federal expenditures were $71.4 billion in 1956, out of total expenditures of $103.6 billion. (See Economic Report of the President, January 1957, table E-49.) A larger proportion of federal expenditures were transfers than is the case with other government units: in 1956 total government expenditures on goods and services (purchased from the business sector or abroad, plus wages and salaries of government employees) were $79.9 billion, of which the federal share was $47.0 billion. These figures are fairly representative of the recent situation.

services, distribution, and construction.[2] Among all the activities of the federal government, we have selected four for examination: taxation; procurement, especially defense procurement; direct aids to small business; and tariffs and commercial policy. These appear to be the types of federal activity which have the most substantial actual or potential effects on competition; and even they must necessarily be treated in a superficial fashion. Other activities which might be of some significance, but are nonetheless ignored here, include the regulation of conditions of labor and minimum wages generally, and in firms performing under government contracts; the disposition of patent rights and know-how accruing to the government through its research activities; and controls on the plane of competition, such as the food and drug regulation, the Federal Trade Commission's oversight of advertising, or the Securities and Exchange Commission's control of exchanges, brokers, and security issues.

TAXATION

High levels of personal and corporate income taxes over the last fifteen years and the continued force of estate and inheritance taxes have contributed substantially to the great change in the structure of the capital markets which has taken place since the twenties.[3] The redistribution of disposable income, accomplished largely by taxation, has reduced the relative importance of the large private saver who tends to invest directly in business, and has increased the importance of the small saver who uses financial intermediaries. Insurance companies and pension funds, particu-

2. For discussion of some of these restrictions, see W. F. Brown and R. Cassady, Jr., "Guild Pricing in the Service Trades," *Quarterly Journal of Economics* (February 1947), 61:311. The spring 1941 issue of *Law and Contemporary Problems* (Vol. 8) was devoted to "Government Marketing Barriers"; the most directly relevant of the papers was that of Silverman, Bennett, and Lechliter on "Control by Licensing over Entry into the Market." See also the monumental *Marketing Laws Survey*, published by the Works Progress Administration. Its ten volumes, appearing from 1940 to 1943, comprise examination of *State Antitrust Laws* (1940, with a supplement, 1942), *State Price Control Legislation* (1940, with two supplements, 1942), *State Milk and Dairy Legislation* (1941), *State Liquor Legislation* (1941), *Interstate Trade Barriers* (1942), *State Occupational Legislation* (1942), and *State Taxation Legislation and Methods* (3 vols., 1943). This work surveys laws and court decisions, but does not attempt to study their economic effects.

3. See "Trends and Structural Changes in Savings in the Twentieth Century," by R. W. Goldsmith, in *Savings in the Modern Economy*, ed. Heller, Boddy, and Nelson (Minn., 1953); "The Changing Importance of Institutional Investors in the American Market," *Law and Contemporary Problems* (Winter 1952); *Direct Placement of Corporate Securities*, by E. R. Corey (Boston, 1951).

larly, have grown rapidly in importance. In general, institutional investors favor debt rather than equity, and the obligations and securities of established, successful enterprises. The high proportion of self-finance through retained earnings in the corporate universe reinforces the advantages of established and large firms as against new and small ones. These changes have tended to increase the relative advantage which old and large firms always have had over new and small ones in access to capital and in the terms on which it is available. The significance of this for the ability of established firms to maintain their position is clear.

There have been some effects of the tax structure operating in the opposite direction. The difference between the capital-gains tax and the marginal rate of personal income tax on high incomes has stimulated a flow of funds into risky investments by investors seeking appreciation rather than dividends.[4] But much of this has been directed to a few industries, especially those in which there were special tax incentives, such as oil and gas; and on balance, the general effects of taxation on the capital markets have been unfavorable to the new and growing firm.

Over and above these very broad — and substantially irreversible — contributions which taxation has made to changing the structure of capital markets, taxes have had more specific and direct effects on market structure. First among these is the unfavorable effect exercised by the present corporate income tax on the survival and growth of new businesses.[5] The high individual income tax rates limit the ability of individuals to accumulate enough money to start a business, and to finance it through its initial unprofitable period when, in the nature of things, institutional or public financing is almost totally unavailable. The impact of corporate income tax becomes important once the firm has passed the stage of initial establishment and reaches the stage of growth. First, the corporate tax reduces the ability of small firms to grow relatively to larger ones. Smaller firms are more dependent on retained earnings for financing growth than are larger ones, and characteristically have retained a much higher proportion of earnings in relation to net

4. See J. K. Butters, L. Thompson, and L. Bollinger, *Effects of Taxation on Investments by Individual* (Boston, 1953).

5. The discussion here draws on the excellent work of J. V. Lintner and J. K. Butters. See *The Effect of Federal Taxes on Growing Enterprises* (Boston, 1945) and "Effects of Taxes on Concentration" in *Business Concentration and Price Policy*, a National Bureau of Economic Research Conference (Princeton, 1955).

worth. Thus a given (high) flat rate tax on corporate income reduces the growth potential of the smaller firms more in comparison to what it would be without the tax (or with a lower tax rate) than it does that of the larger firms. Further, a flat rate corporate tax diminishes the incentive to expand more for the small new firm than for the large established one. This is so for two kinds of reasons. Any particular investment project is likely to be small in size relative to the total activities of the firm in the large established firm; this is not the case for the new and rapidly growing enterprise. For the large firm, the anticipated tax on prospective gains is balanced by the possibility of offsetting losses from an unsuccessful investment against income from other operations, and so reducing taxes proportionately. The small newcomer, however, may not have enough other income fully to offset the losses should a major investment project fail to pay off; thus the calculus of prospective gains and losses after taxes would be less favorable than for the larger firm, given an investment project of intrinsically equal riskiness. Further, the importance of financial stringency in limiting the operations of the small firm is great; the cash drain of high taxes may in itself be an important cause which reduces the prospects of success of a new investment venture, should its course depart from what has been planned, as it so frequently does. Thus high progressive personal income taxes and high corporate income taxes inhibit the entry and rapid growth of new firms, without which existing large firms tend to continue and increase their dominant positions.

Further, the present structure of taxation operates to promote mergers, and so adds another impulse toward greater concentration. The impact of the estate tax on the one hand, and the large difference between capital gains and higher-bracket income tax rates on the other, are stimuli, frequently mutually reinforcing, to the owners of medium-sized, closely-held businesses to sell out.[6] The rationale is simple: the heirs of owners of a closely held corporation with little or no market for its stock often find selling out the whole business the best way of meeting the demands of the estate tax, as well as of serving other purposes, such as, for example, management succession which has not been provided for.

6. See J. K. Butters, J. V. Lintner, and W. L. Cary, *Effects of Taxation on Corporate Mergers* (Boston, 1950), and the paper by Butters and Lintner cited in footnote 5.

Anticipation of the problem may operate on owners during their lifetimes; so does the advantage of building up the enterprise by reinvesting earnings (rather than paying out dividends), selling it, and then paying capital gains rates on the proceeds rather than individual income tax rates on the dividends. In all these situations, the best customers are usually large, well-established concerns in the same or related fields, with publicly traded stocks which are acceptable as payment to the owners of the acquired businesses. These tax forces operate most strongly in the domain of medium-sized closely-held enterprises, with assets of $5 to $25 million. It has been estimated that taxes were of major importance as a motive for mergers in about one fourth the mergers reported in the financial manuals from 1940 to 1947 involving selling companies with assets over $1 million, and such transactions involved one third the assets of all companies in this group.[7]

A narrower aspect of the tax laws which is conducive to mergers in special situations is the availability of previous operating losses of the acquired corporation as an offset to the taxable income of the acquiring corporation. Such carry-overs of loss are available when the stockholders of the acquired corporation come out of the merger transaction with at least 20 percent of the stock of the acquiring corporation. Under these circumstances, of course, the acquisition may be to a substantial extent self-financing. There is some indication that this particular tax motive has been important in the recent mergers in textiles.[8]

It is hardly necessary to argue the significance for competition of forces making for a higher rate of merger, particularly because the greatest effect of taxation falls on enterprises in the size range within which firms already may be significant competitors in national markets, or are growing toward that position.

7. See Lintner and Butters, pp. 272–273. Related to the total of all reported mergers in the period, the ones in which taxes were a primary stimulus amounted to one tenth the total number, and included one fourth the total assets transferred. By size of selling company the figures were as follows:

Asset size (millions of dollars)	Percent of number of mergers in which taxes were of primary importance
Less than 1	Negligible
1–5	20+
5–15	25–33
15–50	40+

8. See *New England Textiles and the New England Economy,* a report to the Conference of New England Governors, by S. E. Harris (1956), pp. 165–167.

One particular excise tax — that on cigarettes — is worth mention in this discussion.[9] The federal excise tax on cigarettes, paid by the manufacturer, is a flat rate per 1000.[10] The flat-rate tax falls more heavily on cheaper brands of cigarettes, and so discourages price competition by narrowing the possible spread in price among brands of different qualities. Most students of the cigarette market have concluded that the substitution of an ad valorem tax for the present flat-rate one would make possible more market competition, by either encouraging the expansion of output of cheaper brands now produced, or forcing producers of major brands to cut their prices.

It is relatively easy to point out problems in the competitive realm created by the tax structure. But in general, proposals for change run into major conflicting policy objectives, including revenue needs and current ideas of equity, and it is difficult to do more than suggest broadly what might be helpful in diminishing the unfavorable repercussions of taxation on competition, without trying to examine in detail how likely it is that these changes will be feasible in the short run. Narrow changes such as that in the cigarette excise tax suggested above, or abolition of the right to transfer loss carry-over privileges through merger, do not involve any grand conflicts of policy; although, to be sure, their present beneficiaries can be counted on to oppose them. But any changes of wide-reaching effect would involve the levels and structure of corporate income, personal income, and capital gains tax, and thus raise the widest issues of fiscal policy.

As long as revenue needs dictate high levels of personal and corporate income tax, the inhibiting effects on the growth of new and small businesses will continue. Some alleviation might be achieved by revising the graduation of the corporate income tax. At present, the first $25,000 of income is taxed at 30 percent, and additional income at 52 percent. The very high concentration of corporate incomes allows scope for reduction of rates on smaller incomes, compensated for by smaller increases in rates on larger ones.[11] A

9. See *Taxation and Business Concentration*, a symposium sponsored by the Tax Institute, 1952, Chapter III, "The Tobacco Industry," by H. M. Robertson; *Price Policies in the Cigarette Industry*, by W. H. Nicholls (1951) pp. 418–423; and *The American Cigarette Industry*, by R. B. Tennant (1950), pp. 382–384.

10. In 1958 the tax was $4.00 per 1000, which was equivalent to 34 percent of the wholesale price for "standard" brands.

11. For example, the 1952 *Statistics of Income*, part 2, showed that the 508 corporate taxpayers with over $10 million net income accounted for about 49 percent

proposal to modify the corporate income tax was submitted to the 85th Congress; the rates on corporate incomes below $100 thousand were graduated from 5 percent for the first $5 thousand of income to 45 percent for the $25 to $100 thousand bracket.[12] The trouble with this proposal is that it concentrates its relief on the very small corporations, roughly those with less than $1 million total assets. This may be helpful to small business as such, but will not reach those businesses which are important as actual and potential competitors of dominant firms in national markets. To have its maximum effect on market competition in major national markets, modification of the tax must extend its benefits to what might be called medium-sized corporations, up to the $50 million total assets size range, or, very roughly, about $5 million income. The difficulties of any such change are clear. The proposal would not benefit from the political support of "small business" and its advocates. It would be a crude measure in industrial terms: the "small" steel firm would be taxed at a higher rate than the "giant" printing establishment or furniture manufacturer. Assets are a far better measure of size than income, but the administrative and legal difficulties of graduating taxes on an asset rather than on an income basis would be great. To some extent, this difficulty could be cured by averaging income; indeed, without some fairly long averaging arrangement, graduation of the tax would bear heavily on firms with fluctuating incomes. With the present rates of corporate taxation, increases of any perceptible magnitude in any brackets seem unlikely; only if a reduction of the average level of corporate taxes is possible is it at all likely that any substantial graduation — say, one producing 15 to 20 percentage points of difference in the tax rate for the $5 million (average) income as against the $100 million (average) income — will be possible. Yet with all these defects, and perhaps

of total taxes paid, and the 854 with over $100 million total assets for over 47 percent. In that year there were some 440 thousand reporting corporations.

12. S. 352, 85 Cong., 1 sess. The complete proposal was:

Income bracket (thousands of dollars)	Tax rate (percent)
First 5	5
5–10	10
10–15	15
15–20	25
20–25	35
25–100	45

Incomes over $100 thousand would be taxed at 55 percent.

many more not mentioned, such a change in the taxation of corporate income would be a powerful force operating against the dominance of large, established sellers in many markets. Whether the urgency assigned to this goal is such as to justify so crude an instrument is another question.

In the area of mergers, the chief problems arise from the rate of graduation of the upper brackets of the personal income tax, and the differential between personal income and capital gains tax rates. A substantial narrowing of that differential would reduce the problem; it may be expected only to the extent that it is likely on other grounds than concern with the effects touched on above.[13]

GOVERNMENT PROCUREMENT

The federal government is our largest single economic unit: its total purchases of goods and services run currently to about $47 or $48 billion, or some 11 percent of the gross national product. Of this total, a little less than half constitutes the compensation of government employees, nearly 40 percent constitutes government purchases from domestic business, and the rest is spent abroad.[14] The way in which the $15 or $16 billion of expenditures directed to the domestic business sector is made can constitute a major influence on many markets. In recent years, nearly 90 percent of federal expenditures have been on national security — defense, atomic energy, foreign aid, and the like. If the same proportions of defense and nondefense expenditures on goods and services goes for purchases to domestic business, this would mean about $1 to $1.5 billion of civilian procurement, and $14 to $15 billion of military procurement.[15] The problems of the two are quite different, and therefore are discussed separately.

13. Recent discussion of equity and efficiency in taxation has raised both these issues, and has suggested changes in the direction of narrowing the differential. See, for example, the papers in Sections VI and VIII of *Federal Tax Policy for Economic Growth and Stability*, papers submitted to the Subcommittee on Tax Policy of the Joint Committee on the Economic Report, 84 Cong., 1 sess., November 1955.

14. The totals are from the Economic Report of the President, January 1957 and January 1956, Table D-1. The breakdown into categories of expenditure is that for 1950; see 1951 National Income Supplement, Department of Commerce, appendix table 9. These figures exclude transfer payments and reflect only the real resource use of the federal government.

15. No precise summary figures are available on this point. Fabricant, in *Trend of Government Activity since 1900* (1952) estimated that in 1939, 48 percent of the military and 52 percent of the nonmilitary expenditures were purchases rather than payments of wages and salaries (table 16). Applying a 50–50 breakdown to the totals for 1956, and distributing the purchases among domestic business and pur-

The bulk of civilian procurement, including the procurement of civilian-type goods such as food and some kinds of clothing, is carried on under procedures designed to maximize the government's utility per dollar spent.[16] Where possible, public advertising of invitations to bid and sealed competitive bids are used. Where possible, specifications are developed for complex products on the basis of extensive research and testing, and the utility of various commercially offered varieties is compared. The government thus appears in markets as an informed buyer, seeking by all the means at its command to foster price competition and reap the benefits in low prices. Where market conditions make it possible for such operations to succeed, they have in fact been highly successful in lowering costs to the government; this is true both in markets for relatively standardized products and in those in which the government has created its own specifications. On the other hand, in buying in such markets as those for electric lamps, where little competition exists, government purchasing, by itself, is not able to create it.

At present, the government does something to make available to other buyers some of the advantages created by its own activities. Bids on sealed-bid contracts are published, and this information is useful both to other buyers and to rival sellers. More might be done, at some additional cost, in making available generally the information resulting from federal testing and from the development of federal specifications.

Military procurement characteristically entails features which make inappropriate or impossible the methods of purchasing used by civilian agencies of the government. The services constitute all or most of the market for many important items of military equipment, and nothing or little that is similar is produced for the ordinary market; this is true, for example, of aircraft, missiles and of electronic equipment. Market prices independent of government purchases of such items cannot exist. Further, equipment of this type often must be bought in large orders and typically involves complex design and engineering problems, and frequently more fundamental scientific ones as well, in addition to the difficulties of

---

chases from abroad according to the 1950 breakdown, gives the estimates presented.

These figures may be compared with Reck's estimate of $865 million of purchases of goods (not including construction) by federal civilian agencies in 1951, when total federal purchases of goods and services were $41 billion. See D. Reck, *Government Purchasing and Competition* (Los Angeles, 1954), p. 7.

16. This discussion draws on Reck, *Government Purchasing and Competition*.

large-scale production of novel, complicated items. For these reasons, the characteristic method of contracting is selection of the suppliers as well as negotiation, usually with frequent modification and renegotiation of the terms of the contract.[17] These same reasons limit the number of possible suppliers; the importance to the services of the expectation of good performance further narrows the number. So does the natural desire of procurement officials to simplify their own tasks, both by dealing with familiar suppliers and so reducing the subjective as well as the objective risks, and by dealing with as few suppliers as possible and reducing the tasks of negotiation and supervision.

Thus a large part of military procurement tends to be concentrated in a relatively small number of suppliers. This gives rise to two kinds of problems: first, its effects on the character and results of the bargaining process in military procurement; second, its effects on the relative position of the favored suppliers in ordinary markets. While the first of these may well be more important, it is only the second which is relevant to the present discussion. Any benefits to their ordinary business which suppliers derive from their military contracts must in general be in the nature of shared overheads, which are not fully traced out by the cost accounting mechanism. Some of these may arise from the supplier's ability to use his facilities more fully and schedule production better simply because of a large, continuing military commitment. Others may be connected with the financial insurance element present in the foreseeable inflows of cash consequent on the contracts, if these are more certain and regular than those arising from ordinary sales. Probably the most important benefits, and the most difficult to allow for in the negotiating and pricing process, are those connected with the gain in research experience, technical knowledge, labor-force and managerial training in areas in which military applications lead a rapidly advancing technology. These gains can provide the small group of contractors with what becomes a continuing lead in technology over rivals and would-be rivals. The atomic energy industry may well provide an example of this type of effect.[18]

17. See J. P. Miller, *The Pricing of Military Procurements* (1949).

18. Originally, the atomic energy program was operated by a very small number of contractors, including General Electric, Du Pont, and Union Carbon and Carbide. The very stringent secrecy rules kept information restricted to the firms which were actually operating. R. Tybout, in "Public Investment in Atomic Power Development," *Law and Contemporary Problems* (Winter 1956), indicates that the prime contrac-

The possibility of concentrated defense procurement having undesirable repercussions in regular markets is clear; an assessment of the extent to which such effects have actually occurred is more difficult. In the first place, factual material that would permit an examination of the allocation of defense contracts by industries, to determine the extent to which output of military goods is more or less concentrated than output of civilian goods produced by the same industry, is not available in appropriate form or with comprehensive coverage. Yet such a determination is basic to any assessment of the net impact of procurement on market structure and functioning. Some pieces of information are available, however, and an examination of them follows.

The Defense Department published a list of the 100 largest prime contractors measured by aggregate contracts over the period July 1950–June 1956.[19] These figures show only prime contracts, not subcontracts, and they are classified by company, lumping together all the contracts of any company, whatever industry or product is involved. The 100 largest contractors received 63 percent of total military contracts let during the period; the largest contractor, General Motors Corporation, received 5 percent; the ten largest — General Motors, General Electric, American Telephone and Telegraph, and seven aircraft producers — 31.5 percent. These figures show an absolutely large concentration of military purchases. A crude measure of whether that concentration is large relative to the general level prevailing in comparable sectors of the economy is given by comparison of the sales of the 10 and 100 largest indus-

---

tors in the period 1952–1955 included five chemical firms, of which four were among the eight largest; and six electrical equipment manufacturers, of which five were among the eight largest. More recently, the atomic power development program and changes in the rules governing access to information have broadened the group of firms with opportunity to acquire knowledge in the field, though it is still small. In 1955, firms with access agreement included the other large chemical firms and 10 to 15 smaller ones, and 10 to 15 smaller electrical equipment manufacturers, as well as 18 study groups, each including electrical utilities and heavy equipment or chemical firms, concerned with atomic power generation. It is still the case that the Commission must grant "access" to the still largely classified technology. When the power program started in May 1951, only four study groups were given access on the grounds that this number exhausted AEC staff facilities. See Northrop, "The Changing Role of the AEC in Atomic Power Development," in *Law and Contemporary Problems* (Winter 1956).

19. *100 Companies and Affiliates Listed According to Net Values of Military Prime Contract Awards,* Office of Assistant Secretary of Defense (Supply and Logistics), 10 April 1957.

trial corporations in 1956 with total manufacturing sales in 1956; the ratios are 13 percent and 35 percent, respectively; for the single large corporation — General Motors — the ratio is 3 percent.[20] But these figures of relative concentration reflect, among other things, the industrial distribution of procurement, and the heavy role of aircraft and equipment, electronics, and other products of concentrated, large-firm industries. For example, more than 40 percent of the total of contracts held by the 100 largest contractors, 26 percent of all military contracts, fell to the 19 aircraft companies on the list. For these, of course, defense was their major or their only business.

In general, the rank order of the companies in the defense contract list was much higher than their rank in the list of the 500 largest industrials. This suggests that the distribution of contracts was not such as to increase concentration.[21]

The second piece of evidence available bears more directly on the question of the effect of military procurement on markets but is less comprehensive. In order to stimulate investment in facilities directly or indirectly useful to military production, the privilege of accelerated amortization for tax purposes has been granted for new facilities certified by the Office of Defense Mobilization. From November 1950, when the program began, to January 1953, certificates covering new investment aggregating $29 billion were issued. An analysis of the effect of this program on industrial concentration was made by R. T. Selden,[22] which indicated that the

20. See *The FORTUNE Directory of the 500 Largest U.S. Industrial Corporations*, a supplementary to *Fortune*, June 1957, and *Survey of Current Business*, February 1957. All the 100 largest industrials were primarily manufacturing companies; at least 7 of the 100 largest defense contractors were not — they included Massachusetts Institute of Technology, several construction companies, and at least one foreign corporation. Thus the base of the relevant comparison should be some larger figure than manufacturing sales, although precisely what is unclear.

21. Thus 18 of the 19 aircraft companies on the list were also on the *Fortune* list; their average rank among defense contractors was 26; among the 500 largest, 250 (as measured by 1956 total assets, selected as a more stable measure of size than a single year's sales).

Of the other 81 companies on the defense list, 74 were identifiable on *Fortune*'s. The average rank of these was 55 on the defense list, and 162 by 1956 total assets on *Fortune*'s. By 1948 total assets, it was 260, thus indicating defense contracts had changed their relative size. The first 37 companies contained 23 with a higher defense rank (33) than general rank (139) and 14 reversed, 32 against 20. The second 37 showed the same division: 23 with an average defense rank of 76 and an average general rank of 338; 14 with an average defense rank of 80 and an average general rank of 42.

22. "Accelerated Amortization and Industrial Concentration," *The Review of Economics and Statistics* (August 1955).

distribution of certificates tended in general to decrease rather than to increase concentration, in the 237 manufacturing industries examined.[23] Selden concludes that the results of the program — an impulse toward deconcentration — were less the result of the deliberate policy of aiding small business or promoting competition, and, in its administration, more the consequences of decisions taken on quite other grounds; this is true especially of the decision of the Secretary of Defense at the outbreak of the Korean War to build a "broad defense base." An effective policy of using certificates to promote deconcentration might have produced an even

23. The share of amortization certificates received by the four largest firms in each of the 237 industries was compared with the share of 1947 output of the same firms. Where the first proportion exceeded the second by more than 10 percentage points (or more than half the difference between zero and the concentration ratio, or the concentration ratio and 100, where the ratio was less than 20 or more than 80), the industry was classified as one in which amortization tended to increase concentration (I); where the difference was in the opposite direction and similarly large, the industry was classified as one in which amortization tended to decrease concentration (D); where it was in either direction, but of smaller size, the industry was classified as unaffected (U). Because of lack of data, not all of the 237 industries could be studied: 53 (four digit SIC) industries, which got 5.6 percent of the total of $14.6 billion certified in manufacturing, had to be excluded. The results for the others (based on 184 industries) were:

Category	Percent of certified	Amortization allowed
I	5.3	4.6
U	38.4	38.1
D	56.3	57.3
Sum	100	100

(The difference between "certified" and "allowed" reflects the fact that accelerated amortization was not given to 100 percent of the cost of all certified facilities, but for varying proportions, averaging about 61 percent for the whole program.)

Among the industries which experienced a significant deconcentration effect were steel, primary copper, primary aluminum, motor vehicles and parts, aircraft, aircraft engines and parts, and heavy electrical equipment. Of the 16 industries receiving $10 million or more in certificates that experienced a significant concentration (I) effect, 4 were already highly concentrated: flat glass, tin cans, tractors, and photographic equipment. It is worth noting that an examination of the aggregate size distribution of certificates, without regard to industry, suggests that the over-all effect of the program was to increase concentration rather than the opposite:

Assets size class (millions of dollars)	Percent of amortization certificates, 1952	Percent of 1952 total assets
Less than 1	2.0	9.6
1–50	23.5	31.5
50–100	6.8	7.4
More than 100	67.7	51.5

stronger effect;[24] a different basic procurement policy might have had the opposite results.[25]

Government selling as well as government buying had an important influence on particular market structures. Some of the vast expansion of industrial capacity during World War II was on government account; since then the plant has been sold to private operators. The disposal operations have all been subject to Congressional direction to promote competition, but also have had as a basic goal sale at a good price. In the three most important disposal operations — aluminum, steel, and synthetic rubber — these somewhat conflicting goals have been given different weights.[26] In the

24. An example of what deliberate policy can do is provided by the expansion of nitrogen capacity from 1951 to 1956, as detailed in the report of the Attorney General pursuant to Section 708(e) of the Defense Production Act of 1950, dated August 1956. In 1951 capacity was 1.5 million tons in the hands of 13 producers operating 19 plants. At the end of the expansion, 32 new plants were constructed with the assistance of accelerated amortization, 11 by new entrants into the industry. A further 11 new plants were constructed by 11 other new entrants. The change in the concentration of capacity was:

	1951	1956
	(percent)	
Largest firm	25	19
5 largest firms	74	48
8 largest firms	85	60

In this case policy was aided by a clear indication of a great permanent expansion of demand. Most of the new entrants were existing large chemical producers or oil refiners. Of the 11 unassisted entrants, 6 were subsidiaries of major oil producers, one was a joint venture of United Gas, Ebasco Services Corporation, and the National Research Corporation, one was U.S. Steel, and three were small chemical producers.

25. The impact of variations in basic procurement policy is indicated by a Report of the Senate Select Committee on Small Business entitled *Case Studies in Government Procurement* (85 Cong., 1 sess., Report No. 1111, 23 August 1957). The committee heard testimony on the effects of the air force's "weapons-system" procurement policy, which shifted entire responsibility for components, auxiliaries, etc., of a particular weapon or weapons system to one single prime contractor, to engage in subcontracting as he saw fit; rather than breaking up the contract into smaller units, some of which might be let to small firms which could not be major contractors. It appeared that this policy led to an expansion of self-supply by prime contractors, including the construction of new capacity for this purpose, to the disadvantage of smaller firms which had received subcontracts and prime contracts for parts, auxiliary equipment, etc., under the previous system.

26. The aluminum disposal program is discussed in Judge Knox's opinion in the Alcoa remedy proceeding, U.S. v. Aluminum Co. of America, 91 F. Supp. 333; in *Public Administration and Policy Development,* ed. H. Stein, pp. 313–362. See also M. J. Peck, *Market Behavior in the American Aluminum Industry,* 1946–1956 (forthcoming). The sale of the Geneva steel plant to U.S. Steel is described in U.S. v. Columbia Steel Co., 334 U.S. 495; and W. Adams and H. Gray, *Monopoly in America,* chapter VI. The synthetic rubber program, completed only in 1956, is described

aluminum case, prime emphasis was given to the effects of disposal on market structure; consequently Alcoa, the prewar sole U.S. supplier, was not allowed to get any of the major new facilities built during the war, and two new producers, Reynolds (who had already been operating some of the plants) and Kaiser, were set up. It is clear that disposal to Alcoa would have been financially more favorable to the government than what was actually done. That Alcoa was an adjudged monopolist, still under the jurisdiction of the Court with respect to remedy, was an important factor in leading to the final outcome.

In the steel case, there was little concern with market structure. Acquisition of the Geneva, Utah, plant increased U.S. Steel's share of West Coast ingot capacity from 17 percent to 51 percent; but U.S. Steel had made the best offer, and the only one not conditional on substantial government financing, and this appeared to determine the outcome.

The disposal of the synthetic rubber plants showed an attempt to balance the two considerations of competitive effects and maximum proceeds to the government. The high bidders — and sometimes the only ones — were the previous operators; the result of the disposal was an industry with a pattern of concentration somewhat lower than that of tires and tubes, and somewhat higher than that of rubber products as a whole.[27] But the larger producers agreed to set aside a portion of their output for sale to independent rubber fabricators; some major producers were not consumers of rubber, and capacity is being expanded.

These three different experiences illustrate the moral of the whole discussion of procurement. It can never be the only or the most important purpose of procurement policy to stimulate compe-

in the *Report to the Congress of the Rubber Production Facilities Disposal Commission*, January 1955, and the *Hearings* of the Senate Banking and Currency Committee, 84 Cong., 2 sess., on S. Res. 197, Disposal of the Institute, W. Va., Synthetic Rubber Plant.

27. After the disposal of the Institute plant, the big four — Goodrich, Firestone, Goodyear, and U.S. Rubber — had about 64 percent of the GRS capacity; General Tire and Rubber, Copolymer, and American Synthetic, about 13 percent; and Shell, Phillips, and Union Carbon and Carbide, 23 percent. Copolymer and American Synthetic were jointly owned ventures of the various minor rubber producers. Firestone and Goodyear operated their GRS plants as wholly owned subsidiaries; Goodrich on a 50 percent joint venture with Gulf Oil, and U.S. Rubber on a 50 percent joint venture with Texas Corporation. At the butadiene level — the major input of the GRS plants — production was more concentrated. One huge joint venture — Goodrich-Gulf and Texas-U.S. — ran the largest single plant, accounting for 32 percent of total capacity.

tition in the markets affected. Yet that may be an important secondary goal; the weight given to it can vary, and so does the extent to which it conflicts with the primary goal of effective and economical procurement. Further, to the extent that procurement policy is directed to a sustained defense effort of roughly the current proportions, rather than to a larger emergency program, the weight to be given the secondary goal without sacrificing the primary one clearly can be increased.

DIRECT AID TO SMALL BUSINESS

The potency of small business as a political force, if nothing else, has been registered in a modest, continuing program of direct federal assistance to small business. The program currently operates under the Small Business Administration, created by the Act of 1955.[28] The agency has a revolving loan fund of $275 million, with powers to lend to small business, as it defines the term. It also has the power to act as a contractor, making contracts with the procurement agencies of the government, and subcontracting them in turn to small businesses. In addition to being banker and contractor, it supplies technical and managerial advice and assistance to small businesses, and acts as liaison agency for them in dealing with the military procurement agencies.

Small business has been defined by the agency as including: any nondominant firms in manufacturing with fewer than 500 employees or any with fewer than 1000 employees declared to be small business firms by the agency; any wholesaler with annual receipts of $5 million or less; any retailer with annual receipts of $1 million or less; any construction firm with average annual receipts of $5 million or less over the last three years.

From October 1953 to February 1957, the SBA made loans of $236 million to some 5000 businesses, selected from more than 11,000 applicants, requesting $627 million in aggregate. Sixty percent of the loans were to trading enterprises, only 22 percent to manufacturing ones. About 70 percent of the loans were made jointly with banks, but the SBA provided most of the money even in these.

28. P.L. 268, 84 Cong., 1 sess. This was the successor to the Small Business Act of 1953, which in turn traces back to the creation of the Smaller War Plants Corporation in 1944, to enable small firms to participate in military supply in World War II. The SBA reports semiannually, the last report being that of 28 February 1957, which is drawn on below.

In the military procurement field, the SBA arranged for set-asides of $750 million of purchases in fiscal 1956. The agency estimated that small business's potential share of defense procurement was about 31 percent of the total, or some $6 billion; its actual sales to the Defense Department were about 18 percent of the total.[29]

What is striking about the present activity of the SBA is its limited scale and scope. What it does has little bearing on the character of competition in most important national and regional markets. To have a substantial effect, the activities of the agency (or some other agency) would have to be considerably enlarged in scale, and would have to be such as to promote the entry and growth of firms into the size range where they would become significant competitive forces, which in many manufacturing industries would involve firms at or above SBA's present limits of operation — 1000 employees.

One possible direction in which these operations might be extended is in the field of capital banking. The much-discussed problems of the finance of expansion for the small enterprise have been referred to above. An extension of some type of participation or guarantee activity, perhaps on the lines of the FHA and FNMA in the housing market, which would make possible readier access to institutional capital by the growing but still relatively new and small firm, might be of first importance in facilitating the successful entry of new sellers into markets now highly concentrated in a few hands.

Another is in the field of industrial research. At present, industrial research expenditures are highly concentrated; a few large firms do most of the nonmilitary as well as a large share of the military research in the United States.[30] This concentration probably makes an important contribution to the continued dominance of the large firms; and, in general, small enterprises may not be able to run economical and efficient research programs themselves. It is possible that government investment in industrial research and in disseminating its results would pay for itself in new products and

29. The "potential" share of small business was defined as consisting of all procurements of less than $10,000, plus all others which were not ruled out for reasons of size, secrecy, or lack of known small-business suppliers.

30. Forty-four firms with 25,000 or more employees spent more than half of the total expenditures on research. See *Scientific Research and Development in American Industry*, Bureau of Labor Statistics, 1953, table C-3.

techniques, as well as in helping promote competition. In agriculture, of course, the federal government has long been the major center of research activity and, in cooperation with the states through the extension service, the major disseminator of its results.[31] In the United Kingdom, a substantial part of industrial research is carried on through the Department of Scientific and Industrial Research. This Department spends the major part of its resources in laboratories of its own; in addition, it works together with trade associations to maintain laboratories partly financed by the users and partly by the government. Altogether, the role of government and cooperative effort is much greater in the United Kingdom than in the United States.[32] Students of British industrial research have found the cooperative and government efforts worth while; their experience may be something from which American policy can learn.

TARIFFS AND COMMERCIAL POLICY

The classic way for governments to limit competition is through the taxation and control of imports. Even though the United States is nearly self-sufficient, especially in manufactured goods, tariff and other trade controls still limit competition significantly in some markets. It was estimated by the staff of the Commission on Foreign Economic Policy that in 1951 the $2.1 billions of dutiable imports for which tariffs were an important barrier would have been some $700 to $1400 million greater in their absence.[33] Affected commodities were divided into those which would experience a slight increase in imports — 10 to 25 percent; a moderate increase — 25 to 50 percent; a substantial one — 50 to 100 percent, and a very large

31. Over the last few years, federal expenditures on agricultural research have been of the order of $100 million per year, including payments to the states for extension work. See *Governmental Cost in Agriculture,* U.S. Agricultural Research Service, May 1956, appendix table C-2. Over the last 50 years, output per resource unit in agriculture has increased about as much as the average of manufacturing industry.

32. See *Applying Science and Technology to the Problems of Industry,* proceedings of a conference at Healesville, Victoria (Australia), October 1954. The major paper was given by Professor R. S. Edwards, of the London School of Economics, the leading student of British industrial research.

33. *Staff Papers,* presented to the Commission on Foreign Economic Policy, February 1954, pp. 298–299. Total merchandise imports in 1951 were $10.8 billion, of which $6 billion were duty free. About 40 percent of the remainder, including petroleum, diamonds, burlap, lumber, nickel, and lead, would be freed by removal of quotas.

one — over 100 percent. The estimated increases were distributed as follows:[34]

Increase	1951 Imports	Estimated Increase	
	(millions of dollars)	(millions of dollars)	
		Minimum	Maximum
Very large	53	53	158
Substantial	607	404	807
Moderate	591	148	296
Small	694	69	174

These estimates all relate to the short-run impact of tariff suspension; in the longer run, undoubtedly, further adaptations both here and abroad would lead to further changes in the pattern of trade. Nonetheless, they give some indication of the degree to which competition is now being restrained in some markets by tariffs.

Another major restraint on import competition, affecting government purchases, is the Buy American Act.[35] This requires the government to purchase from domestic suppliers unless their prices are "unreasonably" above foreign prices; "unreasonable" has been interpreted as 25 per cent or more higher, the computation being made on delivered price, including transportation, tariffs, and supplementary assembly in the United States, of the foreign product. This amounts to an additional tariff, sometimes reaching 60 percent of the foreign price. There are similar enactments with special applications: the Merchant Marine Act which requires vessels built with the aid of federal subsidies to use domestic materials, and those receiving operating subsidies to use domestic supplies; the post office ships mail overseas in American bottoms; the Rural Electrification Act requires borrowers from the REA to buy domestic materials unless their prices are "unreasonable."

34. *Staff Papers*. The major commodities in the three groups were: very large: earthenware and china, leather gloves, leather handbags, fur felt hats, clay tile, clocks, canned tuna fish, linen towels and handkerchiefs, scissors and shears, knives with folding blades; substantial: wool, woolens, and worsteds, fresh or frozen fillets, cigar filler tobacco, sewing machines, shoes, edible nuts, jewelry, optical instruments, bicycles; moderate: watches, canned beef, rayon fiber, whiskey, wool apparel, cotton cloth, stuffed olives, musical instruments; small: cattle and beef, cigarette leaf tobacco, zinc, aluminum, hides and skins, structural steel, fresh fish, tungsten, mercury. See also table 2, *Staff Papers,* pp. 308–309, for lists of products for which imports would account for 10 to 90 percent of total supply in the absence of tariffs.

35. See *Staff Papers,* pp. 315–320. The Act was first passed in 1933, and was extended in the 1954 Defense Department Appropriations Act.

With respect to the restraints on imports discussed, and others, there is no question of conflict between policies directed toward other ends than competition, and that of promoting competition. Rather, the clear aim as well as the effect of the policies in question is the limitation of competition, and the problem is one of policy consistency, rather than one of weighing the competitive effects of public policies directed toward other goals.

VIII

Administration aud Enforcement

In analyzing the comparative merits of various antitrust policy goals and suggesting possible revisions, we have already paid considerable attention to the problems of administration and enforcement. Our purpose in this chapter is twofold: first, to examine in greater detail the impact of administrative and enforcement problems on the choice of statutory standards; and second, to consider possible revisions in the organization and procedures of antitrust enforcement that would be appropriate to alternative policy courses. In other words, we are asking two questions: how workable are the various antitrust policy standards; and how might antitrust policies be more effectively or more appropriately enforced, whether or not any changes are made in substantive law.

STATUTORY STANDARDS

General considerations

A recurring question in the drafting of regulatory statutes is whether to make statutory standards general or specific. Behind this issue lie many competing policy considerations, which in almost all practical situations must be compromised.

A precise and specific statute has many obvious advantages. It clearly marks the boundary between legal and illegal conduct. The law can be more readily and quickly enforced by the enforcement agencies; it also can be more readily enforced by personnel of average capabilities. Clear standards encourage voluntary compliance; the more the certainty the less the temptation to sail close to the wind. The certain standard, other things being equal, is also more palatable in that the regulated are not subject to a range of unpredictable discretion in the hands of the regulators.

However, there are other important goals in the drafting of the statutory standards which precise definition may defeat. A statute should be effective in dealing with the evils sought to be curbed. It should also be fair and reasonable. A statute which strikes down conduct even where that conduct is innocuous or beneficial, or which leaves untouched other forms of conduct having similar ill effects, is neither effective nor fair nor reasonable. It may encourage noncompliance. It may also cause enforcement agencies to wink at violations, which opens up possibilities of graft and abuse; and it may lead courts into bizarre decisions that distort the purpose of the law and prevent its application to clearly bad results.

Moreover, there are often practical considerations that make it impossible or highly undesirable to formulate a precise clear standard. At times it is necessary to commence regulation on the basis of imperfect knowledge of the best ways and means of dealing with the problems involved. At other times, effective regulation necessarily requires a statute couched in general terms. Frequently in the area of economic regulation, the legislature can make precise statutory judgements only within a limited sphere. The greater the need for technical skill and judgement, or the greater the need for a particularized approach to a multitude of individual situations, the greater the necessity for broad statutory standards and broad policy guides.

Utility rate regulation is a prime example of the kind of situation where authority must probably be delegated within fairly broad lines if there is to be any effective regulation at all. It is not only physically impossible for a legislature to make the necessary individual determinations; it is also difficult to determine with any precision the considerations, and the weight to be attached to them, that ought to be applied in each case. A similar approach has been found desirable, or thought necessary, in the following situations among others: the regulation of production, marketing, and pricing of agricultural commodities; the regulation of federal home loan banks; the renegotiation of war and defense contracts for the recovery of excess profits; the regulation of security issues and securities exchanges; the simplification and integration of utility holding company systems; and the licensing of radio and television stations under the Federal Communications Act.

Even though broad statutory standards, for one or more reasons, are adopted at the outset of regulation, it is frequently possible and certainly desirable to amplify and particularize the standards as enforcement develops. Much amplification takes place as more and more cases are decided, by what has been called "a process of reasoned elaboration." Administrative agencies have available the additional device of rule making, which provides clearer guides for enforcement and compliance, and which accelerates the handling of individual cases.

However, none of these devices necessarily insures that continued experience in the enforcement of a vaguely worded statute will reach a high plateau of reason, certainty, and uniformity. Some of the above cited examples of regulation under broad statutes have had unhappy histories — occasionally the results have bordered on the outrageous. In some, much of the blame can be put on the Congress for passing on to enforcement agencies — with barely concealed sighs of relief — political policy conflicts that Congress itself might have, and should have, substantially resolved. But Congress cannot be expected to resolve all of the policy conflicts all of the time; it may well be necessary and appropriate to leave the weighing of potentially competing considerations, such as efficiency of service and low cost to consumers in rate regulation, to the decision of the enforcement agency in individual cases. Moreover, the subject matter may impose intrinsic limitations on the extent to which case precedents and rules can be expected to produce satisfactory clear guides. A standard requiring judgement as to "degree," resting on an assessment of a multitude of facts, is bound to produce some indeterminacy unless the enforcement agency, loathe to grapple with a judgement of this kind, makes certain facts controlling ones regardless of the appropriateness of such "presumptions" in a particular case. The latter approach may be satisfactory if the presumptions are sound in a high proportion of cases, as we suggested in discussing the foundation of per se rules. The approach is unsatisfactory if the presumptions, though clear, are arbitrary. And with rules as with statutes, beyond a point the advantages of certainty are outweighed by the loss in effectiveness and reasonableness. The SEC, for example, developed fairly detailed rules listing the considerations for determining whether or not holding company systems were too complex, and how they should be reorganized, though the rules did not precisely define how any individual case might be decided. In contrast, the SEC steadily refused to amplify by rule-making the statutory term "control" beyond "stating the obvious that 'control' was an issue of fact in any given case and that the mere form in which it might be exercised was, therefore, immaterial."[1]

The antitrust laws

Sixty-odd years of interpretation and enforcement of the antitrust laws have shown some of the difficulties that attend both general statutory guides on the one hand and more specific definitions of offenses on the other.

Little enlightenment can be gleaned from the enforcement of the most general statutory provision of all — Section 5 of the FTC Act. The prohibition of "unfair methods of competition" might well have given us a great deal of experience with the enforcement of an extremely broad and vague statutory proscription. Congress apparently contemplated flexible administrative determination as to what practices might be deemed "unfair," such determinations to be made in the light of administrative expertise and future experience. However, in the *Gratz* case[2] the Supreme Court in effect confined Section 5 to well-recognized offenses, and repressed for nearly two decades whatever creative urges the Federal Trade Commission might otherwise have had. Little in the way of new law has come out of Section 5. With occasional exceptions, such as the *Triangle Conduit & Cable* case,[3] Section 5 has served principally as a jurisdictional cover for FTC proceedings against violations of other provisions of the antitrust laws; and, since 1938, as a basis for attacking unethical practices such as false advertising.

Sherman Act enforcement is a more informative story. "As a charter of freedom," the Supreme Court said in *Appalachian Coals*, the Sherman Act

> has a generality and an adaptability comparable to that found to be desirable in constitutional provisions. It does not go into detailed definitions which might either work injury to legitimate enterprises or through particularization defeat its purposes by proving loopholes for escape.[4]

The "generality and adaptability" of the Act may have prevented loopholes in the law but it has often left considerable doubt as to

1. Landis, *The Administrative Process* (1938), vol. 83 p. 83.
2. FTC v. Gratz, 253 U.S. 421 (1920).
3. Triangle Conduit & Cable Co. v. FTC, 168 F.2d 175 (7 Cir. 1948) *aff'd by an equally divided Court*, 336 U.S. 956 (1949).
4. Appalachian Coals, Inc. v. U.S., 288 U.S. 344, 359–60 (1953).

what the law is. Some certainty has been imparted with respect to activities held illegal per se. There are no doubts as to the ultimate fate of obvious price-fixing or market-sharing agreements. Yet even here there has been an area of doubt as to activities that are not price-fixing or market-sharing on their face. One need only compare *Appalachian Coals* with *Socony-Vacuum*,[5] and note the erratic course of the Supreme Court in the trade association cases. In any event, the interpretations of Section 2 of the Act, from any realistic viewpoint, have fluctuated quite widely.

The generality of the Sherman Act has had the same defects of any generally phrased statute. Lack of precision in statutory standards permits reasonable men to differ, and permits wide swings in the realities of substantive law with changes in judicial temperament. The times of judicial generosity are not forgotten — the level of compliance tends strongly toward the lowest common denominator of what the law has been said to enfold. Moreover, the generality of the act has meant that the scope and variety of relevant evidence have been extremely broad. Most cases require extensive factual investigations, prolonged proceedings, and difficult problems of analysis and proof.

Ostensibly, at least, the Clayton Act embodied a different approach. Specific practices were singled out for harsher treatment. But the Act was still not precise, since the practices were not declared illegal, as such, but only on a showing of probability of harm. Until recent years, the principal effect of the Clayton Act was merely that the denomination of suspect practices prevented courts from treating the practices themselves as being either reasonable or neutral. In other words, the Act raised a mild presumption of illegality. But in prolixity of facts and issues of judgment, Clayton Act cases were not much better than those arising under its predecessor. More recent interpretations of Section 3 of the Act have approached a per se view. But so have parallel determinations under Section 1 of the Sherman Act.

To the extent that it is specific, the Clayton Act has shown the infirmities that often appear in this kind of approach to economic regulation. The principal infirmity is that similar practices, though having identical effects, are left to be dealt with by the Sherman Act standards. Thus, to the extent the standards do differ, form rather than substance determines the law. For example, exclusive require-

5. U.S. v. Socony-Vacuum Oil Co., 310 U.S. 150 (1940).

ments contracts carried out by contract of sale or lease fall within the prohibitions of Section 3 or the Clayton Act, but arrangements with identical effects carried on through agency arrangements are beyond its scope. Acquisition of assets was held not to be covered by original Section 7 of the Clayton Act, a gap not filled until legislative amendment in 1951. Similarly, a "sale" is essential to a violation of the anti-price-discrimination provisions of Section 2, even though some of the most pernicious discriminations involve refusals to sell, or offers so disparate that a sale never takes place.

Clearly the unhappiest experience with semi-specific standards is that under the Robinson–Patman Act. The difficulties have been many, and not entirely related to an absence of generality. The act reflects purposes at least potentially inconsistent with the general body of antitrust laws. It has produced nearly insoluble interpretive problems, and has been extraordinarily difficult to administer. The difficulties are in part due to bad draftsmanship, which reflects among other things the inability of Congress completely to resolve conflicting policy views at the legislative level. But the difficulties have also been due to the task attempted. One fundamental problem is the difficulty of separating invidious discrimination from discrimination that is either neutral or beneficial. Another is that there are myriad ways of discriminating, many being virtually incapable of detection. Inclusive enforcement would require surveillance of day-to-day business operations. The administrative burden is greatly enhanced by the practical problem of determining when unjustified discrimination exists — when price differences are justified by different costs, and when they have been made in good faith to meet competition.

The cost defense posed the dilemma of generality versus precision quite sharply. General rules would have promoted flexibility, fairness, and reasonableness; they would also have led to vagueness and perhaps, although this is arguable, to greater administrative burdens in enforcement proceedings. The FTC until recent years took a harsh approach — requiring fairly precise cost justification — which solved the cases (almost uniformly against defendants) but seemed materially unfair.

The Robinson–Patman Act also contains, in Section 2 (c) as interpreted, the most clear and precise prohibition to be found in the antitrust laws, that making brokerage payments or payments in lieu of brokerage illegal per se. The results have been unfortunate, probably even for those who fully intended that interpretation at the outset, not realizing that its impact would be visited on the small businessman as well as on the large. The prohibition is irrational and, at least in part for that reason, compliance has almost certainly been spotty.

Comments

What general conclusions may be drawn from the past experience? We are primarily interested in three things: the use of "economic" standards generally; the extent to which standards can or should be specific; and different methods of dealing with market power.

Judicial handling of the antitrust laws has tended to concentrate on conduct. One reason for this is obvious — the statutory standards are couched principally in such terms. But there is probably more to account for. At least until more recent years, the courts were hard on practices which historically had been viewed with disfavor; they were comparatively gentle with practices or with situations which had never been thought immoral, and whose ill effects could be appreciated only on the basis of economic analysis of a more refined and less well-known sort than was commonly a part of the courts' intellectual equipment. To be sure there were some cases of unusual insight, such as that of Judge Learned Hand in the *Corn Products*[6] case. But these were comparatively insignificant in the light of such decisions as *U.S. Steel, First Shoe Machinery,* and the old *Cement* case.[7]

It can be argued on the basis of this experience that courts are simply not comfortable with economic issues and cannot be expected to deal with them satisfactorily. There may be some grounds for this argument, but it is hardly a proven proposition. For one thing, economists and economic theory offered little guidance to the courts. There had been little systematic thinking about oligopoly; there were only rudimentary ideas of workable competition; and the testimony of economic experts in antitrust cases was often sterile and usually diametrically conflicting. It seems reasonable to say that the more recent cases have demonstrated a growing concentration on important economic issues, even though the

6. U.S. v. Corn Products Refining Co., 234 Fed. 964 (S.D.N.Y. 1916).

7. U.S. v. U.S. Steel Corp., 251 U.S. 417 (1920); U.S. v. United Shoe Machinery Co., 247 U.S. 32 (1918); Cement Mfrs. Protective Ass'n v. U.S., 268 U.S. 588 (1925).

treatment of those issues and the economic analysis in judicial opinions often leave something to be desired. In any event, there are at least some indications that these issues are susceptible to rational administrative or judicial determination.

A second general conclusion that may fairly be drawn from past antitrust enforcement experience and from the nature of the regulatory area involved, is that there are limits to the specificity with which statutory standards may be or should be drawn. Or, more accurately, there must be *some* statutory standard or standards couched in general terms if antitrust enforcement is to be effective and reasonable.

The antitrust laws have been heavily criticized for their vagueness and uncertainty. But the weight of this criticism must be balanced against the even heavier criticism in recent years of per se doctrines, and the positive praise of the "rule of reason." The demand for certainty often reflects disagreement with the policy results, a demand that certain practices or situations be clearly permitted rather than that they be clearly banned. The support for the "rule of reason" may have similar origins — a desire to expand the grounds on which antitrust charges may be defended. But it also reflects a justifiable fear of irrational results from too extensive a per se approach, a fear which those who want an effective antitrust policy might well share.

As pointed out in Chapter V, per se rules have many advantages which dictate their use in circumstances where the practice to be proscribed has bad effects far more times than it has good. We have suggested that several specific practices not now illegal per se might well be made so. Certainly no administrative considerations would stand in the way; where the per se result is reasonable, all other aims of good statutory draftsmanship — clarity, enforceability, consistency, and the like — are met with no cost.

But there remains an area of practices and the area of "situations" where precision is to a large extent an apparently illusory goal. The comments of Justice Brandeis, dissenting in the *Gratz* case in 1920, would seem sound today:

> Experience with existing laws had taught that definition, being necessarily rigid, would prove embarrassing, and, if rigorously applied, might involve great hardship. Methods of competition which would be unfair in one industry, under certain circumstances, might, when adopted in another industry, or even in the same industry under different circum-

stances, be entirely unobjectionable. Furthermore, an enumeration however comprehensive of existing methods of unfair competition must necessarily soon prove incomplete, as with new conditions arising novel unfair methods would be devised and developed.[8]

As we have pointed out earlier, such practices as exclusive requirements contracts and joint buying agencies are beneficial in a sufficient number of situations that it is unwise to strike them down, per se. Nor does it seem possible, if a program against monopoly power or undue market power is deemed desirable, to carry it out effectively and reasonably by precise, hard-and-fast statutory rules —barring only the possibility that a sufficiently complete dossier of prohibited practices, rigorously enforced, could prevent the growth of undue market power, a possibility which we deem to be remote if for no other reason than that enforcement is unlikely to be continuously rigorous. Some guides can be formulated and have been suggested. But both Section 2 and the suggested outline of a statutory standard against market power concededly leave an area of vagueness with which close cases may be subject to reasonable verdicts either way. However, it does not seem that the vagueness is unusual or "undue" for regulatory problems of this nature. Section 2 is no vaguer than many economic regulatory statutes and perhaps has clearer contours than most. And of course the suggested new standards would not be projected on a clean slate. Moreover, we believe the new standard, though imprecise as to factual determinations, substantially eliminates the problem of balancing competing policy considerations. Nevertheless, a program against market power, whether under Section 2 or under our proposed schemes, has an additional dimension of vagueness not characteristic, in anywhere near the same degree, of prohibitions on conduct. This is the matter of remedy. Planning a structural reorganization is a far more troublesome problem than drafting an injunction. In the history of antitrust enforcement, few reorganizations have been directed. Their paucity may have been due to one or more of the following reasons:

(a) a failure to find the existence of monopoly power where by reasonable test such power existed (*U.S. Steel, First Shoe Machinery*);

(b) a failure of the government to convince the court or a fail-

8. FTC v. Gratz, 253 U.S. 421, 436–37 (1920) (dissenting opinion).

ure of the courts to appreciate fully the probable increase in competition that would result from an addition to the number of independent firms (*National Lead,* where the Supreme Court doubted that four firms would be better than two, or six firms better than four);[9]

(c) a tendency, wherever such a course shows at least some promise of being adequate, to utilize injunctive remedies, which are far simpler to formulate in an actual decree;

(d) a reluctance on the part of individual judges to direct a reorganization program that will have far-reaching and unpredictable effects; and

(e) a failure of the government to present a feasible reorganization plan.

The first two reasons are simply mistakes in advocacy or in judgment. However, the fact that they occur is significant. They may be due in large part to the vagueness of the statute, which again suggests the need for clearer guides to its enforcement. The third reason — a tendency to use the simple rather than the complex — is estimable enough and cannot be objected to. The fourth suggests a relocation of the task, a matter we shall deal with later.

The fifth is a problem of no little consequence. The difficulties of formulating a feasible reorganization plan can be serious, and considerably more complex than those presented by ordinary corporate reorganization, where the sole object is to revise the financial structure of a single firm, or by the reorganization of public utility holding company structures, where the constituent operating companies had monopoly positions in their respective distribution areas. The difficulties facing courts have been enhanced by the inability of the government in some cases to present feasible plans. This is not to say that the government was necessarily at fault. In some cases no plan would have been feasible. And generally government attorneys have neither the business background nor the particular knowledge of the industry necessary to the job. This suggests an improved staffing of the enforcement agency or that some burden of formulating a feasible plan be placed on the defendants in reorganization proceedings, or both.

But this still leaves the question of administrable standards, and there remains considerable doubt that the standards can be sufficiently defined to preclude erratic results. Under existing law, the

9. U.S. v. National Lead Co., 332 U.S. 319 (1947).

plan of reorganization must be "feasible." The term probably comprehends at least the following issues: (a) will the resulting business units have a reasonable chance for survival; (b) will the dissolution eliminate substantial economies of scale; (c) will it destroy efficiencies unique to the particular firm involved; and (d) will it cause serious disruptions elsewhere, and adverse effects on third parties. Finding the answer to the first two questions is not easy — and the answers will be in terms of probabilities. The third is also difficult; there may be no adequate standards of comparison (i.e. the trouble of evaluating performance). As for the fourth, there will always be disruptions of sorts, and the question is "how much is too much?" Each issue invites the presentation of vast amounts of evidence.

Presumptions and burdens of proof, as suggested in Chapter IV, may alter the balance between cases where dissolution is decreed and cases where it is not, but they would not necessarily reduce the adjudicating body's discretion. In other words, their principal effect would be to shift the area of discretion, without compressing its scope. An irrefutable presumption against splitting a single plant does give a specific bench mark, but it will be an infrequent case in which this problem will arise.

Apart from the disadvantages attendant on vagueness, it seems likely that the room for discretion created by uncertain standards would on balance lead to fewer reorganizations rather than to more, if enforcement is left to the courts. This is not to say that judges will disregard their duties. It is merely to say that the complexities of reorganization are so great, and the consequences sufficiently uncertain, that valor will not be the better part of discretion.

We have already, in Chapter IV, drawn some comparisons between the existing law on market power and what we propose. In terms of clarity or, if you like, "enforceability," we believe our proposal is in some respects superior, though the advantages may not be great. Under present law, monopoly power is unlawful only on a showing that it was unlawfully acquired or used. There must be a "combination" or "conspiracy," or in the case of the individual monopolist some kind of "monopolizing" conduct. Proof of conspiracy, or of combination of a sort other than merger or consolidation, typically has involved extensive investigation and proof of conduct and intent over a period of many years, and often of behavior that has no direct bearing on the acquisition or maintenance of monopoly power. Moreover, the scope of individual "monopolizing" conduct still remains unsettled, the issue having been avoided in *Cellophane*.[10]

Our proposal, at least on its face, dispenses with proof of "conspiracy" or "combination" in those situations where market power is jointly possessed. While it might still entail in many cases a thorough review of past behavior to determine whether or not unreasonable market power exists, it would tend to eliminate much of the behavioral evidence that now is relevant. Conduct would also be pertinent, both in "joint" and individual market power cases, because of the justifications which in our view would make market power reasonable. But our formulation makes clearer than present law does what the justifications are. Firms now lacking market power could be reasonably certain as to what course of conduct would insure that any market power acquired would be immune. Our proposal would also narrow somewhat the considerations to be taken into account in determining whether divesture should be decreed; it gives no explicit recognition to transitional disruptions of the companies directly concerned, nor to adverse effects on related concerns.

However, even without change in the law, we have hopes for substantial improvement in the fairness and effectiveness of enforcement from procedural reforms, most of which would be as applicable to present antitrust law as they are to our substantive proposals. It is to procedural matters that we now turn.

ORGANIZATION AND PROCEDURES

The enforcement pattern

Since the creation of the Federal Trade Commission in 1914, we have had a dual enforcement system. The antitrust laws specifically give dual jurisdiction to the courts and to the FTC for the enforcement of Sections 2, 3, 7, and 8 of the Clayton Act (15 U.S.C. Sections 21, 25). In addition, Section 5 of the Federal Trade Commission Act has been interpreted to give the FTC jurisdiction over violations of the Sherman Act.

A third enforcement channel of sorts is private suit by persons injured through violations of the antitrust laws. Injured parties can

10. U.S. v. E. I. du Pont de Nemours & Co., 351 U.S. 377 (1956).

seek treble damages or an injunction against continuing violation (15 U.S.C. Sections 15, 26).

There is a wide variety of available sanctions for actions instituted by the Department of Justice. The action may be either criminal or civil, criminal verdicts resulting in fines and (rarely) imprisonment, and civil judgments entitling the government to a wide range of essentially equitable remedies, including that of divestiture and dissolution.

Short of full litigation, enforcement is also carried out by informal pressures and by consent orders or decrees, devices utilized both by the Department of Justice and by the FTC. There are also more or less informal procedures, most fully developed in the case of mergers, for advance clearance of contemplated arrangements or conduct raising antitrust questions.

Enforcement experience

Experience with advance determination of the legality of proposed actions can be disposed of rather quickly, because there has been no explicit statutory authority for either the Department of Justice or the Federal Trade Commission to give binding advance clearances. The Justice Department has utilized the "railroad release" whereby it purports to bind itself not to institute criminal proceedings. Both the Justice Department and the FTC have procedures for clearing a proposed merger, which, if granted, probably give adequate security for all practical purposes.

However, applications for releases or clearances have been comparatively rare, for reasons which seem largely indigenous to the nature of the matter. Clearance will be sought in any event only where there is substantial doubt. Inevitably, doubt will appear only where the law is vague and where a determination requires extensive knowledge of facts. The greater the range of relevant facts, the less practicable it is for the enforcement agency to give firm advice and the less likely it is that the agency will feel justified in giving a meaningful clearance. If given, the clearance is likely to be so hedged with caveats as to be of limited use. Given this predisposition toward caution, the businessman has little to gain from making a request — if the proposed action is sufficiently innocuous to get a blanket clearance, his lawyer could probably have given him firm advice to begin with; if it is too doubtful for clearance, he will only have called attention to himself. It seems probable that this is about what most lawyers have advised their clients in the past and, with few exceptions, businessmen have taken their chances.

Turning to enforcement of laws against violations that have occurred, the experience has left much to be desired, although antitrust is hardly unique in this respect. On the whole, enforcement has been inadequate even when it is recognized that a large number of local or transient or well-concealed violations would elude the best of federal enforcement programs. Some important violations escape altogether; others are caught up with long after they have occurred or commenced. Second, investigatory and enforcement proceedings, both in the courts and in the FTC, typically are extremely protracted. Finally, enforcement has been uneven and erratic. These are the three general weaknesses that have appeared in antitrust enforcement.

The inadequacy of enforcement has been due in large part to the inadequacy of appropriations, stemming from budgetary considerations, from political sentiment against adequate enforcement, or perhaps from serious doubts that the enforcement appropriation will be efficiently used. Political sentiment against strong enforcement also operates directly on the enforcement agency. An administration less than dedicated to antitrust can considerably dampen the efforts of the Department of Justice, and, by appointments, alter the course pursued by the FTC. As for these political considerations, there is little more that can be said, or that should be done, except to repeat the obvious — that laws of this type do not enforce themselves.

But inadequacy is also due to certain enforcement burdens which, though theoretically conquerable by additional appropriations and staff, impose severe practical limitations on enforcement efficiency. These are the burdens of unearthing violations, of getting information not readily available. They are the burdens of getting the large amount of evidence essential to success in many types of enforcement proceedings, most notably the big Sherman Act case.

These difficulties are also largely responsible for the second weakness in antitrust enforcement — the protracted nature of investigation efforts and enforcement proceedings. In part, the length of enforcement proceedings is due to the nature of the statutory standards, as pointed out earlier; in part, to the character of the procedures themselves. Enforcement would obviously be simplified if less evidence were needed to establish a violation and if evidence did not have to be looked for but were made available by reporting requirements.

In actions against probable violations, both judicial and administrative proceedings reflect a full panoply of procedures and protections — beginning with investigations and ending with full judicial review — which substantially prolong the ultimate disposition of cases. A good part of the delay is not intrinsic to the purposes which full-scale procedures are designed to serve. The reports of the Judicial Conference and of the American Bar Association, recommending steps for speeding the handling of complex cases, illustrate that much of the delay is unnecessary by any standard except that of delay itself being a virtue.

Further shortening of enforcement proceedings would require either one of two approaches: (1) a revision of statutory standards which diminishes the quantity of evidence and the number of issues pertinent to decision; and (2) a substantial alteration in the procedures that heretofore have been demanded both of judicial and administrative enforcement.

We have already discussed, at various points, the problem of simplified standards. The practicalities of enforcement are particularly important in respect to mergers, and sufficiently serious to suggest, among other things, a much more precise statutory standard than we now have. Though hundreds of mergers have taken place since the 1951 amendment to Section 7 of the Clayton Act, proceedings have been instituted in comparatively few cases. Proceedings in those few cases have shown telltale signs of longevity. Yet, from the nature of the problem, speedy determination is highly important both to the parties and to enforcement agencies — to the parties, because the plans for the merger may disintegrate if held up too long; to the government, because lengthy proceedings make it impossible to cover more than a small percentage of violations; to both parties and the government, because the unscrambling of a completed merger may be difficult and costly.

The second approach to more efficient enforcement — shortening procedures — is a difficult one to deal with for several reasons. To begin with, the history of antitrust enforcement seems to show that a mere transfer of proceedings from courts to administrative agencies is no answer. Given cases of comparable scope, Trade Commission proceedings seem to take about the same amount of time as court proceedings. Delays in the handling of FTC cases might be attributed at least in some part to inadequate appropriations and staff, to inefficiency, and to lethargy. But similar excuses could be made for the courts.

Another difficulty, and one which may partially explain the first, is that the kind of proceedings utilized in antitrust cases — whether in the courts or in the FTC — reflects strongly held beliefs as to what is essential and appropriate to all of the aims subsumed in the phrase "due process of law." Full hearings, virtually unlimited right to present evidence within the limits of relevancy, the right to cross-examine opposing witnesses and to attack the validity or weight of opposing evidence — these and other rights are deemed essential both to the protection of litigants and to finding out the truth. Administrative proceedings tend to be less bound by traditional rules of evidence than are proceedings in court. But insofar as time is concerned, this difference cuts both ways. Administrative hearings may waste less time on getting the "best evidence"; but they may and often do also waste more time in the taking of evidence having little conceivable bearing on the issues at stake.

To the extent that existing procedures were devised for and are effective in protecting the basic right of parties to a fair and complete presentation of their side of the case, no criticism is made here. The antitrust problem is not a national emergency in which speed becomes of paramount value. However, some doubts can be raised whether established procedures are in every respect both necessary and appropriate to the purposes which they are designed to serve. Most of the factual evidence relevant to economic issues in antitrust proceedings either is or probably should be undisputed. It is questionable that a full trial adds very much, except a fat record, to the adversary presentation of economic issues. It is at least possible that it decreases the probability of rational decision making. Massive trial records cannot be assimilated in any satisfactory way by most judges or administrators. They tend to be incomprehensible, and some sort of pattern appears only when briefs are prepared and oral argument made. The greater the size of the record, the greater the possibility that decisions will turn on personal predilections or on stray bits of evidence that get far more weight than they reasonably deserve.

We would stress, however, that much of the confusion in trial records is due not to size but to poor case planning and direction.

In many cases, issues have been tried and evidence presented far beyond what was appropriate or reasonably necessary. To some extent, no one is to blame. Some prolixity is intrinsic to adversary proceedings, particularly in areas of the law where principles are vague and unsettled, for parties will tend to argue and present everything that has a reasonable possibility of influencing the result. But even granting these natural propensities, it is hard to escape the impression that there has been much waste motion and much bad case presentation. The government, the courts (or trial examiners), and the defense share the responsibility. Defendants have prolonged antitrust proceedings unduly by insisting on disputing issues of negligible significance, and by contesting facts which they have no serious hope of overturning. Judges may have failed to exert a strong hand in pretrial and trial proceedings, though having wide power, explicitly and implicitly, to rationalize and streamline matters considerably. But perhaps the primary responsibility can be put on the moving party — the government in court proceedings; trial attorneys in FTC hearings. The complaint is of vital importance; so is the organization and presentation of the government's case. It is extremely difficult for defendants or judges to dispel the confusion created by a disorganized ill-thought-out presentation.

The impact of poor planning is particularly severe in matters of remedy. One suspects that many of the inadequacies of remedial decrees are attributable to the government's having spent far more time on ways of winning the case than on relief to be obtained when it is won.

The third weakness in the enforcement of the antitrust laws has been its unevenness, both over the course of time and at any one time. We have already commented on some of the reasons for uneven enforcement from period to period. It is due in part to vagueness in statutory standards, which permit a fairly wide range of plausible interpretations. It also reflects changes in political attitudes, which have affected enforcement whether through the courts or through the Trade Commission. It may also reflect a growth in concepts and understanding.

Unevenness in enforcement at any one time is due in part simply to the inadequacy of enforcement resources. Beyond that, it is a problem largely attributable to enforcement in a variety of district courts. Even if the law were clearly settled by the Supreme Court, which in many important respects it is not, antitrust determinations rest so heavily on fact findings and on interpretations of fact that variety in attitude and experience on the part of district judges would tend to, and does, produce diverse results.

However, reviewing generally the comparative performance of the courts and the Federal Trade Commission, neither one nor the other shows any marked superiority, taking into account the different roles assigned to each. As might be expected when the statutory standards are sufficiently general as to put a premium on insight and judgment, the performance of the courts and the Trade Commission has varied noticeably with the capabilities of the people involved. Peculiar expertise has not played an important enough role to distinguish the performance of the FTC from that of the courts. While the matter is difficult to assess, it would not be hard to conclude that on balance the best "law" has come out of the courts. To some extent, at least, this may be attributable to the fact that what constitutes skill in the making of economic judgments has been less a matter of general agreement than what constitutes skill in other technical areas where administrative enforcement has been superior.

Recommendations

Within recent years, there have been several reports recommending limited changes in enforcement procedures. These include the reports of the Judicial Conference, the Committee on Procedures of the American Bar Association, and the Attorney General's Committee to Study the Antitrust Laws. Many of these proposals are substantially noncontroversial, and will not be discussed here. We shall touch on some but not all of the other problems dealt with in these recent reports. Failure to discuss indicates neither approval nor disapproval.

(1) *Dual enforcement.* We have already assessed, in terms of antitrust experience, the comparative merits and demerits of administrative agencies and of courts as enforcement channels, and have tentatively concluded that neither has shown on balance any marked superiority over the other. Apparently there is little reason to believe that the past antitrust experience is unusual.

Many of the wide differences that once may have existed between courts and administrative agencies have since been narrowed and other differences now existing are more historic than intrinsic in character. Modern federal rules — providing for pretrial discovery and conferences, narrowing of issues, and so forth — permit proceedings closely equivalent to those before administrative agencies. Courts are more and more capable of by-passing exclusionary rules of evidence, and they can take many steps to suit the procedures to the type of case at hand. See, for example, the report of the Judicial Conference.

Nor is expertise a sharply distinguishing factor. Courts can utilize expertise by referrals to special masters. Courts might also be given access to trained economics and statistics staffs. Moreover, expertise does not necessarily mean good judgment. The advantages of the specialist decline the broader the considerations that must be taken into account in making the decision. There is a wide gulf in the importance of expertise between the chemist determining whether or not a food ingredient is harmful, and the administrator who decides that the conversion from VHF to UHF of all television stations in "in the public interest." Judges may have less technical training, but they may also make wiser and more sophisticated decisions. Of course, much rests on the selection of personnel. In some circumstances, carefully selected experts would perhaps be superior to all but a few judges; but poor experts are the nadir. It is in this respect that centralization of enforcement in a single agency would pose both a great opportunity and a great risk.

However, there would seem to be as a general matter two clear advantages in enforcement by administrative agencies — the potentiality depending upon the caliber of the personnel and the now customary restrictions upon the judicial review. First, enforcement by an administrative agency is likely to show a more consistent and rational pattern at any one time. In dealing with subject matter where judgment rests on complex factual considerations, the very variety of courts and judges permits a variety of decision. The basic legal principles may be clear, but the important thing is what is done with the facts, and it is in fact finding that personal attitudes can make a great difference.

The second clear advantage of an administrative agency, particularly in enforcing a broadly defined statutory policy, is that it is capable of developing a new program more rapidly. Case-by-case determination of all of the interpretive problems that will arise tends to be slower and less certain in the courts than through an agency equipped to make a clearly articulated policy and liberal use of rule making. Enforcement of the Wagner Act, for example, took place in circumstances making this advantage peculiarly significant.[11]

The clear disadvantage of the administrative agency (the independent commission more than the executive administrative agency) is that its effectiveness tends to diminish noticeably as time goes by. In the initial stages of a new regulatory scheme, there is pressure on the administration to appoint highly qualified people, and such people tend to be attracted by the nature of the task. But as the period of creativity comes to an end, as routinization sets in, the caliber of personnel tends to decline. There also seems to be a tendency for the regulators and regulated to come together; the perspective of the regulators tends to narrow to that of the industry with which they are concerned.

The claimed advantages of judicial enforcement are that courts command more respect, are more impartial, are less subject to pressures, and are less likely to launch on radical changes of course. The latter claim is at least doubtful. It is not easy to tell, for example, whether the Supreme Court or the FTC has done the most shifting in interpreting the antitrust laws, or whether courts or administrative agencies have embarked more frequently on "radical" changes in utility rate regulation. The claims may be summed up in the shorthand statement that courts are more likely to impose a "rule of law," as opposed to a "rule of men." Again, the difference between courts and administrative agencies is probably less than is usually claimed. Even assuming there is a substantial difference, it may be attributable principally to the fact that administrative agencies typically operate in regulatory areas where broad statutory standards are characteristic and where "partiality" is implicit in statutory policy.

In short, administrative agencies at best have some advantages in certain situations, and courts at best have some advantages in others, and the choice between the two — if one is to be made — depends on what one is trying to do.

In part for the above reasons, we see no strong case for concentrating the whole of antitrust enforcement either in the courts or in the Federal Trade Commission. So long as antitrust law remains a many-sided thing, the potential advantages of each should be utilized.

11. Jaffe, *Administrative Law* (1953), pp. 79, 80.

The principal problems to be avoided are duplication of effort and dual standards. Duplication of effort can be minimized simply by the Department of Justice and the Trade Commission informing each other of what they are doing. Each might make a different decision as to whether it is worth while to proceed in any given case. But this is little cause for serious concern. As for the possibility of dual legal standards, such as appears to have developed in the treatment of exclusive-requirement contracts, disparities can ultimately be resolved by the Supreme Court.

Any attempt to define jurisdictional lines so as to eliminate dual enforcement entirely would cause serious difficulty. A new and often mystifying issue would be introduced into almost every proceeding in both the courts and the FTC. For example, if violations of the Sherman Act were excluded from "unfair methods of competition," each FTC proceeding under Section 5 of the FTC Act would be bedeviled by the problem of determining whether the activities under attack might conceivably be held to be a violation of Section 1 of the Sherman Act.

On the other hand, a reshuffling of responsibilities may be appropriate in particular instances, as suggested in some of the recommendations below.

(2) *"Big" cases.* As has been pointed out, the handling of big Sherman Act cases in district courts has several disadvantages. First, there tends to be a lack of consistent enforcement. Second, big cases throw a tremendous burden on the district courts. Third, the cases put perhaps too heavy a burden of responsibility on individual judges, particularly insofar as such remedies as divestiture or dissolution are concerned.

Assuming no change in the basic antitrust laws, these problems might be substantially mitigated by the creation of a special constitutional court. The court might be given jurisdiction over all Sherman Act cases in which the remedy of divestiture is being sought. This would probably catch most of the big cases. Or, if greater coverage were desired, the special court could be given additional jurisdiction over all complaints in which violations of Section 2 of the Sherman Act are charged, excepting only cases in which an individual firm is charged with an attempt to monopolize. For purposes of review, the court would be considered a district court. Its decisions would be subject to direct appeal to the Supreme Court under the Expediting Act.

Concentration of Section 2 enforcement in a single body would pose risks somewhat similar to those characteristic of the independent commission. On the other hand, assuming that the panel of the special court is made large enough to handle the cases coming before it, we might expect an improvement in this area of antitrust enforcement in several respects. The creation of a special court would enable the appointment of highly qualified judges. Even if the judges initially had no particular familiarity with the field, they would be able to learn through continuous and concentrated experience. Diversity in enforcement would not be eliminated, since results might vary with the make-up of the panel hearing any particular case. But diversity would probably be considerably less than presently exists. A special court could also be supplied with special masters for the hearings of technical issues. It might also be supplied with an economic and statistical staff which could assist the judges in the organization of evidence presented at trial, and could advise the judges in connection with pretrial conferences with counsel for the purpose of streamlining the case and laying down an orderly sequence for presentation of evidence. We are inclined against this; we think it preferable to lodge the expertise in the prosecuting agency; but in any event it would be desirable, if the proposal were adopted, to provide for the appearance of staff as witnesses so that they could be cross-examined by the parties wherever they so desired. Such a special court, confined only to antitrust cases, might also be more capable over the course of time of evolving new procedures and techniques of dealing with cases which will expedite their orderly disposition. We would sacrifice some "stability and experience" by providing for staggered term appointments to the special court, no judge serving for more than, say, eight years.

Another possibility is to use a long dormant provision in the antitrust laws authorizing district courts to refer the formulation of decrees to the Federal Trade Commission acting as a master in Chancery. But this provision has probably lain dormant for the simple reason that in the existing enforcement arrangements it would do no particular good. By the time a judge has heard an antitrust case to the point of rendering judgment of whether or not relief should be granted, he is in most cases sufficiently familiar with the industry and problems involved so that referral to the Federal Trade Commission would probably delay rather than expedite proceedings. Thus whether enforcement of the big case is left with the district courts or transferred to a special tribunal, there seems little to be gained by bringing the FTC into the picture. On the other hand, the FTC and its resources might well be used by the Department of Justice for assistance in the preparation of the government's proposals for remedial decrees.

(3) *Case planning.* The critical importance of case theory and case planning suggests that it be lodged in the best hands, both in the Department of Justice and in the Federal Trade Commission. While both agencies currently have some review procedures in the drafting of complaints and planning of the case, this job by and large is assigned to particular attorneys in charge of particular cases. Centralization in a section staffed with the agencies' best economists and attorneys would improve the drafting of complaints, speed the course of trials, and probably have considerable impact on the interpretation of the law itself.

This is not to say that rational case theory and case presentation would in all cases shorten trials. The rational complaint may in some situations require a longer trial than the irrational one. For example, it is quite possible that some of the more dubious interpretations of the law of recent years came out of a desire on the part of the enforcement agencies to shortcut the route to victory. The government's use of the intracorporate conspiracy doctrine, and its attempts to obtain a holding that vertical integration is illegal per se, may well be instances where this has happened. But even if improved drafting of complaints did little or nothing in speeding up the cases, the prospect of more rational law enforcement is sufficient justification.

(4) *Criminal sanctions.* There seems little doubt that the deterrent value of criminal sanctions in the antitrust laws is considerably greater than that measured by the fines imposed or by the remote possibility of imprisonment. Respectable persons do not wish to be charged with a crime. Criminal sanctions, therefore, should not lightly be tossed aside. Nevertheless, the values underlying the long-honored constitutional prohibitions of undue vagueness in criminal statutes should not lightly be tossed aside either. There is more than a little merit in the complaint that criminal sanctions are inappropriate for those areas of antitrust law where violations depend upon essentially economic judgments on which reasonable Supreme Court justices may and do differ.

Criminal sanctions would seem to be appropriate only in cases where conduct may be unambiguously denominated bad. This would include cases involving specific intent to indulge in bad conduct, and cases where the illegality is so well settled that it is reasonable to impute intent to the conduct itself. Generally speaking, criminal sanctions should be confined to such per se offenses as price-fixing, group boycotts, predatory practices, attempts to monopolize, and the like. The list of criminal offenses should be spelled out as such.

There would, of course, be definitional troubles. Thus price-fixing may be illegal per se, but there is still some doubt as to what activities constitute price-fixing. Presumably, however, the newly defined offenses would work no serious hardship on the government, because the alternative of civil proceeding would still be available. In order to prevent effects akin to *res judicata,* it might be provided that dismissals of criminal indictments would have no effect on subsequent civil determinations.

We make these recommendations apart from the question of whether or not the substantive law is changed. A fortiori, we would have no criminal sanctions attached to a law against unreasonable market power.

(5) *Private actions.* The considerations just raised concerning criminal sanctions are also pertinent to private actions for damages. Vague statutory standards are more tolerable and more fair the more that enforcement has "prospective" effect only. It is unfair for private plaintiffs to collect treble damages for conduct the illegality of which cannot readily be determined in advance.

On the other hand, private suits are becoming more of an important supplementary enforcement device. They may be the most effective way of policing the multitude of comparatively local and insignificant violations that will tend to escape the glance of federal enforcement authorities or that, even if noticed, do not merit the expenditure of limited enforcement resources. Moreover, the prospect of private damage suits is a growing deterrent to illegal conduct, although the difficulties of proving damages remain very great in most situations.

Taking into account these considerations, we are inclined to the following position:

(a) Section 5 of the Clayton Act, making final judgments or decrees in government proceedings prima-facie evidence in subsequent private suits, should be left as is.

(b) Treble damage recovery, as distinct from recovery of "actual" damages, should be limited to violations to which criminal sanctions remain attached (as outlined above).

(c) There should be no private right of action based on the acquisition of "unreasonable market power."

(6) *Mergers.* As has been pointed out, enforcement of the antimerger statute seems hopelessly inadequate. The magnitude of the enforcement task is in large part due to the scope of the investigation required by the existing statutory standards, at least as interpreted by the Commission in the *Pillsbury*[12] case. But even assuming no change in the substantive statutory standard, the effectiveness of enforcement could be substantially increased in several ways.

First, there seems to be no particular reason in this case for dual enforcement. It would seem preferable to concentrate the enforcement of the antimerger statute in the FTC, but only if the Commission, by amendment of Section 7 or otherwise, is induced to subordinate "expertise" to rigorous, speedy enforcement. The Commission should also be given the following powers:

(a) The power (which the Department of Justice has now) to seek a preliminary injunction in any Federal District Court.

(b) The power to compel the filing of a report on any proposed merger involving a company or a to-be-acquired asset in excess of, say, $5,000,000.

Furthermore, it should be provided that no merger for which a report is required can be consummated for a period of 60 days, within which time the Federal Trade Commission may either (1) grant a clearance for the merger, or (2) withhold clearance on the ground that the merger may violate the statute. In the latter event, the Commission's power to obtain a preliminary injunction could be used if the parties showed an inclination to go ahead despite the lack of clearance.

We recognize that the effect of these provisions, because of inherent administrative caution, might effectively block some mergers which might ultimately after full hearing be held legal. In situations where time is of the essence, the law would be similar in effect to the power of the SEC to suspend a registration statement. However, there would be some additional protection in that the Trade Commission would have to make the necessary prima-facie showing of illegality before a preliminary injunction could be obtained;

12. *In re* Pillsbury Mills, FTC Docket No. 6000 (1953).

and the statute might provide that the court, in its discretion, could permit the merger to take place on a showing and assurance that the acquired company would remain a sufficiently distinct entity to enable ready divestiture later on. The justification for the proposals is that adequate enforcement does not otherwise seem possible. Moreover, precisely the same situation would exist under the present law if the Department of Justice had appropriations and staff adequate to keep track of proposed mergers.

(7) *Advance clearance generally.* We have recommended an advance clearance program for mergers, whether existing law is changed or not, principally on the ground that it is needed for effective enforcement, but also on the ground that, in light of the difficulties of unscrambling a merger, advance clearance should be available to those who want it. Is an advance clearance program feasible and appropriate for other areas?

It seems doubtful that there is any strong need felt for such procedures. Significantly, the Attorney General's Committee, heavily represented with antitrust defense counsel, recommended against any amplification of the existing limited devices, without recorded dissent. As we have noted, there are intrinsic limitations on utility and scope of advance clearance. Except in the case of proposed mergers, blanket clearances are likely to be neither possible nor wise. Where legality necessarily turns on effects, the agency will in most cases make the clearance conditional, and might properly insist on a right of surveillance. The latter is particularly unpalatable to most business firms.

Moreover, the need for advance clearance would be considerably diminished if, as we propose, criminal sanctions were removed from all but clearly defined antitrust offenses. To be sure, an adverse civil judgment may have "retroactive" effects where companies have substantially altered their position (i.e., foregone other alternatives or made financial commitments) on an assumption that the conduct, ultimately condemned, was legal. But usually these consequences are not likely to be severe — the loss is the lost opportunity to profit from continuing the violation and presumably, where the remedy is in terms only prospective, the companies, absent damages in private suits, retain the past profits which violation has produced.

(8) *Resources for enforcement.* Before we leave the possibilities of procedural improvements under the present law, it is worth rais-

ing once again, if only for the emphasis it deserves, the question of resources devoted to enforcement. They are at present grossly inadequate on any reasonable standard of the scope and importance of our antitrust policy. In recent years, the two antitrust agencies have spent less than $10 million per year, FTC spending somewhat more and the Antitrust Division somewhat less than half the total.[13] This can be compared with nearly five times that much spent by the five federal regulatory agencies: ICC, SEC, CAB, FCC, and FTC,[14] whose combined jurisdiction covers a far smaller part of the economy than that to which antitrust is applicable. Clearly, more money is a necessary condition of a more effective application of existing law. Further, by laws familiar in the world of government, a large effort may also result in more success in attracting first-rate personnel.

ENFORCEMENT OF A PROGRAM AGAINST UNREASONABLE MARKET POWER

We shall here outline in some detail our recommendations on the mechanism and procedures for enforcing a policy against unreasonable market power. The discussion draws heavily on the preceding parts of this chapter, it is hoped with a minimum of repetition. We shall deal with three general questions: (a) where to locate the prosecuting and adjudicating functions; (b) what procedures should be employed; and (c) how to coordinate enforcement of a market-power statute with the enforcement of antitrust law generally.

The enforcement mechanism

In Chapter III, we suggested that a program against undue market power could be either limited in time, for the sole purpose of clearing up existing concentrations, or, alternatively, made a permanent feature of the antitrust laws. In either event, we would suggest substantially the same enforcement mechanism. Briefly put, we would lodge the prosecuting function in a newly created administrative agency, preferably though not necessarily of the inde-

13. Not all of FTC's expenditures are properly chargeable to antitrust enforcement, since it also polices labelling, advertising, and trade practices, and engages in studies at the request of Congress. The Antitrust Division also has some miscellaneous reporting reponsibilities, but of much smaller total size.

14. The total was $47 million. The figures are annual averages for fiscal 1954–59; taken from the federal budget.

pendent commission type; and would place adjudication in the hands of a special court, along the lines of that suggested for the enforcement of Section 2 cases under existing law.

We believe this scheme would tend to combine the respective advantages of judicial and administrative enforcement.

The decision to locate the prosecuting function in a new independent agency, rather than in an expanded Antitrust Division or in the FTC, is not an obvious answer to a vitally important question. There is something to be said against it. Creating a third antitrust agency would enhance the problem of coordinating policies and efforts, of avoiding conflict and duplication. Presumably the requisite personnel could be added to the Division or to the FTC as well as to a new agency. But we do not think that the difficulties of coordination, about which more shall be said later, are too serious; and we suspect that better personnel could be more readily attracted to a new agency, created to fulfill a single new function, than to a new section of an old-line establishment. Moreover, we believe the function would be more efficiently performed by an independent agency charged with that task only. Finally — as between an independent agency and the Antitrust Division — we would prefer the former because we believe some degree of immunization from day-to-day political currents would produce a greater consistency in the development and application of the program.

We would prefer to place adjudication in the hands of a special court, rather than in the agency itself, for a number of reasons, some of which have been stated or implied previously in this chapter. There are a few others. Splitting off the judging function would enable the agency heads to devote their full attention to directing the tasks of investigation, negotiation, and the preparation and prosecution of cases. It would eliminate the criticism and fears — warranted or unwarranted — that a combination of policy-making, prosecuting, and adjudicating functions tends to produce biased results. It would tend, we believe, to put decisions in the hands of people more qualified, in over-all terms, to make the kind of decisions that would be involved. Finally, it would eliminate at least one of the stages of review that currently characterizes administrative proceedings. The typical administrative agency case goes through four stages: (1) decision by a trial examiner; (2) decision by the Commission; (3) review by a Court of Appeals; and (4) at the discretion of the Supreme Court, review on petition for certiorari. Our scheme would involve but two: (1) decision by a special court, and (2) review by direct appeal to the Supreme Court.

Procedures

In determining appropriate procedures, we deemed certain considerations to be of paramount importance. First, proceedings under a market-power statute, looking to extensive remedies, are almost certain to be major undertakings. For reasons of public interest, conservation of enforcement resources, and simple common sense, it is vitally important that the prosecuting agency, before undertaking proceedings in a particular case, be reasonably convinced not only that undue market power exists in a particular industry, but also that feasible and effective remedies can be imposed. This means that no proceedings should start except after thorough investigation, study, and analysis of the industry concerned.

Second, to save time and to promote rational decisions, every effort should be made to insure a clear, logical formulation of issues and adversary conclusions, to reduce the scope of trials to significant factual issues fairly open to dispute, and to eliminate repetitive or inconsequential offers of proof.

Third, judicial review of special court decisions should be limited to one appeal, and should be narrow in scope. Existence of market power and feasibility of remedy are likely to be related questions: there are clearly many facts of common relevance to both. Piecemeal review of decisions on these two questions seems to have little justification; the cases in which it would save time and effort would likely be far fewer than those in which it would merely cause delay, particularly where the scope of review is narrowly confined and hence the prospect of reversal rather small. And we would narrowly confine the scope of review for the same reasons that it has been confined in similar cases in the past, reasons adding up to the proposition that appellate courts are ill-equipped to remake substantive determinations of highly complex factual questions by judges or agencies who through special knowledge or time have acquired a familiarity with the case that appellate judges, save in cases of obvious error, cannot surpass.

With these considerations and others in mind, we submit the following outline of procedures for enforcing a statute against undue market power.

(a) Staff investigation of the industry which preliminary information indicates may come within the statute. Preparation of a full study, fully annotated to evidentiary sources, and containing (1) conclusions on the presence or absence of market power, and on whether the power is justified; (2) a full statement of the analysis and reasoning in support of those conclusions; and (3) a full discussion, again with reasons, of the feasibility of structural reorganization and other remedies, with general indications as to the lines reorganization might take.

(b) Where undue market power and feasible relief is indicated, informal presentation of the report to the members of the industry concerned, solicitation of written comments and objections, and negotiation with a view toward settlement and voluntary reorganization.

(c) When negotiations fail — or if it is clear beforehand that no voluntary agreement is likely — filing of a complaint with the special court, together with the staff study as a "brief" in support of the complaint, followed by answers and "reply briefs" on behalf of defendants, and written rejoinder by the Agency.

(d) The special court would then:

(i) in the probably rare case where there is no real dispute as to significant facts, proceed to summary judgment that defendant or defendants possess or lack unreasonable market power; and where the decision is for the Agency, direct the Agency and defendants, separately or in concert, to work out and submit proposed plans of reorganization and other relief;

(ii) where there is dispute over significant facts and resolution depends on the reliability of certain evidence or the expertness or method of those who prepared it, direct a trial limited to such factual issues; where the areas of dispute are not clear, endeavor by pretrial proceedings, stipulations, etc., to eliminate those issues not seriously disputed;

(iii) at the conclusion of a trial, direct the submission of trial briefs, hear oral argument, render decision as to the existence of undue market power, and, where such power is found, direct the preparation of remedial decrees;

(iv) enter final decree.

(e) Review by direct appeal to the Supreme Court of a final decision by the special court (a decision that defendants do not possess undue market power, or a final decision incorporating a remedial decree); such review to be limited to (1) correctness of procedures (including questions whether the court followed statutory mandates), and (2) whether critical fact findings rested on substantial evidence.

By way of conclusion, we would stress that the limited judicial review herein suggested is by no means insignificant. It contains the vitally important protection that maintaining a high standard of procedural performance affords; though compelling lower courts or agencies to make clear why and how they reached their results does not guarantee correct decisions, it makes a substantial contribution to that end.

Coordination of enforcement

The needs are to avoid unnecessary duplications of investigations and proceedings; to avoid antitrust proceedings whose results might be made obsolete by the remedies in market power proceedings; and at the same time to leave room for proceedings which have an immediate justification of their own, particularly in light of the fact that market power cases will probably be protracted, and immediate relief under other antitrust provisions may be highly desirable.

Much depends on the character of the conduct that is, or may be made, the subject matter of the other proceedings. Generally speaking, for example, there would seem to be no interference with reorganization proceedings, and little waste motion in moving against price-fixing conspiracies, other per se restraints, and mergers. Price-fixing does current harm, and the quicker it is ended, the better. Injunctions against unlawful mergers would materially aid the ultimate job of reorganizing the industry — there would be fewer eggs to unscramble. At the other end of the line would be a Section 2 monopolization case, which would substantially duplicate a reorganization proceeding and serve no useful purpose. We would meet the last problem by repealing all but the "conspiracy" and "attempt to monopolize" offenses of Section 2.

To a large extent, these considerations are the same whether the court proceedings are criminal or civil, though it is harder to justify the suspension of criminal proceedings against obvious violators.

Our solution to the problem of coordination would run along the following lines, the agency charged with enforcement of the market power statute being identified, simply to give it a name, as the Industrial Reorganization Commission (IRC).

(1) The IRC, FTC, and the Antitrust Division would regularly interchange information as to what industries they were currently investigating, and would supply on request to the others any information they possessed.

(2) The IRC would inform the other agencies of the industries against which market-power proceedings were likely or contemplated, and those Agencies would consult with IRC on the desirability of instituting any other antitrust proceedings against those industries or members thereof.

(3) The Attorney General and the FTC would have final authority in deciding whether to institute antitrust proceedings within their jurisdiction, but only up to the time that the IRC instituted proceedings against the same defendant or defendants under the market-power statute.

(4) From that point, and until final disposition of the market-power proceedings, no civil antitrust proceedings could be instituted by the Antitrust Division or FTC proceedings within the FTC, over the objection of IRC, without written approval of the President.

(5) Similarly, if at the time market power proceedings are commenced, there are civil or FTC proceedings that have not yet gone to trial, the Attorney General should request a court to suspend, and the FTC should suspend, on request by IRC unless the President directs otherwise. We would also give the IRC certain other powers. It would have the power to obtain an injunction against any merger in an industry that has been subjected to market power proceedings. It would be given powers to subpoena books and papers, and to require firms to submit reports covering such matters as financial statements, sales, market areas, etc., provision being made for keeping such information confidential unless and until negotiations are begun for voluntary compliance with the statute.

DRAFT OF A PROPOSED ANTITRUST STATUTE

We conclude this chapter, and our general discussions of antitrust policy, with a draft of a proposed antitrust statute incorporating the bulk of our substantive proposals. It does not cover our proposals on price discrimination, which have already been set forth with some precision; nor does it cover, except by passing reference, our proposals on enforcement machinery and other procedures, which have also been dealt with in detail. The draft is more suggestive than definitive. To each section of the draft statute, we have appended short comments.

DRAFT ANTITRUST LAW

Section 1. *Unreasonable Market Power Injurious to Trade and Commerce*

Possession, by any one or more persons, of unreasonable market power in trade and commerce among the several States or with foreign nations is hereby declared to be injurious to such trade or commerce.

Comments. This is simply a declaration of policy, in preface to provisions providing for proceedings against unreasonable market power.

Section 2. *Market Power Defined. Unreasonable Market Power*

(a) For the purposes of this Act, market power shall mean the persistent ability of a person, or of a group of persons whether or not acting pursuant to agreement or conspiracy, to restrict output or determine prices without losing a substantial share of the market, or without losing substantial profits or incurring heavier losses, because of the increased output or lower prices of rivals. Evidence of market power may include, but shall not be limited to:

(1) persistent failure of prices to reflect substantial declines of demand or costs, or to reflect substantial excess capacity;

(2) persistence of profits that are abnormally high, taking into account such factors as risks and excess capacity; or

(3) failure of new rivals to enter the market during prolonged periods of abnormally high profits or of persistent or recurring rationing.

Comments. The core of market power is the possession of a substantial range of price and output choices, not decisively affected by the response of rivals or would-be rivals. It may be held by a single corporation, or it may be held by several corporations who are able to, or sometimes economically compelled to, behave jointly in such a way as to enhance their profits and/or positions over what would be attained if they competed against each other or if others were able to compete effectively against them. The draft definition specifically states that proof of agreement or conspiracy is not an essential ingredient of "group power." Indeed, the principal purpose of the statute is to cover oligopolistic industries in which effective "shared" market power exists without the ingredient of agreement essential to a Sherman Act charge. The definition technically covers the large-numbers cartel case as well, and in this respect is somewhat redundant. However, we think the coverage is desirable in order to eliminate the possibility that defendants could evade the statute by pointing to minor agreements of one sort or another and arguing that the statute covered wholly noncollusive market power only.

Market power is defined as the ability to restrict output or to determine prices either without losing a substantial share of the market *or* without losing profits or incurring heavier losses. This reflects the fact that sellers with market power usually have a choice between earning high unit profits on a small volume of sales, or lower unit profits on a higher volume of sales. Thus, the mere fact that defendants cannot raise prices without losing a substantial share of the market does not disprove the existence of substantial market power.

The categories of evidence are not exclusive, but probably indicate the most common indicia of substantial market power. The term "abnormally high profits" is admittedly imprecise, but we believe that it is workably determinable in most specific instances. It is often possible to say that profits are abnormally high without determining precisely what normal profits would be. Some cases would be clear, as, for example, a firm or group of firms persistently earning positive profits of any amount during a prolonged period of excess capacity.

Section 2. (continued)

(b) Market power, as defined in Section 2(a), shall be conclusively presumed where, for five years or more, one company has accounted for 50 percent or more of annual sales in the market, or four or fewer companies have accounted for 80 percent of sales.

Comments. We have discussed the pros and cons of this provision in Chapter III. We think it highly likely that this arbitrary definition would cover some situations in which substantial market power did not in fact exist, most likely in declining industries. However, we are inclined to favor it on the ground that it would simplify proof in a large number of cases where fuller study would substantiate the conclusion that these percentage figures would suggest; and on the ground that the enforcement agency, particularly with inevitably limited resources, would have the common sense to avoid inappropriate proceedings.

Section 2. (continued)

(c) Market power shall be deemed unreasonable unless shown by defendant or defendants to have been created and maintained, entirely or almost entirely, by one or more of the following:

(1) such economies as are dependent upon size in relation to the market;

(2) ownership of valid patents, lawfully acquired and lawfully used; provided that, on a showing that market power has been created and maintained by patents, the government shall have the burden of showing invalidity, unlawful acquisition, or unlawful use;

(3) low prices or superior products attributable to the introduction of new processes, product improvements or marketing methods, or to extraordinary efficiency of a single firm in comparison with that of other firms having a substantial share of the market.

Comments. The "justifications" of market power, which defendants have the burden of establishing, closely resemble those suggested by Judge Wyzanski in *United Shoe.* The first and second are fairly obvious. The third deserves some elaboration. We believe that some defense of this kind is essential in order to protect the kind of behavior that competition is thought to foster. On the other hand, we have incorporated some limitations. Low prices or superior products are a justification only if attributable to factors specified. The efficiency justification is available only to a firm having substantial competitors in its market; in other cases, there is no satisfactory standard of comparison.

Section 3. *Jurisdiction of Economic Court. Division and Divestiture*

(a) The Economic Court is invested with jurisdiction to prevent and restrain injuries to trade or commerce resulting from the possession of unreasonable market power; and it shall be the duty of the Industrial Reorganization Commission to institute proceedings in equity before said court to prevent and restrain such injuries. Pending determination of the case, the court may at any time make such temporary restraining order or prohibition as shall be deemed appropriate in the circumstances.

(b) On a judgment that defendant or defendants possess unreasonable market power, the court shall, to the extent that such relief is feasible, order the division or divestiture of assets of defendant or defendants, and, whether or not division or divestiture of assets is ordered, the court may grant such other or further relief as shall be deemed appropriate in the circumstances; provided that:

(1) the court shall not approve a plan involving division of the assets of a single plant;

(2) in determining the feasibility of division or divestiture of assets, the court shall take into account any probable permanent loss of substantial economies intrinsic to the defendant company or companies as currently constituted;

(3) the court shall not order division or divestiture of assets where defendants show that such relief would not materially improve the competitive conditions which other relief, proposed by defendants, would achieve; and

(4) the court shall not approve a proposed plan of divestiture or division of assets where defendants show that one or more companies resulting from the plan would lack reasonable prospects for survival under the competitive conditions likely to prevail.

Comments. Structural reorganization of one or more firms, and creation of new independent companies, would be the usual and normal remedy for unreasonable market power, rather than a last resort. Defendants have the burden of showing that structural reorganization is inappropriate, or that any proposed plan is not feasible, except in the "single plant" case. Whenever it is apparent from evidence received on market power that some reorganization is feasible — which is likely to be the usual case — the court should not allow defendants to pursue the purely negative role of objecting to specific plans proposed by the enforcement agency, but should direct defendants to submit a specific plan or plans of their own.

Section 4. *Amendment and Repeal of Existing Law*

(a) Section 1 of the Sherman Act, 26 Stat. 209, 15 U.S.C. Section 1, as amended, is hereby amended to read in its entirety as follows: "Section 1. Every contract, combination in the form of trust or otherwise, or conspiracy, in restraint of trade or commerce among the several States, or with foreign nations, is declared to be unlawful."

(b) [Similar amendment of Section 3, covering trade and commerce in and with the District of Columbia and the Territories.]

(c) Section 2 of the Sherman Act, 26 Stat. 209, 15 U.S.C., Section 2 is hereby repealed.

(d) The McGuire Act, 66 Stat. 632, 15 U.S.C. 845, is hereby repealed.

Comments. The amendment of Sections 1 and 3 of the Sherman Act removes criminal penalties. The amendment of Section 1 also repeals the Miller-Tydings Act. Parts of Section 2 of the Sherman Act are reinstated in Section 5 of the draft act.

Section 5. *Specific Restraints Prohibited. Criminal Penalties*

(a) It shall be unlawful for any person, in or affecting commerce among the several states or with foreign nations, to agree or conspire with actual or potential competitors for the purpose or with the effect of:

(1) fixing or substantially affecting the price of any goods or services;

(2) dividing or sharing the market for any goods or services;

(3) fixing or limiting the production of goods or services; or

(4) boycotting any other person or persons, whether competitors or not.

(b) It shall be unlawful for any person to attempt to monopolize, or conspire with any other person or persons with an intent to monopolize, any part of the trade or commerce among the several States or with foreign nations.

(c) It shall be unlawful for two or more competitors, in or affecting commerce among the several States or with foreign nations, to agree, through a trade association or otherwise:

(1) to abide by reported list prices;

(2) to report offers at which no sales are made;

(3) to inform each other of the individual buyers and sellers in all transactions;

(4) to refuse to make reports, submitted to each other, available to buyers or buyers' trade associations;

(5) to submit books and accounts to the inspection of any member of the group or representative thereof; or

(6) to report transactions to each other, or to a representative of the group, within a period of seven days or less after said transactions take place.

(d) It shall be unlawful for a patentee or for any person purporting to exercise rights granted to a patentee;

(1) to license the sale, or the manufacture and sale, of patented products, of products incorporating the patent, or of products involving a patented process, on condition that the licensee abide by price restrictions imposed by the licensor;

(2) to license on condition that the licensee assign future patents to the licensor, or grant exclusive licenses under future patents to the licensor; or

(3) to participate in cross-licensing or patent-pooling arrangements containing any restrictions on the participants other than restrictions on fields of use.

(e) The several district courts of the United States are invested with jurisdiction to retrain violations of this section.

(f) Every person who shall willfully violate any provision of this section shall be deemed guilty of a misdemeanor, and on conviction thereof, shall be punished by a fine not exceeding $50,000, or by imprisonment not exceeding one year, or by both said punishments, in the discretion of the court.

Comments. This action sets forth per se offenses. Subparagraph (b) limits existing Section 2 of the Sherman Act to cases involving specific intent.

Section 6. *Private Suits*

(a) Possession of unreasonable market power, as defined in this Act, shall not be deemed a violation of the antitrust laws for the purposes of private suit under Sections 4 and 16 of the Clayton Act, 38 Stat. 731, 15 U.S.C., Sections 15, 26; nor shall a final judgment or decree as to possession of such power be deemed a final judgment or decree under the antitrust laws for the purposes of Section 5 of the Clayton Act, 38 Stat. 731, 15 U.S.C., Section 16.

(b) Violations of Section 1 and 3 of the Sherman Act as amended by Section 4 of this Act, and violations of Section 5 of this Act shall be deemed violations of the antitrust laws for the purposes of private suit under Sections 4 and 16 of the Clayton Act; and final judgments or decrees as to such violations shall be deemed final judgments or decrees under the antitrust laws for the purposes of Section 5 of the Clayton Act; provided, however, that, except as to private suits based on willful violations of Section 5 of this Act, recovery shall be limited to actual damages and the costs of suit, including reasonable attorney's fee.

Comments. This section is self-explanatory. No private suit may be based on a violation of the unreasonable market power prohibition. Recovery of triple damages is limited to the per se offenses.

Statistical Appendix

General Note. In classifying industries by size, by extent of market, and by market structure, the following abbreviations have been used in the tables.

SIZE OF INDUSTRY. I-large; II-medium large; III-medium; IV-small.

EXTENT OF MARKET. 1-national — geographically concentrated supply; 2-national — geographically unconcentrated supply; 3-local and regional; 4-heterogeneous.

MARKET STRUCTURE. A-concentrated; B-unconcentrated.

S.A. Table 1. The classification of manufacturing industries by size, extent of the market, and market structure (national and heterogeneous markets)

Size of industry and extent and structure of market[a]	Industry code	Industry	Value of shipments (thousands of dollars)	Minimum[b] concentration ratio: First 8 firms	Minimum[b] concentration ratio: First 20 firms	Maximum concentration ratio: First 8 firms	Maximum concentration ratio: First 20 firms
I, 1, A							
Type I Oligopolies							
	*3722	Aircraft engines and propellers	3,381,551	76	91 (24)	82	91
	*2111	Cigarettes and tobacco	2,816,216	77	93	95	99
	2823	Plastics materials	1,463,460	61	78		
	2825	Synethic fibers	1,202,343	95	99		
	3351	Copper rolling and drawing	1,123,540	71	89		
	3521	Tractors	1,070,836	84	94		
	3717 (x)	Motor vehicles and parts	(6,620,000)	64	78		
	2085 (x)	Wines and distilled liquors	(1,040,000)				
			18,717,946				
Type II Oligopolies							
	*2834	Pharmaceutical preparations	1,946,672	35	55	47	69
	*3631	Insulated wire and cable	1,772,935	38	61 (24)	54	75
	*2841	Soap, glycerin, cleaning and polishing preparations, and related products	1,590,527	52	66 (28)	64	75
	2721	Periodicals	1,394,073	39	53		
	3614	Motors and generators	1,338,447	56	70		
	3661 (x)	Radios and related products	(1,530,000)	35	54		
	*3585 (x)	Refrigeration equipment	(1,400,000)	53	70	55	73
			10,972,654				
I, 1, B	†*2233	Cotton and synthetic broad-woven fabrics	4,962,646	13	26	35	52
	*3541	Machine tools	2,624,011	15	26 (24)	23	38
	†*3141	Footwear, except rubber	2,021,986	32	42 (24)	36	45
	*2253	Knit outerwear and underwear	1,963,928	06	14	19	32
	*26 misc.	Misc. paper, allied products	1,935,383	19	32	37	53
	†*3439	Heating and cooking equipment	1,931,339	25	42 (28)	34	48
	†*3421	Cutlery, hand tools, and general hardware	1,635,019	26	40 (28)	41	54
	3463	Metal stampings and pressings	1,632,764	18	28		
	*2333	Dresses	1,576,186	06	12	11	46
	*2311	Men's and boys' suits, coats, and trousers	1,323,329	13	23	18	33
	3531	Construction and mining machinery	1,159,170	29	48		
	†*2213	Woolen and worsted manufactures	1,157,863	24	43 (28)	36	56
	*35 misc.	Miscellaneous metal-working machinery	1,117,361	20	35	34	55
	2337	Women's and misses' suits, coats, and skirts	1,101,371	06	12		
			26,142,356				

[a] See General Note, page 274.

[b] In some cases it was not possible to compute the concentration ratio for twenty firms without making special assumptions. In each such case a number of firms near twenty was used, here and in subsequent tables, the number being indicated in parentheses next to the concentration ratio.

* An asterisk indicates consolidations of two or more product class groups. Both minimum and maximum concentration ratios are presented for such markets.

† Cases in which the minimum and maximum concentration ratios for the same market are in different concentration categories are indicated by a dagger sign appearing to the left of the industry code. We have probably understated the number of concentrated industries by classifying all but two industries according to the minimum rate. See the Methodological Appendix, III, for details of our procedure.

(x) An (x) indicates that sales concentration figures were not available and that concentration ratios have been estimated indirectly. See the Methodological Appendix, III, for details.

S.A. Table 1. (Continued)

Size of industry and extent and structure of market[a]	Industry code	Industry	Value of shipments (thousands of dollars)	Minimum[b] concentration ratio: First 8 firms	Minimum[b] concentration ratio: First 20 firms	Maximum concentration ratio: First 8 firms	Maximum concentration ratio: First 20 firms
I, 2, A							
Type I Oligopolies							
	3011	Tires and inner tubes	1,621,917	91	99		
	3411	Tin cans and other tinware	1,340,605	89	96		
	*2932	Coke and by-products	1,247,565	75	92	75	92
	*2062	Sugar	1,217,425	63	94 (28)	87	99
			5,427,611				
Type II Oligopolies							
	†*2011	Meat products	12,682,723	32	43	45	54
	*3721	Aircraft and aircraft equipment	8,412,520	52	70 (24)	62	79
	*2829	Organic chemicals, n.e.c.	3,231,191	43	64	68	84
	†*2092	Oleo, shortening, and cooking oils	2,748,229	28	52	68	88
	*2082	Malt and malt liquors	2,047,945	37	54	44	63
	*2819	Inorganic chemicals, n.e.c.	1,599,859	40	60	47	70
	*2851	Paints, varnishes, and allied products	1,503,728	36	48	37	50
	3522	Farm machinery (except tractors)	1,060,306	49	60		
	3616	Electric control apparatus	1,057,327	59	72		
	*3311 (x)	Blast furnaces, steel works, and rolling mills	(9,400,000)	45	65 (24)	63	83
			43,743,828				
I, 2, B	*2041	Flour and feed	4,899,338	25	38	40	54
	†*2033	Canning, preserving, and freezing	3,245,972	25	37	42	55
	*2511	Household furniture	2,626,819	12	20		
	*2671	Paperboard containers and boxes	2,273,311	24	38	29	43
	*3321	Iron foundries	1,718,373	29	45 (24)	32	48
	*3591	Valves, pipes, and fittings, except plumbers' fittings	1,125,811	20	34	27	44
			15,889,624				
I, 4, A							
Type II Oligopolies							
	*20 misc.	Misc. food and kindred products	3,700,349	36	48	44	58
	*30 misc.	Misc. rubber products	1,956,694	36	53 (24)	45	57
			5,657,043				
I, 4, B	*39 misc.	Misc. manufacturing industries	2,623,673	06	11	36	51
	*34 misc.	Misc. products of steel works	2,447,642	13	23	30	45
	*35 misc.	IMG general industrial machinery, n.e.c.	1,559,974	13	24	35	52
	*28 misc.	Misc. allied chemical products	1,367,347	13	26	44	59
	*23 misc.	Misc. apparel and accessories	1,125,995	05	09	27	41
	3971	Plastic products, n.e.c.	1,085,475	13	22		
			10,210,106				
II, 1, A							
Type I Oligopolies							
	2052	Biscuits, crackers, and pretzels	786,851	73	81		
	3861	Photographic equipment	773,218	70	80		
	3664	Tel. and tel. equipment	755,469	94	97		
	3662	Electronic tubes	709,614	78	92		

S.A. Table 1. (Continued)

Size of industry and extent and structure of market[a]	Industry code	Industry	Value of shipments (thousands of dollars)	Minimum[b] concentration ratio First 8 firms	Minimum[b] concentration ratio First 20 firms	Maximum concentration ratio First 8 firms	Maximum concentration ratio First 20 firms
	*3581	Dry cleaning and laundry equipment	672,986	72	91 (24)	79	95
	3641	Engine electrical equipment	564,325	79	87		
	3593	Ball and roller bearings	533,796	78	91		
	3571	Computing and related machines	501,311	84	96		
			5,297,570				
Type II Oligopolies							
	*2871	Fertilizers	855,196	45	64	45	64
	2893	Toilet preparations	701,532	42	63		
			1,556,728				
II, 1, B	†*2522	Nonhousehold partitions and fixtures	916,900	14	24	34	48
	†*2392	House furnishings, n.e.c.	906,967	29	45 (24)	35	49
	*2731	Books, publishing, and printing	896,559	21	35	31	48
	†*3611	Wiring devices and supplies	767,676	26	50 (24)	42	62
	*2328	Men's and boys' rough clothing	719,077	17	29	23	37
	2321	Men's dress shirts and nightwear	717,031	26	40		
	*2361	Children's and infants' outerwear	640,450	09	17	18	31
	3471	Lighting fixtures	632,327	24	53		
	3111	Leather tanning and finishing	618,177	30	48		
	*3941	Games and toys	596,857	16	34 (28)	28	94
	3566	Power transmission equipment	595,019	32	50		
			8,007,040				
	*2551 (x)	Hosiery mills	(858,279)				
			8,865,319				
II, 2, A							
Type I Oligopolies							
	3519	Internal combustion engines	923,115	61	82		
	3352	Aluminum rolling and drawing	760,416	87	93		
	3615	Transformers	628,917	86	93		
	3221	Glass containers	628,916	78	92		
			2,941,364				
Type II Oligopolies							
	2024	Ice cream and ices	954,337	41	52		
	3561	Pumps and compressors	867,400	34	51		
	3821	Mechanical measuring instruments	856,318	37	56		
	2023	Concentrated milk	836,908	52	62		
	3341	Secondary nonferrous metals	826,739	58	73		
	3811	Scientific instruments	644,457	60	73		
	2661	Paper bags	634,594	43	63		
	*3613	Electrical industrial apparatus, n.e.c.	574,264	33	53 (28)	43	96
	*36 misc.	Misc. electrical products	514,989	34	55	63	78
	*3292	Asbestos products	507,205	44	69 (24)	59	81
			7,217,211				

S.A. Table 1. (Continued)

Size of industry and extent and structure of market[a]	Industry code	Industry	Value of shipments (thousands of dollars)	Minimum concentration ratio[b]		Maximum concentration ratio	
				First 8 firms	First 20 firms	First 8 firms	First 20 firms
II, 2, B	2070	Confectionary products	982,501	26	41		
	3361	Nonferrous castings	843,090	27	37		
	2022	Cheese	613,197	28	35		
	3323	Steel castings	535,054	28	46		
	2432	Plywood	504,725	24	40		
			3,478,567				
II, 4, A *Type II Oligopolies*							
	*34 misc. F.	Misc. fabricated metal products	631,133	33	47	51	63
II, 4, B	*22 misc.	Misc. textile mill products	973,788				
	*32 misc.	Misc. nonmetallic mineral products	878,993	31	41	50	64
	*23 misc. F.	Misc. fabric and textile products	842,715	22	28	34	44
	*31 misc.	Misc. leather products	655,951	12	20	31	45
	*24 misc. W	Misc. wood products	631,383	12	22 (28)	24	38
	3559	Special industry machinery, n.e.c.	604,535	25	39		
			4,587,365				
III, 1, A *Type I Oligopolies*							
	3211	Flat glass	499,267	99	100		
	2072	Chocolate and cocoa products	471,965	76	90		
	3742	Railroad and street cars	468,233	74	94		
	3334	Primary aluminum	464,754	99	100		
	2094	Corn wet milling products	435,966	90	97		
	3511	Steam engines and turbines	426,197	94	99		
	3229	Pressed and blown glass, n.e.c.	416,997	75	86		
	2121	Cigars	333,273	64	81		
	2043	Cereal breakfast foods	330,970	89	98		
	3651	Electric lamps (bulbs)	309,650	96	99		
	3871	Watches and blocks	293,353	66	98		
	3359	Rolling and drawing, n.e.c.	275,067	70	85		
	2223	Thread	166,979	73	88		
	2274	Hard-surface floor coverings	159,679	97	100		
	2073	Chewing gum	153,524	93	99		
	3584	Vacuum cleaners	144,182	76	93		
	3572	Typewriters	141,677	98	99		
	3562	Elevators and escalators	128,102	65	77		
	3583	Sewing machines	107,492	89	95		
	*2271 (x)	Carpets and rugs	(480,000)	53	76 (28)	63	82
			6,207,327				
Type II Oligopolies							
	*3842	Surgical, medical, and dental instruments and supplies	481,056	33	60 (28)	56	70
	2025	Special dairy products	474,735	55	64		
	*2031	Canned and cured seafood	434,074	34	47	48	64
	2342	Corsets and allied garments	351,258	36	55		
	3552	Textile machinery	304,053	44	59		
	*35 misc.	Misc. office and store machinery	286,407	39	65 (24)	63	73
	†3231	Products of purchased glass	239,810	61	68		
	3555	Printing trades machinery	228,774	49	65		
	2771	Greeting cards	217,501	51	66		
	3554	Paper industries machinery	176,172	42	61		

S.A. Table 1. (Continued)

Size of industry and extent and structure of market[a]	Industry code	Industry	Value of shipments (thousands of dollars)	Minimum[b] concentration ratio		Maximum concentration ratio	
				First 8 firms	First 20 firms	First 8 firms	First 20 firms
	*3872	Instruments and related products, n.e.c.	156,270	46	68 (24)	59	77
	3851	Opthalmic goods	136,482	56	72		
	*3263	China and earthenware food utensils	118,579	40	77 (28)	61	90
	*2281	Hats (excluding millinery)	111,352	38	59	66	86
			3,716,473				
III, 1, B	*3911	Jewelry	342,259	18	31 (24)	29	42
	2331	Blouses	315,658	17	27		
			657,917				
III, 2, A *Type I Oligopolies*							
	*3272	Gypsum products and mineral wool	434,902	79	95 (28)	89	96
	3339	Primary nonferrous metals, n.e.c.	396,004	86	95		
	2824	Synthetic rubber	392,194	79	100		
	3741	Locomotives and parts	365,169	97	99		
	3333	Primary zinc	205,039	83	99		
	2896	Compressed and liquefied gases	195,390	83	90		
	3951	Pens and mechanical pencils	118,110	67	80		
	3331 (x)	Primary copper[c]	(490,000)	100 (9)			
	3332 (x)	Primary lead[c]	(305,000)	100 (6)			
			2,901,808				
Type II Oligopolies							
	2095	Flavorings	464,166	56	69		
	3431	Plumbing fixtures and fittings	423,984	51	67		
	2393	Textile bags	210,191	55	69		
	3589	Service and household machinery, n.e.c.	184,477	36	53		
			1,282,818				
III, 2, B	3551	Food products machinery	371,408	25	41		
	†*2563	Venetian blinds and window shades	171,811	32	52 (28)	45	57
	3732	Boat building and repairing	163,605	24	37		
			706,824				
III, 4, A	(none)						
III, 4, B	*32 misc. V.	Misc. vitreous products	462,566	29	46	59	79
IV, 1, A *Type I Oligopolies*							
	3751	Motorcycles and bicycles	88,340	72	93		
	3586	Measuring and dispensing pumps	85,094	76	96		
			173,434				

[c] Concentration data are based on the 1947 *Census of Manufactures*. Value of shipments listed is for 1954, but in order to avoid disclosure of data for individual firms, the 1954 data do not give concentration ratios. Both industries are extremely concentrated.

S.A. Table 1. (Continued)

Size of industry and extent and structure of market[a]	Industry code	Industry	Value of shipments (thousands of dollars)	Minimum[b] concentration ratio		Maximum concentration ratio	
				First 8 firms	First 20 firms	First 8 firms	First 20 firms
IV, 1, B	(none)						
IV, 2, A							
Type I Oligopolies							
	3663	Phonograph records	80,224	78	86		
	2898	Salt	71.636	93	99		
			151,860				
IV, 2, B	*24 misc. T.	Misc. timber basic products	73,881	27	47	49	
IV, 4, A							
Type I Oligopolies							
	2999	Petroleum and coal products, n.e.c.	61,241	68	89		
IV, 4, B	(none)						

S.A. Table 2. Frequency distribution of manufacturing industries by size, extent of the market, and market structure (national and heterogeneous markets)

Markets	No. of industries		Total value of shipments (thousands of dollars)	
National markets				
I. Large				
a. Concentrated, Type I	12		24,145,557	
b. Concentrated, Type II	17		54,716,482	
Subtotal		29		78,862,039
c. Unconcentrated		20	42,031,980	
II. Medium large				
a. Concentrated, Type I	12		8,238,934	
b. Concentrated, Type II	12		8,773,939	
Subtotal		24		17,012,873
c. Unconcentrated		17	12,343,886	
III. Medium				
a. Concentrated, Type I	29		9,109,135	
b. Concentrated, Type II	18		4,999,291	
Subtotal		47		14,108,426
c. Unconcentrated		5	1,364,741	
IV. Small				
a. Concentrated, Type I	4		325,294	
b. Concentrated, Type II	0		0	
Subtotal		4		325,294
c. Unconcentrated		1	73,881	
Total, concentrated				110,308,632
Total, unconcentrated				55,814,488
Total, all national markets		147		166,123,120
Heterogeneous markets				
I. Large				
a. Concentrated, Type I	0		0	
b. Concentrated, Type II	2		5,657,043	
Subtotal		2		5,657,043
c. Unconcentrated		6	10,210,106	
II. Medium large				
a. Concentrated, Type I	0		0	
b. Concentrated, Type II	1		631,133	
Subtotal		1		631,133
c. Unconcentrated		6	4,587,365	
III. Medium				
a. Concentrated, Type I	0		0	
b. Concentrated, Type II	0		0	
Subtotal		0		0
c. Unconcentrated		1	462,566	
IV. Small				
a. Concentrated, Type I	1		61,241	
b. Concentrated, Type II	0		0	
Subtotal		1		61,241
c. Unconcentrated		0		
Total, all heterogeneous markets		17	21,609,454	

S.A. Table 2. (Continued)

Markets	No. of industries		Total value of shipments (thousands of dollars)	
Total, national and heterogeneous markets				
I. Large				
a. Concentrated, Type I	12		24,145,557	
b. Concentrated, Type II	19		60,373,525	
Subtotal		31		84,519,082
c. Unconcentrated		26	52,242,086	
II. Medium large				
a. Concentrated, Type I	12		8,238,934	
b. Concentrated, Type II	13		9,405,072	
Subtotal		25		17,644,006
c. Unconcentrated		23	16,931,251	
III. Medium				
a. Concentrated, Type I	29		9,109,135	
b. Concentrated, Type II	18		4,999,291	
Subtotal		47		14,108,426
c. Unconcentrated		6	1,827,307	
IV. Small				
a. Concentrated, Type I	5		386,535	
b. Concentrated, Type II	0		0	
Subtotal		5		386,535
c. Unconcentrated		1	73,881	
Total, concentrated			116,658,049	
Total, unconcentrated			71,074,525	
Total, all national and heterogeneous markets		164	187,732,574	

S.A. Table 3. National concentration ratios for regional and local industries (by market structure and size)

Industry code	Industry	Value of shipments (thousands of dollars)	Minimum[a] concentration ratio: First 8 firms	Minimum[a] concentration ratio: First 20 firms	Maximum[a] concentration ratio: First 8 firms	Maximum[a] concentration ratio: First 20 firms
Type I Oligopolies						
2911	Petroleum refining products	11,865,167	52	77	56	83
3731	Shipbuilding and repairing	972,154	59	74		
2812	Alkalies and chlorine	362,712	88	99		
3691	Storage batteries	336,118	80	90		
3491	Metal drums, barrels, and pails	202,617	64	84		
Type II Oligopolies						
3443	Boiler shop products	1,089,948	36	50		
3241	Cement, hydraulic	901,279	43	65	49	74
2952	Roofing felts and coatings[b]	508,954	50	65	55	74
3532	Oilfield machinery and tools	468,716	46	63		
2097	Manufactured ice	132,979				
Possible Type II Oligopolies						
2612	Paper and paperboard	6,252,932	19	32	37	53
3713	Truck and bus bodies	752,603	25	36	41	57
Unconcentrated						
2027	Fluid milk and other products	3,969,143	27	33		
2751	Commercial printing	3,645,648	27	33		
2421	Sawmill and planning mill products	3,595,598	07	13 (24)	11	17
2051	Bread and related products	3,012,109	32	42		
2711	Newspapers	2,899,842	25	36		
3441	Structural and ornamental work	2,355,031	19	29 (28)	23	31
2431	Millwork	1,152,113	11	21 (28)	17	28
2081	Bottled soft drinks	1,096,065	14	20		
3271	Concrete products	1,035,166	09	15	18	26
3599	Machine shop products	919,258	15	25		
2021	Creamery butter	858,525	19	28		
3444	Sheet metal work	727,620	24	31		
2411	Logs, bolts, pulpwood, etc.	590,805	18	27		
2793	Photoengraving	580,480	06	12	17	28
3594	Industrial patterns and molds	236,582	12	20		

[a] Numbers in parentheses indicate more than or less than the stated number of firms.
[b] Possibly Type I.

S.A. Table 4. "National" and regional market structures for selected industries

Industry	Structure on basis of national concentration ratio	Type or number of regional markets	Range[a] of regional concentration ratios: First 8 firms	Range[a] of regional concentration ratios: First 20 firms	Typical regional structure	Comments
Petroleum refining	Type I Oligopoly	17	48–99 (4)	51–100 (15)	Type I Oligopoly	Concentration ratios shown are for national majors, not always the largest sellers in each region.
Commercial printing	Unconcentrated	(a) National	(a) n.a.	n.a.	(a) Type II (?) Oligopoly	(a) The national submarket includes the firms which do large magazine orders, mail order catalogues, directories, securities prospectuses, direct mail advertising, etc.
		(b) Metropolitan areas	(b) n.a.	n.a.	(b) Unconcentrated	(b) The metropolitan area market handles the printing of local firms.
		(c) Small cities and towns	(c) n.a.	n.a.	(c) Type I Oligopoly	(c) Outside of metropolitan areas there are only a few firms in each county.
Sawmills and planing mill products	Unconcentrated	West, South, Northeast	n.a. n.a.	5–20 (40)	Unconcentrated	West and South both produce surpluses over local demand. Northeast is a deficit area supplied by both.

S.A. Table 4. (Continued)

Industry	Structure on basis of national concentration ratio	Type or number of regional markets	Range[a] of regional concentration ratios: First 8 firms	Range[a] of regional concentration ratios: First 20 firms	Typical regional structure	Comments
Bread and related products	Unconcentrated	Metropolitan areas; 100 mile radius from towns	n.a. n.a.	n.a. n.a.	Type II Oligopoly	Average number of large firms in the metropolitan area is 3; New York had 10. Outside metropolitan areas, there are even fewer establishments (or firms) in the typical regional market.
Newspapers	Unconcentrated	Metropolitan area or city	60–100	100	Type I Oligopoly	Forty percent of national circulation is in one-firm markets. These figures refer to English language dailies.
Cement	Type II Oligopoly				Type I Oligopoly	

Sources. PETROLEUM REFINING: L. Cookenboo, *Crude Oil Pipelines* (1955), Federal Trade Commission, *Report on Distribution Methods and Costs* (1948). COMMERCIAL PRINTING: *Standard and Poors Industry Surveys*, vol. 122, no. 46, sec. 2, 1954 *Census of Manufactures*, vol. I (*General Statistics*), vol. III (*Statistics by States*). SAWMILL AND PLANING MILL PRODUCTS: Interstate Commerce Commission, Bureau of Transport Economics and Statistics, *Carload Waybill Analyses, 1949, State to State Distribution of Products of Forests* (1951), U.S. Department of Commerce, Office of Domestic Commerce, *Lumber, Plywood and Allied Products* (1949). BREAD AND RELATED PRODUCTS: Federal Trade Commission, *The Wholesale Baking Industry* (1946), 1954 *Census of Manufactures*, vol. III. NEWSPAPERS: "Monopoly in the Newspaper Industry," *Yale Law Journal* (June 1952). CEMENT: S. Loescher, *Imperfect Collusion in the Cement Industry* (1959).

[a] Numbers in parentheses indicate more than or less than the stated number of farms.

S.A. Table 5. The classification of mineral industries by size, extent of the market, and market structure
(source: *Census of Mineral Industries, 1939*)

Size of industry and structure of market[a]	Industry	No. of mines, quarries, pits	No. of preparation plants	Value of all products (thousands of dollars)	Concentration[b] ratios — mines		Concentration[b] ratios — plants	
					First 8 firms	First 20 firms	First 8 firms	First 20 firms
I, 1, B	Coal			920,462				
	Bituminous			727,357				
	Lignite			3,457				
	Anthracite			189,648				
III, 1, A								
Type I Oligopolies								
	Iron ore	177	41	150,872	28.3 (7)	61.8 (38)	61.8 (7)	76.1 (18)
	Copper	51	27	141,635	54.4 (6)	74.9 (20)	68.0 (10)	75.4 (21)
Type II Oligopolies								
	Gold	1180	329	114,090	33.4 (9)	46.3 (30)	33.4 (9)	46.3
III, 3, B	Oil- and gas-field services performed by contractors			203,844				
	Limestone — crushed and broken			77,147				
	Common sand and gravel			69,130				
IV, 3, A								
Type I Oligopolies								
	Granite — crushed and broken	79	74	7,030	59.3 (13)	76.2 (21)	59.3 (12)	76.2 (20)
	Granite — rough dimension	163	12	5,846	38.5 (6)	60.7 (20)	60.7 (4)	100.0 (12)
	Foundry sand	144	105	4,136	36.1 (6)	50.4 (15)	36.1 (7)	50.4 (16)
	Sandstone — crushed and broken	68	50	2,930	34.7 (8)	65.0 (12)	34.7 (5)	65.0 (15)
	Sandstone — rough dimension	59	5	1,515	59.5 (5)	75.5 (12)	100.0 (5)	
Type II Oligopolies								
	Basalt — crushed and broken	116	115	9,632	42.9 (13)	68.9 (33)	42.9 (13)	68.9 (33)
IV, 2, A								
Type I Oligopolies								
	Lead	76	29	31,467	77.7 (8)	93.6 (21)	77.7 (8)	94.4 (19)
	Silver	163	32	19,716	66.0 (7)	82.8 (24)	71.6 (6)	88.4 (19)

	Kaolin and ball clay	95	53	7,239	47.1 (5)	76.5 (23)	47.4 (5)	76.5 (19)
	Rock salt	17	17	6,896	87.9 (9)	100.0 (17)	87.9 (9)	100.0 (17)
	Glass sand	39	40	6,136	55.8 (5)	83.6 (15)	55.8 (5)	83.6 (16)
	Gypsum	59	25	4,569		75.5 (20)	75.5 (9)	96.6 (22)
IV, 2, A								
Type I Oligopolies								
	Limestone — rough dimension	64	21	3,509	54.3 (8)	81.7 (21)	54.3 (8)	100.0 (21)
	Fluorspar	61	53	3,398	70.3 (12)	90.6 (23)	70.3 (12)	90.6 (24)
	Talc and soapstone	38	26	3,269	40.3 (5)	61.3 (20)	40.3 (6)	61.3 (19)
	Native asphalt and bitumens	23	15	2,968	83.8 (9)	100.0 (23)	83.8 (7)	100.0 (15)
	Marble — rough dimension	38	3	2,532	68.0 (8)	93.7 (22)	100.0 (3)	
	Slate — crushed and broken	11	11	2,137	98.6 (8)	100.0 (11)	98.6 (8)	100.0 (11)
	Fuller's earth	22	18	2,107	62.5 (10)	66.7 (16)	62.5 (10)	66.7 (16)
	Barite	47	32	2,065	55.7 (8)	79.6 (22)	55.7 (7)	79.6 (19)
	Slate — rough dimension	68		2,025	23.9 (4)	75.9 (24)		
	Bentonite	29	20	1,982	66.3 (7)	83.4 (18)	95.6 (9)	100.0 (20)
	Feldspar	59	2	981	23.7 (4)	62.2 (16)	100.0 (2)	
	Mica	21	10	327	54.6 (5)	100.0 (21)	100.0 (10)	
Type II Oligopolies								
	Zinc	170	91	31,184	46.0 (11)	64.2 (24)	46.0 (12)	64.2 (26)
IV, 3, B	Fine clay			7,178				
	Common clay and shale			6,341				
	Misc. stone			2,528				
IV, 1, B	Phosphate rock			12,286				
IV, 1,[c]	Sulphur			31,812				
	Molybdenum ore			15,411				
	Potash			13,946				
	Tungsten ore			3,354				
	Natural sodium compounds			3,067				
	Bauxite			2,527				
	Diatomite			2,018				
	Mercury			1,830				
	Vanadium and uranium ore			1,473				

[a] See General Note, page 000.
[b] Numbers in parentheses indicate more than or less than the stated number for each form.
[c] Data from U.S. Census not available for the calculation of concentration ratios for structure of market.

S.A. Table 5. (Continued)

Size of industry and structure of market[a]	Industry	No. of mines, quarries, pits	No. of preparation plants	Value of all products (thousands of dollars)	Concentration[b] ratios — mines: First 8 firms	Concentration[b] ratios — mines: First 20 firms	Concentration[b] ratios — plants: First 8 firms	Concentration[b] ratios — plants: First 20 firms
	Magnesite			1,396				
	Natural abrasives			1,295				
	Manganese ore			945				
	Pyrites			602				
	Asbestos			492				
	Titanium ore			458				
	Tripoli			427				
	Peat			378				
	Greensand			285				
	Crushed and broken marble			177				
	Vermiculite			150				
	Kyanite			139				
	Graphite, etc.			96				
	Chromite and antimony ore			47				
	Rough dimension basalt			26				

S.A. Table 6. Exempt industries, showing the character of their regulation and their market structure

Industry or industries	Primary regulatory agency or agencies	Nature and extent of regulation	Present market structure	Market structure in absence of regulation
1. Agriculture				
Agriculture includes three major areas of exemption which together account for slightly more than half farm cash receipts. (1) Certain commodities classified by law as basic, and designated nonbasic. These made up 45 percent of total farm cash receipts in 1953. (2) Fluid milk and other crops — largely regional fruit crops. All these accounted for 6.5 percent of total 1953 farm cash receipts. (3) Sugar production and imports. Sugar accounted for 0.6 percent of farm cash receipts in 1952.	Department of Agriculture	(1) Prices are supported at levels up to 90 percent of parity. (2) Market agreements and orders which are, respectively, voluntary and involuntary cartels. Price either controlled directly, as milk, or indirectly through quotas. (3) Import and production quotas are set.	Extremely unconcentrated in nearly all exempt and nonexempt areas.	Same
2. Transportation				
Railroads — both freight and passenger traffic.	Interstate Commerce Commission	Common carrier status. Rate-setting, authorization of joint rate-making by competing roads, approval of mergers.	Narrow Type I Oligopoly for most traffic. Competition is effective for high-value traffic, and water competition provides effective competition for bulk traffic in limited areas.	Same
For-hire trucking	Interstate Commerce Commission	Control of rates, entry, mergers, and service for common carriers. Minimum rate-setting and entry controls for contract carriers.	Typically Type II Oligopoly in smaller markets. Unconcentrated in largest markets.	Removal of entry barriers would probably result in an unconcentrated structure on nearly all routes.
Urban transit	State and local commission	Complete regulation of rates, service, expenses, etc.	Natural monopoly subject to strong competitive pressure from private autos.	Same
Intercity bus transport	Interstate Commerce Commission	Control over entry, mergers, rates.	Narrow Type I Oligopoly subject to heavy competition from passenger cars.	Same

S.A. Table 6. (Continued)

Industry or industries	Primary regulatory agency or agencies	Nature and extent of regulation	Present market structure	Market structure in absence of regulation
2. Transportation (cont.)				
Inland and coastal shipping	Interstate Commerce Commission	Most traffic unregulated. Some common carriers, which set rates through a rate bureau, but regulation has little effect because of competition from unregulated carriers and railroads.	On borderline between loose Type II Oligopoly and unconcentrated structure for most traffic. Great Lakes structure complicated by predominance of captives and semicaptives of industrial concerns. Coastal tanker fleet is distributed among eleven oil companies and three independents.	Same
International shipping, composed of: (1) liners, (2) tankers, (3) tramps.	Federal Maritime Board	No rate-setting or entry controls. Regulation by Board is of little importance because of dominance of foreign firms. Rate conferences, sanctioned by board, dominate liner market, which is not competitive with other forms of shipping. Tramp shipping is competitive in behavior.	(1) Liner markets oligopolistic. (2) Tramps are unconcentrated. (3) Tankers are more concentrated than tramps owing to captive fleets of oil companies.	Same
Airlines	Civil Aeronautics Board	Regulation of rates, mergers, entry, and service of common carriers. Registration and limitation on frequency of service of supplemental carriers.	Narrow Type I Oligopoly.	Still oligopolistic but significantly less concentrated.
Pipelines	Interstate Commerce Commission for crude oil and gasoline. Federal Power Commission for natural gas pipelines.	ICC powers — which accord common carrier status to pipelines — have rarely been exercised. FPC regulates resale price of natural gas by pipelines, entry, service, accounting, and financial practices.	Usually natural monopoly. Oil companies own more than 80 percent of crude oil pipeline capacity.	Same
3. Local and communications utilities				
Electricity and gas	Federal Power Commission, local and state commissions	FPC regulates rates for interstate power sales as well as financial and accounting practices of interstate firms. State and local commissions have extensive control over rates, entry, service, etc.	Natural monopoly in transmission and distribution stages.	Same
Telephone and telegraph	Federal Communications Commission, state and local commissions	FCC regulates interstate charges. Extensive control over rates service, entry, and accounting at local level.	Natural monopoly.	Same

Radio broadcasting and television	Federal Communications Commission	Primarily control of entry through allocation of radio frequencies.	Type I Oligopoly, mainly because of existence of networks.	Same
4. Commercial banking and insurance				
Commercial banking	Federal Reserve System, Comptroller of Currency, and state banking commissions	Federal Reserve controls general level of interest rates and availability of credit. Federal and state authorities control bank operations through entry controls and examinations. Limitation of competition is considered by regulation authorities as necessary to stability of banking systems.	National credit market is oligopolistic, as are most local markets.	Concentration might be reduced, but oligopolistic structures would probably still dominate.
Insurance[a]	State agencies	Rate bureaus are enforced in most states and permitted in others. Some bureaus operate on a national level.	Type I Oligopoly in life insurance. Other forms of insurance are less concentrated.	Life insurance still probably oligopolistic. Other forms might be competitive in absence of rate bureaus.
5. Natural resource industries				
Crude oil	Interstate Crude Oil Compact, state commissions	A system of quotas, with conservation as the alleged purpose, has the effect (together with import restrictions) of protecting the price of crude from market pressure.	Type I Oligopoly in regional markets.	Same
Natural gas production	Federal Power Commission, state commissions	Status uncertain.[b] Minimum well-head prices set by states for conservation purposes are apparently legal.	Type II Oligopoly. Markets are regional.	Same
Anthracite coal	Committee set up under Pennsylvania Commerce Act. Committee consists of representatives of labor, the producers, and the commonwealth.	"Voluntary" cartel which has been effective in controlling prices through limiting output. Conservation is alleged goal.	Type I oligopoly subject to heavy pressure from competing fuels.	Same

[a] Under the McCarran Act [59 Stat. 33 (1945), 15 U.S.C., 1011–1015 (1946) as amended by 61 Stat. 888 (1947)] insurance is subject to the antitrust laws to the extent that it is not regulated by the states. Where protective legislation does not exist, insurance companies could undoubtedly generate enough political pressure to provide for friendly regulation should antitrust action become imminent. Therefore, we classify the industry as exempt.

[b] In 1954 the Supreme Court [Phillips Petroleum Co. v. State of Wisconsin, 347 U.S. 672 (1954)] held that it was the duty of the FPC to fix the prices that interstate pipelines pay independent producers for gas. FPC regulation of production has been ineffective, owing to Congress' failure to appropriate any funds for that purpose, and there has been continuing pressure in Congress to remove FPC control over wellhead prices.

Methodological Appendix

General Note. In classifying industries by size, by extent of market, and by market structure, the following abbreviations have been used in the tables.

Size of Industry. I-large; II-medium large; III-medium; IV-small.

Extent of Market. 1-national — geographically concentrated supply; 2-national — geographically unconcentrated supply; 3-local and regional; 4-heterogeneous.

Market Structure. A-concentrated; B-unconcentrated.

Methodological Appendix

I. NOTE ON INDUSTRY CLASSIFICATION

In order to have any economic meaning the figures of concentration of sales must be stated in terms of a market. The market is defined as a group of firms relatively insulated from competition from other firms in the economy, where competition is defined to include both competition among different products and among alternative actual or potential sources of supply. The market is then defined in terms of the buyers' substitution of one product for another and in terms of producers' substitution of one product for another in their output mix in response to relative price, cost, or product variation. In order to define a market we attempt to obtain information on cross elasticities of both demand and supply. Such information is rarely available directly, but must be approximated by evidence on consumer behavior (is poultry considered a substitution for meat?) and on the degree of specialization of equipment (can cotton looms easily be shifted to rayon weaving?). The substitution process is properly defined in quantitative terms, but we must separate significant and nonsignificant substitution by various types of nonquantitative evidence.[1]

As the text notes, our basic source of data is by four-digit census product class groups, which are grouped primarily on the basis of similarity of products and processes. These criteria are in accord with our own criteria of supply and demand substitutability for defining a market. In practice, however, the four-digit product class groups are often narrower in scope than the extent of the market. In identifying competing products, insufficient attention is paid to alikeness in terms of consumers' reaction as distinct from physical or technical alikeness. Indeed, in some cases, the similarity of products is made to turn entirely on technical processes, e.g., beet sugar is classified separately from cane sugar. On the supply side, insufficient attention is paid to potential channels of production as

1. In making such decisions the most important source was the industry descriptions in the census itself. Other frequently used sources were Alderfer and Michl, *Economics of American Industry* (N.Y., 1950); and Glover and Cornell, *The Development of American Industries* (N.Y., 1951).

distinct from actual channels of production. The emphasis is on the existing organization of production rather than on the potential response to price changes. Thus men's and boys' suits are in a different four-digit group from separate trousers.

Finally, there is a separate problem which arises because the census statistics are in value of shipments rather than value added. As a result, industries which are partially integrated require some special adjustment. For example, establishments in the iron and steel industry may produce only a proportion of the final product, the other proportion being produced by nonintegrated producers which are a separate industry. The concentration computed for either industry is by itself meaningless, since the two industries produce competing products.

We have combined census groups, then, in the following situations to produce a revised industry classification:

1. When products defining two or more census industries appear to be close substitutes for the consumer, the product groups are combined. For example, cane and beet sugar are combined and metal and wood office furniture are combined. On the other hand, we have not adopted a low enough value of the substitution coefficient to combine cigarettes with cigars or chewing gum with confectionery products.

2. Two product groups are combined when there is close supply substitution. For example, men's suits are combined with separate trousers. On the other hand, cigars and cigarettes have not been combined (even though there is some occasional movement of firms between the two) since such production changes require considerable investment in new equipment.

3. Where the census has separated vertically integrated firms from nonintegrated firms producing the same product, and the integrated sector is a larger producer of the product than the nonintegrated sector, the two sectors are combined. For example, steel works and rolling mills are combined with welded and heavy riveted pipe.

4. Where the value of shipment of a product group is small, it has often been combined with other products on a less strict basis. For example, children's bicycles and dolls are combined with toys *n.e.c.*, although according to the three criteria above these would have been retained as separate markets.

We have been relatively liberal in our consolidations so that the

440 four-digit census manufacturing product classes are combined into 191 markets; 83 of these represent consolidations.

It should be noted that all these adjustments are in the direction of producing a wider market classification. In cases where the census industries are broader than the market, no adjustment is possible. Likewise when only part of two industries produce competing products, the only possible action is to combine or retain them as separate industries, according to the character of the product accounting for the larger share of the sales.

The procedure of these consolidations can best be explained by an example. The flour and feed industry is a consolidation of three census product class groups whose concentration data appear below. In order to obtain a single set of concentration ratios, we must make

Code	Title	Total value of shipments (thousands of dollars)	Values of shipments for leading firms (thousands of dollars)		
			First 4	Next 4	Next 12
2041	Flour and meal	1,653,581	628,361	214,966	264,573
2042	Prepared animal feeds	2,843,114	597,054	227,449	398,036
2045	Blended and prepared flour	402,643	217,427	52,344	44,291
	Total	4,899,338	1,442,842	494,759	

some assumption about the relationship of the top companies. One possibility would be to assume that the top companies in each product class group were identical, in which case the concentration ratio for the first eight firms would be a weighted average of the concentration ratios of the first eight firms in the individual product class groups. We would simply add up the two columns giving values of shipments for the first four and second four leading firms and divide this total (1,442,842 + $494,759 = $1,937,601) by the total value of shipments for the markets ($4,889,338). This gives us the maximum possible concentration ratio (40 percent) for the eight leading companies.

Alternatively, we could assume that the top companies in each four-digit group are independent of the top companies in each other four-digit group. We also make the assumption that if one set of four firms has a larger sales total than another set of firms, then any individual firm in the first set is larger than any individual firm in the second. These two assumptions give us the minimum possible concentration ratio for the market. To get the minimum ratio for the first eight firms in our example, we would add the values of shipments for the two blocks of four firms with the largest total shipments. These would be the first four in group 2041 ($628,361) and the first four in group 2042 ($597,054). Adding these we get $1,225,415. We divide this figure by the market total to get a minimum ratio of 25 percent.

Those markets in which both the maximum and minimum ratios fall into the same structural category (either concentrated or unconcentrated) present no classification problem. Fortunately, 61 of our 83 consolidations are of this type. Of the 22 markets which have unconcentrated minimum ratios and concentrated maximum ratios, nine are miscellaneous industries, which fit our minimum assumptions fairly well. We listed the others as unconcentrated except in two cases where we had direct evidence of sufficient overlap of firms between product groups to place the markets in our concentrated category.[2] All 13 cases of nonmiscellaneous industries with concentration ratios straddling our dividing lines are indicated by a † appearing to the left of the product code in S.A. Table 1 of the Statistical Appendix. It should be emphasized that all of the error in classification which has been made as a result of consolidation is in the direction of understating the number of concentrated industries.

Concentration data for 1954 is not available for certain four-digit product class groups whose components bear a vertical relation to one another, so that the total value of shipments for each four-digit group involves a large element of double counting. We have estimated the concentration ratios indirectly in such cases.[3]

2. The two cases were (a) 2011 (meat packing) in which the overlap of leading firms is substantial and the minimum and maximum ratios for eight firms are 32 percent and 45 percent; and (b) 2092 (oleo, shortening, and cooking oils), also with substantial overlap. In (b) the minimum and maximum ratios for the top eight firms are 28 percent and 68 percent. Our principal source for evidence on overlap is *Report of the Federal Trade Commission on Industrial Concentration and Product Diversification in the Largest Manufacturing Companies: 1950* (U.S. Government Printing Office, 1957).

3. Estimation procedure was as follows. For unconsolidated markets, 1947 value-added concentration ratios for the relevant census industries were used. For consolidated markets, 1954 value-added weights were used to combine the concentration ratios of component product class groups. In the cases of the components for which sales concentration ratios were not available, 1947 value-added weights for the relevant census industries were used. In two markets, 1954 value-added weights were not available for all components, and 1947 value-added weights were used for these components. It should be noted that value-added weights and value-added concentration data are for census industries, whereas the 1954 sales concentration ratios are based on total shipments of the primary products of census industries. Value-added

The markets involved are indicated in S.A. Table 1 in the Statistical Appendix by an "(x)" appearing to the right of the market code. Size classification of these markets is based on 1947 sales figures for census industries. M.A. Table 1, which follows lists the results of our consolidation procedure.

---

data for 1954 were taken from the Advance Industry Reports, 1954 *Census of Manufactures,* and 1947 value-added data were taken from Industry Reports, 1947 *Census of Manufactures.* The 1947 value-added concentration ratios were taken from *Hearings before the Subcommittee on Study of Monopoly Power of the Committee on the Judiciary, House of Representatives,* 81 Cong., 1 sess., Serial No. 14, Part 2-B, p. 1453.

M.A. Table 1. The consolidation of census manufacturing industries

Standard industrial classification			
Three digit	Four digit	Classified under —	Characteristics[a]
	Major group 20 — Food and kindred products		
201	2011	2011	I, 2, A
	2013	2011	I, 2, A
	2015	2011	I, 2, A
202	2021	2021	II, 3
	2022	2022	II, 2, B
	2023	2023	II, 2, A
	2024	2024	II, 2, A
	2025	2025	III, 1, A
	2027	2027	I, 3
203	2031	2031	III, 1, A
	2032	2031	III, 1, A
	2033	2033	I, 2, B
	2034	2033	I, 2, B
	2035	2033	I, 2, B
	2036	2031	III, 1, A
	2037	2033	I, 2, B
204	2041	2041	I, 2, B
	2042	2041	I, 2, B
	2043	2043	III, 1, A
	2044	20 misc.	I, 4, A
	2045	2041	I, 2, B
205	2051	2051	I, 3
	2052	2052	II, 1, A
206	2061	2062	I, 2, A
	2062	2062	I, 2, A
	2063	2062	I, 2, A
207	2071	2071	II, 2, B
	2072	2072	III, 1, A
	2073	2073	III, 1, A
208	2081	2081	I, 3
	2082	2082	I, 2, A
	2083	2082	I, 2, A
	2084	2085	I, 1, A
	2085	2085	I, 1, A
209	2091	20 misc.	I, 4, A
	2092	2092	I, 2, A
	2093	2092	I, 2, B

[a] See General Note, page 294. Data for regional industries are listed in the Statistical Appendix, S. A. Table 2. Since the A and B classifications are based on national concentration data, we do not apply this classification to regional industries.

M.A. Table 1. (Continued)

Standard industrial classification			
Three digit	Four digit	Classified under —	Characteristics[a]
	2094	2094	III, 1, A
	2095	2095	III, 2, A
	2097	2097	III, 3
	2098	20 misc.	I, 4, A
	2099	20 misc.	I, 4, A
	Major group 21 — Tobacco manufacturers		
211	2011	2111	I, 1, A
212	2121	2121	III, 1, A
213	2131	2111	I, 1, A
214	2141	2111	I, 1, A
	Major group 22 — Textile mill products		
221	2211	2213	I, 1, B
	2212	2213	I, 1, B
	2213	2213	I, 1, B
222	2222	2213	I, 1, B
	2223	2223	III, 1, A
	2224	2233	I, 1, B
223	2233	2233	I, 1, B
	2234	2233	I, 1, B
224	2241	22 misc.	II, 4, B
225	2251	2251	II, 1, B
	2252	2251	II, 1, B
	2253	2253	I, 1, B
	2254	2253	I, 1, B
	2255	2253	I, 1, B
	2256	2253	I, 1, B
	2259	2253	I, 1, B
226	2261	2233	I, 1, B
227	2271	2271	III, 1, A
	2273	2271	III, 1, A
	2274	2274	III, 1, A
228	2281	2281	III, 1, A
	2282	2281	III, 1, A
	2283	2281	III, 1, A
	2284	2281	III, 1, A

[a] See General Note, page 294. Data for regional industries are listed in the Statistical Appendix, S.A. Table 2. Since the A and B classifications are based on national concentration data, we do not apply this classification to regional industries.

M.A. Table 1. (Continued)

Standard industrial classification			
Three digit	Four digit	Classified under —	Characteristics[a]
229	2291	22 misc.	II, 4, B
	2292	22 misc.	II, 4, B
	2293	2251	II, 1, B
	2294	22 misc.	II, 4, B
	2295	22 misc.	II, 4, B
	2298	22 misc.	II, 4, B
	2299	22 misc.	II, 4, B
	Major group 23 — Apparel and related products		
231	2311	2311	I, 1, B
	2312	2311	I, 1, B
232	2321	2321	II, 1, B
	2322	2253	I, 1, B
	2323	23 misc. (A)[b]	I, 4, B
	2325	23 misc. (A)[b]	I, 4, B
	2326	23 misc. (A)[b]	I, 4, B
	2327	2311	I, 1, B
	2328	2328	II, 1, B
	2329	2328	II, 1, B
233	2331	2331	III, 1, B
	2333	2333	I, 1, B
	2334	2333	I, 1, B
	2337	2337	I, 1, B
	2338	23 misc. (A)[b]	I, 4, B
	2339	23 misc. (A)[b]	I, 4, B
234	2341	2253	I, 1, B
	2342	2342	III, 1, A
235	2351	23 misc. (F)[c]	II, 4, B
236	2361	2361	II, 1, B
	2363	2361	II, 1, B
	2369	2361	II, 1, B
237	2371	23 misc. (A)[b]	I, 4, B
238	2381	23 misc. (A)[b]	I, 4, B
	2382	23 misc. (A)[b]	I, 4, B
	2383	23 misc. (A)[b]	I, 4, B
	2384	23 misc. (A)[b]	I, 4, B
	2385	23 misc. (A)[b]	I, 4, B

[a] See General Note, page 294. Data for regional industries are listed in the Statistical Appendix, S.A. Table 2. Since the A and B classifications are based on national concentration data, we do not apply this classification to regional industries.
[b] Apparel and accessories.
[c] Fabric and textile products.

Standard industrial classification			
Three digit	Four digit	Classified under —	Characteristics[a]
	2386	23 misc. (A)[b]	I, 4, B
	2387	23 misc. (A)[b]	I, 4, B
	2388	23 misc. (A)[b]	I, 4, B
	2389	23 misc. (A)[b]	I, 4, B
239	2391	2392	II, 1, B
	2392	2392	II, 1, B
	2393	2393	III, 2, A
	2394	23 misc. (F)[c]	I, 4, B
	2396	23 misc. (F)[c]	II, 4, B
	2397	23 misc. (F)[c]	II, 4, B
	2398	23 misc. (F)[c]	II, 4, B
	2399	23 misc. (F)[c]	II, 4, B
Major group 24 — Lumber and wood products			
241	2411	2411	II, 3
242	2421	2421	I, 3
	2422	2421	I, 3
	2423	24 misc. (T)[d]	IV, 2, B
	2424	24 misc. (T)[d]	IV, 2, B
	2425	24 misc. (T)[d]	IV, 2, B
	2429	Not used in '47 Census	
243	2431	2431	I, 3
	2432	2432	II, 2, B
	2433	2431	I, 3
244	2441	24 misc. (W)[e]	II, 4, B
	2442	24 misc. (W)[e]	II, 4, B
	2443	24 misc. (W)[e]	II, 4, B
	2444	2421	I, 3
	2445	2421	I, 3
249	2491	24 misc. (W)[e]	II, 4, B
	2492	24 misc. (W)[e]	II, 4, B
	2493	24 misc. (W)[e]	II, 4, B
	2499	24 misc. (W)[e]	II, 4, B

[a] See General Note, page 294. Data for regional industries are listed in the Statistical Appendix, S.A. Table 2. Since the A and B classifications are based on national concentration data, we do not apply this classification to regional industries.
[b] Apparel and accessories.
[c] Fabric and textile products.
[d] Timber basic products.
[e] Wood products.

M.A. Table 1. (Continued)

Standard industrial classification			
Three digit	Four digit	Classified under —	Characteristics[a]
	Major group 25 — Furniture and fixtures		
251	2511	2511	I, 2, B
	2512	2511	I, 2, B
	2514	2511	I, 2, B
	2515	2511	I, 2, B
	2519	2511	I, 2, B
252	2521	2522	II, 1, B
	2522	2522	II, 1, B
253	2531	2522	II, 1, B
	2532	2522	II, 1, B
254	2541	2522	II, 1, B
256	2561	2431	I, 3
	2562	2563	III, 2, B
	2563	2563	III, 2, B
259	2591	2522	II, 1, B
	2599	2522	II, 1, B
	Major group 26 — Paper and allied products		
261	2611	2612	I, 3
	2612	2612	I, 3
	2613	2612	I, 3
264	2641	2612	I, 3
265	2651	26 misc.	I, 1, B
266	2661	2661	II, 2, A
267	2671	2671	I, 2, B
	2674	2671	I, 2, B
269	2691	26 misc.	I, 1, B
	2693	26 misc.	I, 1, B
	2694	26 misc.	I, 1, B
	2699	26 misc.	I, 1, B
	Major group 27 — Printing, publishing, and allied industries		
271	2711	2711	I, 3
272	2721	2721	I, 1, A

[a] See General Note, page 294. Data for regional industries are listed in the Statistical Appendix, S.A. Table 2. Since the A and B classifications are based on national concentration data, we do not apply this classification to regional industries.

M.A. Table 1. (Continued)

Standard industrial classification			
Three digit	Four digit	Classified under —	Characteristics[a]
273	2731	2731	II, 1, B
	2732	2751	I, 3
274	2741	2731	II, 1, B
275	2751	2751	I, 3
276	2761	2751	I, 3
277	2771	2771	III, 1, A
278	2781	2793	II, 3
	2782	2751	I, 3
	2783	2751	I, 3
	2789	2751	I, 3
279	2791	2793	II, 3
	2792	2793	II, 3
	2793	2793	II, 3
	2794	2793	II, 3
Major group 28 — Chemical and allied products			
281	2811	2819	I, 2, A
	2812	2812	III, 3
	2819 (incl. 2811)	2819	I, 2, A
282	2821	2829	I, 2, A
	2822	2829	I, 2, A
	2823	2823	I, 1, A
	2824	2824	III, 2, A
	2825	2825	I, 1, A
	2829	2829	I, 2, A
283	2831	2834	I, 1, A
	2832	2834	I, 1, A
	2833	2834	I, 1, A
	2834	2834	I, 1, A
284	2841	2841	I, 1, A
	2842	2841	II, 1, A
	2843	2841	I, 1, A
285	2851	2851	I, 2, A
	2852	2829	I, 2, A
	2853	2851	I, 2, A

[a] See General Note, page 294. Data for regional industries are listed in the Statistical Appendix, S.A. Table 2. Since the A and B classifications are based on national concentration data, we do not apply this classification to regional industries.

M.A. Table 1. (Continued)

Standard industrial classification			
Three digit	Four digit	Classified under —	Characteristics[a]
286	2861	28 misc.	I, 4, B
	2862	28 misc.	I, 4, B
	2863	28 misc.	I, 4, B
	2865	28 misc.	I, 4, B
287	2871	2871	II, 1, A
	2872	2871	II, 1, A
288	2881	2092	I, 2, A
	2882	2092	I, 2, A
	2883	2092	I, 2, A
	2884	2092	I, 2, A
	2886	2011	I, 2, A
	2887	2841	I, 1, A
	2889	2011	I, 2, A
289	2891	28 misc.	I, 4, B
	2892	28 misc.	I, 4, B
	2893	2893	II, 1, A
	2894	28 misc.	I, 4, B
	2895	28 misc.	I, 4, B
	2896	2896	III, 2, A
	2897	28 misc.	I, 4, B
	2898	2898	IV, 2, A
	2899	28 misc.	I, 4, B
	Major group 29 — Products of petroleum and coal		
291	2911	2911	I, 3
293	2931	2932	I, 2, A
	2932	2932	I, 2, A
295	2951	2952	II, 3
	2952	2952	II, 3
299	2992	2911	I, 3
	2999	2999	IV, 4, A
	Major group 30 — Rubber products		
301	3011	3011	I, 2, A
302	3021	30 misc.	I, 4, A
303	3031	30 misc.	I, 4, A
309	3099	30 misc.	I, 4, A

[a] See General Note, page 294. Data for regional industries are listed in the Statistical Appendix, S.A. Table 2. Since the A and B classifications are based on national concentration data, we do not apply this classification to regional industries.

M.A. Table 1. (Continued)

Standard industrial classification			
Three digit	Four digit	Classified under —	Characteristics[a]
Major group 31 — Leather and leather products			
311	3111	3111	II, 1, B
312	3121	31 misc.	II, 4, B
313	3131	3141	I, 1, B
314	3141	3141	I, 1, B
	3142	31 misc.	II, 4, B
315	3151	31 misc.	II, 4, B
	3152	31 misc.	II, 4, B
316	3161	31 misc.	II, 4, B
317	3171	31 misc.	II, 4, B
	3172	31 misc.	II, 4, B
319	3192	31 misc.	II, 4, B
	3199	31 misc.	II, 4, B
Major group 32 — Stone, clay, and glass products			
321	3211	3211	III, 1, A
322	3221	3221	II, 2, A
	3229	3229	III, 1, A
323	3231	3231	III, 1, A
324	3241	3241	II, 3
325	3251	3271	II, 4, B
	3253	32 misc. (V)[f]	III, 4, B
	3254	3271	I, 3
	3255	32 misc. (V)[f]	III, 4, B
	3259	3271	I, 3
326	3261	32 misc. (V)[f]	III, 4, B
	3262	3263	III, 1, A
	3263	3263	III, 1, A
	3264	3611	II, 1, B
	3265	3263	III, 1, A
	3269	32 misc. (V)[f]	III, 4, B

[a] See General Note, page 294. Data for regional industries are listed in the Statistical Appendix, S.A. Table 2. Since the A and B classifications are based on national concentration data, we do not apply this classification to regional industries.

[f] Vitreous products.

M.A. Table 1. (Continued)

Standard industrial classification			
Three digit	Four digit	Classified under —	Characteristics[a]
327	3271	3271	I, 3
	3272	3272	III, 2, A
	3274	3241	II, 3
	3275	3272	III, 2, A
328	3281	32 misc. (N)[g]	II, 4, B
329	3291	32 misc. (N)[g]	II, 4, B
	3292	3292	II, 2, A
	3293	3292	II, 2, A
	3295	32 misc. (N)[g]	II, 4, B
	3297	32 misc. (N)[g]	II, 4, B
	3298	32 misc. (N)[g]	II, 4, B
	3299	32 misc. (N)[g]	II, 4, B
	Major group 33 — Primary metal industries		
331	3311	3311	I, 2, A
	3312	3311	I, 2, A
	3313	3311	I, 2, A
332	3321	3321	I, 2, B
	3322	3321	I, 2, B
	3323	3323	II, 2, B
333	3331	3331	III, 2, A
	3332	3332	III, 2, A
	3333	3333	III, 2, A
	3334	3334	III, 1, A
	3339	3339	III, 2, A
334	3341	3341	II, 2, A
335	3351	3351	I, 1, A
	3352	3352	II, 2, A
	3359	3359	III, 1, A
336	3361	3361	II, 2, B
339	3391	3311	I, 2, A
	3392	3631	I, 1, A
	3393	3311	I, 2, A
	3399	3311	I, 2, A
	Major group 34 — Fabricated metal products		
341	3411	3411	I, 2, A

[a] See General Note, page 294. Data for regional industries are listed in the Statistical Appendix, S. A. Table 2. Since the A and B classifications are based on national concentration data, we do not apply this classification to regional industries.

[g] Nonmetallic mineral products.

M.A. Table 1. (Continued)

Standard industrial classification			
Three digit	Four digit	Classified under —	Characteristics[a]
342	3421	3421	I, 1, B
	3422	3421	I, 1, B
	3423	3421	I, 1, B
	3424	3421	I, 1, B
	3425	3421	I, 1, B
	3429	3421	I, 1, B
343	3431	3431	III, 2, A
	3439	3439	I, 1, B
344	3441	3441	I, 3
	3442	3441	I, 3
	3443	3443	I, 3
	3444	3444	I, 3
346	3461	32 misc. (V)[h]	III, 4, B
	3463	3463	I, 1, B
347	3471	3471	II, 1, B
348	3481	34 misc. (P)[i]	I, 4, B
	3489	34 misc. (P)[i]	I, 4, B
349	3491	3491	III, 3
	3492	34 misc. (F)[i]	II, 4, A
	3493	34 misc. (P)[i]	I, 4, B
	3494	34 misc. (P)[i]	I, 4, B
	3495	34 misc. (P)[i]	I, 4, B
	3496	34 misc. (F)[j]	II, 4, A
	3497	34 misc. (F)[j]	II, 4, A
	3499	34 misc. (F)[j]	II, 4, A
Major group 35 — Machinery (except electrical)			
351	3511	3511	III, 1, A
	3519	3519	II, 2, A
352	3521	3521	I, 1, A
	3522	3522	I, 2, A
353	3531	3531	I, 1, B
	3532	3532	III, 3

[a] See General Note, page 294. Data for regional industries are listed in the Statistical Appendix, S.A. Table 2. Since the A and B classifications are based on national concentration data, we do not apply this classification to regional industries.
[h] Vitreous product.
[i] Product of steel works.
[j] Fabric metal products.

M.A. Table 1. (Continued)

Standard industrial classification			
Three digit	Four digit	Classified under —	Characteristics[a]
354	3541	3541	I, 1, B
	3542	34 misc. (M)[k]	I, 1, B
	3544	3541	I, 1, B
	3545	3541	I, 1, B
355	3551	3551	III, 2, B
	3552	3552	III, 1, A
	3553	35 misc. (M)[k]	I, 1, B
	3554	3554	III, 1, A
	3555	3555	III, 1, A
	3559	3559	II, 4, B
356	3561	3561	II, 2, A
	3562	3562	III, 1, A
	3563	35 misc. (I)[l]	I, 4, B
	3564	35 misc. (I)[l]	I, 4, B
	3565	35 misc. (I)[l]	I, 4, B
	3566	3566	II, 1, B
	3567	35 misc. (I)[l]	I, 4, B
	3568	35 misc. (I)[l]	I, 4, B
	3569	35 misc. (I)[l]	I, 4, B
357	3571	3571	II, 1, A
	3572	3572	III, 1, A
	3576	35 misc. (O)[m]	III, 1, A
	3579	35 misc. (O)[m]	III, 1, A
358	3581	3581	II, 1, A
	3582	3581	II, 1, A
	3583	3583	III, 1, A
	3584	3584	III, 1, A
	3585	3585	I, 1, A
	3586	3586	IV, 1, A
	3589	3589	III, 2, A
359	3591	3591	I, 2, B
	3592	3591	I, 2, B
	3593	3593	II, 1, A
	3594	3594	II, 3
	3599	3599	II, 3
	Major group 36 — Electrical machinery, equipment, and supplies		
361	3611	3611	II, 1, B
	3612	3611	II, 1, B

[a] See General Note, page 294. Data for regional industries are listed in the Statistical Appendix, S.A. Table 2. Since the A and B classifications are based on national concentration data, we do not apply this classification to regional industries.

[k] Metalworking machine.

[l] Industrial machinery, general.

[m] Office and store machinery.

M.A. Table 1. (Continued)

Standard industrial classification			
Three digit	Four digit	Classified under —	Characteristics[a]
	3613	3613	II, 2, A
	3614	3614	I, 1, A
	3615	3615	II, 2, A
	3616	3616	I, 2, A
	3617	35 misc. (M)[n]	I, 1, B
	3619	3613	II, 2, A
362	3621	3439	I, 1, B
363	3631	3631	I, 1, A
364	3641	3641	II, 1, A
365	3651	3651	III, 1, A
366	3661	3661	I, 1, A
	3662	3662	II, 1, A
	3663	3663	IV, 2, A
	3664	3664	II, 1, A
	3669	36 misc. (E)[o]	II, 2, A
369	3691	3691	III, 3
	3692	36 misc. (E)[o]	II, 2, A
	3693	36 misc. (E)[o]	II, 2, A
	3699	36 misc. (E)[o]	II, 2, A
	Major group 37 — Transportation equipment		
371	3713	3713	II, 3
	3715	3713	II, 3
	3716	3713	II, 3
	3717	3717	I, 1, A
372	3721	3721	I, 2, A
	3722	3722	I, 1, A
	3723	3722	I, 1, A
	3729	3721	I, 2, A
373	3731	3731	II, 3
	3732	3732	III, 2, B
374	3741	3741	III, 2, A
	3742	3742	III, 1, A
375	3751	3751	IV, 1, A

[a] See General Note, page 294. Data for regional industries are listed in the Statistical Appendix, S.A. Table 2. Since the A and B classifications are based on national concentration data, we do not apply this classification to regional industries.
[n] Metalworking machinery.
[o] Electrical products.

M.A. Table 1. (Continued)

Standard industrial classification			
Three digit	Four digit	Classified under —	Characteristics[a]
379	3799	3713	II, 3
	Major group 38 — Professional, scientific, and controlling instruments, photographic and official goods, watches and clocks		
381	3811	3811	II, 2, A
382	3821	3821	II, 2, A
383	3831	3872	III, 1, A
384	3841	3842	III, 1, A
	3842	3842	III, 1, A
	3843	3842	III, 1, A
385	3851	3851	III, 1, A
386	3861	3861	II, 1, A
387	3871	3871	III, 1, A
	3872	3872	III, 1, A
	Major group 39 — Miscellaneous manufacturing industries		
391	3911	3911	III, 1, B
	3912	3911	III, 1, B
	3913	3911	III, 1, B
	3914	39 misc. (M)[p]	I, 4, B
393	3931	39 misc. (M)[p]	I, 4, B
	3932	39 misc. (M)[p]	I, 4, B
	3933	39 misc. (M)[p]	I, 4, B
	3939	39 misc. (M)[p]	I, 4, B
394	3941	3941	II, 1, B
	3942	3941	II, 1, B
	3943	3941	II, 1, B
	3949	39 misc. (M)[p]	I, 4, B
395	3951	3951	III, 1, A
	3952	39 misc. (M)[p]	I, 4, B
	3953	39 misc. (M)[p]	I, 4, B
	3954	39 misc. (M)[p]	I, 4, B
	3955	39 misc. (M)[p]	I, 4, B

[a] See General Note, page 294. Data for regional industries are listed in the Statistical Appendix, S.A. Table 2. Since the A and B classifications are based on national concentration data, we do not apply this classification to regional industries.

[p] Manufacturing industries.

M.A. Table 1. (Continued)

Standard industrial classification			
Three digit	Four digit	Classified under —	Characteristics[a]
396	3961	39 misc. (M)[p]	I, 4, B
	3962	39 misc. (M)[p]	I, 4, B
	3963	39 misc. (M)[p]	I, 4, B
	3964	39 misc. (M)[p]	I, 4, B
397	3971	3971	I, 4, B
398	3981	39 misc. (M)[p]	I, 4, B
	3982	39 misc. (M)[p]	I, 1, B
	3983	39 misc. (M)[p]	I, 4, B
	3984	39 misc. (M)[p]	I, 4, B
	3985	39 misc. (M)[p]	I, 4, B
	3986	39 misc. (M)[p]	I, 4, B
	3987	39 misc. (M)[p]	I, 4, B
	3988	39 misc. (M)[p]	I, 4, B
399	3991	39 misc. (M)[p]	I, 4, B
	3992	39 misc. (M)[p]	I, 4, B
	3993	39 misc. (M)[p]	I, 4, B
	3994	39 misc. (M)[p]	I, 4, B
	3995	39 misc. (M)[p]	I, 4, B
	3996	39 misc. (M)[p]	I, 4, B
	3997	3585	I, 1, A
	3999	39 misc. (M)[p]	I, 4, B

[a] See General Note, page 294. Data for regional industries are listed in the Statistical Appendix, S.A. Table 2. Since the A and B classifications are based on national concentration data, we do not apply this classification to regional industries.

[p] Manufacturing industries.

II. NOTE ON GEOGRAPHICAL CLASSIFICATION

The computations of the concentration ratios by the Department of Commerce are for the country as a whole. Such national concentration ratios are relevant for the functioning of the industry only when the market for its principal product is nationwide. In cases where the product has several distinct regional or local markets, the concentration ratio must be computed on a regional or local basis in order to retain its significance for market behavior. The objective of this second section of the Methodological Appendix is to distinguish between industries with national markets and those with regional and local markets.

We have done so by the following procedure. National concentration ratios clearly apply to industries with geographically concentrated supply, since it is a necessary condition of a regional market that there be geographically dispersed suppliers. Of course, there may still be market-sharing with the various firms selling to different consuming markets, but this is a behavior characteristic which is not relevant to an investigation of market structure. Geographic concentration is considered to occur when over three quarters of the national production occurs in one or two contiguous regions. In a few cases, lower values were accepted when other evidence suggested a predominantly national market. A further check on this classification was provided by a comparison of our classifications with those made by Gardiner Means[4] and by Willard Thorp and Walter Crowder.[5] In the few cases where our judgments differ from these authors we have indicated the rationale of our classification.

However, the geography of the United States creates one complication in this procedure. The West Coast market is separated from the East Coast manufacturing areas by a considerable area of sparse population density, and because of this bimodal population distribution, the West Coast has somewhat the characteristic of a regional market, with its own manufacturing capacity even for industries otherwise geographically concentrated. However, the California capacity is typically a small percentage of the total and a sufficient deficit exists on the West Coast so that the area still imports from other regions. In this way the region remains part of the national market, although there may be some of the characteristics of a distinct West Coast market. We have ignored this phenomenon in our geographical classification when there was no positive evidence of a separate West Coast market.

There remain some industries whose products have national markets, yet do not present clear-cut cases of geographically concentrated supply. These industries have been checked against those made by Means and by Thorp and Crowder. Since our judgments are more subjective for this category, we have distinguished between national market classification on this basis and those by geographical concentration.

This category also includes industries which are regional or local in terms of the movement of product, but are characterized

4. Gardner Means, *The Structure of the American Economy,* National Resource Committee (Washington, 1939).

5. Willard Throp and Walter Crowder, *The Structure of the American Economy,* Temporary National Economic Committee, Monograph No. 27 (Washington, 1941).

by large national firms which operate in each local market. The tin can industry exemplifies such a situation.[6] Each canning region contains tin can plants which supply primarily the local market. There are two firms, American and Continental, which make between them 83.7 percent of the nationwide sales. Each of these firms operates almost every market and distributional sales, and the share of these two firms together in each market is similar enough to the national shares that the specification of local markets would not change the classification of the industry as a Type I Oligopoly. In such cases of multiplant firms operating in each of the regional markets, the national concentration ratios serve as adequate approximations to the regional concentration ratio, and therefore these industries have been called national market industries. It should be recognized that for any other analytical purposes than the establishment of concentration ratios such industries should be classified as regional.

The remaining industries are of course regional and local. Such industries have been identified by correspondence between the location of the probable demand and production. The presumption is that if the geographical distribution by census regions of demand and supply are in approximate balance, each locality will supply its own demand, so that it is unlikely that there will be the nationwide shipment of the product which characterizes a national market.[7] As a further check, we have utilized industry studies and previous classification of industries to make the final judgment. From such material, an attempt has been made to define the boundaries of regional markets. These range in size from East and West Coast markets to a metropolitan area.

It should be recognized that in making geographical classifications, as with other types of market classifications, the problem is making sharp distinctions when in fact markets vary almost continually in the degree to which they are regional. Thus, in borderline cases we have been forced to somewhat arbitrary classifications.

Furthermore, some of the evidence, particularly from the industries studies, is impressionistic and subject to varying interpretations. Other economists might make different judgments about particular classifications, but we believe the geographical classification

6. See C. H. Hession, "The Tin Can Industry," in *The Structure of American Industry*, ed. Walter Adams (New York, 1954, rev. ed.), pp. 403–442.

7. The geographical distribution of demand was estimated by population in the cases of consumers goods and by the location of the consuming industry in cases of producers goods.

has sufficient accuracy to make our basic concentration tables meaningful.

M.A. Table 2 lists the geographical classifications and includes information on particular decisions where the evidence is not clear.

M.A. Table 2. The classification of manufacturing industries by geographic extent of market

Census category	Commodity	Probable market boundaries for regional and local industries	Sources of geographic classification[a] TNEC	NRC
Type I Oligopolies				
	National market — geographically concentrated supply			
20	Biscuits, crackers, and pretzels			N
	Chewing gum			N
	Wines and distilled liquors		N	N
	Corn products		N	N
	Cereal preparations			N
	Chocolate and cocoa products			N
21	Cigars and tobacco		N	N
	Cigarettes		N	N
22	Thread mills			
	Carpets and rugs			N
	Hard-surface floor coverings		N	N
27	Greeting cards			
28	Soap and glycerin, cleaning and polishing products and related products			N
	Plastic materials		N	
	Synthetic fibers		N	N
32	Flat glass		N	N
	Pressed and blown glassware, n.e.c.			
33	Copper rolling and drawing		N	
	Nonferrous metal rolling			
35	Steam engines and turbines		N	N
	Tractors		N	
	Printing trades machinery			N
	Paper industry machinery			
	Elevators and escalators			
	Typewriters		N	N
	Laundry and dry-cleaning equipment machinery		N	
	Ball and roller bearings			
	Sewing machines			N
	Measuring and dispersing pumps			
36	Engine electrical equipment			
	Electric lamps		N	
	Telephone and telegram equipment		N	
	Electronic tubes			
	Motors and generators		N	
37	Motor vehicles and parts		N	N
	Aircraft engines and propellers			N
	Locomotives and parts			N
	Railroad and street cars			
	Motorcycles and bicycles			N
38	Ophthalmic goods			
	Photographic equipment		N	N
	Watches and clocks			N
39	Pens and mechanical pencils			N

[a] *TNEC* indicates the geographic classification made by Willard Thorp and Walter Crowder in *The Structure of Industry* (TNEC Monograph 27; Washington, 1941); *NRC* indicates the geographic classification made by Gardiner C. Means in *The Structure of the American Economy* (National Resources Committee, Washington, 1939). Key to classification: N = national; R = regional; L = local. If there is no entry in the last column it indicates that the industry has been broadly classified by the authors.

M.A. Table 2. (Continued)

Census category	Commodity	Probable market boundaries for regional and local industries	Sources of geographic classification[a] TNEC	NRC
	National market — geographically unconcentrated supply			
20	Concentrated milk			N
	Sugar		N	N
23	Textile bags[b]		N	
26	Paper bags			
28	Salt			N
	(Inorganic chemicals, n.e.c.)			
	Synthetic rubber		N	N
	(Organic chemicals, n.e.c.)			
	Compressed and liquefied gases[c]		R	L
29	Coke and by-products			R
30	Tires and inner tubes		N	N
31				
32	Glass containers			
	Gypsum products and mineral wool			
33	Primary nonferrous metals, n.e.c.			N
	Primary zinc		N	N
	Primary aluminum		N	N
	Primary copper		N	N
	Primary lead		N	N
	Aluminum rolling and drawing		N	N
34	Tin cans and other tin ware[d]		R	N
	(Metal plumbing fixtures and fittings)		Mixed	N
35	Internal combustion engines		N	
	Computing and related machines		N	N
36	Transformers		N	
	Electrical control apparatus		N	
	Phonograph records		N	
37	Aircraft and equipment			N
	Regional and local market			
28	Alkalies and chlorine	1) The South 2) The West 3) The rest of the U.S.		N
	Explosives	1) The West 2) The rest of the U.S.		
29	Petroleum refining	1) The West 2) The Midcontinent 3) The Gulf and Eastern U.S.	N	N

[a] *TNEC* indicates the geographic classification made by Willard Thorp and Walter Crowder in *The Structure of Industry* (TNEC Monograph 27; Washington, 1941); *NRC* indicates the geographic classification made by Gardiner C. Means in *The Structure of the American Economy* (National Resources Committee, Washington, 1939). Key to classification: N = national; R = regional; L = local. If there is no entry in the last column it indicates that the industry has been broadly classified by the authors.

[b] The concentrations are in West North Central and West South Central; and, by and large, the production pattern is in accordance with demand; but there is (presumably) a surplus in the Middle Atlantic and a chain linking of markets.

[c] Production is highly decentralized, but it is a case of multiplant production by a few firms with the local concentration ratio very little different from the national ratio.

[d] Production is decentralized, but it is a case similar to that of compressed and liquefied gases (above).

M.A. Table 2. (Continued)

Census category	Commodity	Probable market boundaries for regional and local industries	Sources of geographic classification[a] TNEC	NRC
	Paving and roofing materials	1) The East 2) The West	N	
34	Metal barrels, drums, and pails	1) Pacific Coast 2) West South Central 3) The rest of the U.S.	R	R
35	(Oil field machinery and tools)			
36	Storage batteries	1) The East 2) The West	N	
37	Ship building and repairing			
Type II Oligopolies				
	National market — geographically concentrated supply			
20	Canned and cured fish			N
22	Hats			N
23	House furnishings			N
27	Periodicals			
28	Fertilizers		R	R
	Toilet preparations			
	Drugs and medicines		N	N
	Soap and glycerin, cleaning and polishing preparations and related products			N
31	Leather tanning and polishing		Mixed	N
32	China and earthenware food utensils			N
	Products of purch. glass		N	all glassware
35	Textile machinery			N
	Power transmission equipment			N
	Office and store machines and devices, n.e.c.		N	N
	Refrigeration machinery		N	N
	Printing trades machinery			N
	Paper industries machinery			
30	Insulated wire and cable		N	N
	Radios and related products		N	N
37	Surgical, medical, and dental instruments			N
	Instruments and related products, n.e.c.			N
	National market — geographically unconcentrated supply			
20	Meat products		N	N
	Cheese			N
	Ice cream and ices[e]			L
	Flavorings			N
24	Misc. timber basic products			cooperage (R) excelsior (N)
	Window shades and venetian blinds			

[a] *TNEC* indicates the geographic classification made by Willard Thorp and Walter Crowder in *The Structure of Industry* (TNEC Monograph 27; Washington, 1941); *NRC* indicates the geographic classification made by Gardiner C. Means in *The Structure of the American Economy* (National Resources Committee, Washington, 1939). Key to classification: N = national; R = regional; L = local. If there is no entry in the last column it indicates that the industry has been broadly classified by the authors.

[e] This industry is classified as national even though production is highly decentralized, but it is a case of multiplant production by national firms.

M.A. Table 2. (Continued)

Census category	Commodity	Probable market boundaries for regional and local industries	Sources of geographic classification[a] TNEC	NRC
28	Paints and varnishes			N
	Industrial organic chemicals, n.e.c.			
	Industrial inorganic chemicals, n.e.c.			
32	Asbestos products		N	N
33	Blast furnaces, steel works, and rolling mills[f]		Mixed	N
	Steel foundries			
	Secondary nonferrous metals			
	Nonferrous metals			
	Metal plumbing fixtures and fittings		Mixed	N
	Farm machinery (except tractors)		N	N
	Pumps and compressors			
36	Service and household machinery, n.e.c.			
	Electrical industrial apparatus, n.e.c.			
	Electrical products, n.e.c.			
37	Boat building and repairing[g]			
38	Mechanical measuring instruments		N	
	Regular and local market			
32	Cement	highly localized	R	R
35	Oil field machinery and tools	{ The West The rest of the U.S.		
37	Ship building and repairing	{ The East including Gulf The West	N	
Unconcentrated industries				
	National market — concentrated supply			
23	Men's and boys' suits, coats, and trousers		N	
	Men's dress shirts and nightwear		N	N
	Men's and boys' rough clothing		N	
	Women's and misses' dresses		N	
	Women's and misses' dresses		N	
	Women's and misses' suits, coats, and skirts		N	N
25	Nonhousehold furniture; partitions and fixtures		N	N
26	Pulp goods and misc. converted paper products		N	N
27	Publishing (except newspaper publishing and magazines)			N
31	Footwear (except rubber)		N	N
34	Cutlery, hand tools, and general hardware			N
	Metal stampings			
35	Construction and mining machinery			N
	Machine tools and cutting tools		N	N
	Metal working machinery, n.e.c.		N	N
	Wiring devices		N	

[a] *TNEC* indicates the geographic classification made by Willard Thorp and Walter Crowder in *The Structure of Industry* (TNEC Monograph 27; Washington, 1941); *NRC* indicates the geographic classification made by Gardiner C. Means in *The Structure of the American Economy* (National Resources Committee, Washington, 1939). Key to classification: N = national; R = regional; L = local. If there is no entry in the last column it indicates that the industry has been broadly classified by the authors.

[f] This industry is classified as national although the West does have 5 percent of value added in steel products.

[g] Although production is highly decentralized, this is classified as a national industry, partly because national firms are involved — and partly because it is not really clear what else to do with it.

M.A. Table 2. (Continued)

Census category	Commodity	Probable market boundaries for regional and local industries	Sources of geographic classification[a] TNEC	NRC
	National market — unconcentrated supply			
20	Canning, preserving and freezing		N	N
	Oleo, shortening, and cooking oils		N	N
	Malt and malt liquors			R
	Confectionary products[h]			N
	Flour and feed[i]			Flour N Feed R
25	Household furniture		N	N
26	Paper containers and boxes		N	N
33	Iron foundries[j]		N	
34	Heating and cooking apparatus		Mixed	N
35	Valves, fabricated pipe, and fittings			
	Regional and local			
20	Creamery butter			N
	Bread and other bakery products	East West		L
	Bottled soft drinks			L
24	Sawmills and planing mills	East West		
	Structural products	East West		
26	Paper and paper mills		N	N
27	Newspapers			L
	Commercial printing and lithographing			L
	Service industries for the printing trade			L
32	Structural clay and concrete products			R
34	Boiler shop products,[k] structural and ornamental products		R	R
37	Motor vehicles and parts, n.e.c.	East West		
	Unclassifiable			
	Misc. food products			
	Misc. textile goods			
	Misc. apparel and accessories			
	Misc. fabric textile products			
	Misc. chemical products			
	Misc. rubber industries			
	Misc. products of steel works			
	Special industry machinery, n.e.c.			
	General industrial machinery, n.e.c.			
	Plastic products, n.e.c.			
	Misc. leather goods			

[a] *TNEC* indicates the geographic classification made by Willard Thorp and Walter Crowder in *The Structure of Industry* (TNEC Monograph 27; Washington, 1941); *NRC* indicates the geographic classification made by Gardiner C. Means in *The Structure of the American Economy* (National Resources Committee, Washington, 1939). Key to classification: N = national; R = regional; L = local. If there is no entry in the last column it indicates that the industry has been broadly classified by the authors.

[h] This industry is classified as national even though production is decentralized (with the exception of a concentration in Illinois — 32 percent of total shipments). But this is a case of predominantly national producers setting up numerous local plants and there is only a (fairly sizable) periphery of small local firms.

[i] This industry is classified as national even though the West appears to be self-supporting in flour (Pacific with 8 percent of total shipments, Mountain with 4 percent) and even though the production of feed is consistent with the demand for it. But feed production is simply a matter of mixing together various products from the flour industry.

[j] This is classified as national, but it is important not to overemphasize the degree of concentration of South. It is pretty much in the Northeast iron and steel area, but this is partly (at least) because this is where the market lies and (apart from the multiplant firms) there is a considerable number of small local producers.

[k] With some doubts, this is classified as regional. Production follows pretty much the distribution of presumable demand. It seems that it is composed of big multiplant firms (with a national spread) and small local firms.

III. NOTE ON ECONOMIC TYPE CLASSIFICATION

Individual markets are classified in this study into four economic types: consumer nondurables, consumer durables, industrial material inputs, and investment goods. These categories are intended to represent two attributes of an industry's position in the economic process: its proximity to the consumer, and the postponability of the decision to purchase its product. The first characteristic is recognized by distinguishing between intermediate industries selling to other industries and consumer industries selling directly to the household. Industrial material inputs and investment goods are defined as the intermediate industries, with the other two being the consumer industries. The criterion of the classification of an industry as an intermediate or consumer type is the distribution of particular industry sales between households and other industries as shown by the Leontief input-output table.[8] Industries which made over 50 percent of their sales to households were considered consumer-good industries, and the others as intermediate industries. However, when a material input industry made over 50 percent of its sales to one other industry, then its economic type follows that of the purchasing industry. This, of course, recognizes that the arguments for the special economic significance of intermediate industries rests on the supplying of several industries. In cases where the Leontief industry classification and our classification do not correspond, it was necessary to determine the economic type from the industry's description either in the preceding section (II) of this Appendix or elsewhere.

The twofold classification within the intermediate and consumer industries has no such quantitative basis and as a result contains a larger arbitrary element. The essential difference between consumers' durables and nondurables and material inputs and investment goods is the postponability of purchase for the durables and investment goods, although these two also share other economic characteristics such as the importance of credit and of obsolescence in the purchase decisions. The classification here was according to the characteristics of the products as given in the preceding section and elsewhere.

We recognize that this limited classification scheme is a very

8. The table utilized was the 1947 *Industry Flow of Goods and Services of Origin and Destination*, compiled by the U.S. Department of Labor, Bureau of Labor Statistics, Division of Interindustry Economics (October 1952).

crude way of measuring the economic significance of an industry. Economic significance is, of course, a very subtle general equilibrium concept to which very little economic analysis has been applied.

The individual classification of each manufacturing industry is given in M.A. Tables.

M.A. Table 3. Classification of Industries by Economic Type

Size of industry and extent and structure of market[a]	Industry code	Industry	Economic type classification[b]
I, 1, A			
Type I Oligopolies			
	3722	Aircraft engines and propellers	IG
	2111	Cigarettes and tobacco	CN
	2823	Plastic materials	MI
	2825	Synthetic fibers	CN
	3351	Copper rolling and drawing	MI
	3521	Tractors	IG
	3717	Motor vehicles and parts	CD
	2085	Wines and distilled liquors	CN
Type II Oligopolies			
	2834	Pharmaceutical preparations	CN
	3631	Insulated wire and cable	MI
	2841	Soap, glycerin, cleaning and polishing preparations, and related products	CN
	2721	Periodicals	CN
	3614	Motors and generators	IG
	3661	Radios and related products	CD
	3585	Refrigeration equipment	CD
I, 1, B	2233	Cotton and synthetic broad woven fabrics	CN
	3541	Machine tools	IG
	3141	Footwear, except rubber	CN
	2253	Knit outerwear and underwear	CN
	26 misc.	Misc. paper and allied products	MI
	3439	Heating and cooking equipment	UNC.
	3421	Cutlery, hand tools, and general hardware	UNC.
	3463	Metal stampings and pressings	MI
	2333	Dresses	CN
	2311	Men's and boys' suits, coats, and trousers	CN
	3531	Construction and mining machinery	IG
	2213	Woolen and worsted manufactures	CN
	35 misc.	Misc. metalworking machinery	IG
	2337	Women's and misses' suits, coats, and skirts	CN
I, 2, A			
Type I Oligopolies			
	3011	Tires and inner tubes	CD
	3411	Tin cans and other tinware	MI
	2932	Coke and by-products	MI
	2062	Sugar	CN

[a] See General Note, page 294.
[b] The abbreviations used are as follows: CD = consumer durables; CN = consumer nondurables; MI = material inputs; IG = investment goods.

M.A. Table 3. (Continued)

Size of industry and extent and structure of market[a]	Industry code	Industry	Economic type classification[b]
Type II Oligopolies			
	2011	Meat products	CN
	3721	Aircraft and aircraft equipment	IG
	2829	Organic chemicals	MI
	2092	Oleo, shortening, and cooking oils	CN
	2082	Malt and malt liquors	CN
	2819	Inorganic chemicals, n.e.c.	MI
	2851	Paints, varnishes, and allied products	MI
	3522	Farm machinery (except tractors)	IG
	3616	Electric control apparatus	MI
	3311	Blast furnaces, steel works, and rolling mills	MI
I, 2, B	2041	Flour and feed	CN
	2033	Canning, preserving, and freezing	CN
	2511	Household furniture	CN
	2671	Paperboard containers and boxes	MI
	3321	Iron foundries	MI
	3591	Valves, pipe, and fittings, except plumbers fittings	MI
I, 4, A			
Type II Oligopolies			
	20 misc.	Misc. food and kindred products	CN
	30 misc.	Misc. rubber products	MI
I, 4, B	39 misc.	Misc. manufacturing industries	UNC.
	34 misc.	Misc. products of steel works	MI
	28 misc.	Misc. allied chemical products	MI
	23 misc.	Misc. apparel and accessories	CN
	3971	Plastic products, n.e.c.	MI
	35 misc.	General industrial machinery, n.e.c.	IG
II, 1, A			
Type I Oligopolies			
	2052	Biscuits, crackers, and pretzels	CN
	3861	Photographic equipment	CD
	3664	Tel and tel equipment	IG
	3662	Electronic tubes	MI
	3581	Dry cleaning and laundry equipment	IG
	3641	Engine electrical equipment	MI
	3593	Ball and roller bearings	MI
	3571	Computing and related machines	IG
Type II Oligopolies			
	2871	Fertilizer	MI
	2893	Toilet preparations	CN
II, 1, B	2522	Nonhousehold partitions and fixtures	MI
	2392	House furnishings, n.e.c.	CD
	2731	Books, publishing, and printing	CN
	3611	Wiring devices and supplies	MI

M.A. Table 3. (Continued)

Size of industry and extent and structure of market[a]	Industry code	Industry	Economic type classification[b]
	2328	Men's and boys' rough clothing	CN
	2321	Men's dress shirts and nightwear	CN
	2361	Children's and infants' outerwear	CN
	3471	Lighting fixtures	CD
	3111	Leather tanning and finishing	CN
	3941	Games and toys	CN
	3566	Power transmission equipment	IG
	2251	Hosiery mills	CN
II, 2, A			
Type I Oligopolies			
	3519	Internal combustion engines	IG
	3352	Aluminum rolling and drawing	MI
	3615	Transformers	IG
	3221	Glass containers	MI
Type II Oligopolies			
	2024	Ice cream and ices	CN
	3561	Pumps and compressors	MI
	3821	Mechanical measuring instruments	IG
	2023	Concentrated milk	CN
	3341	Secondary nonferrous metals	MI
	3811	Scientific instruments	IG
	2661	Paper bags	CN
	3613	Electrical industrial apparatus, n.e.c.	IG
	36 misc.	Misc. electrical products	UNC.
	3292	Asbestos products	MI
II, 2, B	2071	Confectionery products	CN
	3361	Nonferrous castings	MI
	2022	Cheese	CN
	3323	Steel castings	MI
	2432	Plywood	MI
II, 4, A	34 misc.	Misc. fabricated metal products	MI
II, 4, B	22 misc.	Misc. textile mill products	CN
	32 misc.	Misc. nonmetallic mineral products	MI
	23 misc. F.	Misc. fabric and textile products	MI
	31 misc.	Misc. leather products	CN
	24 misc. WP.	Misc. wood products	MI
	3559	Special industrial machinery, n.e.c.	IG
III, 1, A			
Type I Oligopolies			
	3211	Flat glass	MI
	2072	Chocolate and cocoa products	CN
	3742	Railroad and street cars	IG
	3334	Primary aluminum	MI
	2094	Corn wet milling products	CN
	3511	Steam engines and turbines	IG
	3229	Pressed and blown glass, n.e.c.	MI
	2121	Cigars	CN

M.A. Table 3. (Continued)

Size of industry and extent and structure of market[a]	Industry code	Industry	Economic type classification[b]
	2043	Cereal breakfast foods	CN
	3651	Electric lamps (bulbs)	CD
	3871	Watches and clocks	CD
	3359	Rolling and drawing, n.e.c.	MI
	2223	Thread	CN
	2274	Hard-surface floor coverings	CD
	2073	Chewing gum	CN
	3584	Vacuum cleaners	CD
	3572	Typewriters	UNC.
	3562	Elevators and escalators	IG
	3583	Sewing machines	CD
	2271	Carpets and rugs	CN
Type II Oligopolies			
	3842	Surgical, medical, and dental instruments and supplies	IG
	2025	Special dairy products	CN
	2031	Canned and cured seafood	CN
	2342	Corsets and allied garments	CN
	3552	Textile machinery	IG
	35 misc.	Misc. office and store machinery	IG
	3231	Products of purchased glass	MI
	3555	Printing trades machinery	IG
	2771	Greeting cards	CN
	3554	Paper industries machinery	IG
	3872	Instruments and related products, n.e.c.	IG
	3851	Opthalmic goods	CD
	3263	China and earthenware food utensils	CD
	2281	Hats (excluding millinery)	CN
III, 1, B	3911	Jewelry	CD
	2331	Blouses	CN
III, 2, A			
Type I Oligopolies			
	3272	Gypsum products and mineral wood	MI
	3339	Primary nonferrous metals, n.e.c.	MI
	2824	Synthetic rubber	MI
	3741	Locomotives and parts	IG
	3333	Primary zinc	MI
	2896	Compressed and liquefied gases	MI
	3951	Pens and mechanical pencils	CD
	3331	Primary copper	MI
	3332	Primary lead	MI
Type II Oligopolies			
	2095	Flavorings	CN
	3431	Plumbing fixtures and fittings	MI
	2393	Textile bags	CN

M.A. Table 3. (Continued)

Size of industry and extent and structure of market[a]	Industry code	Industry	Economic type classification[b]
	3589	Service and household machinery, n.e.c.	CD
III, 2, B	3551	Food products machinery	IG
	2563	Venetian blinds and window shades	CD
	3732	Boat building and repairing	IG
III, 4, B	32 misc. V.	Misc. vitreous products	MI
IV, 1, A *Type I Oligopolies*			
	3751	Motorcycles and bicycles	CD
	3586	Measuring and dispersing pumps	MI
IV, 2, A *Type I Oligopolies*			
	3663	Phonograph records	CN
	2898	Salt	MI
IV, 2, B	24 misc. TBP	Misc. timber basic products	MI
IV, 4, A *Type I Oligopolies*			
	2999	Petroleum and coal products, n.e.c.	MI

IV. HETEROGENEITY OF CONCENTRATION WITHIN MARKETS

Because there is rarely perfect supply and demand substitutability between the component products of any given market, the existence of large differences in the degree of concentration of different sectors of the same market acts to limit the meaning of our over-all structural classification. Other things being equal, the greater the difference in structure between a given submarket and the remaining members of its parent market, the greater will be the difference in market behavior between the submarket and the rest of the market. The significance of a given amount of dispersion in submarket structures is greatest where the supply and demand cross-elasticities are low for the products involved. Even though a market may have a low over-all concentration ratio, some members of the market may possess a substantial degree of market power as a result of extreme concentration in certain sectors of the market which are relatively insulated from immediate competition by other market members. A case in point is furnished by the metal stampings industry Code 3463), which is classified as unconcentrated on the basis of an 18 percent concentration ratio for eight firms. This market includes nine five-digit census products with individual concentration ratios ranging from 14 percent to 98 percent for eight firms. The concentration figures are reproduced below.[9]

Code	Industry	Value of shipments (thousands of dollars)	Concentration ratios of eight largest firms
3463	Metal stampings	1,632,764	18
34631	Job stampings, except automotive	510,422	14
34632	Stamped and spun cooking and kitchen utensils	200,902	61
34633	Pails, ash cans, garbage cans	44,652	56
34634	Metal home canning closures	17,673	—[a]
34635	Metal commercial closures, except crowns	94,949	77
34636	Crowns	78,443	98
34637	Job stampings, automotive	474,349	39
34638	Other stamped or pressed metal products	184,188	19

[a] Figure not given in order to avoid disclosing data for individual firms.

It is fairly clear that the supply substitutability between, say, kitchen utensils and the rest of the market is sufficiently imperfect to give economic meaning to concentration in this particular submarket.

Fortunately for our purposes, the varied concentration pattern which exists within the metal stampings industry is not typical. A crude idea of the extent to which concentration may vary among the component products of individual markets is furnished by a frequency distribution of ranges in eight-firm concentration ratios for the five-digit census products within each market. Such a distribution appears in M.A. Table 4.

A high range is a necessary but not a sufficient condition for the existence of economically significant dispersion within a market. It may be that the great bulk of a market's sales are in similarly concentrated products but that extremely high or low concentration in relatively small submarkets has given the market a high range in product concentration ratios. Therefore, in classifying industries according to the existence or nonexistence of economically significant dispersion, it is necessary to decide two things. First, how far apart must any two-product concentration ratios be before the dif-

9. The data appear on p. 55 of the *Senate Report*.

M.A. Table 4. Ranges in eight firm concentration ratios for census products within individual markets

	Number of markets			
	All markets		Nonmiscellaneous markets	
Range class, one-product markets	Class frequencies	Cumulative frequencies	Class frequencies	Cumulative frequencies
	37	37	37	37
0–39	87	124	85	122
40–49	18	142	17	139
50–59	26	168	19	158
60–69	8	176	5	163
70 and over	15	191	10	173

ference is to be significant? In short, we must set upper and lower limits for the concentration ratios of "nondispersed" products in each market. And second, once we have established the bounds of acceptable dispersion, how large a share of the market must lie outside these boundaries in order for the market to be classed as "dispersed"?

We have compiled a list of dispersed markets on the basis of the following procedure. In order to be classed as dispersed, a market must have at least 20 percent of its sales in products having concentration ratios which are at least 20 percentage points greater or less than the market concentration ratio.[10] The difficulty with using this standard exclusively is that it tends to overstate dispersion in those cases in which the market concentration ratio is considerably lower than the concentration ratios for the bulk of the industry's products, so that most of the product concentration ratios lie above the upper limit of acceptable dispersion.[11] In those industries in which firms tend to specialize in particular products, this is often the case. We have relied on visual inspection to spot the more flagrant examples of this "false dispersion" and have eliminated these cases from our list of dispersed industries. Another difficulty with our dispersion standard is that a given point difference in concentration ratios is more meaningful for low ratios than for high ones.

10. In the cases of consolidated markets we used the maximum market-concentration ratio.

11. Use of a weighted average of product-concentration ratios in place of the market-concentration ratio would eliminate this difficulty. However, the small gain in accuracy that this would provide was not considered sufficient to compensate for the increased effort involved.

For instance, the difference between ratios of 65 and 85 is not as impressive as the difference between ratios of 15 and 35. Accordingly, we did not classify as dispersed any market in which the component products all had ratios of 40 percent or more. Our list of dispersed industries appears in M.A. Table 5.

M.A. Table 5. Markets showing significant dispersion in product concentration ratios (regional markets excluded)

Code	Industry	Code	Industry
	Range class: 70 and over		*Range class: 60 to 69*
2033	Canning, preserving, and freezing	2522	Nonhousehold partitions and fixtures
2392	House furnishings, n.e.c.	3661	Radios and related products
3421	Cutlery, hand tools, and general hardware		*Range class: 50 to 59*
3463	Metal stampings	2023	Concentrated milk
3541	Machine tools	3721	Aircraft and aircraft equipment
3613	Electric industrial apparatus, n.e.c.		*Range class: 40 to 49*
		3971	Plastic products, n.e.c.

Crude as it is, this list should be taken only as a warning that the over-all market concentration figures for the indicated industries should be interpreted conservatively. The economic significance of the dispersion varies from market to market and requires detailed knowledge of the component products of each industry for its evaluation.

Index

Bei Fragen zur Produktsicherheit wenden Sie sich bitte an:
If you have any questions regarding product safety,
please contact:

Walter de Gruyter GmbH
Genthiner Straße 13
10785 Berlin
productsafety@degruyterbrill.com